Lecture Notes in Computer

Edited by G. Goos, J. Hartmanis, and J

Springer
Berlin
Heidelberg
New York
Barcelona
Hong Kong
London
Milan
Paris
Tokyo

Fabio Crestani   Mark Girolami
Cornelis Joost van Rijsbergen (Eds.)

Advances in Information Retrieval

24th BCS-IRSG European Colloquium on IR Research
Glasgow, UK, March 25-27, 2002
Proceedings

Springer

Series Editors

Gerhard Goos, Karlsruhe University, Germany
Juris Hartmanis, Cornell University, NY, USA
Jan van Leeuwen, Utrecht University, The Netherlands

Volume Editors

Fabio Crestani
University of Strathclyde, Department of Computer and Information Sciences
26 Richmond Street, Glasgow G1 1XH, UK
E-mail: fabio.crestani@cis.strath.ac.uk

Mark Girolami
University of Paisley, School of Information and Communication Technologies
High Street, Paisley PA1 2BE, UK
E-mail: mark.girolami@paisley.ac.uk

Cornelis Joost van Rijsbergen
University of Glasgow, Computing Science Department
17 Lilybank Gardens, Glasgow G12 8RZ, UK
E-mail: keith@dcs.gla.ac.uk

Cataloging-in-Publication Data applied for

Die Deutsche Bibliothek - CIP-Einheitsaufnahme

Advances in information retrieval : proceedings / 24th BCS IRSG European
Colloquium on IR Research, Glasgow, UK, March 25 - 27, 2002. Fabio Crestani
... (ed.). - Berlin ; Heidelberg ; New York ; Barcelona ; Hong Kong ; London ;
Milan ; Paris ; Tokyo : Springer, 2002
    (Lecture notes in computer science ; Vol. 2291)
    ISBN 3-540-43343-0

CR Subject Classification (1998): H.3, H.2, I.2.3, I.2.6, H.4, H.5.4, I.7

ISSN 0302-9743
ISBN 3-540-43343-0 Springer-Verlag Berlin Heidelberg New York

Springer-Verlag Berlin Heidelberg New York
a member of BertelsmannSpringer Science+Business Media GmbH

http://www.springer.de

© Springer-Verlag Berlin Heidelberg 2002
Printed in Germany

Typesetting: Camera-ready by author, data conversion by PTP-Berlin, Stefan Sossna
Printed on acid-free paper   SPIN: 10846377   06/3142   5 4 3 2 1 0

Preface

The annual colloquium on information retrieval research provides an opportunity for both new and established researchers to present papers describing work in progress or final results. This colloquium was established by the BCS IRSG (British Computer Society Information Retrieval Specialist Group), and named the Annual Colloquium on Information Retrieval Research. Recently, the location of the colloquium has alternated between the United Kingdom and continental Europe. To reflect the growing European orientation of the event, the colloquium was renamed "European Annual Colloquium on Information Retrieval Research" from 2001.

Since the inception of the colloquium in 1979 the event has been hosted in the city of Glasgow on four separate occasions. However, this was the first time that the organization of the colloquium had been jointly undertaken by three separate computer and information science departments; an indication of the collaborative nature and diversity of IR research within the universities of the West of Scotland.

The organizers of ECIR 2002 saw a sharp increase in the number of good-quality submissions in answer to the call for papers over previous years and as such 52 submitted papers were each allocated 3 members of the program committee for double blind review of the manuscripts. A total of 23 papers were eventually selected for oral presentation at the colloquium in Glasgow which gave an acceptance rate of less than 45% and ensured a very high standard of the papers presented.

The colloquium consisted of well-attended sessions on IR Models, Document Categorization, Web IR, Soft Computing and IR, Interactive IR Systems, Multimedia IR, Structured Document Retrieval, Cross Lingual IR, and Query Modification.

Browsing through the table of contents the reader will also note that in addition to contributions from European authors just over 20% of the papers presented were authored by researchers from the USA and Asia which added a slight international flavor to ECIR 2002.

Acknowledgements

The organizing committee would like to thank all the authors who submitted their work for consideration and the participants of ECIR 2002 for making the event a great success. Special thanks are due to the members of the program committee who worked very hard to ensure the timely review of all the submitted manuscripts, and to the invited speaker Rik Belew, of the University of California at San Diego. We also thank the sponsoring institutions CEPIS-IR, BCS-IRSG, and Memex Technology for their generous financial support of the colloquium, and Glasgow City Council for civic hospitality.

Thanks are also due to the editorial staff at Springer-Verlag for their agreement to publish the colloquium proceedings as part of the Lecture Notes in Computer Science series.

Finally thanks are due to the local team of student volunteers (in particular Heather Du and Puay Leng Lee), secretaries (Linda Hunter and Anne Sinclair), and information officers (Paul Smith, Jon Ritchie, and Naveed Khan) whose efforts ensured the smooth organization and running of the colloquium.

March 2002

Fabio Crestani
Mark Girolami
Keith van Rijsbergen

Organization

Organizing Institutions

ECIR 2002 was jointly organized by the Department of Computer and Information Sciences of the University of Strathclyde, the School of Information and Communication Technologies of the University of Paisley, and the Department of Computer Science of the University of Glasgow.

Conference Chairs

Fabio Crestani (University of Strathclyde, UK)
Mark Girolami (University of Paisley, UK)
Keith van Rijsbergen (University of Glasgow, UK)

Sponsoring Institutions

British Computer Society – Information Retrieval Specialist Group
CEPIS-IR (Special Interest Network on Information Retrieval of the Council of European Professional Informatics Societies)
Memex Technology, East Kilbride, Scotland
Glasgow City Council

Program Committee

Gianni Amati (Fondazione Ugo Bordoni, Italy)
Micheline Beaulieu (University of Sheffield, UK)
Mohand Boughanem (IRIT Toulouse, France)
David Carmel (IBM, Israel)
Matthew Chalmers (University of Glasgow, UK)
Yves Chiaramella (IMAG Grenoble, France)
Stavros Christodoulakis (Technical University of Crete, Greece)
Pablo de la Fuente (University of Valladolid, Spain)
Arjen de Vries (CWI, The Netherlands)
Sandor Dominich (University of Veszprem, Hungary)
Steve Draper (University of Glasgow, UK)
Mark Dunlop (University of Strathclyde, UK)
Leo Egghe (Limburgs Universitair Centrum, Belgium)
Hans Peter Frei (Inforcons, Switzerland)
Norbert Fuhr (University of Dortmund, Germany)
Ayse Goker (Robert Gordon University, Aberdeen, UK)

David Harper (Robert Gordon University, Aberdeen, UK)
Theo Huibers (KPMG, The Netherlands)
Peter Ingwersen (Royal School of Library and Information Science, Denmark)
Gareth Jones (University of Exeter, UK)
Joemon Jose (University of Glasgow, UK)
Cornelis Koster (University of Nijmegen, The Netherlands)
Mounia Lalmas (Queen Mary, University of London, UK)
Monica Landoni (University of Strathclyde, UK)
David Losada (San Pablo-CEU University, Spain)
Massimo Melucci (University of Padova, Italy)
Dieter Merkl (Technical University of Vienna, Austria)
Elke Mittendorf (SYSTOR, Switzerland)
Josiane Mothe (IRIT Toulouse, France)
Frank Nack (CWI, The Netherlands)
Iadh Ounis K(University of Glasgow, UK)
Gabriella Pasi (ITIM CNR, Italy)
Victor Poznanski (Sharp, UK)
Steve Robertson (Microsoft, UK)
Tony Rose (Reuters, UK)
Fabrizio Sebastiani (IEI CNR, Italy)
Alan Smeaton (Dublin City University, Ireland)
Eero Sormunen (University of Tampere, Finland)
John Tait (University of Sunderland, UK)
Ulrich Thiel (GMD Darmstadt, Germany)
Ozgur Ulusoy (University of Bilkent, Turkey)
Kenneth Wood (AT&T, UK)

Previous Venues of the Annual Colloquium

2001 Darmstadt (organized by GMD)
2000 Cambridge (organized by Microsoft Research)
1999 Glasgow (organized by Strathclyde University)
1998 Grenoble (organized by CLIPS-IMAG)
1997 Aberdeen (organized by Robert Gordon University)
1996 Manchester (organized by Manchester Metropolitan University)
1995 Crewe (organized by Manchester Metropolitan University)
1994 Drymen (organized by Strathclyde University)
1993 Glasgow (organized by Strathclyde University)
1992 Lancaster
1991 Lancaster
1990 Huddersfield
1989 Huddersfield
1988 Huddersfield
1987 Glasgow

1986 Glasgow
1985 Bradford
1984 Bradford
1983 Sheffield
1982 Sheffield
1981 Birmingham
1980 Leeds
1979 Leeds

Table of Contents

Models

Categorization

Structured Documents

Cross-Language

Interactive Systems

Evaluating a Melody Extraction Engine

Thomas Sødring and Alan F. Smeaton

School of Computer Applications

Dublin City University
Glasnevin
Dublin 9
Ireland

tsodring@compapp.dcu.ie

Abstract. This paper introduces the CEOLAIRE Music Information Retrieval System; a system which stores, indexes and provides content-based retrieval on a collection of over 7,000 music files. What makes CEOLAIRE different from most other music information retrieval systems is that it indexes actual raw compressed or uncompressed audio rather than just indexing MIDI, which is effectively instructions for generating musical notes. The paper includes an overview of the CEOLAIRE system and includes an evaluation of the effectiveness of its melody extraction engine, the crucial part of CEOLAIRE which recognises the notes and melody being played. Our results show that for the type of melody matching used in CEOLAIRE's retrieval engine, the performance of our melody recognition is quite acceptable.

1   Introduction

One of the advantages of having information in digital form is that it lends itself readily to content-based access. This applies to information stored in any media, though content searching through information stored in a structured database or as text is more developed then content searching through information stored in other media such as music, which is what we are concerned with here. In practice, the most common way to index and provide retrieval on digital music is to use its metadata such as title, performer, etc., as has been done in Napster [Napster].

However, in the face of ever increasing availability of music resources, especially on the web, the inadequacy of searching on metadata rather than directly on content, becomes apparent. People want to search through music databases based on content which includes melody and beat.

To address this, we have built a Musical Information Retrieval System called CEOLAIRE, which allows for search of the actual content of raw digital monophonic music files, rather than simple meta-data searching. This paper explores the components which make up the CEOLAIRE Music Retrieval System and how we quantified the correctness of its extraction engine.

F. Crestani, M. Girolami, and C.J. van Rijsbergen (Eds.): ECIR 2002, LNCS 2291, pp. 1–21, 2002.

The organisation of this paper is as follows. In the next section we give a brief overview of other systems which provide content-based music IR. We then follow that with an overview of how digital audio information is created and some fundamentals on what makes music the way it is. In section 5 we describe the CEOLAIRE system and in sections 6 and 7 we present our experimental evaluation and our results.

2   Previous Research

Retrieval of digital music based on content, i.e. melody, has been implemented in several systems, some of which we briefly review.

2.1   MELDEX

MELDEX is the New Zealand Digital Library Melody Index [McNab et al., 97]. It was designed to retrieve melodies from a database on the basis of a few notes sung into a microphone. A user inputs a query into a microphone and uploads a file, which contains a sampled acoustic signal to MELDEX. MELDEX performs automatic melody transcription on the query file, looking for notes. Individual note beginnings and endings are determined after pitches are identified. MELDEX depends on the user separating each note by singing "da" or "ta". This melody is then compared against a musical database of North American, British and Irish folksongs, German ballads and folksongs and Chinese ethnic and provincial songs. The database consists of publicly available MIDI files.

2.2   Query by Pitch Dynamics

Query by Pitch Dynamics was developed at The Link Group at Carnegie Mellon University [Beeferman, 97]. This system allows for the indexing of music by its tonal content, so that a user can search by content and also perform off-line analysis. It indexes a one-dimensional time series sequence of elements, based on the relative values of nearby elements rather than absolute values. Like MELDEX, this system currently uses only MIDI files.

2.3   Query by Humming

Query by Humming (QBH) was developed at Cornell University [Ghias et al., 95] to allow musical information retrieval on an audio database. The QBH system consists of three parts, the pitch tracking module, the melody database and the query engine. Songs in the database are pre-processed into a string database with the melody to be tracked as notes. Notes are defined in terms of their relationship to the previous note in the tune as being either up (U), down (D) or same (S) as the previous note so instead of representing the melody of a song with features such as beat, rhythm and timing information, the tracking of the melody is represented instead. A query is processed into the same notation for comparison. The search is 'fuzzy' pattern matching, 'fuzzy' because errors may be introduced by the way people hum and in the representation of the song itself, as well as in the matching.

Recent efforts have been in the area of feature extraction from and working with polyphonic music sources [Pye, 00][Lenström et al., 00].

2.4 SEMEX

SEMEX [Lenström et al., 00] is an efficient music retrieval prototype which uses bit-parallel algorithms for locating transposition invariant monophonic queries within monophonic or polyphonic musical databases. SEMEX uses pitch levels for music representation. Pitch levels are represented as small integers, making up the language of the system.

2.5 ARTHUR

ARTHUR [Foote, 00] is an audio retrieval-by-example system designed for orchestral music. It is named after Arthur G. Lintgen who was able to identify phonographic recordings by the softer and louder passages, which are visible in the grooves of an LP. ARTHUR was designed to the same, retrieve audio based on its long term structure. Audio energy versus time in one or a number of frequency bands is one way to determine the long-term structure of audio. At the core of ARTHUR is the use of a dynamic programming algorithm called "Discrete Time Warping", which is used in speech recognition to help account for variations in speech timing and pronunciation. Dynamic Programming is useful where signal amplitudes do not match exactly and relative timing is divergent. Two signals are aligned to each other via a lattice, the test signal on the vertical axis and the reference on the horizontal. Every point (i, j) in the lattice corresponds to how well the reference signal at time i corresponds to the test signal at time j. The Dynamic Programming algorithm returns the best aligned path that converts one signal into the other and the cost of that path. If the 2 signals are identical, the cost will be 0 and the resulting line will be diagonal. Increasing dissimilarity will have increased costs associated with them.

For the interested reader, an excellent review of audio information retrieval including music information retrieval can be found in [Foote, 99].

2.6 OMRAS

Online Music-Recognition and Searching (OMRAS) is a cross-disciplinary research project covering computational musicology, computer science and library science to answer the problem of a digital music library, the inability to search the content of the collections for music itself. One of the goals of OMRAS is to offer access to and retrieval of polyphonic sources [Plumbley et al., 01] and [Dovey, 01].

In the last few years the field of music information retrieval has been extended by incorporating the use of raw or compressed music files as basis for experimentation [Foote, 00][Plumbley et al., 01]. The current trend is towards building systems which can successfully negotiate features or structures from polyphonic sources. The use of MIDI as a musical format for music information retrieval is of particular use in testing proof of concepts for both polyphonic and monophonic music sources as its structure is easily extracted.

MELDEX, Query by Pitch Dynamics and QBH represent the early music information retrieval systems. What they have in common is that they generate their musical database index from music stored as MIDI files and effectively this reduces the problem of retrieval by content to that of text searching. The reason for this is that MIDI is a format which encodes instructions on how to synthesise music, instructions such as which note to play and for how long, rather than a digital version of the actual music. While systems such as MELDEX and QBH allow progress with the information retrieval aspects, not all music is available in MIDI format; human singing, for example cannot be represented as MIDI and there is no robust and reliable mechanism to transcode digital audio into MIDI as MIDI is normally generated at the time that the audio itself is first played.

Our work targets the development of a music information retrieval system based on indexing raw or compressed audio but not dependent on it being in MIDI format. Currently it is limited to monophonic music sources but that is just a starting point, which we hope to build on.

3   Audio

Audio is generated by a sound creating source and it exists as pressure waves travelling through a medium, air for example. The human ear has a frequency range between roughly 20 Hz and 20,000 Hz and the human voice box produces sounds between 50 Hz and 5,000 Hz. Audio is a continuous signal and therefore must be sampled to be stored digitally. Sampling involves measuring and recording pressure waves at successive moments in time quantifying the continuous signal as a series of discrete values. The parameters of sampling are the sampling rate (the number of times per second that the signal is sampled), the sample size (number of bits used in each sample) and whether the signal is a mono or stereo signal.

The *sampling rate* is the number of times per second that the continuous signal is quantised. Figure 1 shows that the greater the sampling rate, the truer the stored representation is to the original sound.

Sampling is subject to the Nyquist theorem which states that, to be able to reproduce a signal accurately, at least two samples of each cycle of its waveform needs to be stored. This is important because the sampling rate has to be twice the maximum frequency present in the signal to be recorded. So, for speech quality recordings, a sampling rate of 11,025 samples per second (Maximum frequency range 5,512 Hz) is sufficient and for CD quality recordings 44,100 samples per second (Maximum frequency range 22,050 Hz) is needed.

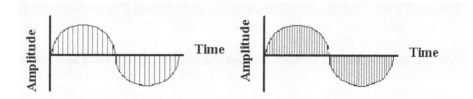

Fig. 1. Different sampling rates

Sampled audio is normally stored using 8 or 16 *bits per sample*. Using 8 bits per sample allows audio to be represented with values ranging from -128 to 127. Using 16 bits per sample gives a sample range of -32,768 to 32,767 per sample.

It should be obvious that sampling audio with 16 bits gives better resolution, that is, it gives a better representation of the continuous pressure waves which means that at playback time, a more accurate rendition of the original audio can be generated.

To store stereo quality sound every sample must be sampled twice, one for each channel, left and right. A typical sampling application will, for CD quality sound, sample the pressure waves 44,100 times per second, twice for stereo sound, using 16 bits per sample (see Figure 2). Sampled audio is stored in a format known as PCM which is also referred to as raw or uncompressed audio.

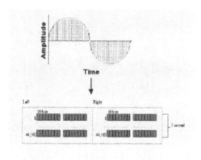

Fig. 2. Sampling CD quality audio

There are many different formats available for encoding music. These include AIFF, AU, WAV, VOC, Real Audio, MP3, Windows Media Format and MIDI. Formats like AIFF and WAV contain uncompressed raw audio data with an associated file header. WAV can be divided into blocks with headers for each block. Microsoft and IBM designed the WAV format while AIFF was developed by Apple. AU was developed by Sun Microsystems and is mu-law encoded PCM. Kientzle [Kientzle, 98] provides an excellent insight into the different sound formats that are commonly used today. Real Audio, MP3, Windows Media Format and Ogg Vorbis are all examples of audio formats that can be compressed and streamed over the Internet. Compressing audio files can be achieved by applying techniques such as psychoacoustic principles, sub-band coding and bit rate reduction [Pan, 95].

Among the different formats for encoding audio, MIDI format files are unique in that they do not actually store audio, rather they store instructions that a synthesiser can interpret to synthesise music. This means that MIDI files are much smaller than their equivalent, generated audio files, and it is trivial to gain access to features of the audio such as the melody or timing information. Other formats exist for storing music in stave notation, abc format for example.

4   Music Fundamentals

Audio, whether digital or analogue, exists in both the time and frequency domains. The time domain data relates directly to the pressure waves created by a sound source, a human voice box or a speaker. This domain is useful if we want to scale a song up or down (make it louder/ quieter), edit it (copy, cut and paste sections) etc. A time domain representation of audio is shown in Figure 3.

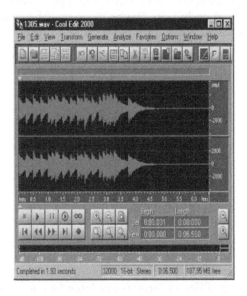

Fig. 3. Time domain, represented in the audio editing software CoolEdit 2000

The frequency domain contains all the frequency data, and it is here the presence of a particular frequency at a particular moment in time can be observed. CD quality music is sampled at 44,100 samples per second, giving a frequency range for the sampled audio from 0 Hz to 22,050 Hz which corresponds roughly to the frequency range of the human ear, 20 Hz to 20,000 Hz. A Fourier transformation can be used to convert sampled music from the time domain to the frequency domain.

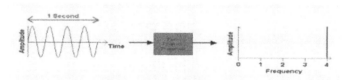

Fig. 4. A 4 Hz Sin wave with its frequency spectrum

A Fourier transform takes a number of PCM samples as input and generates the frequency spectrum for those samples. For example, on the left-hand side of Figure 4 there is a sampled sound. This is demonstrated by a sine wave, with a frequency of 4 Hz, that is the signal repeats 4 times every second. Applying a Fourier transform on this sound generates the output on the right, a frequency spectrum. A frequency domain representation is shown in Figure 5.

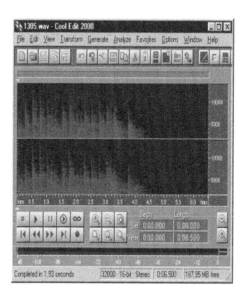

Fig. 5. Frequency domain, represented in the audio editing software CoolEdit 2000

The frequency spectrum generated by a Fourier transform is the frequency range (from 0 Hz to the maximum frequency) divided up into a number of equal sized bins. Each bin contains the amplitude or loudness of the frequency that the bin represents. The greater the number of bins, the more informative a frequency spectrum that can be generated. This is shown in Figure 6.

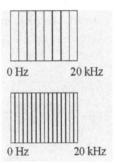

Fig. 6. The difference between an 8 and 16 point Fourier transform

Analysing the frequency spectrum of a sound created by an instrument will show a strong presence of the fundamental frequency followed by a decaying amplitude presence at integer multiples of the fundamental frequency. Harmonics of the note C in the first octave are shown in Table 1.

Table 1. Harmonics of the note C (Octave 1)

Fundamental Frequency	32.70 Hz
Harmonic 1	65.41 Hz
Harmonic 2	130.81 Hz
Harmonic 3	261.63 Hz
Harmonic 4	523.25 Hz
Harmonic 5	1046.50 Hz
Harmonic 6	2093.00 Hz

Western music is played by tuning instruments to a musical system known as "Equal Tempering". The Equal Tempering system evolved from the music theories of the ancient Greek mathematicians. [Kientzle, 98, p14]. The Equal Tempering system is divided into octaves with 12 notes between each octave. A piano standard, for example, has 88 notes across 8 octaves. The Equal Tempering system assumes that the note known as middle A is 440Hz, the first note C starting 32.70 Hz. This is shown in Figure 7.

5   The Ceolaire System

CEOLAIRE is a music information retrieval system which we built to support information retrieval on digital music by matching user's music queries directly against the melody content of recorded songs. The CEOLAIRE user interface is a graphical web-based Java applet which is accessible using any conventional web browser over the WWW. Songs are represented in CEOLAIRE as a string of letters where each letter represents the type of change in pitch from one note in

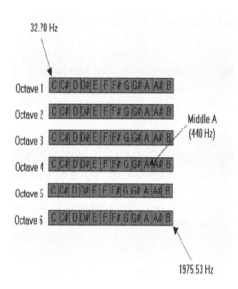

Fig. 7. Part of the Equal Tempering System and corresponding frequencies

the song to the next. A note can have a higher, lower or repeated value when compared to its predecessor and this allows songs to be represented as simple strings of the 3-letter alphabet (U) up, (D) down or (S) same. The sequence of note changes are used to represent both songs and user's queries and matching occurs between these. CEOLAIRE runs on an IBM S/390 mainframe machine running virtual instances of the SuSE Linux operating system.

5.1 Melody Extraction

CEOLAIRE reads in music files stored in PCM or MP3 format into its database and in order to generate an internal representation of the actual notes played from which we can then compute the string of note changes used to represent a song, we must automatically extract the melody from the song file. The first step of the melody extraction process is to generate frequency spectra for the music file. CEOLAIRE uses Fast Fourier Transforms (FFT) to generate these, one of the reasons being for speed. These spectra are then subject to a filtering process which filters out equal tempering notes. Initially, the music files are analysed for meta-data, sampling rate etc. before the detailed note analysis is performed.

Frequency Spectra Generation. The music file is processed in windows incrementaly. Each window is 2,205 samples in size, resulting in 20 windows per second. The window is passed to a hamming function to converge any sharp jumps at the beginning or the end of the window towards zero, minimising the introduction of noise. The window of PCM samples are then passed to a 32, 768 point fast Fourier routine which computes the frequency spectrum for that window. The computed spectrum is divided up into bins which are 1.3 Hz in size, that is, the spectrum is in increments of 1.3 Hz. The difference between Note C (32.70 Hz) and C# (34.65 Hz) of the first octave is 1.95 Hz and CEOLAIRE needs to be able to distinguish between the two notes, which is why we use a 32,768 point Fast Fourier Transform for the spectrum analysis.

Note Filtering. Note filtering is achieved with the use of a 72 note look-up table. As stated earlier, each musical note comprises a fundamental frequency with corresponding harmonics at integer multiples of that fundamental. Each column in the filtering table corresponds to a note and every row entry constitutes the presence or absence of the amplitude of the fundamental frequency or one of the harmonics for that note. An example of the note filtering table is shown in Figure 8.

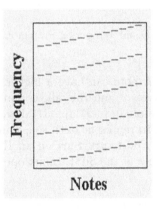

Fig. 8. Note filtering table

Using the table CEOLAIRE takes the computed spectrum and filters out the notes that are present in the spectrum. This output of the filter is the calculated intensity of all 72 notes. The output forms the basis of a melody representation for the given music file, which can be used to build a index for a musical search engine, for subsequent queries.

Music as Text Strings. The melody representation used is UDS (Up, Down, Same) notation which was first proposed by Dowling [Dowling, 78] who discovered that the perceived change in pitch was enough to match tunes from memory. The melody of a song is defined by comparing the change from one note to the next, throughout the entire file. These changes are recorded as a note either going up (U), going down (D), or repeated (S) relative to the previous note, irrespective of any timing information. As the first note has no previous note, the UDS notation starts with the change from the first note to the second. The calculated UDS string for the entire file is then segmented into varying length overlapping sub-strings or *n-grams* from 2 up to 20, 20 being an arbitrary limit. These varying length n-grams are then used to identify the song, i.e. a term in the song's index is a single instance of one of the n-grams, i.e. 'UDDUU' contained within the song.

When faced with the task of generating a music query which will itself be in a music format, a user will find it easier to generate a query using UDS notation than to be able to recall exact note values. This is shown in Figure 9.

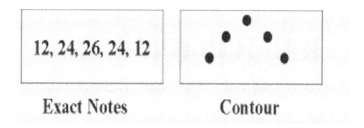

Fig. 9. Exact notes versus contour

5.2   The Ceolaire User Interface

CEOLAIRE has a web interface which uses a Java applet to aid the user when generating a music query. The interface is shown in Figure 10.

Query Formulation. CEOLAIRE's query generation interface helps the user when generating a query. This is achieved by displaying the query graphically to the user as it is being formulated. A query note is assumed to be a candidate note and is drawn in red on the painting screen until it is committed as an actual query note. The query screen is split up into three parts; the virtual keyboard, the paint area and the command buttons. The command buttons are used to delete notes, reset the query, and submit the query to the search engine. A query can be formulated by either playing notes on the virtual keyboard or by drawing the notes on the painting screen.

Virtual Keyboard. When formulating a search query, the user is presented with a virtual keyboard. As a user moves the mouse pointer over the keyboard the display is updated with the position of the candidate note on the paint area. This is depicted by the presence of a red circle which moves up and down as the user moves the mouse pointer over the keyboard. When the user presses a key, the note is no longer assumed to be a candidate note and is committed as a query note. The note is then played and drawn in blue on the paint area. The

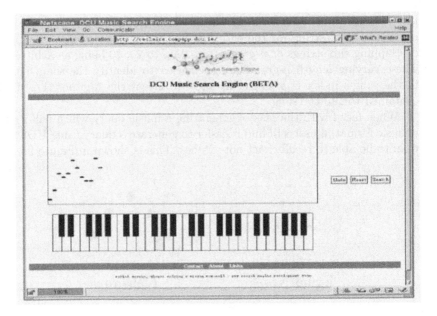

Fig. 10. CEOLAIRE's interface

piano key also gives an impression that it has been pushed down. The red helper ball then moves on to the next note position helping the user to guide the note to its next position.

Paint Area. The paint area can be used to draw a query. The user achieves this by either clicking or dragging the mouse inside the drawing area. The paint area can also be used to refine a query that was generated using the keyboard.

Support for Query Formulation. In comparison with text retrieval, when formulating a music search query, there is no such thing as a "spelling error" which can be detected at the time of query formulation. However, given the difficulties we have in formulating music queries, it can be expected that there is some proportion of spelling errors in query tunes. A text search engine does not normally try to accommodate misspelled words in the search, although the web search engine Google [Google] can offer the user a close alternative to a misspelled word if it believes a misspelling has occurred in the query.

One way that misspelling in queries can be accommodated is by using n-grams. When using n-grams all indexable terms are first broken up into overlapping fragments of the original term, or n-grams. Before submitting a query to the search engine it also is broken up into the same size n-grams. The retrieval process then ranks the documents in the order of documents that have the most matches.

Misspelling can also be accommodated by using string matching or dynamic programming techniques to evaluate how close a misspelled word is to a dictionary of correctly spelled words. In fact a lot of the techniques applied to matching music in different systems are based on string matching algorithms [McNab et al., 97][Ghias et al., 95].

When a user creates a musical query, errors can also be introduced. These errors include forgetting a note in the query, inserting an incorrect note, or repeating a note. These types of errors are referred to as *insertion*, *deletion* and *duplication* and are shown in Figure 11.

Insertion	Deletion	Duplication
marmal**x**ade	mar**ml**ade	marmal**aa**de

Fig. 11. Examples of *insertion, deletion* and *duplication* errors of the word 'marmalade'

Whether or not a music information system should accommodate these errors is debatable, but it is something that a user-friendly system should strive to achieve. One of the ways that such a system can achieve this is by using n-grams of notes to introduce a notion of 'fuzziness'. CEOLAIRE's interface also helps to combat the introduction of this error at the source using a strategy of *hear, view* and *review*. The user *hears* the melody of the query as it is being generated. He/she can also *view* the graphical representation of the query on the paint area and finally the user can play the query back (*review*) before submitting it to the search engine. By adding these extra features, the CEOLAIRE query handler puts a lot more emphasis on the query generation stage than one would normally find in a information retrieval system.

5.3 Retrieval

A query is broken into a set of query n-grams before being submitted to the search engine via the query handler. The similarity between a query and a tune is calculated using the OKAPI probabilistic model. An example result set of the query from Figure 10 is shown in Figure 12. There is currently no opportunity for relevance feedback in the current version of CEOLAIRE although we are working on this as future work. No use is made of timing information from either the query or the database tune, that is the duration of the notes are deemed irrelevant. In the current operational system there are 7,718 music files. CEOLAIRE supports sub second retrieval.

6   Engine Evaluation

The reason we have developed the CEOLAIRE system has been to allow us to work with audio and to develop retrieval techniques which stem from analysis at the signal level and to observe the impact of variations in our melody extraction and

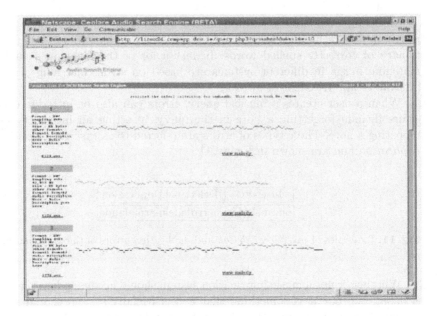

Fig. 12. Ranked list of returned results

indexing technique. To measure the efficacy of CEOLAIRE and how accurately it really represents the melody being indexed, we needed to determine what representation was suitable for use in the index and whether that representation was in fact true to the original, and any evaluation of a music retrieval system should first start with an evaluation of how it generates its index. As our index is based on encoded digital music, we must be able to quantify its performance or 'correctness'. CEOLAIRE underwent a number of experiments as part of this evaluation. The goal was to compare CEOLAIRE's music representation derived from automatically extracted melodies, against a music representation which we knew to be correct. This we accomplished by using MIDI files.

MIDI files store music as *note on* and *note off* "events" which can be readily extracted automatically. These start and end times for notes were used to generate note files which were compared to note files derived from CEOLAIRE's automatic melody extraction engine.

6.1   The Data Set

The data set used in our experiments to measure the effectiveness of melody extraction was made up of files taken from the NZDL MIDI folk song collection which consists of about 10,000 type 0 MIDI files i.e. they are monophonic (have single notes playing at all points in time). The music files are all folk songs belonging to the following categories:

- North American and British folk songs
- Irish folk songs
- German ballads and folk songs
- Chinese ethnic and provincial songs

The NZDL MIDI folk song collection was chosen because of its size and ease of access to the musical data (MIDI events etc.). A MIDI file contains all the information needed by a synthesiser to synthesise a sound - note, start time, end time, instrument, etc. The information we needed, which is easily extracted was *note, start time* and *end time*. Using the start time, end time and note played, a time versus note representation of the song was obtained. This is shown in Figure 13. This representation is the same that the CEOLAIRE melody extraction output uses and is referred to as a notes file.

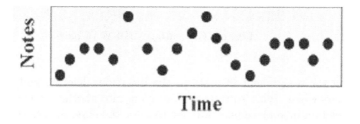

Fig. 13. Note versus Time representation

6.2   Pre-analysis

Before any experiments could be run, notes files had to be generated. The MIDI files were synthesised using an open source MIDI synthesiser called *Timidity* [Timidity]. Instead of playing the output on a sound card, it was captured and converted into PCM encoded WAV files.

The WAV files were then subject to CEOLAIRE's melody extraction engine to generate a notes file for each WAV file. A notes file for each MIDI file was also generated by analysing the start and end events of individual notes. This process is shown in Figure 14. All the experiments listed below use some form of the MIDI-WAV pair of files. Timidity was only able to process 7,718 of the files. It had trouble reading the rest.

The search engine accommodates the melody of the song files by using n-grams to hold their structure, rather than just storing their exact notes. The notes files were all converted into a set of n-grams of notes for each file, with a sliding window of notes, using one note as an offset.

In all, four sets of experiments were carried out to measure the melody extraction engine's level of correctness. The comparison operator chosen for the experiments was a simple string comparison algorithm and the minimal edit distance function which can evaluate how similar two strings are. It does this by

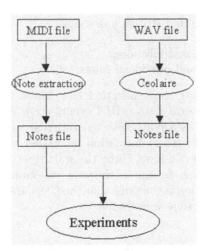

Fig. 14. Generating MIDI-WAV pairs

allowing the assignment of costs to the insertion, deletion and replacement of characters when trying to convert one string into another. The cost of an insertion, deletion or replacement was set to 1 for the experiments that use minimal edit distance. The total cost of an individual MIDI-WAV comparison was divided by the length of the longest string giving a percentage figure indication of the similarity of the two strings. Rather than doing a simple difference comparison of the files to see if they are similar, processed representations of both MIDI-WAV outputs were used to generate a more informative comparison.

6.3   Exact and Note Modulo 12 Experiments

The first experiment we did was to evaluate the similarity between the notes file generated directly from the MIDI file and the notes file generated automatically from the PCM WAV file, generated in turn from the MIDI synthesised audio of the original file. This was computed based on the precise notes and tested for exact matches. The purpose of this was to determine if at any given time in the WAV notes file, does a corresponding similar n-gram exist with its counterpart created from the MIDI file. Both sets of n-grams used the same value for n, n=5. N-gram pairs were compared using a string comparison function. The total number of matching n-grams was computed for every n-gram pair. This total was then divided by the total number of n-grams to give a percentage of how close the sets of n-grams actually are. This is shown in figure 15.

The second set of experiments undertaken was to evaluate similarity using *note modulo 12*. This would bring the current alphabet of notes of size 72 down to a size of 12 by mapping each note occurrence into a single octave, or computing it modulo 12. The use of a smaller alphabet enhances the search engine by allowing for octave-irrelevant melody searches. The note C in any octave would

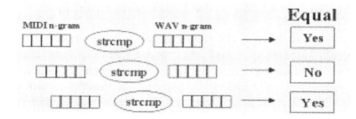

Fig. 15. n-gram comparison

simply be represented as C. A jump from note C in the first octave to note C in the second would be noted as *CC* rather than *C1C2*. A query would be treated exactly the same way at retrieval. As with the first experiment a string comparison function was used to compute a equal match. The results we got in the first two experiments are shown in Table 2 and in summary, these are not very impressive. What we can see from these results is that the majority of note file pairs, which emanate from the same original MIDI file, are not being identified as the same. The reduction of the allowable song space down to 12 notes, i.e. 1 octave, making the analysis invariant to octave choice, improves the results only marginally. Analysis of these results has shown that there is a problem with timing in the way that the Timidity synthesiser generates audio in that it ends a note before its prescribed time. Our guess as to why this is so is that the human ear will hear a note even after its generation has ceased and the Timidity synthesiser is taking account of that by not reproducing notes exactly as prescribed in the MIDI file.

Table 2. Results of Exact and Note modulo 12

	Note%12	Exact Note
Number of files/songs	7,718	7,718
Average dissimilarity	20.87%	18.52%
Standard deviation	16.2	14.35
Number of notes files with perfect match	0	61
Total number of ngrams	3,502,464	3,502,464
Total Number of ngrams that match	2,688,625	2,791,679

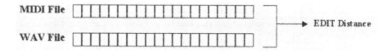

Fig. 16. Edit distance used for exact note and note contour

6.4   Measuring Similarity by Exact Note Contour

In an attempt to address the timing problem introduced by the Timidity synthesiser, the third set of experiments we did was to evaluate similarity between
notes files based on exact note contour. This experiment simplifies the structure
of the representation of melody by ignoring the duration of notes (See example
in Figure 17). It records only the fact that a note has changed and what that
note is. This experiment will show how well CEOLAIRE extracts individual notes
irrespective of the note's duration. This is important if the timing or duration
of the original notes differ from that produced by the extraction engine, as we
have found above. Any user friendly music information retrieval system should
minimise the imposition of restrictions on the user due to user inability to recall
music or formulate a musical query. As mentioned before, Dowling showed that
the change in pitch is sufficient for retrieval [Dowling, 78], thus reducing the
importance of the duration of the note when it comes to melody retrieval. In our
experiments, string sequences were created for both sets of notes files, but there
was no guarantee that the strings would be the same length so the edit distance
was used as normal, with costs for insertion, deletion and replacement. The cost
was set to 1 for all the operations.

Given the following sequence of notes

12, 12, 12, 23, 23, 34, 36, 36, 42, 42, 42, 16, 16

it is reduced to

12, 23, 34, 36, 42, 16

Fig. 17. Reading notes by exact note contour

These results (see Table 3) show a marked improvement in the measured
similarity between sets of notes files generated directly from MIDI and from
automatically recognised melody taken, in turn, from synthesised versions of the
same MIDI files.

Table 3. Results from the Exact Contour experiment

	Exact Contour
Number of files/songs	7,718
Average dissimilarity	0.88%
Standard deviation	4.76
Number of notes files with perfect match	7,233

6.5   Measuring Similarity Based on Contour

The fourth set of experiments undertaken was to evaluate similarity between notes files based on contour. This experiment simplifies a notes file even further than above by bringing it to a representation of contour over time (see example in Figure 18). Again, actual note duration and timing information is deemed irrelevant and discarded, and just the fact that a note has changed is used as the index representation. Here the MIDI-WAV pairs of files are converted into a simple up / down structure based on how the notes change. Costs were the same as with experiment 3, a value of 1 for any of the operations. The results of this experiment are shown in Table 4.

Given the following sequence of notes

12, 12, 12, 23, 23, 34, 36, 36, 42, 42, 42, 16, 16

it is reduced to

UP, UP, UP, UP, DOWN

Fig. 18. Reading notes by contour

Table 4. Results from the Contour experiment

	Contour
Number of files/songs	7,718
Average dissimilarity	0.88%
Standard deviation	4.76
Number of notes files with perfect match	7,233

The fact that tables 3 and 4 are identical shows that no extra similarity benefits are to be gained by using note contour rather than exact note contour. It can be observed that the 0.88% dissimilarity from the exact note contour experiment show that the extraction engine is good at extracting the correct note. This is confirmed by the fact that if the extraction engine was finding incorrect notes, these two dissimilarity figures would not be the same. Comparing tables 2 and 3 the dissimilarity figures differ by two orders of magnitude. The reason for this was observed to be the fact that the notes files generated by Timidity constantly finished earlier than the prescribed time. Removing the duration of notes as was done for the exact note contour experiment eliminated this problem, hence the low dissimilarity figure.

7   Conclusion

This paper has presented an introduction to the CEOLAIRE Music Information Retrieval System and has also presented a series of experiments which measure the effectiveness of the system's melody extraction engine.

The results show that CEOLAIRE works well on the automatic extraction of melody from monophonic music sources when the similarity measure used is based on melodic contour or melodic exact note contours. Initially, this may seem somewhat of a cop-out as in our series of experiments we appear to have simplified the similarity measure we use until we get strong enough similarities between notes files generated from the same MIDI sources but using two different approaches. This approach is justified by us when we consider that others [McNab et al., 97][Beeferman, 97] have already shown (when working with MIDI files) that such melody contours are a sufficient base for good quality retrieval from digital music. Using MIDI as format for generating PCM files for comparison purposes has also been carried out by [Plumbley et al., 01].

Our contribution in this paper is to report that the melody extraction engine in CEOLAIRE, while perhaps not perfect in recognising the absolute notes played in a music file, is good enough to calculate the melodic contour and even the exact note melodic contour with enough accuracy to allow subsequent retrieval to proceed. Measuring the effectiveness of such retrieval will allow us to refine and improve upon the retrieval engine we have developed and that will be the subject of further work.

A further stage of our work will be to develop and then evaluate the extraction engine on polyphonic music sources where the notes being played at any single point in time could be a combination of harmonies with an underlying melodic thread. Currently the identification of single notes, let alone the complete melody, from polyphonic music is beyond what we can currently achieve. Work such as that reported in [Plumbley et al., 01] gives a good review of polyphonic music analysis and shows that analysis of chords of up to three notes is now possible, but only on very small data sets whereas in our work we are interested in working with much larger volumes.

Acknowledgments. We would like to thank David Bainbridge for giving us access to the NZDL MIDI folksong collection.

References

[Beeferman, 97]   Beeferman, D. "QPD: Query by Pitch Dynamics, Indexing Tonal Music By Content", 15-829 Course Project, School of Computer Science, Canegie Mellon University - December 1997.

[Dovey, 01]   Dovey, M. "A technique for 'regular expression' style searching in polyphonic music". *Proceedings of the 2nd ISMIR*, Bloomington, Indiana, USA, 15 - 17 October, 2001, 179-185.

[Dowling, 78]   Dowling, W. "Scale and contour: Two components of a theory of memory for melodies". *Psychological Review*, 85(4), 1978, 341-354.

[Foote, 99]   Foote, J. "An overview of audio information retrieval" *In Multimedia Systems*, 7 (1), pp.January 1999, 2-11.

[Foote, 00]   Foote J., "ARTHUR: Retrieving Orchestral Music by Long-Term Structure". *Proceedings of the 1st ISMIR*, Plymouth, Massachusetts, USA, 23-25 October, 2000.

[Ghias et al., 95]   Ghias, A., Logan, J., Chamberlain, D. and Smith, B. "Query by Humming - Musical Information Retrieval in an Audio Database". *Proceedings of ACM Multimedia 95, San Francisco, CA USA*, 5 - 9 November, 1995, 231 - 236.

[Google]   Google. http://www.google.com/ (Last visited - January 2002).

[Kientzle, 98]   Kientzle, T. *A Programmers Guide to Sound*. Addison Wesley, 1998.

[Lenström et al., 00]   Lemström K. and Perttu S., "SEMEX - An efficient Music Retrieval Prototype". *Proceedings of the 1st ISMIR*, Plymouth, Massachusetts, USA, October 23-25, 2000.

[McNab et al., 97]   McNab, R., Smith, L., Bainbridge, D. and Witten, I. "The New Zealand Digital Library MELody inDEX", *D-Lib Magazine*, May 1997.

[Napster]   Napster Inc. http://www.napster.com/ (Last visited - January 2002).

[Pan, 95]   Pan, D. "A tutorial on MPEG / Audio Compression". *IEEE Multimedia*, 2 (2), 1995, 60 - 74.

[Plumbley et al., 01]   Plumbley, M., Abdallah, S., Bello J., Davies, M., Klingseisen J., Monti, G. and Sandler, M. "ICA and Related Models Applied to Audio Analysis and Separation". To appear in *Proceedings of the 4th International ICSC Symposium on Soft Computing and Intelligent Systems for Industry*, Paisley, Scotland, 26 - 29 June, 2001.

[Pye, 00]   Pye, D. "Content-Based Methods for the Management of Digital Music". *Proceedings of the International Conference on Audio, Speech and Signal Processing (ICASSP)*, Istanbul, Turkey, 5-9 June 2000.

[Timidity]   Timidity Synthesiser. MIDI to WAVE converter/player. Available at http://www.goice.co.jp/member/mo/timidity/ (Last visited - January 2002).

[Wold et al., 96]   Wold, E., Blum, T., Keislar, D. and Wheaton, J. "Content-Based Classification, Search, and Retrieval of Audio", *IEEE Multimedia*, 3 (3), 1996, 27-36.

Organising and Searching Partially Indexed Image Databases

Gérald Duffing and Malika Smaïl

UMR 7503 LORIA
Campus Sciences BP 239
54506 Vandoeuvre-Les-Nancy France,
{duffing,malika}@loria.fr

Abstract. This paper addresses the issue of efficient retrieval from image corpora in which only a little proportion is textually indexed. We propose a hybrid approach integrating textual search with content-based retrieval. We show how a preliminary double clustering of image corpus exploited by an adequate retrieval process constitutes an answer to the pursued objective. The retrieval process takes advantage of user-system interaction via relevance feedback mechanism whose results are integrated in a virtual image. Experimental results on the PICAP prototype are reported ed and discussed to demonstrate the effectiveness of this work.

1 Introduction

Whereas collecting thousands of images is now possible, an accurate and comprehensive image indexing is still a time-consuming and an error-prone process. We claim, however, that *partially indexed* corpora can be organised in a way that allows interesting retrieval performance.

Two main categories of image retrieval systems exist. Systems allowing only *keyword querying* only take into account manually indexed images, and performance will depend on the quality of indexing. Many indexing schemes are available, from classical keyword vectors to more complex data structures. Of course, the difficulty of the indexing task varies accordingly [4]. *Content-based retrieval* systems use visual similarity to retrieve relevant images [21]. The main advantage of this approach is that features can be computed off-line [25,9,22,12].

We notice that content-based systems give little attention to the semantic part of the query. However, we believe that keywords remain an important mediating object between users' desires and image content. Therefore, we propose a new retrieval strategy based on a prior corpus organisation that takes into account both textual and visual aspects. Our work applies to domain-independent corpora, in which few images are actually manually indexed. This is crucial, as image corpora easily include large amounts of images.

This paper includes a brief description of some related works (§ 2). We examine in § 3 how a corpus may be characterised and organised. Then we show

F. Crestani, M. Girolami, and C.J. van Rijsbergen (Eds.): ECIR 2002, LNCS 2291, pp. 22–40, 2002.

how a retrieval process can be designed to take advantage of this organisation (§ 4). Finally, current experimentations and results are presented and discussed (§ 5).

2   Related Work

Drawbacks of pure visual retrieval systems have already been pointed out [1] and the combination of visual and textual features has been addressed in several ways. Those hybrid approaches try to fulfill a double objective of textual and visual relevance.

Working on a restrictive domain helps achieving good results. For example, locating and naming faces on images or movies is possible by combining very specialised visual features with textual features extracted from captions [7,19]. When no particular assumption can be made on the domain, textual description can be attached to images by means of keywords, and pictorial content can be characterised by visual features, whereas no link is established between these two different spaces: some systems rely on keywords, shape, colour and texture to build a similarity measure [13]. Textual annotations have to be provided by hand. As an attempt to bring together textual and visual properties, keywords can be associated to a combination of visual features [14]. These associations are not established automatically. In the web context, images come with texts in HTML pages. Assuming that the text is related to the content of images, the latent semantic indexing technique allows the automatic computation of descriptors including both textual and visual features [20]. Other statistical methods can be utilised in order to associate words to images, based on some learning processes [11].

These approaches do not consider partially indexed corpora. They give little attention to feedback mechanism. We believe, however, that valuable information can be extracted from user interaction.

3   Corpus Organisation

In our approach, images are characterised on a visual and *possibly* textual point of view. Indeed, not all images need to come with a textual annotation, whereas some visual features are automatically computed on each image. Our first goal is to select some relevant features, that can highlight image similarities, and be used thereafter for classification purposes.

3.1   Textual Description of Images

We assume that the collection of images is partially and roughly indexed with text. In other words, a small number of images are associated with textual description, and, when this description is available, three or four words are sufficient.

The lexical reference system WordNet [6] is used as a knowledge source to help dealing with synonyms, namely. In WordNet, words are organised into synonym sets called "synsets". Each synset represents a lexical concept and is connected to other synsets with different kinds of semantic relationships that provides access, for example, to "generic", "specific", "antonym" concepts.

The classical vector model and its associated cosine measure have been chosen as a textual similarity measure [18], and will be used for both clustering and retrieval.

3.2   Visual Description of Images

Image analysis techniques provide us with many possible features to describe colour, texture or shape [16]. Each image can be automatically characterised by a set of features, but numerous problems remain. For example, it is well known that some features are particularly well adapted to a given domain, whereas they achieve poor results in other ones. Useful visual features are close to human perception, in order to take easily into account user judgements [15]. In our environment, we cannot assume domain-dependent knowledge that could help selecting relevant features, or defining specific ones, and thus we have to use "generic" features.

As a very general — though powerful — feature, we chose colour histogram [23], represented in L*u*v* colour space. L*u*v* is a device-inde–pendent and perceptually uniform colour model, thus well suited for comparisons. We considered three different colour spaces: RGB, L*u*v*, HVC. Not surprisingly, L*u*v* achieved the best results for colour comparisons.

A subset of 128 representative colours can be selected from the entire corpus, so that each image can be quantised according to this reduced colour map, and represented by a 128-components vector.

To improve localisation and to allow "layout" comparison, features are not only computed over the entire image, but also on small image areas: a fixed grid is applied on the image, defining 32x32 pixels squares called *tiles*. A colour histogram is computed for each tile of each image in the corpus. The spatial organisation of visually homogeneous areas (according to the colour feature) provides for a rough sketch of the "shapes" contained in the image.

This basic visual characterisation is intended to test the validity of our approach. As a second step, we are planning to introduce more powerful features, such as texture and shape, that will capture other visual properties of images. These are, however, difficult issues. On one hand, extraction of the "relevant" shape is not straightforward [1]. Many approaches exist, some of them being more adapted to object recognition purposes (*i.e.*, when "known objects" have to be carefully characterised, before attempting to identify them in various images). On the other hand, while it is easy to give a rough description of texture, we believe that fine texture characterisation has to be achieved on homogeneous zones. In both cases, some kind of image segmentation will be required.

3.3   Classification-Based Corpus Organisation

For corpus organisation purposes we focused on clustering techniques [3], which aim at grouping similar objects. These techniques have been extensively used and studied in the field of Information Retrieval [8,24,5,26]. It is also worth noting that these techniques have been mainly applied to textual information organisation; we intend to use them for *image* classification as well, based on visual features. In our approach, agglomerative hierarchical clustering (AHC) has been chosen to classify the corpus. Other works suggested alternative classifications of images based on visual features [10].

Two classifications have been constructed over the corpus: a textual and a visual classification, based on features described in sections 3.1 and 3.2 above; the resulting structure is called "dendrogram".

The textual dendrogram includes only textually indexed images, that is, potentially few images. The visual dendrogram, however, includes all images, as the colour feature computation can be carried out automatically.

The advantage of hierarchical structure is that the cluster size can be controlled by a cut-off value (cf. fig. 1): at lower levels, clusters contain few, very similar images. The cluster size grows as we consider higher levels, and this suggests a simple way to balance precision against recall (*Precision* is defined as the proportion of the retrieved documents which are relevant, whereas *recall* is the proportion of relevant documents that are actually retrieved). The cut-off value is determined during retrieval session, and is thus context-adaptive.

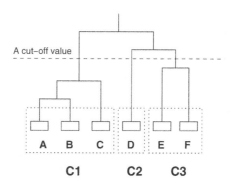

Fig. 1. The dendrogram: a hierarchic structure produced by Agglomerative Hierarchic Clustering.

4   Image Retrieval Process

4.1   Process Outline

In our point of view, textual query the best way for the user to launch a retrieval process. Of course, the visual aspect is important for image search, but it seems difficult to assume that the user has already found a good example of the image(s) he/she is looking for or that he/she is able to sketch the desired images.

Figure 2 shows the overall image retrieval process. The initial textual query allows the retrieval system to propose a first set of images. An important characteristic of our approach is that this initial image set contains both textually indexed and not indexed images thanks to the tunnel mechanism (§ 4.3).

The user can then express his visual needs or preferences by providing precise feedback. This is performed by giving examples and counter-examples of what is relevant in respect with textual aspect and visual aspect (colours, layout...). Indeed, users find it more comfortable to provide interactively examples of relevant and irrelevant images. This feedback is exploited by the system in order to build a *virtual image* which gathers its understanding of the user's current need.

A graphical interface allows user to pick words and to browse through synsets, using *generic/specific*, *synonym* and *part of* relationships to navigate. The vocabulary is limited to nouns from *WordNet*. Each selected item is then qualified : "absolutely", "rather" or "possibly" *present* or *absent* in the image.

Section 4.3 describes the cluster collecting process and our image ranking scheme. Section 4.2 explains how the virtual image constitutes a support for the relevance feedback mechanism (feedback criteria and modalities will be given). To improve the legibility of the paper, we present this section before the collecting and ranking section (since the latter operation, in the general case, assumes a visualisation phase and user's feedback gathering).

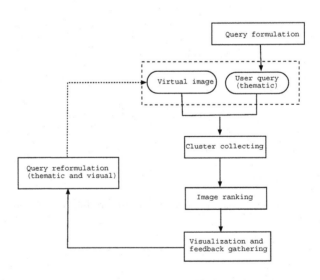

Fig. 2. The overall image retrieval process

4.2   Virtual Image as a Support for Relevance Feedback

After a visualisation step, it is important to gather information as precise as possible from user. Actually, images may have been judged relevant in only one point of view (textual or visual): the system needs to know in what extent a retrieved image is relevant or not to the user. To achieve this, we propose a twofold judgement on each image.

The theme. – This kind of judgement is used to determine what themes are to be searched or avoided. A relevant image may feature new interesting themes that should be included in the next query, by means of reformulation.

The colour. – Colour has been chosen as the most representative among visual indices. It is a fundamental visual property of images, as users are very sensitive to colour; it has also a great discriminant power [23].

For each judgement type, user can "accept", "reject" or have "no idea" about each selected image, and can moderate his judgement with a weight ranging from 1 to 10.

Furthermore, **the layout** seems to be an additional good criterion candidate, as it captures the whole "composition" of the image, and then some shape properties. In this work, "layout" refers to spatial localisation of blobs, each blob featuring some homogeneous visual feature. The user has the possibility to choose, among the proposed images, the most representative one (if any) according to the layout. This "typical" layout will be used for image ranking purposes at the next retrieval step.

From this judgement data, the system derives a representation of its understanding of user's needs. Practically, we are looking for discriminating information : we will try to find both colours and themes that are in common in the set of relevant images, and then in the set of irrelevant ones.

To handle this information, we introduce the **virtual image** concept. From the user feedback and from the features associated with displayed images, we can build two parts for wanted and unwanted image features, respectively. This applies both on textual and visual features. The reformulation allows the "filling" of these different parts of the virtual image as follows:

- **textual reformulation**: the thematic positive (resp. negative) feedback can be handled by a simple weighted averaging of the vectors representing the index of the user-relevant (resp. irrelevant) images.

- **visual reformulation**: as image colours are also represented by vectors, the same method can be applied to handle the positive and the negative feedback on the colour aspect as for textual reformulation.

4.3   Cluster Collecting and Image Ranking

The retrieval process consists in searching the textual dendrogram and the visual one in order to select some clusters likely to contain relevant images. The selected images are then ranked before being presented to the user.

Searching the textual or visual dendrogram is done by an ascendant method which performs a constrained generalisation of the low level clusters (adapted from [17]). We use constraints that control the minimum/max–imum size of the cluster, its dispersion rate, and the maximum distance. Depending on the collecting result, these constraints can be weakened.

Step 1 – Textual dendrogram search. — The thematic hierarchy is searched using the textual part of the virtual image (cosine measure is evaluated between "positive" part of the query and the cluster centroid). Depending on clusters size, though, not all images may be equally relevant to the query: this motivates an additional textual ranking process that will be used for the *tunnel* mechanism (see below). Let us suppose that cluster $C1$ is selected, in which image A is the best ranked.

Step 2 – Visual dendrogram search (direct). — The visual hierarchy is searched using the visual (colours) part of the virtual image (The "positive" part of the query and the cluster centroid are matched). This results in some likely interesting clusters.

Step 3 – Visual dendrogram search using tunnels. — The corpus organisation process (§ 3) has led to two different images classifications, and we believe that links can be established between the thematic classification and the visual one, yielding to a textual and visual synergy, which is based on the following hypothesis: "Textual similarity and visual similarity are not independent". Figure 3 illustrates this textual and visual cooperation called *tunnel*.

We assumed that image A from thematic cluster $C1$ is particularly relevant (step 1, above). The tunnel hypothesis tells us to consider visually similar images, which consists in locating image A in the visual dendrogram, and to consider that some "neighbourhood" around A as relevant. In our example, A also belongs to visual cluster $C2$, and all images in $C2$ will be selected as likely relevant (visually and textually). Some of them are indexed whereas others are not.

The overall advantage of this collecting process is that **non-indexed images have a chance to be retrieved** thanks to the tunnel mechanism even at the first retrieval attempt (*i.e.*, with a textual query). Retrieved images in all the selected clusters can now be **ranked** in a unique list. The following formula is used to rank images:

$$S = w * S_t + (1 - w) * S_v.$$

where the visual score (S_v) and thematic score (S_t) may be weighted by the user (w factor) so that it is possible to give more or less importance to visual search against textual search.

This ranking uses both positive and negative parts of the virtual image *i.e.*, what is wanted or unwanted by the user. Again, the cosine measure can be used for S_t and S_v after merging the positive and negative parts of the query in one vector (by affecting positive weights to wanted criteria and negative weights to unwanted ones).

Furthermore, if a typical layout has been chosen by the user, retrieval precision can be considerably improved by introducing a local visual matching (as opposed to the global colour-based matching). The term S_v above is then defined

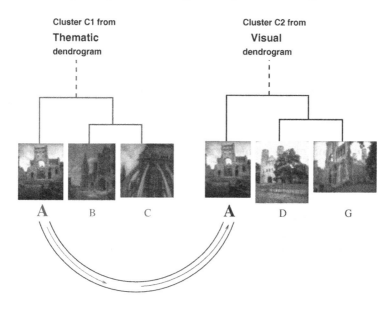

Fig. 3. The "tunnel" mechanism.

as a linear combination between a local term and a global term (the w_l factor gives less or more importance to the local visual term against the global one):

$$S_v = w_l * S_{l,v} + (1 - w_l) * S_{g,v}.$$

5   Experiments

5.1   Corpus Characteristics and Indexing

Experiments reported in this paper are based on an image corpus containing 2470 heterogeneous images (pictures, paintings, ...). In fact, almost every image is indexed with text, but the conducted experiments aim at evaluating the impact of partial indexing on retrieval in our approach. Therefore, we added to the PICAP prototype the facility to "hide" some of the textual indexing.

In this context, the text descriptions to hide have been chosen randomly, or by hand. *Random indexing* consists in choosing randomly a certain amount of images, and to make their indexing keywords "visible" to the system. *Ad hoc indexing* relies on manual selection of images for which indexing should be kept visible. We define three different indexing conditions:

- *Random indexing* of 20% of the total amount of images.
- *Random indexing* of 40% of the total amount of images.
- *Ad hoc indexing* of 5% of the total amount of images.

It is worth noting that *ad hoc* indexing concerns far less images than random indexing: this is on purpose, since we want to prove that our approach can achieve good performance, provided few images — chosen by hand — are indexed.

5.2   Experiment Description

To assess performance of the textual and visual approach, we let the user conduct an entire session (*i.e.*, consisting in as many iterations as he wants). Our goal is to determine whether the system allows retrieval of interesting images, that is, thematically and visually relevant images. As a retrieval session may return numerous images, and as each image is ranked according to its expected visual and textual relevance, we say that a retrieval session is "successful" whenever a certain amount of best ranked images are thematically and visually relevant.

We assume that images are presented to the user by groups of n images. We consider only the k first groups for evaluation. Each of these $k \times n$ images is evaluated by the user from a visual and textual point of view. Therefore, a symbolic grade is assigned to each image: A (very relevant), B (relevant), C (rather relevant), D (irrelevant), and E (totally irrelevant), according to its visual and textual user-relevance. Our decision rules are as follows: an image visually and thematically relevant gets grade A; an image visually or thematically relevant only gets grade C; finally, an image that is not thematically nor visually relevant gets grade E (of course, other decision rules may be adopted, depending on a particular search context).

We define a quality measure, noted Q, to evaluate the retrieval session performance, based on relevance judgements of the user (as described above), and on ranking:

$$Q = N \sum_{b=1}^{k} \left((k - b + 1) \sum_{p=1}^{n} v_{b,p} \right) \tag{1}$$

With:

> b group number,
> p image position within a group,
> $v_{b,p}$ relevance value associated with image
> at position p in group b,
> N normalisation factor.

The numerical value $v_{b,p}$ is derived from symbolic grades. In this experiment, we chose the values reported on table 2. Constant N may be set to 1, so that Q is a "general quality measure", or to $1/nk$, to obtain an "average quality measure".

A collection test of 11 queries has been defined, in order to evaluate system performance on the corpus. Table 1 lists these queries, along with a manual evaluation of the amount of potentially relevant images in the corpus.

Given the collection test described above, retrieval sessions have been conducted in different indexing conditions, namely 20%, 40% and *ad hoc* indexing. Only the 10 first images are taken into account (we consider 2 groups of 5 images, that is, $k = 2$ and $n = 5$ in equation 1), yielding a global performance measure Q. As the user may tune visual against textual weights to optimise the results, we also indicate the visual weight (in a range from 0 to 100). Table 3

Table 1. Collection test.

Query Number	Query Formulation	Total nbr of relevant images
1	People at the airport	6
2	Military aircrafts	116
3	Sea birds	33
4	Boats	55
5	Soldiers in the desert	11
6	A cliff and a river	13
7	Cities views	70
8	Mountain sports	21
9	Trains or locomotives	43
10	Old cars	41
11	Fruits sales at the market	11

Table 2. Numerical values for symbolic grades.

Symbol	Value
A	+5
B	+3
C	0
D	−1
E	−2

shows the results corresponding to our 11 queries under different indexing conditions. The information provided in these tables corresponds to whole retrieval sessions, that is, after feedback, if any. It is organised as follows: for each query (col. 1), and under various indexing conditions — that is, 20%, 40% or ad hoc indexing — (col. 2), relevance judgements are reported for the 10 best ranked images (col. 3 to 12): "T" stands for "thematically relevant", "V" for "Visually relevant". A session quality score Q is computed according to equation 1, with $k = 2$, $n = 5$, $N = 1$ (col. 13). Finally, the visual weight used to produce the reported results is given (col. 14).

5.3   Discussion

In our approach, the *tunnel* mechanism has been devised to allow collaboration of textual and visual retrieval techniques. Experiments show that, for each query, an interesting set of images has been retrieved, by means of textual and/or visual similarity measures (see table 3 for a complete report of our results, and tables 4 and 5 for a visual representation of our retrieval results for some queries).

Figure 4 reveals the contribution of textual, visual, and tunnel techniques. In this histogram, the average number of images retrieved using each technique is plotted. The lower part of the bar represent the number of images that are actually considered as thematically and visually relevant by user. We observe that the *tunnel* mechanism is fairly reliable: 62.5% of tunnel-retrieved images

Table 3. Query results (5% indexing is *ad hoc* indexing).

Qry Nbr	Index Cond.	1	2	3	4	5	6	7	8	9	10	Qual. Sc.	Vis. Wght
1	20%	TV	TV	TV	V	TV			TV	TV		44	70
	40%	TV	TV	TV	TV	TV						40	100
	5%	TV	TV	TV	TV	TV		TV				47	70
2	20%	TV	TV	T	TV	T	T		T			24	60
	40%	TV	TV	TV	TV	TV	TV	T				49	70
	5%	TV	TV	TV	TV	TV	T	T	T		T	48	90
3	20%	TV	TV	TV	TV	V	TV	V	V			41	70
	40%	TV	TV	TV	TV	V	V	V		T	T	38	30
	5%	TV	TV	T	TV	TV	T	T	T			36	40
4	20%	TV	V	T	V	TV	V		V	TV		16	60
	40%	TV	T	T	TV	TV	T				T	24	50
	5%	TV	TV	TV	TV	T		T	T	T	T	38	80
5	20%	TV	TV	TV	TV	TV	V		TV			49	100
	40%	TV	TV	TV	TV				T			32	50
	5%	TV	TV	TV	TV	TV	TV		TV	T	TV	63	70
6	20%	TV	TV	TV	TV				TV			37	100
	40%	TV	TV	TV	TV	TV	TV	V	V	V	TV	60	100
	5%	TV	TV	TV	TV	TV	TV	T	V	V	V	55	60
7	20%	TV	TV	V	TV	TV	V	T				34	90
	40%	TV	TV	TV	TV	TV					TV	47	100
	5%	TV	TV	TV	TV	TV	TV	T	V	TV	V	60	60
8	20%	TV	TV	TV	TV							26	60
	40%	TV	TV	TV		TV						26	70
	5%	TV	TV	TV	TV	TV	TV	TV			TV	61	100
9	20%	TV	TV	TV								12	60
	40%	TV	TV	TV	TV	TV		T			T	44	70
	5%	TV	TV	TV	TV	T	TV		TV	T		46	20
10	20%	TV	TV		TV	TV	TV			TV	TV	47	95
	40%	TV	TV	TV	TV	TV	TV	TV	TV			61	60
	5%	TV	TV	TV	TV	TV	T	T	T		T	48	70
11	20%	TV	TV	TV	TV	TV	TV	V	T	V	V	55	90
	40%	TV	TV	TV	TV	TV		TV	TV			54	50
	5%	TV	TV	TV	TV	TV	TV	TV		T	V	58	100

turned out to be relevant, whereas only 30% of images retrieved from visual technique only proved to be relevant.

The hypothesis associated to the *tunnel* mechanism turned out to be verified: we observe that most of the images retrieved by means of *tunnel* have been judged as relevant by the user. In this way, the *tunnel* can be used to *confirm* image relevance. As a heuristic, we can say that an image retrieved by means of visual techniques *and* by means of *tunnel* is more likely to be relevant than another.

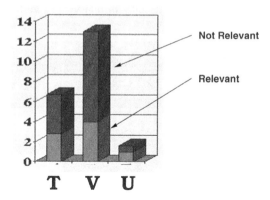

Fig. 4. Performance of (T)extual, (V)isual, and t(U)nnel retrieval techniques.

Query Reformulation Performance. We shall focus here on visual reformulation, that permitted retrieval results improvement. Global colour-based reformulation allows the system to focus on a certain kind of images, namely those which are closer to the user's desires. As a complement, layout-based reformulation allows the system to refine image ranking (see results on table 5(a) and 5(b)).

Visual retrieval favours recall against precision. As a consequence, "noise" is the main drawback of this approach. We think, however, that this is necessary, as the corpus is not totally indexed. Actually, relevant images may not be indexed, and visual retrieval — combined with the *tunnel* mechanism — is the only chance we have to retrieve those images. Figure 5 gives an example of our results: whereas textual descriptions allows the retrieval of two interesting images only (step 1), the *tunnel* mechanism (step 2) acts as a relay and allows retrieval of 6 more images, that are not actually indexed. The virtual image and the relevance feedback process are responsible for improving image ranking, and therefore to allow those non-indexed images to be presented.

Pure Visual Similarity Experiment. To evaluate the contribution of our textual and visual approach, we conducted an additional experiment to show in what extent pure visual retrieval could bring back interesting images on its own.

For each query, we chose to select among all relevant images an example that could be used to retrieved similar images in a "query by example" strategy, based only on visual similarity (*i.e.* the use of colour histogram intersection).

Figure 6 compares this pure visual retrieval to our textual and visual retrieval approach. For each query and each method, our quality measure is computed: vertical bars report pure visual retrieval score, where as the combined textual and visual score is represented by a cross (for readability purposes, crosses have been joined by a solid line). In two cases, visual retrieval achieved as good results as our combined method. In fact, very similar images existed in the database,

Table 4. Results for queries 1, 4 and 9.

(a) Query #1 (*ad hoc* indexing)

(b) Query #4 (40% indexing)

(c) Query #9 (40% indexing)

and the colour histogram feature could easily retrieve them. In all other cases, the combined method yielded better results as:

– Many images can be relevant, although very different on a visual point of view. Query by visual example focuses on one possible representation.

Table 5. Results for queries 9 and 11.

(a) Query # 11 (20% indexing) without layout feedback

(b) Query # 11 (20% indexing) after layout feedback

– Global colour histogram is a rough visual feature. We are dealing with complex images, that would require more accurate features.

As a consequence, texture and shape features ought to be incorporated in an efficient visual similarity measure. This yields, however, to additional problems. Texture feature is only relevant for a small, homogeneous image clip: if various textures are present in this clip, then the texture feature will capture a "blurred" vision of this sub-image. When it comes to shape description, the difficult problem of shape identification arises. Before trying to characterise some shape, we need to determine what should be considered as a shape, that is, what is important to the user's eyes. This can vary, however, from a user to another, and it depends also on user's information need.

As we mentioned earlier, texture and shape features require some fine image segmentation to be efficient. We think however that this process can hardly be carried out automatically, as it depends on user's feeling, in a given retrieval situation. In our opinion, a possible solution is to allow him to draw onto an

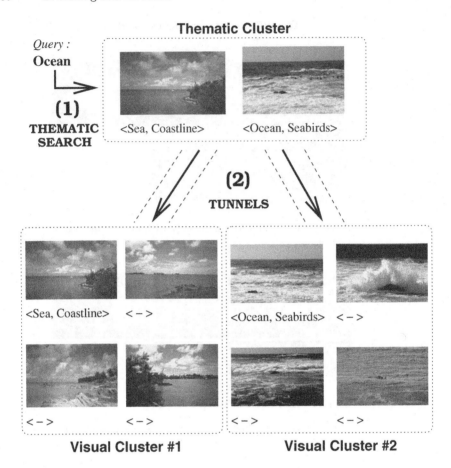

Fig. 5. An example of textual and visual retrieval results.

interesting image a region that he considers as relevant, and to further analyse this particular clip with more powerful visual features. This is to be implemented in a more sophisticated relevance feedback mechanism.

The Impact of Initial Indexing. Initial textual indexing is of particular importance. We obtained the following average scores according to the three indexing conditions we considered: 35 at random 20%, 42 at random 40%, and 51 at *ad hoc* indexing. Figure 7 compares our results (detailed information is reported on table 3). *Ad hoc* indexing achieved often the best results, even if far less images are actually indexed in this case. Moreover, indexing more images does not systematically lead to better results.

It is clear that retrieval techniques based on visual similarity evaluation only are not sufficient, since visual indices are often not powerful enough to characterise accurately *all* kind of images. In this case, part of the corpus may be

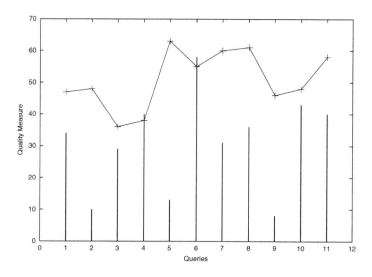

Fig. 6. Pure visual retrieval compared to textual and visual retrieval.

"invisible" to the system. Similar situation occurs when images are not indexed, and therefore not accessible from a textual point of view.

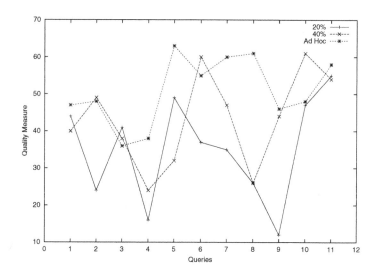

Fig. 7. Results under three different indexing conditions.

These remarks highlight the need for a textual and visual approach, that tries to avoid both of these situations. Indeed, the relevance feedback mechanism, based on both textual and visual aspects allows the user to choose what type of feedback (textual and/or visual) is to be applied at a particular step of his retrieval session. It is then possible to first focus on some very precise theme. During this stage, relevance feedback suggests more indexing terms that could help retrieving new interesting images. Thereafter, the user can choose between different visually homogeneous classes of images, taking into account some visual expectations (this two-step process was illustrated in figure 5).

6   Conclusion and Future Work

We have presented an integrated method that allows textual and visual image retrieval in a partially indexed corpus. Our strategy relies on a preliminary corpus organisation into two hierarchical structures by a clustering process. An adapted retrieval process was designed that takes advantage of the user-system interactions: precise feedback data are gathered and processed within a *virtual image*. We also defined an original evaluation method suitable to the proposed approach.

This approach for image retrieval is well suited to large corpora in which a little proportion is textually indexed: visual index is computed off-line, fast image filtering is allowed by hierarchical clustering, and new images may be easily added to the existing hierarchies.

First experimentation results with the PICAP prototype confirm the relevance of our approach. We believe that PICAP could be improved by the integration of powerful visual characteristics which will make possible to refine not only the user query but also the similarity measure. This could be achieved by selecting the best characteristics according to the user and his preferences (see for example [2,15]), or by setting up a more sophisticated relevance feedback mechanism.

Finally, we think that off-line session analysis is likely to produce interesting indexing hypothesises. Indeed, non-indexed images may have been retrieved during a session and user feedback is precise enough to allow us to determine if an image is relevant to a given query. Assuming some good properties of the query (such as compactness, i.e. few items are specified in the query), a temporary label can be attached to the image. Repeated successful retrievals of this image will increase the hypothesis confidence until it becomes a regular indexing item.

Furthermore, as initial visual clustering allows the identification of homogeneous images, we think that the *ad hoc* indexing process can be facilitated: each cluster is examined, and at least one image of a representative theme is manually indexed. Our process ensures that if this cluster is retrieved based on some textual query, all images in this cluster get a chance to be retrieved by means of the *tunnel* mechanism.

References

1. P. Aigrain, H. Zhang, and D. Petkovic. Content-Based Representation and Retrieval of Visual Media: A State-of-the-Art Review. *Multimedia Tools and Applications*, 3:179–202, 1996.

2. G. Ciocca and R. Schettini. A relevance feedback mechanism for content-based image retrieval. *Information Processing and Management*, 35:605–632, 1999.

3. R. Duda and P. Hart. *Pattern Classification and Scene Analysis*. John Wiley and Sons, 1973.

4. M. Dunlop. *Multimedia Information Retrieval*. PhD thesis, Glasgow University, Scotland, 1991.

5. A. El-Hamdouchi and P. Willett. Techniques for the measurement of clustering tendency in document retrieval systems. *Journal of Information Science*, 13:361–365, 1987.

6. C. Fellbaum, editor. *WORDNET: An Electronic Lexical Database*. MIT Press, 1998.

7. V. Govindaraju. Locating human faces in photographs. *International Journal of Computer Vision*, 19(2):129–146, 1996.

8. N. Jardine and C.J. van Rijsbergen. The use of hierarchical clustering in information retrieval. *Information Storage and Retrieval*, 7:217–240, 1971.

9. T. Kato. Database architecture for content-based image retrieval. In *Image Storage and Retrieval Systems*, volume 1662, pages 112–123, San Jose, CA, 1992. SPIE.

10. A. Lakshmi-Ratan, O. Maron, E. Grimson, and T. Lozano-Perez. A Framework for Learning Query Concepts in Image Classification. In *IEEE Proc. of Conf. on Computer Vision and Pattern Recognition*, volume I, pages 423–429, 1999.

11. Y. Mori, H. Takahashi, and R. Ohta. Automatic word assignment to images based on image division and vector quantization. In *RIAO 2000*, volume 1, pages 285–293, Paris, France, April 2000.

12. C. Nastar, M. Mischke, C. Meilhac, N. Boudjemaa, H. Bernard, and M. Mautref. Retrieving images by content: the surfimage system. In *Multimedia Information Systems*, Istanbul, 1998.

13. W. Niblack, R. Barber, W. Equitz, M. Flickner, E. Glasman, D. Petkovic, P. Yanker, C. Faloutsos, and G. Taubin. The QBIC project: querying images by content using color, texture and shape. In Wayne Niblack, editor, *Storage and Retrieval for Image and Video Databases*, pages 173–181, San Jose, CA, 1993. SPIE.

14. V. E. Ogle and M. Stonebraker. CHABOT: Retrieval from a relational database of images. *IEEE Computer*, 28(9):40–48, 1995.

15. R.W. Picard and T.P. Minka. Vision Texture for Annotation. *Multimedia Systems*, 3:3–14, 1995.

16. W.K. Pratt. *Digital Image Processing*. John Wiley & Sons, New York, second edition, 1991.

17. C.J. van Rijsbergen and W.B. Croft. Document clustering: an evaluation of some experiments with the Cranfield 1400 collection. *Information processing and management*, 11:171–182, 1974.

18. G. Salton and M.J. McGill. *Introduction to Modern Information Retrieval*. McGraw-Hill, 1983.

19. S. Satoh, Y. Nakamura, and T. Kanade. Name-It: Naming and detecting faces in news videos. *IEEE MultiMedia*, 6(1):22–35, January-March 1999.

20. S. Sclaroff, M. La Cascia, S. Sethi, and L. Taycher. Unifying textual and visual cues for content-based image retrieval on the world wide web. *Computer Vision and Image Understanding*, 75(1–2):86–98, 1999.

21. A. Smeulders, M. Worring, S. Santini, A. Gupta, and R. Jain. Content-Based Image Retrieval at the End of the Early Years . *IEEE Transactions on pattern analysis and machine intelligence*, 22(12):1349–1379, 2000.

22. J. R. Smith and S.-F. Chang. Querying by color regions using the VisualSEEk content-based visual query system. In Mark T. Maybury, editor, *Intelligent Multimedia Information Retrieval*, pages 23–41. AAAI Press, Menlo Park, 1997.

23. M.J. Swain and D.H. Ballard. Color indexing. *International Journal of Computer Vision*, 7(1):11–32, 1991.

24. E. Voorhees. *The Effectiveness and Efficiency of Agglomerative Hierarchic Clustering in Document Retrieval*. PhD thesis, Cornell University, Ithaca, NY, Etats-Unis, 1985. Rapport Technique TR 85-705.

25. T. Whalen, E.S. Lee, and F. Safayeni. The Retrieval of Images from Image Databases. *Behaviour & Information Technology*, 14(1):3–13, 1995.

26. P. Willett. Recent trends in Hierarchic Document Clustering. *Information processing and management*, 24(5):577–597, 1988.

Combining Features for Content-Based Sketch Retrieval – A Comparative Evaluation of Retrieval Performance

Daniel Heesch and Stefan Rüger

Department of Computing, Imperial College
180 Queen's Gate, London SW7 2BZ, England
{dh500,srueger}@doc.ic.ac.uk

Abstract. We study three transformation-invariant shape descriptors and evaluate their relative strengths in the context of content-based retrieval of graphical sketches. We show that the use of a combination of different shape representations may lead to a significant improvement of retrieval performance and identify an optimal combination that proves robust across different data sets and queries.

1 Introduction

Over the previous ten years there has been a growing interest in content-based image retrieval (CBIR), a trend that coincides and appears to be causally linked with the rise of the world-wide web and the spread of digital technologies for image creation. Research into CBIR has resulted in a number of commercial systems such as IBM's QBIC, Convera's (formerly Excalibur) Visual RetrievalWare and Virage's VIR Image Engine to name but a few of the most prominent. The practical applications of CBIR are multifarious and range from medical diagnosis over remote sensing to journalism and home entertainment. A special area of application is in architecture and engineering where information is often in the form of graphical sketches.

Sketches constitute a special type of image with a few characteristics that impinge on the kind of techniques employed for successful retrieval. First, in contrast to a fully-fledged image that often requires segmentation to separate local objects from their context, sketch objects are already well-defined since spatial context and background are typically trivial. Secondly, the object shape captures most of the semantic information present in a sketch. With little, if any, semantic contribution from colour and texture, the performance of a sketch retrieval system is essentially determined by its ability to capture the shapes detectable in the sketch.

The issue of shape-based object recognition has long been one central interest in the area of computer vision. Traditionally, most research has aimed at finding ever more powerful shape descriptors [1]. Little work has been done, however, on how to combine different representations in an attempt to boost retrieval performance.

F. Crestani, M. Girolami, and C.J. van Rijsbergen (Eds.): ECIR 2002, LNCS 2291, pp. 41–52, 2002.

The number of shape representations developed over the past fifty years is bewildering. Each representation differs in applicability and complexity. The simplest representations are based on so called "shape factors," which are single values that capture but the minimal information of the object. These factors include, *inter alia*, the perimeter, the area, the radius, the elongation, the compactness, the number of corners, the circularity and the convexity of the object. The first three of these measures suffer from the fact that they vary with the object size and lose important information. Although the remaining measures provide scale invariance, they still do not provide sufficient information for reliable object recognition and retrieval when used in isolation [2].

An early attempt to achieve a boundary representation that can be used for recognition purposes is the chain coding method proposed by Freeman [3, 4]. A chain code approximates a curve with a sequence of directional vectors lying on a square grid. The technique is computationally efficient but suffers from digitisation noise. A well-established technique to describe closed planar curves is the use of Fourier descriptors (see for example [5] and [6]). Using the Fourier descriptors one can achieve representational invariance with respect to a variety of affine transformations; these descriptors have successfully been used for recognition tasks (eg [7]). Among area-based representations, moments are the most notable. They can be made invariant and have variously been used for recognition and retrieval tasks ([8], [9] and [10] for aircraft recognition, [2] for trademark retrieval).

All of the above-mentioned representations have in common that they lend themselves very well to comparison as they can be stored as a simple vector. More elaborate shape representations have been introduced some of which are the curvature scale space representation or the spline curve approximation which require sophisticated shape matching techniques ([11]). Even though they can provide very powerful shape representations, their computational costs make them ill-suited for the purpose of interactive retrieval of objects from large databases where performance becomes an issue.

For the present study we have selected three descriptors, namely Fourier descriptors, moment invariants and difference chain codes. The choice was based on three criteria: (i) suitability of the descriptor for large databases, (ii) efficiency of extraction from image and (iii) retrieval efficiency as documented in the literature. We describe how descriptors can be combined with one another in a retrieval model to produce retrieval results superior to any of the single-descriptor models.

With the increasing number of shape descriptors and the growing need for sketch retrieval, formal evaluation of retrieval performance becomes a major desideratum. Using standard information retrieval measures we evaluate the retrieval performance under different feature regimes for a database of 238 black-and-white sketches (see Appendix A). Section 2 describes in detail the methods we used, and Section 3 the results we obtained.

2   Methods

2.1   Shape Descriptors

Chain Code Histograms. Freeman chain codes are derived by reading the contour in a consistently clock-wise or counter-clockwise direction starting at position 0 and noting for each pixel i of the contour its relative position c_i with respect to its neighbour. Specifically, a 0, 2, 4 or 6 is noted for right, top, left, bottom, respectively. The chain-code $c_1 c_2 \ldots c_n$ thus obtained is invariant with respect to translation. Encoding the change in direction $d_i = (c_{i+1} - c_i) \bmod 8$ at any one pixel yields invariance under rotation. In the last step this sequence of difference chain codes is reduced to a 4-bin percentage histogram resulting in a four-number representation of the contour that is invariant with respect to translation and starting points as well as, though to a lesser extent owing to digitisation noise, to rotation and scaling.

Moment invariants. Moments capture distributional properties of a random variable. The first moment is equivalent to the expected value, while the second central moment yields the variance of that variable. For 2-d black-and-white images of size $N \cdot M$, nth order moments are defined as

$$M_{pq} = \sum_{i=1}^{N \cdot M} x_i^p y_i^q f(x_i, y_i),$$

where $p, q \in \mathbb{N}$ with $p + q = n$ and $f(x_i, y_i) = 1$ if the pixel i at position (x_i, y_i) is set and 0 otherwise. Translation invariance can be achieved by central moments

$$C_{pq} = \sum_{i=1}^{N \cdot M} (x_i - \bar{x})^p (y_i - \bar{y})^q f(x_i, y_i),$$

where $\bar{x} = M_{10}/M_{00}$ and $\bar{y} = M_{01}/M_{00}$. Further normalisation renders the moments scale-invariant:

$$\mu_{pq} = \frac{C_{pq}}{(M_{00})^\lambda},$$

where $\lambda = 1 + (p + q)/2$. Finally, there are seven terms made from 2nd and 3rd order moments which are also invariant under rotations [8]:

$$m_1 = \mu_{20} + \mu_{02}$$
$$m_2 = (\mu_{20} - \mu_{02})^2 + 4\mu_{11}^2$$
$$m_3 = (\mu_{30} - \mu_{12})^2 + (3\mu_{21} - \mu_{03})^2$$
$$m_4 = (\mu_{30} + \mu_{12})^2 + (3\mu_{21} - \mu_{03})^2$$
$$m_5 = (\mu_{30} - 3\mu_{12})(\mu_{30} + \mu_{12})[(\mu_{30} + \mu_{12})^2 - 3(\mu_{21} + \mu_{03})^2] +$$
$$(3\mu_{21} - \mu_{03})(\mu_{21} + \mu_{03})[3(\mu_{30} + \mu_{12})^2 - (\mu_{21} + \mu_{03})^2]$$
$$m_6 = (\mu_{20} - \mu_{02})[(\mu_{30} + \mu_{12})^2 - (\mu_{12} + \mu_{03})^2] + 4\mu_{11}(\mu_{30} + \mu_{12})(\mu_{21} + \mu_{03})$$
$$m_7 = (3\mu_{21} - \mu_{03})(\mu_{30} + \mu_{12})[(\mu_{30} + \mu_{12})^2 - 3(\mu_{21} + \mu_{30})^2] +$$
$$[(3\mu_{12} - \mu_{30})(\mu_{21} + \mu_{03})][3(\mu_{30} + \mu_{12})^2 - (\mu_{21} + \mu_{03})^2]$$

The above seven moments vary considerably as the last two moments are exceedingly small. To grant each moment invariant an equal weight, they need to be normalised such that they cover approximately the same range. In the approach taken in this study the moment invariants computed for each sketch are normalised using

$$m_i \mapsto \frac{m_i - \overline{m}_i}{\sigma_i},$$

where $\overline{m}_i$ and σ_i denote the mean and the standard deviation, respectively, of the ith moment invariant (taken over the sketch database). The majority of the resulting values will now range between -1 and 1; these 7 numbers constitute the feature vector.

Fourier Descriptors. For the computation of Fourier descriptors the contour pixels need to be represented as complex numbers $z = x + iy$ where x and y are the pixel coordinates. As the contour is closed we get a periodic function which can be expanded into a convergent Fourier series. Specifically, let Fourier Descriptor C_k be defined as the kth discrete Fourier transform coefficient

$$C_k = \sum_{n=0}^{N-1} (z_n e^{\frac{-2\pi i k n}{N}}),$$

$-N/2 \leq k < N/2$, which we compute from the sequence of complex numbers $z_0, z_1, \ldots, z_{N-1}$ where N is the number of contour points. To characterise contour properties any constant number of these Fourier descriptors can be used. The most interesting descriptors are those of the lower frequencies as these tend to capture the general shape of the object. Translation invariance is achieved by discarding C_0, rotation and starting point invariance by further using only absolute values of the descriptors, and scaling invariance is brought about by dividing the other descriptors by, say, $|C_1|$. The final feature vector has the form

$$\left(\frac{|C_{-L}|}{|C_1|}, \ldots, \frac{|C_{-1}|}{|C_1|}, \frac{|C_2|}{|C_1|}, \ldots, \frac{|C_L|}{|C_1|} \right)^T,$$

where L is an arbitrary constant between 2 and $N/2 - 1$. In this study L is 10 resulting in 19 descriptors per object.

2.2   Evaluation

Evaluation of retrieval systems is a critical part in the process of continuously improving the existing techniques. While text information retrieval has long been using a sophisticated set of tools for user-based evaluation, this does not as yet apply to image retrieval. Only the minority of systems provide evaluation that goes beyond simple common-sense judgements. And yet, when applied with care, evaluation techniques from information retrieval can profitably be applied to image retrieval as well. For the present study we deploy the two measures *recall* and *precision*. Owing to the potential polysemy of images, the use of these measures in the context of image retrieval is not free from difficulties. The problem of polysemy can be resolved, however, if the image database relies on the strong semantics provided by a label or other textual descriptions [12]. In the present study all 238 images have been assigned to 34 categories. Each of these images corresponds to only one category (see Appendix A for some example categories), and categories vary in size from as few as 3 to as many as 23 objects. Removing semantic ambiguities, we obtain an image which is regarded as relevant with respect to a query from the database if and only if both share the same category.

We compute a *precision-against-recall* graph by, firstly, ranking all items of the database (with exception of the query) with respect to their similarity to the query. Then, the precision and recall values are determined for the sequence of relevant items and the values interpolated as described in [13]. Each query results in one characteristic precision-against-recall graph and an average measure capturing the performance for the entire database can be obtained by averaging the precision-against-recall graphs over all queries. From the final graph, a more concise measure of performance can be derived in the form of *average precision* which can be thought of the area under the *precision-against-recall* curve. A high value indicates a good trade-off between high precision and high recall.

2.3   Similarity Functions

Each shape descriptor reduces the image information to a vector of real numbers. For any one descriptor the similarity between two images is then computed as the similarity between the two corresponding vectors. The most commonly used measures are based on the Euclidean distance measure, the cosine similarity measure and the intersection distance measure. Experiments performed on the sketch database (the results are omitted in this paper) have suggested the use of the cosine similarity measure for all descriptors:

$$\text{Sim}(u, v) = \frac{\sum_i u_i v_i}{|u| \cdot |v|}$$

2.4   Combination of Shape Descriptors

Descriptors are combined in an integrated retrieval model such that the overall similarity between two sketches Q and T is given by a convex combination

$$S(Q, T) = \sum_f w_f \text{Sim}_f(Q_f, T_f)$$

of the similarity values calculated for each descriptor. Here $\text{Sim}_f(Q_f, T_f)$ denotes the similarity between the respective feature vectors Q_f and T_f for feature f of images Q and T using a possibly feature-specific similarity function and weighted by a factor $w_f \in \mathbb{R}$ with $0 \le w_f \le 1$ and $\sum_f w_f = 1$.

2.5   Comparison between Shape Descriptors

One of the aims of our investigation is empirically testing the hypothesis that some combination of the descriptors can outperform the most successful single-descriptor model in retrieval performance. Each image in the database is used as query and produces a corresponding average precision value. We perform a paired t-test on the 238 average precision values for each of the two models to be compared in order to test the hypothesis whether the models are significantly different in performance.

2.6   Robustness of the Optimal Weight Combination

The optimal combination of descriptors is achieved when a particular combination of weights for which the mean average precision averaged over all 238 queries reaches a maximum. We find this optimum by raster scanning with a resolution of 0.01 as not too many weights and queries are involved in our experiments. It is natural to ask whether this optimum varies with the data set or whether it proves to be a generic feature that is largely unaffected by the type of objects present in the database. In the latter case the optimal combination of weights for the entire data set may be taken as an estimate of the optimal combination for an unknown dataset.

To evaluate the robustness of the optimal combination, the optimum is determined not only for the entire database but, in addition, for a sample of 12 smaller subsets. Each subset contains all the sketches from 20% of the categories selected randomly from the total of 34 categories. The inverse of the scatter of the optimal combination can be regarded as a reasonable measure of the robustness.

3   Results

3.1   Single-Descriptor Models

Figure 1 depicts the precision-against-recall graphs for each of the descriptors using the method described in 2.2. Fourier descriptors prove most successful for the given retrieval task followed by moment invariants and difference chain codes. Despite the considerable standard deviation, the difference between the performance of Fourier descriptors and those of the other descriptors is significant at $\alpha = 0.05$ ($p < 0.001$).

3.2   Multi-descriptor Model and Robustness

When the three descriptors are combined as described in 2.4, overall performance can be plotted in a three-dimensional space against the weights of two descriptors (note that the third is determined by the first two). Using an equilateral triangle *all* three weights can be represented as axes in two dimensions. For any given point within the triangle, the contribution of a particular descriptor is given as the distance between the point and the respective side of the triangle. Since the

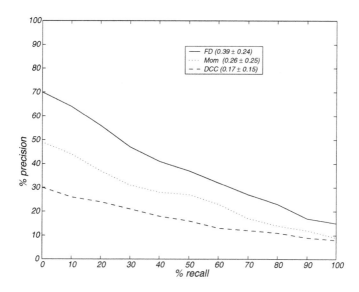

Fig. 1. Precision-against-recall graphs for the single-descriptor models (FD = Fourier descriptors, Mom = moment invariants, DCC = difference chain codes). Mean average precision and the corresponding standard deviation is given in brackets.

sum of the perpendiculars from any point onto the three sides is a constant, the condition $\sum_f w_f = 1$ is satisfied.

Figure 2 shows the mean average precision values (averaged over all 238 queries) as grey value for all possible combinations of the three weights. Note that the performance of the single-value models is found at the respective corners of the triangle (where two of the three weights are zero).

The large circle near the base of the moment invariants represents the combination of descriptor weights for which average precision reaches the global maximum. The optimal weights are 0.63 for Fourier descriptors, 0.35 for difference chain code histograms and 0.02 for moment invariants. The precision-against-recall graph corresponding to this optimal combination of weights is depicted in Figure 3. The difference in performance between this model and the best single-descriptor model is highly significant ($\alpha = 0.05$, $p < 0.001$).

To answer the question to what extent the optimum is independent of the query set, we determined the optimum weight sets for a number of subsets. The optima are plotted in Figure 2 (smaller circles). As can be seen, the scatter defines an elongated region close to and along the base of the moment invariants. Fourier descriptors vary between 0.95 and 0.45 and hence there exists query sets for which difference chain codes outperform Fourier descriptors. The consistently low weights assigned to moment invariants suggests that their weakness in a multi-descriptor model is of a fairly generic nature.

These results are corroborated by additional experiments (not shown) in which a fourth descriptor (angle co-occurrence matrix) has been added to the

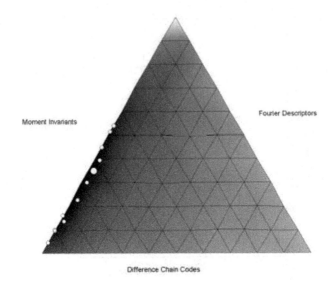

Fig. 2. Mean average precision values for model combinations.

previous three. The contour points are sampled equidistantly, successive angles in the arising polygon are quantised into 4 bins and their co-occurrence summarised in a $4 \cdot 4$ percentage histogram, which is used as feature vector [14]. When used in isolation the angle co-occurrence matrix has a marginal advantage over difference chain codes. When used in conjunction with the other three descriptors its contribution to the boost of retrieval performance is almost zero. Hence, it does not upset the optimum weight set, ie, moment invariants remain negligible with the weights for Fourier descriptors and difference chain codes adding up to one.

4   Discussion

As can be seen in Figures 1 and 3 the standard deviation of the average precision values are considerable which implies that retrieval performance varies quite substantially with the query. This is to be expected since the image collection used in the present study shows a high degree of heterogeneity. In addition, categories range in size from as few as 3 to as many as 23 objects. As average precision values tend to increase with the size of the category the query belongs to, one must expect variation in category size to further inflate the standard deviation. It is interesting to note that, despite the large standard deviation, retrieval performances differ significantly between the three single-descriptor models as revealed in a paired t-test. This observation suggests that retrieval performance of different descriptors co-vary with the query, in other words, a "difficult" query will be difficult to handle by *any* descriptor. One reason for this co-variance is, once again, variation in category size: a query from a common category will tend

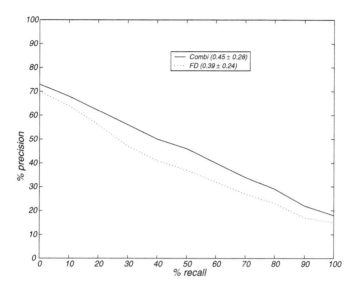

Fig. 3. Performance of the optimal combination model (Combi) in comparison to the best single-descriptor model (FD = Fourier descriptor).

to result in better performance, no matter which descriptor is used. In addition, some categories are quite "unique" while others are not. Members of the "sea-stars" category, for example, are very different from all other database sketches. By contrast, there are a number of categories that are very close in feature space to other categories (eg the categories "vans" and "trucks," "cars" and "fishes," "cats" and "dogs" etc). Retrieval of these categories is generally more difficult.

One of the most notable findings of our experiments is the non-additive, synergetic interaction between descriptors in multiple-descriptor models. Although moment invariants perform significantly better than difference chain codes when considered in isolation, it is only the latter that improves performance beyond the level of the best single-descriptor model when the three descriptors are allowed to combine with one another. One may want to argue that both Fourier descriptors and moment invariants capture similar aspects of the shape and will therefore offset with each other rather than complement each other. Likewise, difference chain codes and Fourier descriptors are probably sufficiently orthogonal to each other in order to allow for some degree of complementation. Also, as their name suggests, the strength of moment invariants lies in their invariance with respect to all three affine transformations. Because they are based on the area rather than the contour of an object, moment invariants are less affected by digitisation noise than, for example, difference chain codes. The sketches within each category are presently of similar scale and are aligned in a consistent manner, so that no reward is given to descriptors that are highly invariant. This may help to explain the performance of moment invariants in the single and multiple-descriptor models.

Appendix A: Example Sketches and Categories

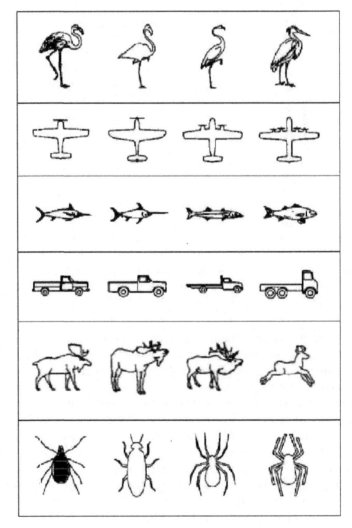

Fig. 4. Example sketches from six of the 38 categories in the database. Other categories include, *inter alia*, rockets, airbusses, sea-stars, deers and other types of animals.

Appendix B: Example Run of the System

Figure 5 shows the query sketch and the associated contour used for a particular retrieval problem. The user can choose one or more contours by double-clicking on them. In this case, the user chose the outer contour of the car and ignores the hub-caps. Figure 6 shows the system output for our four models. Note that the respective performance results of our study are clearly exhibited in this example.

Fig. 5. The query (left) and the contours of the objects found by our segmentation algorithm (right). The black contour is the one that has been activated by the user.

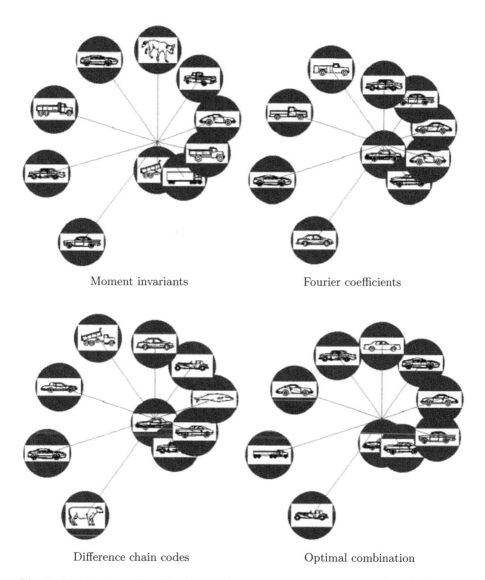

Fig. 6. Retrieval results. The ten most similar images are arranged such that the distance to the centre reflects the dissimilarity between that image and the query.

References

1. T S Rui, T S Huang, M Ortega, and S Mehrota, "Relevance feedback: a power tool for interactive content-based image retrieval," *IEEE Trans. Circuits and Systems for Video Technology*, pp. 123–131, 1998.
2. B M Mehtre, "Shape measures for content-based image retrieval: a comparison," *Information Processing and Management*, vol. 33, no. 3, pp. 319–337, 1997.
3. H Freeman, "On the encoding of arbitrary geometric configurations," *IEEE Trans. Electron. Comput.*, vol. 10, no. 2, pp. 260–268, 1961.
4. H Freeman and L S Davis, "A corner finding algorithm for chain coded curves," *IEEE Transactions on Computers*, vol. 26, pp. 297–303, 1977.
5. C T Zahn and R Z Roskies, "Fourier descriptors for plane closed curves," *IEEE Trans. Comput.*, vol. C-21, no. 3, pp. 269–281, 1972.
6. E Peerson and K S Fu, "Shape discrimination using fourier descriptor," *IEEE Trans. Syst., Man, Cybern.*, vol. SMC-7, no. 3, pp. 170–179, 1977.
7. T P Wallace and P A Wintz, "An efficient three dimensional aircraft recognition algorithm using normalized fourier descriptors," *Computer Graphics and Image Processing*, vol. 13, pp. 99–126, 1980.
8. M K Hu, "Visual pattern recognition by moment invariants.," *IRE Transactions on Information Theory*, vol. 8, pp. 179–187, 1962.
9. S Dudani, "Aircraft identification by moment invariants," *IEEE Transactions on Computers*, vol. 26, pp. 39–45, 1977.
10. J Flusser and T Suk, "Pattern recognition by affine moment invariants," *Pattern Recognition*, vol. 26, no. 1, pp. 167–174, 1993.
11. A del Bimbo and P Pala, "Visual image retrieval by elastic matching of user sketches," *IEEE Trans. Pattern Analysis and Machine Intelligence*, vol. 19, no. 2, pp. 121–132, 1997.
12. J R Smith and C S Li, "Image retrieval evaluation," in *Proc. Workshop Content-Based Access of Image and Video Libraries*, 1998, pp. 343–353.
13. E M Voorhees and D Harman, "Overview of the eigth text retrieval conference (TREC-8)," in *Proc. TREC*, 1999, pp. 1–33 and A.17 – A.18.
14. A L Reno, *Object recognition by stochastic model adaptation and selection*, Ph.D. thesis, Imperial College, London, 1998.

Combining Web Document Representations in a Bayesian Inference Network Model Using Link and Content-Based Evidence

Theodora Tsikrika and Mounia Lalmas

Department of Computer Science, Queen Mary, University of London,
Mile End Road, E1 4NS London, UK.
{theodora, mounia}@dcs.qmul.ac.uk

Abstract. This paper introduces an expressive formal Information Retrieval model developed for the Web. It is based on the Bayesian inference network model and views IR as an evidential reasoning process. It supports the explicit combination of multiple Web document representations under a single framework. Information extracted from the content of Web documents and derived from the analysis of the Web link structure is used as source of evidence in support of the ranking algorithm. This content and link-based evidential information is utilised in the generation of the multiple Web document representations used in the combination.

1 Introduction

The advent of the *World Wide Web* (Web) was accompanied by an explosion of the amount of easily accessible information. This triggered the need for the development of efficient Information Retrieval (IR) systems that would assist the users in locating the pieces of information that interest them, so that they could satisfy their information needs. Web IR adopted models, algorithms and heuristics previously developed in traditional and/or hypertext/hypermedia IR environments. In the early stages of their development, the majority of Web search engines used variations of the classic IR models, typically the Boolean and the vector space model. However, these content-based retrieval strategies soon proved to be quite ineffective and this led to the development of novel IR algorithms, mainly *ad hoc* approaches, which attempted to increase the effectiveness of the retrieval process on the Web. These Web IR strategies mainly followed two different paths in order to achieve improvements in the effectiveness.

The first path was through the analysis of the link structure, which is one of the most important features of the Web and also its main difference from traditional IR environments. The derived link-based information was utilised usually in conjunction with the content-based information provided by the Web documents. Several approaches either relying solely on link-based information [20] or using it in combination with content-based information [6, 9], have presented experimental results that indicated enhancements in the effectiveness.

F. Crestani, M. Girolami, and C.J. van Rijsbergen (Eds.): ECIR 2002, LNCS 2291, pp. 53-72, 2002.
© Springer-Verlag Berlin Heidelberg 2002

The second path was to use a standard technique for improving the effectiveness, which has been applied in both traditional and hyperlinked environments: the combination of evidence in IR. This method consists of two separate approaches: i) the combination of different document and information need representations and ii) the combination of the results of distinct search strategies. The first approach refers to the development of IR models that explicitly support the combination of multiple document representations and/or information need representations (queries) under a single framework. The second approach refers to the development of systems and models that support the combination of the results of distinct search strategies based on different IR models. This combination is referred to as *data fusion* and IR research has shown, in many cases, that the application of *data fusion*, both in traditional IR environments [5, 29] and on the Web, performed by metasearch engines [17, 30, 33], yields improvements in the effectiveness over that of a single representation scheme or a single retrieval strategy. A summary of research in the area of combining approaches in IR is presented in [10].

1.1 Aim

Our aim is to introduce an expressive Web IR approach that integrates, into a single framework, these two ways of improving the effectiveness. We achieve this by generating multiple representations of Web documents, each representation capturing a different perspective of the information associated with a document, such as its content-based and its link-based information. The link-based evidence incorporated into these document representations is extracted through the analysis of the Web link structure, by considering, not only the mere existence of a link between two documents, but by also attempting to identify the relationship it represents.

We base our framework on a formal model because, as stated by [24], "the setting up of a (mathematical) model generally presupposes a careful formal analysis of the problem and specification of the assumptions and explicit formulation of the way in which the model depends on these assumptions". This explains why models with a sound theoretical basis have played an increasingly justified role in IR research [32]. Therefore, a formal model for our Web IR approach will enable us to rationalise and analyse these assumptions, as well as the retrieval results.

In the field of the application of formal models in IR, research [36] suggests that improvements in the retrieval effectiveness will require techniques that, in some sense, 'understand' the content of documents and queries and use it in order to infer probable relationships between them. Therefore, IR can be considered to be an evidential reasoning process, in which we estimate the probability that a user's information need, expressed as one or more queries, is satisfied given a document as 'evidence'.

To model the retrieval process as inference, Bayesian networks [22] can be used in order to provide a sound framework, which allows the combination of distinct sources of evidence. Bayesian networks have been applied to the IR domain for modelling the document retrieval, resulting to the development of, namely, the *inference network* model [11, 34, 35] and the *belief network* model [26, 31]. Both of these models have shown improvements in the effectiveness, especially when incorporating additional pieces of evidence.

Our goal is to develop a formal Web IR model, which views IR as an evidential reasoning process, using Web documents as sources of evidence in support of the ranking algorithm. The purpose of this model is the incorporation of more of the available information accompanying Web documents in their representations. This is achieved by utilising content-based and link-based information in multiple document representations, which are then integrated through their combination. Our Web retrieval model uses Bayesian networks, and more specifically the *inference net* model [11, 34, 35], as its underlying formal framework in order to support the explicit combination of multiple document representations.

1.2 Outline

This paper is organised as follows: *Section 2* presents a literature review and background information on the combination of multiple document representations and on the Web IR approaches analysing the Web link structure. *Section 3* presents a classification of Web links based on the relationships they represent, in order to provide the foundation for the generation of the representation of Web documents based on link-based evidence. *Section 4* provides a detailed description of our Web document retrieval model. *Section 5* presents an example of the application of our model and *Section 6* describes how our model could be extended. Finally, in *Section 7*, our conclusions and suggestions for further work are discussed.

2 Related Work

Numerous IR models, such as the vector space model [28], the probabilistic model [25] and others [36, 35], have been developed and extensive experiments have been performed in order to test their effectiveness. The results of these experiments revealed that there was a low overlap among the retrieved documents and more specifically among the retrieved relevant documents, when different IR strategies or different document representations within one single IR model, were employed [15, 19]. This led to the introduction of the technique of combining distinct document representations in order to improve the effectiveness and to find more of the relevant documents.

Distinct document representations within a single IR model can be generated using a variety of approaches. A first approach could be to consider each time only a subset of the information associated with each document, where, for instance, one representation consists of the title of the document and a second one of its abstract [15]. A second approach could be to adopt different indexing schemes, where one representation is generated by using index terms automatically extracted from the text of the document and a second one by using terms from a controlled vocabulary [19]. Finally, citations [16, 34], hypertext links [11] and Web links [7] have also been used as alternative documents representations.

Large-scale evaluation experiments [19, 23, 34] showed that the combination of these document representations led to improvements in the retrieval effectiveness over single representations. These experiments were performed using IR systems [23, 34] based on probabilistic models and capable of supporting combination of multiple sources of evidence. These approaches [11, 34, 35] led to the introduction of Bayesian networks as a sound and formal framework for combining document representations.

To apply the combination of multiple document representations on the Web, its link structure was analysed to extract information that could be incorporated into alternative document representations. Kleinberg [20] introduced the HITS algorithm which exploits the information inherent in the Web links to find the most "important" documents among the thousands of relevant Web documents returned in response to a broad-topic query. There are two measures reflecting the importance of a Web document: its degree of *authority* and its degree of *hub*. A good authority page is one pointed to by many good hubs and a good hub page is one pointing to many good authorities. These two qualitative measures, with respect to a query, are computed for a set of Web documents, called the *base set*, which contains the k top-ranked documents (e.g. $k=200$) generated by a content-based IR approach and the pages pointing to or pointed to by these documents. The iterative algorithm used in estimating the hub and authority values of a Web document is presented in [20]. Variations of the initial HITS algorithm have also been applied, including the incorporation of keyword-based evidence in the computation of these two metrics [6, 9].

3   Web Links : Syntax and Semantics

Our aim is to incorporate link-based evidential information into the Web document representations by considering not only the presence of a link between two documents, signifying that there is a relationship between them, but also by taking into account the nature of that relationship. For that reason, we present a classification of Web links based on the relationship existing between the documents they connect, so that links can be differentiated according to their type.

Web links can be differentiated by considering either their *syntax* or their *semantics*. The syntactic analysis is based on the relationship of the source and destination Web pages that the link connects, in terms of their relative location in the Web structure, i.e. if they belong to the same domain or to the same site, etc. A very basic classification of this kind can be introduced by characterising links as being *structural* when the source and destination documents belong to the same Web domain (e.g *.qmul.ac.uk*) and as being *semantic* otherwise. However, this taxonomy is very simplistic and it captures more the semantics of the links than their syntactic properties. That is why a more detailed syntactic analysis, introduced in [18], is presented.

Based on the syntactic analysis of links, as this is presented in [18], links can be classified as being:

- *internal* (inside – page) : when the link points to the Web page it belongs to
- *hierarchical* : when the source and the destination Web pages belong to the same directory path. These types of links can be further categorised as:
  - *horizontal* : when the source and the destination Web pages belong to the same directory

- *up* : when the source Web page is "deeper" in the directory path than the destination Web page
- *down* : when the source Web page is "higher" in the directory path than the destination Web page
- *transversal* : when the destination Web document is neither in the ascendant nor in the descendant directories, however, it still belongs to the same site as the source Web document
- *cross site*: when the destination Web document belongs to the same domain as the source Web document, but is part of another site
- *outside domain* : when the source and destination documents belong to different Web domains

By attempting to identify the semantics of a link, the aim is to discover the reasons why this link exists. Link semantics should also signify how the observation of the destination document affects our knowledge or understanding of the source document. Therefore, [18] suggested that there are 3 fundamental relationships existing between Web documents and established by the links connecting them:

- *composition* : this relation expresses the forming of an entity consisting of simpler components. For instance, a book consists of many chapters, which in turn consist of sections and subsections. If a Web page corresponds to a section, a chapter can be defined as a composition of these Web pages, usually in a hierarchical manner.
- *sequence* : this relation expresses the order in which some Web documents are organised. For instance, *chapter 2* of a book precedes *chapter 3* and follows *chapter 1*. This order provides to the user a path he has to follow in order to achieve better understanding.
- *reference* : this relation expresses the fact that the source and destination documents are similar in some way. For instance, the author of the source document might have found the destination document to be valuable source of information or he might reference it, because it provides a counter-argument to what he is claiming.

The *composition* and *sequence* relations are well defined, while the notion of the *reference* relation is broad. The question asked is whether it is possible to define a link's semantics given only its syntactic specification. For instance, *outside domain* links are classified [20] as *semantic* links expressing the *reference* relation defined above. [18] further suggested that *hierarchical down* links reflect the *composition* relation and *hierarchical horizontal* links the *sequence* relation. Finally, contrary to the approach mostly followed on the Web [20] that only *outside domain* links capture the *reference* relation, [18] claimed that also *transversal* and *cross site* links could be candidates for expressing the *reference* relation.

In summary, Web links can be classified into three types according to the relationship they represent: i) links expressing the *reference* relation, ii) links expressing the *composition* relation and iii) links expressing the *sequence* relation.

4   Web Retrieval Model

Our goal is to develop a formal Web IR model, which utilises content-based and link-based information in multiple document representations. This Web retrieval model uses Bayesian networks, and more specifically the *inference net* model [11, 34, 35], as its underlying formal framework in order to support the explicit combination of the multiple document representations.

This section presents the way the multiple Web document representations are generated (section 4.1), how the combination of these representations and the retrieval of Web documents is modelled using the inference net as the underlying framework (section 4.2) and finally how the probabilities reflecting the dependencies among the document and query representations and the index terms are estimated (section 4.3).

4.1 Web Document Representations

Different Web document representations can be generated by considering each time, a subset of the available information regarding the document, by taking into account, for instance, only the title of the document for one representation and only its abstract for another [15]. Web documents, however, are associated with much more information and several document representations can be generated by exploiting content-based and link-based information. Each of these representations corresponds to a different perspective of how the document could be viewed with respect to the available information taken into account.

Multiple document representations are generated by considering each Web document's *content*, *metadata* and *links*.

Content. A straightforward way of representing a document is by considering its *content*, i.e. the terms it contains. This is the approach followed in traditional IR and in many Web IR models. The significance of a term contained in a document is determined by a weight assigned to it, reflecting the 'goodness' of that term at discriminating the document's content. We can use the two standard IR weighting functions: the *term frequency* of a term t in a document d, $tf(t, d)$ and *inverse document frequency* of the term in the document collection, $idf(t)$.

Additional term characteristics can also be employed in the calculation of these weights, such as those presented in [27]. The motivation behind their introduction is that IR techniques should not only take into account the absence, presence and frequency information of query terms in the documents, but they should also consider information on how these terms are used within the documents. The term characteristics that capture that (apart from tf, idf) are:

- *noise* – measures how important a term is within a collection, but it is based on within-document frequency
- *theme* – based on the distribution of term occurrences within a document to define whether the term is related to the main topic of a document or to a localised discussion

- *context* – such as co-occurrence information about the logical structures in which the term appears

These term characteristics were proposed as additional weighting schemes and not as alternative to *tf*, *idf* and this is justified by the results of experiments [27], showing that the weighted combination of these characteristics (including *tf*, *idf*) improved the effectiveness.

In the case of HTML documents, which constitute the majority of Web documents, the use of HTML tags allows us to extract more information about a term. For instance, the part of the document in which as term appears can be easily determined by examining the HTML tags denoting the internal structure of the document. Therefore, if we follow the rationale that terms appearing in different parts of a document may have a different significance in identifying that document, the occurrence of a term in the document title would result in the assignment of a higher weight to it, compared to the weight assigned to the same term occurring in the body of the document. Furthermore, the visual presentation details of a term, if, for instance, is displayed in **bold** or in *italics*, can be easily determined. This approach of exploiting the HTML tags in the assignment of weights has been tested [12] and the results indicated that it is a useful strategy for improving the effectiveness of retrieving HTML documents. This approach has been applied in major search engines, such as Google [7].

Metadata. The meta-information accompanying each Web document, such as its author and the keywords describing it, can be used in representing a document. This information can be exploited by the retrieval function to improve its effectiveness, especially in database-like queries. However, it has been suggested [7] that since this meta-information is invisible to the user, it could be easily manipulated for spamming purposes and therefore should be used with caution. This can be achieved by adjusting the influence of the *metadata* representation to the final combination of Web document representations.

Links. Each Web document constitutes a node on the Web graph connected with the other nodes via the Web links. To generate a document representation based on link-based evidential information, the links are differentiated according to their direction with respect to a Web document. Links pointing to a document are referred to as *inlinks* of that document, whereas links contained in a Web document are referred to as its *outlinks*. Following the classification presented in section 3, where links are characterised based on the relationship they represent, *inlinks* and *outlinks* can be further subdivided into the following categories: *inlinks_ref*, *inlinks_comp*, *inlinks_seq*, *outlinks_ref*, *outlinks_comp* and *outlinks_seq*. The *inlinks_ref* refer to inlinks representing the reference relationship between the linked documents, the *inlinks_comp* the composition relationship and the *inlinks_seq* the sequence relationship. The same applies for the outlinks. The following sections discuss how a Web document representation can be generated by considering its *inlinks*, its *outlinks* and its *hub* and *authority* values.

Inlinks. To represent a Web document using its inlinks, their anchor text, which is the text associated with each link pointing to a Web page, can been used. The basis of this approach lies on the assumption that the anchor text usually provides a more accurate and concise description of the Web page that it is associated with, than the actual Web page itself, by probably using more significant terms than those contained in the document [4]. This assumption forms the foundation of many approaches [2, 3, 4, 7, 9] and it has been tested empirically on a relatively large Web corpus [13]. The results of the experiments indicated that this idea holds true and therefore the anchor text of links can be used to describe the page these links reference and may also be employed as a useful discriminator among unseen pages. Furthermore, they can be used to represent non-indexable pages, such as images [7], and this method is analogous to the one proposed by Dunlop [14] in hypertext/hypermedia environments in which the context of non-textual documents is used to represent their content.

Therefore, the anchor text of links can be used in the document representation of the document these links reference. It has been suggested [4, 6, 9] that if the anchor text is not sufficiently self-descriptive, then the text surrounding the link should be also considered.

However, not all inlinks of a Web page and their associated anchor texts should be treated uniformly. Different weights could be assigned to the links (and their associated anchor texts) reflecting their suitability for representing these Web documents. These weights could be based on:

- Type of inlink: *inlinks_ref*, *inlinks_comp*, *inlinks_seq*
- Similarity between the linked documents
- Position of link in referencing document. A number of studies [2, 3] have analysed the conventions with which Web documents are being written and it has been suggested that there is a pattern in the way people describe and link to other documents. To be more specific, there are 4 patterns of linking Web documents to each other within the limits of a paragraph, which can be described as follows (each case constitutes a paragraph):
    1. Anchor ...text....text.
    2. Text .... Anchor... text.
    3. Text ... text... Anchor.
    4. Anchor ... Anchor... Anchor.

A series of experiments indicated that when a link is in the beginning of a paragraph and is followed by text, then this text is most useful in describing the topic of the linked document.

Finally, since we are dealing with text, any of the methods discussed previously can be used in assigning weight to the terms themselves.

Out-links. Each Web document can be represented by the anchor (and possibly the surrounding) text of the outlinks it contains. The rationale of this approach lies on the assumption that the text associated with the outlinks could be used to extract information about the topics of the documents. The weights assigned to these links, reflecting their suitability for representing these Web documents, could be based on:

- Type of outlink: *outlinks _ref, outlinks _comp, outlinks_seq*
- Similarity between the linked documents
- Position of link in the document
- The distribution of the links. The less evenly the terms in the anchor text associated with the outlinks, are distributed within a document, the more likely they are to correspond to a localised discussion and not to the main topic of the document.

Similarly, since we are dealing with text, any of the methods discussed previously can be used in assigning weight to the terms themselves.

Authority & Hub Values. Using the HITS algorithm, described in section 2, or any of the approaches [6, 9], the hub and authority values of the Web documents in the base set, generated by a content-based IR strategy, can be estimated. These two values provide link-based evidential information regarding the quality of these documents and can be combined with content-based document representations in order to yield improvements in the retrieval effectiveness.

4.2 Retrieval through Combination of Web Document Representations

This section introduces the concept of Bayesian networks and then describes our Web document retrieval model, using the *inference net* [34, 35] as its basis. This determines how the document and queries are represented and how the actual retrieval is achieved.

Network representations have been used in IR since the early 1960s for a variety of applications [35]. However, since IR can be viewed as an *inference* or *evidential reasoning* process [36] and the probability that a user's information need is satisfied, can be estimated given a document as 'evidence', these network representations can be employed as *mechanisms for inferring these kinds of relationships* [35] between the documents and the queries. Bayesian networks provide a sound framework and can be applied to IR, allowing the combination of distinct sources of evidence.

A Bayesian network [22] is a directed acyclic graph (DAG) in which the nodes represent variables and the arcs between them signify causal dependencies between these variables. The strengths of these dependencies are expressed by conditional probabilities. If there is a directed arc from node p to node q, then p is the *parent* node, q is the *child* node and p is considered to '*cause*' q. This causal dependency is quantified by the conditional probability $P(q|p)$. The nodes that do not have parents are referred to as the *root* nodes of the network. When a node x of a Bayesian network has more than one parent nodes, which form a set P, then to quantify their influences, one would need to specify any function F that satisfies the following:

$$\sum_{\forall x} F(x,P) = 1, 0 \leq F(x,P) \leq 1. \tag{1}$$

The function $F(x,p)$ provides a numerical quantification for $P(x|p)$ [26].

The first ones to introduce the use of Bayesian networks to model the document retrieval procedure were Turtle and Croft [11, 34, 35]. The proposed model is called *inference net* and forms the basis of our approach. The main contributions of their model to IR research was the development of a formal retrieval model based on a sound theoretical framework that allows the combination of multiple document representations and information need representations (queries), as well as the combination of the rankings produced by different retrieval algorithms. Moreover, the inference net model has been turned into an efficient implementation by the *INQUERY* system [8] and has shown significant improvements in the retrieval effectiveness over conventional models, demonstrating, in that way, both its practical and theoretical value.

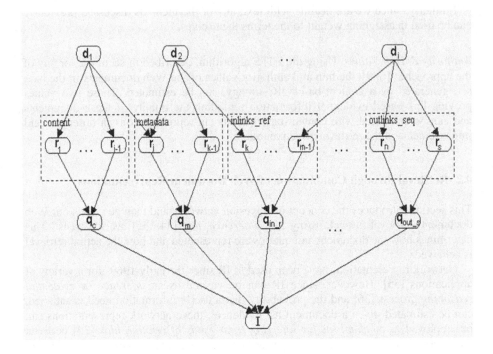

Fig. 1. A Web document retrieval inference model

The Web document retrieval inference net model is illustrated in Figure 1. It consists of a *document network* and of a *query network*. The document network is built once and represents the Web documents' collection, which are indexed using a number of representation techniques. The query network is built every time a user submits a request to the system and represents the user's information need expressed as one or more queries. All the nodes on the inference network are either *true* or *false* and they represent the random variables that are associated with the documents, the queries and the concepts used to represent them. The values of the root nodes can be determined by observation, whereas the values of the rest of the nodes must be determined by inference. Finally, the values assigned to the links are interpreted as beliefs.

Document Network. The *document network*, shown in Figure 1, is a simple two-level DAG containing two different types of nodes: the document nodes (d_i's) and the concept representation nodes (r_k's). If we denote D to be the set of documents, R the set of representation concepts and their cardinalities are n_d and n_r respectively, then the event space of the document network is $E_d = D \times R$. The size of this event space is $2^{n_d} \times 2^{n_r}$, because the nodes of the document network represent propositions associated with binary-valued variables.

The document nodes are the root nodes of the network and they represent the Web documents constituting the document collection. The document nodes correspond to the event that a particular Web document has been observed. In principle, a Web document can consist of any number of Web pages, but we will follow the simple approach adopted in Web IR research [1] of considering each Web document to correspond to a single Web page. Furthermore, each Web page usually contains a number of different media, such as text, images, sound etc., but here we will focus on their textual aspect. The prior probabilities $P(d_i)$ associated with each document d_i are generally set to be equal to $1/n_d$.

A content representation node r_k represents the proposition that a concept has been observed. For the model to support multiple document representation schemes, the set of representation concepts is divided into as many disjoint subsets, as the number of representation schemes supported [34, 35]. Each of these subsets corresponds to an individual representation technique and contains the representation concepts used to index each document using this particular representation scheme. In principle, the model allows for an unlimited number of representation schemes, however, our model currently supports the representation techniques, discussed in section 4.1. Consequently, there are eight sets of representation concepts, each consisting of the nodes representing the keywords, which were considered by any one of the following indexing schemes: *content, metadata, inlinks_ref, inlinks_comp, inlinks_seq, outlinks_ref, outlinks_comp, outlinks_seq*. For instance, the *inlinks_ref* subset consists of the keywords extracted by considering the *anchor* (and possibly the surrounding) *text* of links representing the *reference* relationship, pointing to the Web documents in the collection.

Therefore, each representation concept corresponds to the event that this concept has been automatically extracted from the Web documents in the collection, through the application of one of the proposed representation schemes. Therefore, when a concept r_k is assigned to a document d_i, this assignment is represented by a directed link from that document to that concept, signifying that by observing a document, an increased belief is caused on that concept node. The value of the link is the conditional probability $P(r_k \mid d_i)$, which is specified given the set of parent nodes and their influence on that concept. This specification can then express any term weighting function, such as the *idf* associated with each representation concept node. For a node with n parents, this would require $O(2^n)$ space, but the use of canonical representations reduces that to $O(n)$ space, as discussed in section 4.3.

To incorporate the link-based evidence in the form of the hub and authority values, the *base set* [20] of Web documents with respect to the user's information need should be generated. This can be achieved by employing a content-based IR approach, such as the Web document retrieval model in Figure 1, with only the *content* representation scheme activated. Two new representation concept nodes are then added to the document network (as illustrated in Figure 2) in order to model the hub and authority values associated with each document belonging to the base set. Each of these two nodes r_a and r_h represents the terms extracted from the user's query and each of the documents d_j in the base set is linked to them, so that the conditional probabilities $P(r_h \mid d_j)$ and $P(r_a \mid d_j)$ correspond respectively to the hub and authority values of document d_j with respect to the given query. This approach of incorporating link-based evidence, in the form of the hub and authority values, has been applied to the Web using the *belief network* [26] as the underlying formal framework and the combination of content and link-based evidence has led to significant improvements in the retrieval effectiveness [31].

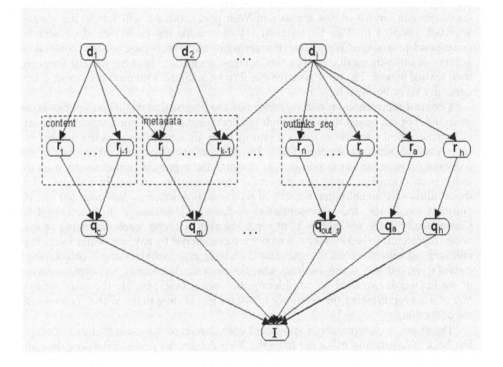

Fig. 2. The Web document retrieval network including link-based evidence

Query Network. The *query network*, as shown in Figure 1, is an 'inverted' DAG consisting of two levels: the information need level and the queries level. If we denote Q to be the set of queries expressing the information need I and its cardinality is n_q, then the event space of the query network is $E_q = I \times Q$. The size of this event space is 2^{n_q+1}, since the nodes of the network represent propositions associated with binary-valued variables. Therefore, the event space of the whole network is $E_d \times E_q$.

The user's information need is represented by node I, which corresponds to the event that this information need is met. A query node represents a specific query formulation and corresponds to the event that this query representation is satisfied. Each of these query formulations is associated with each of the representation schemes supported by the model and is constructed using the representation nodes of this particular representation technique. Therefore, the combination of these query formulations leads to combination of the different document representations, as done in the INQUERY system. Therefore, if we consider, for example, the *content* and *inlinks_ref* representation schemes supported by our model, there will be at least two query nodes $q_{content}$ and $q_{inlinks\_ref}$. These query formulations are generated using the query terms corresponding to the representation concepts belonging, respectively, to the *content* and *inlikins_ref* subsets.

The query and document networks are connected by the directed links from the content representation nodes to the query nodes. These links signify that an increased belief is caused to this particular query formulation by the observation of the concepts belonging to a representation scheme.

To produce a ranking of the documents in the collection with respect to a given information need *I*, we compute the probability that this information need is satisfied given that document d_i has been observed, $P(I|\ d_i)$. This is referred to as *instantiating* d_i and corresponds to attaching evidence to the network, by stating that $d_i = true$, whereas the rest of the document nodes are set to *false*. By adding this new evidence, the probability distribution represented by the network remains the same, whereas the beliefs do change in order to be consistent with that distribution [22]. When the probability $P(I|\ d_i)$ is computed, this evidence is removed and a new document $d_j, j \neq i$, is instantiated. By repeating this computation for the rest of the documents in the collection the ranking is produced.

The inference network intends to capture how a user's information need is met given the Web documents' collection and the way this depends on the document and query representations. If these dependencies are characterised correctly, then the results provided are good estimates of the probability this information need is met.

4.3 Conditional Probabilities

For any of the non-root nodes *A* of the network, the dependency on its set of parent nodes $\{P_1, P_2, ..., P_n\}$, quantified by the conditional probability $P(A|\ P_1, P_2, ..., P_n)$, must be estimated and encoded.

Encoding the Probabilities Using Link Matrices. To encode the probability that a value is assigned to a node *A* given any combination of values of its parent nodes, *link matrices* are used. However, all the random variables (r_k, q_j, I), represented by the non-root nodes in the network, are binary and therefore, when a node has *n* parents, the link matrix associated with it is of size 2×2^n.

Canonical link matrix forms, which allow us to compute for *A* any value $L_A[i, j]$ of its link matrix L_A, where $i \in \{0,1\}$ and $0 \leq j \leq 2^n$, will be used (as done in [34, 35]). The row number $\{0,1\}$ of the link matrix corresponds to the value assigned to the node *A*, whereas the binary representation of the column number is used so that the highest order bit reflects the value of the first parent, the second highest order bit the value of the second parent and so on.

We will use the *weighted-sum* canonical link matrix form [34, 35]. This allows us to assign a weight to the child node *A*, which is, in essence, the maximum belief that can be associated with that node. Furthermore, weights are also assigned to its parents, reflecting their influence on the child node. Consequently, our belief in the node is determined by the parents that are true.

If we suppose that node *A* has only two parents P_1, P_2 and that the weights assigned to them are w_1, w_2 respectively and we denote w_A to be the weight of node *A* and $P(P_1 = true) = p_1$ and $P(P_2 = true) = p_2$, then the link matrix L_A is as follows:

$$L_A = \begin{bmatrix} 1 & 1-\dfrac{w_2 w_A}{w_1 + w_2} & 1-\dfrac{w_1 w_A}{w_1 + w_2} & 1-\dfrac{(w_1 + w_2)w_A}{w_1 + w_2} \\ 0 & \dfrac{w_2 w_A}{w_1 + w_2} & \dfrac{w_1 w_A}{w_1 + w_2} & \dfrac{(w_1 + w_2)w_A}{w_1 + w_2} \end{bmatrix}. \tag{2}$$

If we evaluate this link matrix, we get the following results:

$$P(A = true) = \frac{(w_1 p_1 + w_2 p_2)w_A}{w_1 + w_2} \qquad P(A = false) = 1 - \frac{(w_1 p_1 + w_2 p_2)w_A}{w_1 + w_2}. \tag{3}$$

In the more general case of the node A having n parents, the derived link matrix can be evaluated using the following closed form expression:

$$bel(A) = \frac{w_A \sum_{i=1}^{n} w_i p_i}{\sum_{i=1}^{n} w_i}. \tag{4}$$

Finally, since only a weight for each of the parents is required, the space complexity is reduced to $O(n)$.

Estimating the Probabilities. For our Web document retrieval model, we need to provide estimates that characterise the following three dependencies:

1. the dependence of the representation concepts upon the Web documents containing them
2. the dependence of a query formulation upon the representation concepts in the Web document collection
3. the dependence of the user's information need upon the different query formulations

To estimate the probability that a representation concept is good at discriminating a Web document's content, several weighting functions can be incorporated in the weighted-sum link matrix. Experiments using the basic inference network model [34, 35] indicated that a good belief estimate can be achieved by employing the *tf, idf* weighting strategies. This estimate is given by:

$$P(r_k \mid d_i = true) = 0.4 + 0.6 \times tf \times idf \qquad P(r_k \mid all\ parents\ false) = 0.4. \tag{5}$$

Our aim is to also incorporate additional term characteristics, such as those discussed in section 4.1, in the calculation of these estimates, to capture other aspects of the usage of terms within the documents. This approach excludes the case of the representation concepts r_h and r_a, associated with the hub and authority link-based evidence, where the conditional probabilities correspond to the values of these metrics.

Similarly, the weighted-sum link matrix can be used to encode the dependency of an individual query formulation upon the representation concepts associated with a particular representation scheme, through the employment of appropriate query term weighting functions. Finally, since the user's information need is represented by multiple query representations, their combination can be achieved using a weighted-sum link matrix, with weights expressing the importance of each query representation, which reflects the importance of the representation scheme associated with that particular query.

5   Example

We now present an example to demonstrate the retrieval process using the model introduced in the previous section.

We consider only two of the Web documents in the document collection and two representation schemes (*content* and *inlinks_ref*). The fragment of the Web document retrieval model illustrating these two documents and a small portion of the representation concepts associated with them is displayed in Figure 3. Let us suppose that document d_1 discusses the research in the area of information retrieval and fusion from distributed data and knowledge sources and contains, among others, the terms *extraction*, *data* and *fusion*. The anchor texts of the links representing the reference relation and pointing to d_1 are used in the *inlinks_ref* representation scheme and contain, among others, the phrase *information retrieval*. Let us further assume that document d_2 presents the compilation of atomic and molecular collision data, relevant to fusion energy research and will be represented using the terms *data*, *fusion* and *energy*. The term *collection* will be considered for its *inlinks_ref* representation. The user's information need is about *information retrieval* and *data fusion*. To provide a ranking of these two documents, we need to estimate the probabilities $P(I|d_1)$ and $P(I|d_2)$.

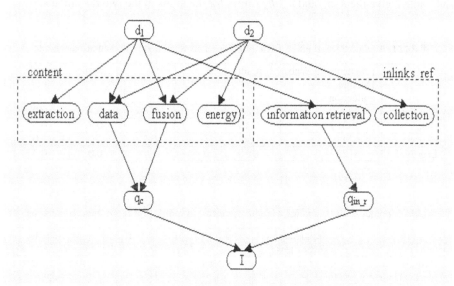

Fig. 3. Web document retrieval network fragment

We assume that the conditional probability of the representation concept r_i belonging to the subset associated with the representation scheme k for $k \in \{content, inlinks\_ref\}$, when d_j is instantiated, can be estimated using the following formula:

$$P(r_{ik} \mid d_j = true) = 0.5 + 0.5 \times n\_tf_{ijk} \times idf_{ik} \qquad P(r_{ik} \mid all\ parents\ false) = 0.0 \qquad (6)$$

where n_tf_{ijk} is the normalised term frequency and n_idf_{ik} the normalised inverse document frequency of concept r_i associated with document d_j when considering the subset of information about that document, taken into account by the representation scheme k. When $k = content$, n_tf_{ijk} corresponds to the normalised term frequency of concept r_i in document d_j and n_idf_{ik} to the normalised inverse document frequency of concept r_i in the Web document collection. When $k = inlinks\_ref$, however, n_tf_{ijk} refers to the normalised term frequency of concept r_i by considering the anchor text of the reference type inlinks of document d_j and n_idf_{ik} to the normalised inverse document frequency of concept r_i in the termspace created by the anchor text of these inlinks for all the Web documents in the collection.

The normalised term frequency n_tf_{ijk} and inverse document frequency n_idf_{ik} values are estimated using the following formulas (as done in [34]):

$$n\_tf_{ijk} = \frac{tf_{ijk}}{max\_tf_{ik}} \qquad n\_idf_{ik} = \frac{\log\left(collection\ size_k \big/ df_{ik}\right)}{\log(collection\ size_k)} \ . \qquad (7)$$

Let us assume that our Web document collection contains 100,000 documents and that they are all pointed to by at least one Web document. If, for the *content* representation scheme, we assume that $max\_tf_{d1} = 5$ and $max\_tf_{d2} = 4$ and for the *inlinks_ref* representation scheme that $max\_tf_{a1} = 10$ and $max\_tf_{a2} = 5$, then Table 1 and Table 2 give the n_tf_{ijk} and n_idf_{ik} values for the terms in the two documents.

Table 1. Frequencies, tf and idf wieghts for terms in content representation scheme

	Frequency in Web Document collection	n_idf	tf_{d1}	tf_{d2}	n_tf_{d1}	n_tf_{d2}
Extraction	92	0.61	2	0	0.4	0.0
Data	18515	0.15	4	2	0.8	0.5
Fusion	624	0.44	5	4	1.0	1.0
Energy	3122	0.30	0	3	0.0	0.75

Table 2. Frequencies, tf and idf wieghts for terms in inlinks_ref representation scheme

	Frequency in anchor text	n_idf	tf_{a1}	tf_{a2}	n_tf_{a1}	n_tf_{a2}
Information retrieval	115	0.59	8	0	0.8	0.0
Collection	35	0.69	0	2	0.0	0.4

When d_1 is instantiated we obtain the following results (using 6):
- *Content* representation scheme:
  bel$_c$ (extraction) = 0.622   bel$_c$ (data) = 0.56
  bel$_c$ (fusion) = 0.72   bel$_c$ (energy) = 0.000
- *Inlinks_ref* representation scheme:
  bel$_{in\_r}$(information retrieval) = 0.736   bel$_{in\_r}$ (collection) = 0.000

When d_2 is instantiated we obtain the following results:
- *Content* representation scheme:
  bel$_c$ (extraction) = 0.000   bel$_c$ (data) = 0.537
  bel$_c$ (fusion) = 0.72   bel$_c$ (energy) = 0.612
- *Inlinks_ref* representation scheme:
  bel$_{in\_r}$ (information retrieval) = 0.000   bel$_{in\_r}$ (collection) = 0.638

The link matrices associated with the two query formulations can be estimated using query term frequency weights, but for the example we assume that they are:

$$L_{qc} = \begin{bmatrix} 0.9 & 0.7 & 0.4 & 0.2 \\ 0.1 & 0.3 & 0.6 & 0.8 \end{bmatrix} \qquad\qquad L_{qin\_r} = \begin{bmatrix} 0.9 & 0.3 \\ 0.1 & 0.7 \end{bmatrix}$$

Therefore : $P(q_c| d_1) = 0.1 \times 0.44 \times 0.28 \ + \ 0.3 \times 0.44 \times 0.72 \ +$
                        $0.6 \times 0.56 \times 0.28 \ + \ 0.8 \times 0.56 \times 0.72 \ = 0.524$
$P(q_{in\_r}| d_1) = 0.542$ $P(q_c| d_2) = 0.512$ $P(q_{in\_r}| d_2) = 0.1$

Let us assume that we assign weights to the two query formulations represented by the following link matrix:

$$L_I = \begin{bmatrix} 0.9 & 0.3 & 0.3 & 0.2 \\ 0.1 & 0.7 & 0.7 & 0.8 \end{bmatrix}$$

This results in the following estimates: bel$(I \mid d_1) = 0.597$ bel$(I \mid d_2) = 0.442$

Further work is needed to investigate the usage of additional term characteristics, such as those described in section 4.1, in the estimation of the conditional probabilities $P(r_{ik} \mid d_j = true)$. Experimental evaluation will allow us to determine the weights assigned to the different query formulations in order to obtain improvements in the effectiveness.

6   Extended Model

Additional evidence can be incorporated in our model. It has been suggested [21] that the next generation Web search engines should take into account *context* information. This means that the results they provide in response to a query should depend on the user who submitted the query and also on the context in which the user made the request. This can be done either explicitly, by asking the user to provide additional information, or implicitly, by automatically inferring this information for the user's profile, preferences and current interests. This additional context information can then be used in our model in order to improve the ranking.

It has also been proposed [37] that metrics quantifying the quality of each Web document should be incorporated in the retrieval process. That should happen because Web documents differ in their quality, since there is usually no control of how these documents are created and maintained, as is usually the case in traditional IR environments. Six quality metrics were proposed:

- *currency* – measures how recently the Web document has been updated
- *availability* – measures the number of broken links contained in a Web page
- *information-to-noise* - measures the proportion of useful to non-useful content of within a Web document
- *authority* – measures the reputation of the organisation that produced the Web page
- *popularity* – measures the number of Web pages citing this page
- *cohesiveness* – measures the degree to which the content is focused on one topic

A document can be further characterised through the usage of terms in the document by estimating its *specificity*, which is a measure of the technical complexity of the document, introduced in [27]. These document characteristics, which are query independent, can be taken into account by our model, either for all the documents in the collection or for only the documents containing at least one of the query terms, as done in [27]. Finally relevance feedback and thesaurus information can be incorporated in our model.

7   Conclusions and Further Work

We have presented a formal Web IR model which uses the *Bayesian inference network* model as its underlying framework and supports the explicit combination of multiple Web document representations. These representations are generated by considering content and link-based evidential information. Our model currently supports eight representation schemes based on the *content, metadata, inlinks* and *outlinks* of the Web documents. The link-based analysis considers not only the presence of a link between two documents, signifying that a relationship exists between them, but also the nature of that relationship. This leads to a classification of the Web links, according to the relationship they represent. Additional link-based information, in the form of the *hub* and *authority* values of the Web documents, are also incorporated in the model.

Further work will investigate the effect onto the retrieval effectiveness, of the different possible combinations of the Web document representation schemes and of the incorporation of additional sources of evidence, such as *context* information. Additional term weighting functions, such as those discussed in section 4.1, will be considered to estimate the conditional probabilities. Our aim is to research these aspects by performing evaluation experiments using a large corpus of Web documents.

References

1. Agosti, M. & Melucci, M. Information Retrieval on the Web. Lectures on Information Retrieval: Third European Summer-School ESSIR 2000, Varenna, Italy, September 11-15, 2000, Agosti, M. Crestani, F. & Pasi, G. eds. Revised Lectures, Springer-Verlag, Berlin/Heidelberg, 2001, 242-285.
2. Amitay, E. Using common hypertext links to identify the best phrasal description of target Web documents. In *Proceedings of the SIGIR Post-Conference Workshop on Hypertext Information Retrieval for the Web*, Melbourne, Australia, 1998.
3. Amitay, E. InCommonSense – Rethinking Web Results. *IEEE International Conference on Multimedia and Expo (ICME 2000)*, New York City, NY, USA.
4. Attardi, G., Gullì, A. & Sebastiani, F. Automatic Web Page Categorization by Link and Context Analysis. *European Symposium on Telematics, Hypermedia and Artificial Intelligence*, Varese, 1999.
5. Belkin, N. J., Kantor, P., Fox, E. A. & Shaw, J. A. Combining the evidence of multiple query representations for information retrieval. *Information Processing & Management*, 31(3), pp. 431-448, 1995.
6. Bharat, K. & Henzinger, M. Improved algorithms for topic distillation in hyperlinked environments. *In Proceedings of the Annual International ACM SIGIR Conference on Research and Development in Information Retrieval, 1998, pp. 104-111.*
7. Brin, S. & Page, L. The Anatomy of a Large-Scale HyperTextual Web Search Engine. In *Proceedings of the Seventh International World Wide Web Conference*, Brisbane, Australia, 1998.
8. Callan, J.P., Croft, W.B., & Harding, S.M. The INQUERY Retrieval System. In *Proceedings of the 3rd International Conference on Database and Expert Systems Applications*, Valencia, Spain, 1992, pp. 78-83.
9. Chakrabarti, S., Dom, B., Gibson, D., Kleinberg, J., Raghavan, P. & Rajagopalan, S. Automatic resource list compilation by analysing hyperlink structure and associated text. In *Proceedings of the 7th International World Wide Web Conference,* 1998.
10. Croft, W.B. Combining Approaches to Information Retrieval, *Advances in Information Retrieval: Recent Research from the CIIR*, W. Bruce Croft, ed., Kluwer Academic Publishers, Chapter 1, pp.1-36, 2000.
11. Croft, W.B. & Turtle, H. A Retrieval Model Incorporating Hypertext Links. In *Proceedings of the second annual ACM conference on Hypertext,* Pittsburgh, PA USA, 1989, pp. 213-224.
12. Cutler, M., Deng H., Manicaam S., & Meng W. A New Study on Using HTML Structures to Improve Retrieval. *The Eleventh IEEE International Conference on Tools with Artificial Intelligence (ICTAI99),* Chicago IL, November 9-11, 1999
13. Davison, B. D. Topical Locality in the Web. In *Proceedings of the 23rd Annual International ACM SIGIR Conference on Research and Development in Information Retrieval*, Athens, Greece, July 24-28, pages 272-279.
14. Dunlop, M. D. & van Rijsbergen, C. J. Hypermedia and free text retrieval, *Information Processing and Management*, vol. 29(3), May 1993.
15. Fischer, H. & Elchesen, D. Effectiveness of combining title words and index terms in machine retrieval searches, *Nature*, 238:109-11, 1972.
16. Fox, E., Nunn, G. & Lee, W. Coefficients for combining concept classes in a collection. In *Proceedings of the 11ᵗʰ Annual International ACM SIGIR Conference on Research and Development in Information Retrieval*, pp. 291-308, 1988.
17. Gauch, S., Wang, H. & Gomez, M. ProFusion: Intelligent Fusion from Multiple, Distributed Search Engines. *Journal of Universal Computing*, Springer-Verlag, Volume 2 (9), September 1996.

18. Géry, M. & Chevallet, J. P. Toward a Structured Information Retrieval System on the Web: Automatic Structure Extraction of Web Pages. In *International Workshop on Web Dynamics*. In conjunction with the *8th International Conference on Database Theory*. London, UK, 3 January 2001.
19. Katzer, J., McGill, M., Tessier, J., Frakes, W. & DasGupta, P. A study of the overlap among document representations. *Information Technology: Research and Development*, 1(4): 261-274, 1982.
20. Kleinberg, J. Authoritative sources in a hyperlinked environment. In *Proceedings of the 9th ACM-SIAM Symposium on Discrete Algorithms*, 1998. Extended version in Journal of the ACM 46[1999]. Also appears as IBM Research Report RJ 10076, May 1997.
21. Lawrence, S. Context in Web Search. *IEEE Data Engineering Bulletin*, Volume 23, Number 3, pp.25-32, 2000.
22. Pearl, J. *Probabilistic Reasoning in Intelligent systems: Networks of plausible inference.*, Revised second printing, Morgan Kaufmann Publishers Inc., 1997.
23. Rajashekar, T. & Croft, B. Combining automatic and manual index representation in probabilistic retrieval. *Journal of the American Society for Information Science*, 46(4):272-283, 1995.
24. Robertson, S.E. Theories and models in Information Retrieval. *Journal of Documentation*, 33, pp. 126-148, 1977.
25. Robertson, S. & Sparck-Jones, K. Relevance weighting of search terms. *Journal of American society for Information Science*, 27:129-146, 1976.
26. Ribeiro-Neto, B., daSilva, I. & Muntz, R. Bayesian Network Models for IR. In *Soft Computing in Information Retrieval: Techniques and Applications*, Crestani, F. & Pasi, G. editors. Springer Verlag, 2000. pp 259-291
27. Ruthven, I., Lalmas, M. & van Rijsbergen, K. Combining and selecting characteristics of information use. *Journal of the American Society of Information Science and Technology*, 2002 (To appear).
28. Salton, G., Yang, C. & Wong, A. A vector space model for automatic indexing, *Communications of the ACM*, 18(11), pp. 613-620, 1975.
29. Savoy, J., Le Calvé, A. & Vrajitoru, D. Report on the TREC-5 Experiment: Data Fusion and Collection Fusion. *Proceedings TREC5*, 1996.NIST Publication 500-238, Gaithersburg (MD), 489-502, 1996.
30. Selberg, E. & Etzioni, O. The MetaCrawler Architecture for Resource Aggregation on the Web. *IEEE Expert*, January / February 1997, Volume 12 No. 1, pp. 8-14.
31. Silva, I., Ribeiro-Neto, B., Calado, P., Moura, E. & Ziviani, N. Link-Based and Content-Based Evidential Information in aBelief Network Model. In *Proceedings of the 23rd Annual International ACM SIGIR Conference on Research and Development in Information Retrieval*, Athens, Greece, July 2000, pp 96-103
32. Sparck Jones, K. & Willett, P. *Readings in Information Retrieval*, Sparck Jones, K. & Willett, P. eds, Morgan Kaufmann Publishers, 1997.
33. Tsikrika, T. & Lalmas, M. Merging Techniques for Performing Data Fusion on the Web. *Proceedings of the Tenth International Conference on Information and Knowledge Management (ACM CIKM 2001)*, Atlanta, Georgia, November 5-10, 2001.
34. Turtle H. R. Inference Networks for Document Retrieval. Ph.D. dissertation.
35. Turtle, H. & Croft, W.B. Evaluation of an Inference Network-Based Retrieval Model. *ACM Transactions on Information Systems*, 9(3), pp. 187-222.
36. van Rijsbergen, C. J. A Non-Classical Logic for Information Retrieval. In *Readings in Information Retrieval*, Sparck-Jones, K. & Willett, P. editors. The Morgan Kaufmann Series in Multimedia Information and Systems, Edward Fox Series Editor, 1997.
37. Zhu, X. & Gauch, S. Incorporating quality metrics in centralized/distributed information retrieval on the World Wide Web. In the *Proceedings of the 23rd Annual International ACM SIGIR Conference on Research and Development in Information Retrieval*, July 24 - 28, 2000, Athens, Greece, pp. 288-295.

An Improved Computation of the PageRank Algorithm[1]

Sung Jin Kim and Sang Ho Lee

School of Computing, Soongsil University, Korea
lace@nowuri.net, shlee@computing.ssu.ac.kr
http://orion.soongsil.ac.kr/

Abstract. The Google search site (http://www.google.com) exploits the link structure of the Web to measure the relative importance of Web pages. The ranking method implemented in Google is called PageRank [3]. The sum of all PageRank values should be one. However, we notice that the sum becomes less than one in some cases. We present an improved PageRank algorithm that computes the PageRank values of the Web pages correctly. Our algorithm works out well in any situations, and the sum of all PageRank values is always maintained to be one. We also present implementation issues of the improved algorithm. Experimental evaluation is carried out and the results are also discussed.

1. Introduction

Web information retrieval tools typically make use of the text on the Web pages as well as the links of the Web pages that contain valuable information implicitly. The link structure of the Web represents a considerable amount of latent human annotation, and thus offers a starting point for structural studies of the Web. Recent work in the Web search area has recognized that the hyperlink structure of the Web is very valuable for locating information [1, 2, 3, 4, 5, 9, 13, 14, 15].

The Google search site (http://www.google.com), which emerged in 1998, exploits the link structure of the Web to measure the relative importance of Web pages. The ranking method implemented in Google is called PageRank [3]. PageRank is an objective measure of citation importance that corresponds with people's subjective idea of importance. Pages that are well cited from many places are worth looking at. PageRank postulates that a link from page u to v implies the author of u recommends to take a look at page v. A page has a high PageRank value if there are many pages that point to it, or if there are pages that point to it and have a high PageRank value. It is known that PageRank helps to rank pages effectively in the Google site.

The PageRank algorithm and implementation details are described in [7, 12]. The PageRank algorithm represents the structure of the Web as a matrix, and PageRank values as a vector. The PageRank vector is derived by computing matrix-vector multiplications repeatedly. The sum of all PageRank values should be one during the computation. However, we learned that the sum becomes less than one as the computation process continues in some cases. In those cases, all PageRank values become smaller than they should be.

---

[1] This work was supported by grant No. (R-01-2000-00403) from the Korea Science and Engineering Foundation.

F. Crestani, M. Girolami, and C.J. van Rijsbergen (Eds.): ECIR 2002, LNCS 2291, pp. 73-85, 2002.
© Springer-Verlag Berlin Heidelberg 2002

In this paper, we present an improved PageRank algorithm that computes the PageRank values of the Web pages correctly. Our algorithm works out well in any situations, and the sum of all PageRank values is always maintained to be one. We also present implementation issues of the improved algorithm. Experimental evaluation is carried out and the results are also discussed.

This paper is organized as follows. The PageRank algorithm is presented in section 2. Section 3 identifies drawbacks of the original PageRank algorithm [7] and presents an improved PageRank algorithm. In section 4, we discuss experimental evaluation of algorithms and its results. Section 5 contains closing remarks.

2. PageRank Computation

Let v be a Web page, F_v be the set of pages v points to, and B_v be the set of pages that point to v. Let $N_v = |F_v|$ be the number of links from v. The PageRank (PR) equation [12] for v is recursively defined as:

$$PR(v) = \sum_{u \in B_v} \frac{PR(u)}{N_u}.$$ (1)

The pages and hyperlinks of the Web can be viewed as nodes and edges in a directed graph [10]. Let M be a square matrix with the rows and columns corresponding to the directed graph G of the Web, assuming all nodes in G have at least one outgoing edge. If there is a link from page j to page i, then the matrix entry m_{ij} has a value $1/N_j$. The values of all other entries are zero. PageRank values of all pages are represented as an $N \times 1$ matrix (a vector), $Rank$. The ith entry, $rank(i)$, in $Rank$ represents the PageRank value of page i.

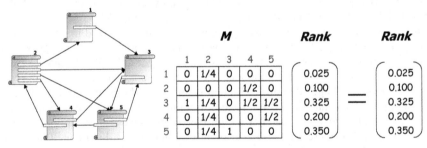

Fig. 1. A small Web, its matrix, and its PageRank values

Fig. 1 shows a simple example of M and $Rank$. The rectangular shape like a document denotes a page. A page identifier appears above each page. The small rectangle represents a URL in a page. The directed line denotes a link from one page to another. For an instance, page 5 has two outgoing edges to page 3 and 4 ($N_5 = 2$), m_{35} and m_{45} of M are $(1/2)$, and m_{15}, m_{25}, and m_{55} are 0. Page 5 is pointed by page 2 and 3, so its PageRank value is determined by PageRank values of page 2 and 3. Since page 2 and 3 have four links and one link respectively, the PageRank of page 5, $rank(5)$, is the sum of a fourth of $rank(2)$ and $rank(3)$. Such computation corresponds to the matrix-vector multiplication.

Computation of the equation (1) can be represented by the following matrix calculation: *Rank* = *M* × *Rank*. The vector, *Rank*, is the principle eigenvector of the matrix *M*. *Rank* can be computed by applying *M* to an initial *Rank* matrix $[1 / N]_{N×1}$ repeatedly, where $[1 / N]_{N×1}$ is an $N × 1$ matrix in which all entries are *(1/N)* [7, 12]. Let $Rank_i$ be the ith intermediate *Rank*, $Rank_I$ be the initial *Rank*, and $Rank_{i+1}$ be *M* × $Rank_i$ (i.e., $Rank_{i+1}$ = *M* × $Rank_i$). $Rank_i$ is converged to a fixed point as *i* increases. The converged $Rank_i$ (i.e., *Rank*) contains PageRank values of all pages.

A vector in which all entries are zero is a zero vector. A page with no outgoing edge is a dangling page. If page *j* is a dangling page, then the jth column of *M* is called a dangling column. A dangling column of *M* is represented as a zero vector. An L_1 norm (simply norm) represents the sum of all entries in a vector. A matrix *M* is irreducible if and only if a directed graph is strongly connected. All columns in an irreducible *M* have norms of value one.

Consider two Web pages that point to each other but to no other pages (i.e., a loop). Suppose there are some Web pages that point to one of them. Then, during the matrix-vector multiplication process, the loop accumulates PageRank values but never distributes any PageRank values (since there are no outgoing edges) [12]. The loop forms a sort of trap, which is called RankSink. Consequently, pages in the loop are likely to have higher PageRank values than they should be.

To overcome the RankSink problem, they [7, 12] introduce another matrix *M'*, where transition edges of probability *(d/N)* between every pair of nodes in *G* are added to *M*. Let *N* be the number of total pages and $[1 / N]_{N×N}$ be an $N × N$ square matrix in which all entries are *(1/N)*. The equation (2) shows a new matrix *M'*.

$$M' = (1-d)M + d \, [\frac{1}{N}]_{N × N} .$$ (2)

The constant *d* is called a dampening factor, and it is less than one. With Fig. 1, *M'* is constructed as below:

	1	2	3	4	5
1	(1-d)(0) + d(1/N)	(1-d)(1/4) + d(1/N)	(1-d)(0) + d(1/N)	(1-d)(0) + d(1/N)	(1-d)(0) + d(1/N)
2	(1-d)(0) + d(1/N)	(1-d)(0) + d(1/N)	(1-d)(0) + d(1/N)	(1-d)(1/2) + d(1/N)	(1-d)(0) + d(1/N)
3	(1-d)(1) + d(1/N)	(1-d)(1/4) + d(1/N)	(1-d)(0) + d(1/N)	(1-d)(1/2) + d(1/N)	(1-d)(1/2) + d(1/N)
4	(1-d)(0) + d(1/N)	(1-d)(1/4) + d(1/N)	(1-d)(0) + d(1/N)	(1-d)(0) + d(1/N)	(1-d)(1/2) + d(1/N)
5	(1-d)(0) + d(1/N)	(1-d)(1/4) + d(1/N)	(1-d)(1) + d(1/N)	(1-d)(0) + d(1/N)	(1-d)(0) + d(1/N)

The definition of *M'* has an intuitive basis in random walks on graphs. The "random surfer" keeps clicking on successive links at random, but the surfer periodically "gets bored" and jumps to a random page. The probability that the surfer gets bored is a dampening factor.

Even though the matrix *M'* is not sparse, there is no need to store it explicitly. When the equation of *M'* × *Rank* is computed, *M'* is replaced with the right side of the equation (2). The replacement and matrix transformation produce an equation (3). Equation (3) is used to compute PageRank values of all pages.

$$M' × Rank = (1-d)M × Rank + d \, [\frac{1}{N}]_{N × 1} .$$ (3)

3. Improved PageRank Computation

We note that there is a drawback of the original PageRank algorithm. Consider the Web structure in Fig. 2. Because there is no outgoing edge in page 1, it becomes a dangling page.

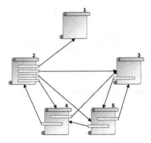

Fig. 2. A small Web with a dangling page

With Fig. 2, M' is represented as:

	1	2	3	4	5
1	(1-d)(0) + d(1/N)	(1-d)(1/4) + d(1/N)	(1-d)(0) + d(1/N)	(1-d)(0) + d(1/N)	(1-d)(0) + d(1/N)
2	(1-d)(0) + d(1/N)	(1-d)(0) + d(1/N)	(1-d)(0) + d(1/N)	(1-d)(1/2) + d(1/N)	(1-d)(0) + d(1/N)
3	(1-d)(0) + d(1/N)	(1-d)(1/4) + d(1/N)	(1-d)(0) + d(1/N)	(1-d)(1/2) + d(1/N)	(1-d)(1/2) + d(1/N)
4	(1-d)(0) + d(1/N)	(1-d)(1/4) + d(1/N)	(1-d)(0) + d(1/N)	(1-d)(0) + d(1/N)	(1-d)(1/2) + d(1/N)
5	(1-d)(0) + d(1/N)	(1-d)(1/4) + d(1/N)	(1-d)(1) + d(1/N)	(1-d)(0) + d(1/N)	(1-d)(0) + d(1/N)

Let $Rank_i$ be $(\alpha, \beta, \gamma, \delta, \varepsilon)^T$, T stands for transposition. Then $Rank_{i+1}$ and its norm are represented as follows:

$$M' \times \begin{pmatrix} \alpha \\ \beta \\ \gamma \\ \delta \\ \varepsilon \end{pmatrix} = \begin{pmatrix} m_{11}\alpha + m_{12}\beta + m_{13}\gamma + m_{14}\delta + m_{15}\varepsilon \\ m_{21}\alpha + m_{22}\beta + m_{23}\gamma + m_{24}\delta + m_{25}\varepsilon \\ m_{31}\alpha + m_{32}\beta + m_{33}\gamma + m_{34}\delta + m_{35}\varepsilon \\ m_{41}\alpha + m_{42}\beta + m_{43}\gamma + m_{44}\delta + m_{45}\varepsilon \\ m_{51}\alpha + m_{52}\beta + m_{53}\gamma + m_{54}\delta + m_{55}\varepsilon \end{pmatrix}$$

The norm of $Rank_{i+1}$ = $(m_{11} + m_{21} + m_{31} + m_{41} + m_{51})\alpha + (m_{12} + m_{22} + m_{32} + m_{42} + m_{52})\beta +$
$(m_{13} + m_{23} + m_{33} + m_{43} + m_{53})\gamma + (m_{14} + m_{24} + m_{34} + m_{44} + m_{54})\delta +$
$(m_{15} + m_{25} + m_{35} + m_{45} + m_{55})\varepsilon$

Note that the norm of the first column vector of M' (i.e., $m_{11} + m_{21} + m_{31} + m_{41} + m_{51}$) is not one, but d, and that all other columns of M' have the norm with one. The norm of $Rank_{i+1}$ is $(d*\alpha + \beta + \gamma + \delta + \varepsilon)$. Because d is less than one, the norm of $Rank_{i+1}$ is less than the norm of $Rank_i$ by $(1-d)*\alpha$. This is contrary to the property that the norm of $Rank$ should be maintained to be one during the entire computation process. During the iteration of matrix-vector multiplication, $Rank_i$ loses a part of its norm continuously. We call this phenomenon norm-leak. This phenomenon takes place when there are dangling pages.

The norm-leak phenomenon has critical implications in terms of computation: First, PageRank values are likely to be smaller than they should be, and might become all zero in the worst case. Second, the iteration process might not converge to a fixed point, because the norms of $Rank_i$ and $Rank_{i+1}$ are not the same.

In order to put an emphasis on the original link structure of the Web (ignoring the virtual links at the same time) in the computation of PageRank values, we need to use a small vaiue of the dampening factor and use a large number of iterations. Interestingly enough, the problems caused by the phenomenon become evident when we use a small value of the dampening factor and a large number of iterations. Consequently, the norm-leak problem does not allow us to consider the original link structure significantly in the computation.

In the original Google computation [7, 12], all dangling pages are simply removed from the system, and then the PageRank values are calculated for the remaining Web pages. After that, dangling pages are added back in a heuristic way. This paper presents a simple but elegant technique to solve the norm-leak phenomenon in a detailed level.

3.1 A New Matrix, $M*$

Before introducing a new computation technique, we need to define a matrix M^+. The matrix M^+ is the same as M, except that a dangling column of M is replaced by $[1 / N]_{N \times 1}$. Let D be a set of dangling pages. Let $<1 / N>_{N \times N,p}$ be an $N \times N$ matrix in which entry m_{ij} is $(1/N)$ if j is equal to p and m_{ij} is zero otherwise. The pth column of $<1 / N>_{N \times N,p}$ is exactly $[1 / N]_{N \times 1}$. Then M^+ can be expressed as follows:

$$M^+ = M + \sum_{p \in D} < \frac{1}{N} >_{N \times N, p} \cdot \qquad (4)$$

When a node i has outgoing edges to each of all nodes including itself, then node i is said to have a complete set of edges. The matrix M^+ implies that each dangling page has a complete set of edges, and that a dampening factor is not used. Given Fig. 2 ($N = 5$), M^+ is expressed as:

	1	2	3	4	5
1	1/N	1/4	0	0	0
2	1/N	0	0	1/2	0
3	1/N	1/4	0	1/2	1/2
4	1/N	1/4	0	0	1/2
5	1/N	1/4	1	0	0

Now we are ready to propose a synthesized matrix M^*:

$$M^* = (1-d)M^+ + d\,[\frac{1}{N}]_{N \times N} . \tag{5}$$

Since M^* is based on M' and M^+, the matrix M^* can be viewed in two aspects: a dampening factor is applied to M^+, and complete sets of edges are applied to M'. A dangling column of M^* is represented as $[1 / N]_{N \times 1}$, no matter what a dampening factor d is. Note that the norm of each column of M^* is always one. Consequently, it is guaranteed that M^* is irreducible. Given Fig. 2, the matrix M^* is described as:

	1	2	3	4	5
1	(1-d)(1/N) + d(1/N)	(1-d)(1/4) + d(1/N)	(1-d)(0) + d(1/N)	(1-d)(0) + d(1/N)	(1-d)(0) + d(1/N)
2	(1-d)(1/N) + d(1/N)	(1-d)(0) + d(1/N)	(1-d)(0) + d(1/N)	(1-d)(1/2) + d(1/N)	(1-d)(0) + d(1/N)
3	(1-d)(1/N) + d(1/N)	(1-d)(1/4) + d(1/N)	(1-d)(0) + d(1/N)	(1-d)(1/2) + d(1/N)	(1-d)(1/2) + d(1/N)
4	(1-d)(1/N) + d(1/N)	(1-d)(1/4) + d(1/N)	(1-d)(0) + d(1/N)	(1-d)(0) + d(1/N)	(1-d)(1/2) + d(1/N)
5	(1-d)(1/N) + d(1/N)	(1-d)(1/4) + d(1/N)	(1-d)(1) + d(1/N)	(1-d)(0) + d(1/N)	(1-d)(0) + d(1/N)

Both M' and M^* imply that each page in G has its own links and a complete set of edges. When a page in both M' and M^* is non-dangling, it distributes d of its importance to all pages, and *(1-d)* of its importance to pages along with original links. However, a dangling page in M^* evenly distributes all of its importance to all pages, while a dangling page in M' distributes *(1-d)* of importance to all pages.

Now, consider the difference of M' and M^* in terms of random surfer model. When a random surfer reaches a dangling page, the surfer in M^* jumps to a page with *(1/N)* probability (note that it is independent of a dampening factor), while the surfer in M' jumps to a page with *(d/N)* probability.

3.2 Computational Efficiency

The improved computation for PageRank uses a matrix M^*, which is not sparse. A non-sparse matrix generally requires a large amount of spatial and computational overhead. We describe an efficient computation of $M^* \times Rank$, which does require a little overhead.

In our algorithm, a leaked value of a dangling page should be distributed to all pages additionally. If we distributed the value whenever we found a dangling page, it would not be an efficient approach to compute PageRank values. Instead, we compute the sum of all leaked values from all dangling pages and distribute them to all pages at once. An expression that corresponds to the accumulation and distribution of leaked values needs to be added to equation (3). Equation (6) shows the final equation. On computation of *(1-d) M × Rank*, we accumulate all *(1-d) rank(p)* (leaked values). After the computation of *(1-d) M × Rank*, the sum is redistributed to all pages.

$$M^* \times Rank = (1-d)M \times Rank + (1-d)[\frac{1}{N}]_{N \times 1} \times \sum_{p \in D} rank(p) + d[\frac{1}{N}]_{N \times 1} \cdot \quad (6)$$

There is one matrix-vector multiplication in the equation (6). Because the matrix M is generally sparse, only non-zero entries in the matrix can be stored and used to compute the matrix-vector multiplication. The matrix M should be stored in a disk, because of its huge size. Given Fig. 2, a data structure for M, referred to as *Links* (see Fig. 3 [7]), is stored on disk. *Links* is scanned only once for the matrix-vector multiplication.

Source Node	Out Degree	Destination Nodes
2	4	1, 3, 4, 5
3	1	5
4	2	2, 3
5	2	3, 4

Fig. 3. Data structure of *Links*

Information of dangling pages has to be stored in *Links* in our computation. The value of *Destination Nodes* of a dangling page is null, representing all pages. This additional information doesn't affect the matrix-vector multiplication. Given Fig. 2, Fig. 4 shows *Links* for our algorithm.

Source Node	Out Degree	Destination Nodes
1	5	Null
2	4	1, 3, 4, 5
3	1	5
4	2	2, 3
5	2	3, 4

Fig. 4. *Links* for the improved PageRank algorithm

Now consider the size of the additional space for dangling pages. For each dangling page, we need to know *Source Node*, *Out Degree*, and *Destination Nodes*. *Source Node* is a sequential number, which does not need to be stored explicitly. The value of *Destination Nodes* is null, which is of length zero. The pure space overhead for n dangling pages is 'n * *the length of Out Degree*', which is *(4*n)* presuming an integer value is represented by 4 bytes.

4. Evaluations

In order to show that the improved PageRank algorithm can solve the norm-leak and the RankSink problem, we implemented and evaluated the improved PageRank algorithm and the original one. We performed two experiments; one with real Web pages and one with a small set of artificial Web pages. The hardware we used was PentiumII-350 with 192MB main memory, running the Accel Linux Version 6.1 operating system.

4.1 An Experiment Using the Real Web

We applied the both algorithms to over 10 million Web pages that had been collected from most of Korean sites. It is simply not feasible to show all PageRank values of the pages. In order to show the distribution of values of PageRank among the pages, we did as follows. We grouped the pages into 1000 groups randomly. With over 10 million, a single group contained approximately over 10,000 pages. The PageRank values of the pages that belonged to the same group were accumulated into a variable. There were 1000 groups, each of which has the accumulated PageRank value. We plotted all the 1000 accumulated PageRank values graphically, as shown in Fig. 5 and 6. The maximum number of iterations and the dampening factor for computation were set as 30 and 0.15, respectively.

Fig. 5 shows the distribution of the accumulated PageRank values that were derived using the original algorithm. Since there were 1000 groups and most of the accumulated PageRank values were smaller than 0.001, we can inference that the sum of all values might be less than one. The sum of all the PageRank values was indeed 0.52 in our experiment. It shows that the norm-leak phenomenon occurs in the original algorithm.

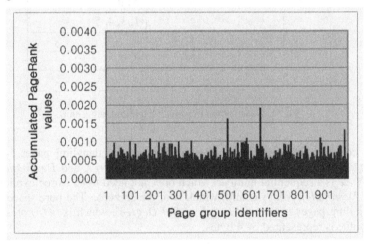

Fig. 5. Accumulated PageRank values by the original algorithm

Fig. 6 shows the distribution of PageRank values that were derived using the proposed algorithm. Note that most of the accumulated PageRank values were plotted around 0.001. The sum of all PageRank values was indeed exactly one in our experiment, as it should be. The norm-leak phenomenon didn't take place in the improved algorithm.

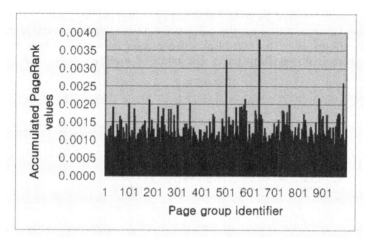

Fig. 6. Accumulated PageRank values by the improved PageRank algorithm

4.2 An Experiment Using Artificial Small Webs

Ten pages are used for our testing. These pages are appropriately linked each other to simulate the RankSink problem and the norm-leak problem. Fig. 7 shows a basic organization of the pages. Our experiments performed under four cases. The maximum number of iteration for computation was set to 20. Three dampening factors were considered.

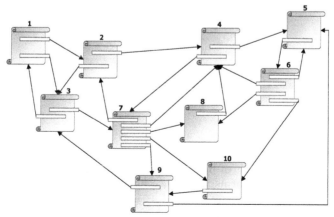

Fig. 7. A basic structure of a ten page Web

(1) Case 1: No RankSink, No Dangling Pages
The basic organization in Fig. 7 is tested. The ten pages have no RankSink and no dangling page. This case serves as a baseline of our testing. Fig. 8 shows the results of the two algorithms. Two algorithms behaved identically in this case, as expected. See the line with $d = 0$. Page 5 and 6 have the highest PageRank value and page 1 has the lowest one. The PageRank value of page 6 is the same as one of page 5, because page 6 is linked by page 5 that has one outgoing edge only. The smaller a dampening factor is, the bigger the difference between the highest PageRank and the lowest PageRank is. The norm-leak phenomenon does not happen in this case, because there is no dangling page. The norm of *Rank* is always one in the both algorithms.

Page ID	$d = 0$	$d = 0.15$	$d = 0.5$
1	.045 403 000	.059 643 500	.078 636 400
2	.047 125 000	.061 079 100	.080 842 000
3	.090 870 700	.105 046 000	.114 545 000
4	.153 046 000	.146 574 000	.132 772 000
5	.161 537 000	.145 503 000	.121 727 000
6	.161 381 000	.138 672 000	.110 863 000
7	.121 940 000	.121 983 000	.111 829 000
8	.064 798 600	.065 199 400	.075 040 800
9	.089 100 000	.091 146 100	.098 703 400
10	.064 798 600	.065 199 400	.075 040 800
Norm	1	1	1
Iterations	20	20	20

(a)   (b)

Fig. 8. Case 1 result

(2) Case 2: No RankSink, One Dangling Page
Suppose that the link from page 10 to 9 is removed in Fig. 7, so that page 10 is a dangling page. Ten pages have no RankSink, but have one dangling page. Case 2 shows that our algorithm can solve the norm-leak phenomenon, which the existing PageRank algorithm cannot solve.

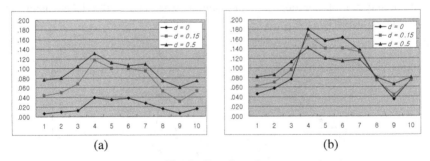

(a)   (b)

Fig. 9. Case 2 results

Fig. 9(a) shows the result of the existing PageRank algorithm. Because page 10 confers a fraction (here *d*) of its importance to all pages, *(1-d)* of the importance is lost at each iteration. The norm of *Rank* is always less than one. The smaller a dampening factor value is, the smaller values of PageRank are. If the number of iteration were set to a much higher value, the PageRank values would be much smaller.

Fig. 9(b) shows the result of the improved PageRank algorithm. Although page 10 is a dangling page, the norm of $Rank_i$ is always kept as one. The norm of $Rank$ is one, independent of a dampening factor and the number of iterations. It is interesting to note that the distributions of PageRank values vary depending on dampening values.

(3) Case 3: No RankSink, Three Dangling Pages
Suppose that the links from pages 5, 8, and 10 are removed in 7. Pages 5, 8, and 10 become dangling. Ten pages have three dangling pages and no RankSink. Case 3 shows that our computation exhibits noticeable difference when there are many dangling pages.

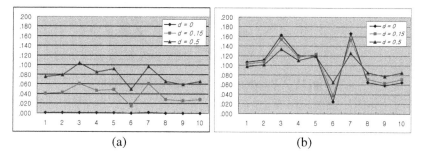

(a)   (b)

Fig. 10. Case 3 results

Fig. 10(a) shows the result of the existing PageRank algorithm. Since the norm-leak takes place at three dangling pages, PageRank values in Fig. 10(a) are much smaller than those in Fig. 9(a). With many dangling pages, the norm of $Rank$ leaks severely. See the broken line with $d = 0$. The line cannot tell us importance of pages, since all PageRank values are virtually zero. If we applied many extra iterations of matrix-vector multiplication additionally, the PageRank values with $d = 0.5$ would converge to zero.

Fig. 10(b) shows the result of the improved PageRank algorithm. Although there are three dangling pages, the norm-leak phenomenon does not happen. Fig. 10 shows that the effect of our algorithm becomes evident as the number of dangling pages increases.

(4) Case 4: RankSink, No Dangling Page
Suppose that the links from pages 2, 3, and 7 to pages 4, 7, and 2 are removed in Fig. 7. Fig. 11 shows the resulting Web. Pages 1, 2, and 3 form a group 1, and the rest of the pages form a group 2. Note that a link from page 9 to page 3, which is an only link from a group 2 to a group 1, exists. Each of the ten pages has at least one outgoing edge, so that there is no dangling page. Case 4 shows that the improved PageRank algorithm handles the RankSink phenomenon, just as the PageRank algorithm does.

The two algorithm works identically. Fig. 12 shows the result. In both algorithms, the norm of $Rank$ was always maintained as one. Pages in group 1 have relatively high PageRank values, whereas pages in group 2 have low values. This is due to the fact that pages of group 1 received most of the importance of pages in group 2. We see that the improved PageRank can also solve the RankSink phenomenon by choosing an appropriate d.

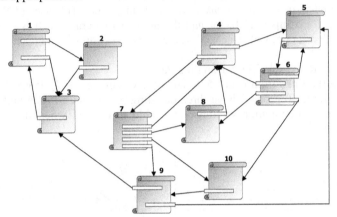

Fig. 11. A RankSink structure of a ten page Web

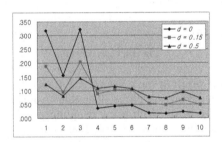

Fig. 12. Case 4 result

5. Conclusion

In the paper, we presented an improved PageRank algorithm that solves the norm leak phenomenon. In the new PageRank algorithm, pages have the right PageRank values and the iteration process always converges to a fixed point. We also described efficient implementation issues of our algorithm. The implementation of our algorithm does not require a large amount of spatial and computational overhead. Recently, we learned that our approach had been very briefly mentioned in [7, 11]. However, the description of this paper about the problem is much more detailed than those of [7, 11] are, and implementation issues were also discussed in this paper.

We applied our algorithm to over 10 million Web pages that had been collected from most of Korean sites. The elapsed times of the both algorithms to compute PageRank values were less than an hour in a medium-sized server machine. Our algorithm only needs a few mega-byte disk spaces to store the information of dangling pages additionally. It took less than minutes to read the additional space.

We have learned that a number of pre-processing operations are recommended to compute the PageRank values correctly. These operations may affect PageRank values and computing time significantly. Examples of these pre-operations include how to extract URLs in Web pages (in particular a URL associated with an image in a script language), how to convert a relative URL to an absolute URL, how to map a URL to a page identifier, and so on. The effectiveness of a Web crawler affects PageRank values significantly, too. In order for the link graph to represent the real Web exactly, a crawler should collect all Web pages. Crawling all Web pages is not a simple job in our experience.

References

1. G. O. Arocena, A. O. Mendelzon, and G. A. Mihaila: Applications of a Web Query Language, Proceedings of WWW6 (1997), 1305-1315
2. K. Bharat and M. Henzinger: Improved Algorithms for Topic Distillation in Hyperlinked Environments, Proceedings of the 21st ACM SIGIR Conference (1998), 104-111
3. S. Brin and L. Page: The Anatomy of a Large-Scale Hypertextual Web Search Engine, Proceedings of WWW7 (1998), 107-117
4. J. Carriere and R. Kazman: Webquery: Searching and Visualizing the Web through Connectivity, Proceedings of WWW6 (1997), 1257-1267
5. J. Dean and M. R. Henzinger: Finding Related Web Pages in the World Wide Web, Proceedings of WWW8 (1999), 1467-1479
6. D. Gibson, J. Kleinberg, and P. Raghavan: Inferring Web Communities from Link Topology, Proceedings of the 9th ACM Conference on Hypertext and Hypermedia (1998), 225-234
7. T. H. Haveliwala: Efficient Computation of PageRank, unpublished manuscript, Stanford University (1999)
8. E.-J. Im and K. Yelick: Optimizing Sparse Matrix Vector Multiplication on SMPS, Proceedings of the 9th SIAM Conference on Parallel Processing for Scientific Computing (1999), 127-136
9. J. Kleinberg: Authoritative Sources in a Hyperlinked Environment, Proceedings of the 9th ACM-SIAM Symposium on Discrete Algorithms (1998), 604-632
10. J. Kleinberg, S. R. Kumar, P. Raghavan, S. Rajagopalan, and A. Tomkins: The Web as a Graph: Measurements, Models and Methods, Invited survey at the International Conference on Combinatorics and Computing (1999), 1-17
11. A. Y. Ng, A. X. Zheng, and M. I. Jordan: Stable Algorithms for Link Analysis, Proceedings of the 24th ACM SIGIR Conference (2001), 258-266
12. L. Page, S. Brin, R. Motwani, and T. Winograd: The PageRank Citation Ranking: Bringing Order to the Web, unpublished manuscript, Stanford University (1998)
13. J. Pitkow and P. Pirolli: Life, Death, and Lawfulness on the Electronic Frontier, Proceedings of the Conference on Human Factors in Computing Systems (CHI 97) (1997), 383-390
14. P. Pirolli, J. Pitkow, and R. Rao: Silk from a Sow's Ear: Extracting Usable Structures from the Web, Proceedings of the Conference on Human Factors in Computing Systems (CHI 96) (1996), 118-125
15. E. Spertus: ParaSite: Mining Structural Information on the Web, Proceedings of WWW6 (1997), 1205-1215
16. S. Toledo: Improving the Memory-system Performance of Sparse-matrix Vector Multiplication, IBM Journal of Research and Development, volume 41 (1997)
17. Google Search Engine: http://www.google.com

Serving Enhanced Hypermedia Information

George Lepouras[1], Costas Vassilakis[1], and George R.S. Weir[2]

[1] Department of Informatics and Telecommunications, University of Athens, 157 84 Athens, Greece
{G.Lepouras, C.Vassilakis}@di.uoa.gr
[2] Department of Computer and Information Sciences, University of Strathclyde, Glasgow G1 1XH, UK
gw@cis.strath.ac.uk

Abstract. An apparent limitation of existing Web pages is their inability to accommodate differences in the interests and needs of individual users. The present paper describes an approach that dynamically customises the content of public Web-based information via an interceding 'enhancement server'. The design and operation of this system is described with examples drawn from two current versions. Indications from early trials support the view that this approach affords considerable scope for accommodating the needs and interests of individual Web users.

Introduction

Perhaps the major advantage afforded to designers by the Web is the facility to create hyperlink documents and so produce an interconnected pool of information. Users commonly use links to navigate in the WWW. In a recent user survey [1], most users (17.2%) in responding to the question "How Users Find out About WWW Pages" indicated that they follow hyperlinks from other Web pages. The same survey indicates that users are often unable to find the information they seek (7.1%) and a smaller percentage (4.7%) failed to find a page that they knew existed. Search engines are a significant aid in finding information, however, as pointed out by the Science Magazine survey [2], these have some shortcomings, such as low percentage of Web page coverage (in the best case, only 34% of the total web pages are indexed), inclusion in the result set of pages not containing the search terms and dangling links. Moreover, in many cases search engines fail to take into account the *semantic context* of the search, returning thus pages that *do* contain the search terms but are irrelevant to the desired result, even in the presence of category-guided searches; additionally much of the Web's dynamically generated content is not being indexed satisfactorily [3].

This observation suggests that some difficulties that arise during users' navigation could be alleviated if the visited web pages contained hyperlinks to the information web surfers were looking for. However, this cannot always be achieved. When a web developer creates a web page, it is customary that only links relevant to the hosting site's main purpose are included. For instance, within a site providing geographic

F. Crestani, M. Girolami, and C.J. van Rijsbergen (Eds.): ECIR 2002, LNCS 2291, pp. 86–92, 2002.

information, the word "Italy" might be linked to the prefectures or the neighbouring countries of Italy, but not to pages about its culture or economy. It is simply impractical to accommodate all user preferences and all links to related information.

On the other hand if the web user had a defined set of preferences, the visited page could have been enhanced with information pertaining to the individual's interests. In what follows, we outline a system that will enhance the content of web pages in accommodation of user preferences. Thereafter, we propose an architecture for such a system and discuss issues related to customisation of user information and presentation. Our fourth section describes the current system development status and the last section draws conclusions and sets goals for future work.

Objectives

Shneiderman [4] points to four key phases in the operation of any integrated framework for creativity support:

- *Collect*: learn from previous works stored in digital libraries, the web, etc.
- *Relate*: consult with peers and mentors at early, middle and late stages
- *Create*: explore, compose, discover and evaluate possible solutions
- *Donate*: disseminate the results and contribute to digital libraries, the web, etc.

A web page enhancement system can support the collection and donation phases and even during the creation phase. Such an enhancement system would aim to enrich web pages according to user preferences, aid in the *collection* of appropriate information, facilitate the annotation and ranking of pages by web surfers and enable the *donation* of the collated results to other users.

Enhancement Server

To accommodate these objectives we propose an enhancement server - a server that adds 'enhancements' in conjunction with 'standard' Web services. This facility will provide a locus for Web interaction that enables users to define their own preferences for content and presentation. The service will also co-ordinate user ranking of web pages and manage annotations on Web information. An additional primary role for the enhancement server will be dissemination of user-collated data to other users with similar preferences.

System Architecture

Responsible for keeping track of users' navigation and enriching web pages, the enhancement server has to intercede between the user's browser and the web server that hosts the 'public' web pages. Users will login once to the enhancement server in order to create a profile of their individual preferences. A creation form for user profiles is shown in Figure 1. This illustrates an enhancement facility based on second language support (cf. [5]), offering local language support for a variety of linguistic features and associated presentation characteristics.

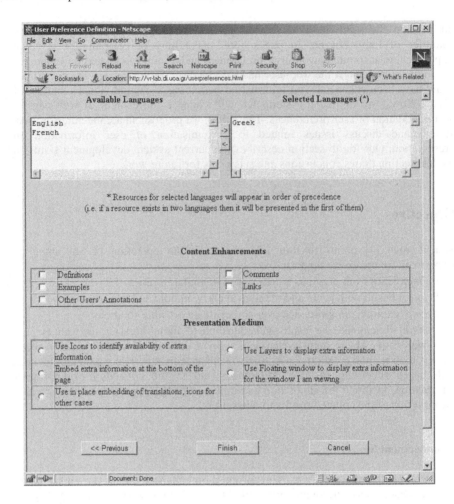

Fig. 1. Setting User's Preferences

Having set their options for available enhancements (e.g., choice of local language supplements, content targets, and presentation modes) the user's browser acquires a cookie. This is the mechanism whereby returning users are subsequently identified by the enhancement server.

The enhancement server may be deployed in two user modes. In normal operation, users set their browsers to treat the enhancement server as a *proxy server*. Alternatively, users who are otherwise required to use a local proxy server (e.g., if the local administration policy requires all web traffic to pass through this proxy) may connect directly to the enhancement server and type the URL they want to view. Operation of the enhancement server is illustrated in Figure 2.

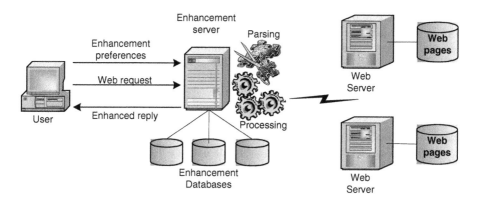

Fig. 2. System Architecture

As depicted in Figure 2, the user requests a web page via the enhancement server. In response, the user receives the requested page affected by the enhancement preferences. The enhancement server scans the incoming requested web page for keywords matching user's preferences and annotates the incoming page 'on the fly' to add links to the supplemental information. On conclusion of the process, the enhanced page is sent to the user. The enhancement server comprises a parsing subsystem, a processing subsystem and several databases.

Parsing Subsystem

When the enhancement server retrieves a requested web page, the *parsing subsystem* is invoked to search for patterns that accord with the individual user's preferences. The simplest form of a pattern is a *text fragment* - either a single word or a sequence of words. If seeking to enrich pages with geographical information about countries, the text patterns *France*, *U.K.* and *United Kingdom* might be sought within the document and annotations added that link from the modified (requested) page to appropriate 'enriching' related material.

Of course, simple string searches have limited application. For instance, the European Union's legislation is commonly referred to within documents as *"EU law 02.10.10"*, *"law 05.20.10.30/EU"* or simply *"09.50.10.30/EU"*. In this case, the portion providing the document identity varies, and it is clearly infeasible to list all document identities exhaustively. Such cases are accommodated through patterns that include a *regular expression* [6]. This affords a flexible means of specifying desired text portions. In this notation, the text portion corresponding to the earlier document identity can be coded as *[0-9][0-9](.[0-9][0-9]){0,3}*. This is interpreted as *two digits, followed by zero to three strings, each consisting of a dot and two digits*. The document identifier may be combined with constant text portions to formulate a complete regular expression that matches the desired document text, e.g. *"law [0-9][0-9](.[0-9][0-9]){0,3}/EU"*.

Processing Subsystem

Upon completion of the parsing phase, the results are forwarded to the processing subsystem. This operational phase inserts extra information in the page (according to user's preferences) and makes any necessary alterations for the enhancements to be displayed correctly. The processing subsystem also creates new header information and sends the enhanced Web page back to the user.

Our approach to presentation aims to leave retrieved web page looking as close to the original as possible. At the same time, the presence of extra information should be evident to the user. The presence of additional links should not interfere or obscure any original links (placed in the document by its author). To this end, the user has a number of choices regarding the presentation method for the newly embedded information:

1. An *icon* may be applied to the corresponding location in the returned document, directly **linking** to the related resource. This method works best when a small number of matches are found and there is only a single resource related to each match. Depending on the type of resource (i.e. translation, definition, example, etc) different types of icon may be used to indicate the availability of the corresponding resource.

2. An *icon* may be embedded to the corresponding location, **popping up** a new layer when the mouse hovers over this area. The new layer may host multiple items, so this method can cater for situations where multiple resources are related to each match. However, problems may arise when the document already contains layers or when the web browser does not support them.

3. Added resources may be placed at the bottom of the page (or at the top), separated from the actual page content via a horizontal line. This method is quite similar to the format used by *Google* (www.google.com) to display *cached versions* of pages or HTML versions of resources in other formats (e.g. PDF and Postscript). This technique has the advantage of supporting large volumes of added information without altering the page appearance, but, on the down side, separates the additional resources from their actual anchors within the page.

4. Extra resources may appear in a floating window. This technique preserves the appearance of the original page, but it exhibits two drawbacks. Firstly, extra information is displayed 'out of place'. Secondly, if the user has more than one browser window open, the floating window will display information for the last window opened.

5. Translations of key terms can be placed in the web page, since they stand out from the rest of the document. Other resources can use icons as described in the first approach. This alternative was used in the evaluation version of the enhancement server.

The user may select the desired style of enhancement from the user preference definition dialogue (see figure 1). If the user has left all choices blank, the system defaults to placing information at the bottom of the page. In all cases, however, a shortcut is provided at the bottom of the returned page, which allows the users to conveniently switch between the available presentation options.

An additional task addressed by the processing subsystem is to apply the tags required for correct display of multi-lingual resources. When an additional resource in some language needs to be added to the result page, the required character set for the resource presentation is compared to the page's primary character set, designated in the *<meta http-equiv="content-type">* header tag. If these character sets are different, the inserted data are enclosed between the tags *<span lang="LANG">* and *</span>*, signifying to the browser which fonts are required to display these pieces of information.

When all supplemental information has been embedded within the retrieved page, the enhancement server computes the new document size, changes the HTTP headers accordingly and forwards the document to the user (strictly, to the user's browser).

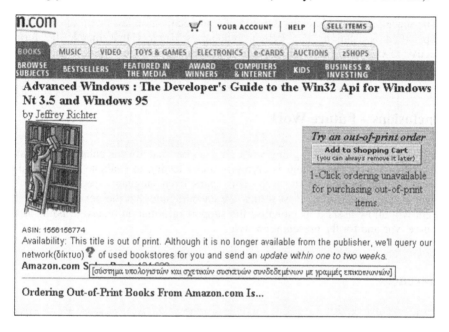

Fig. 3. Web page enhanced with translation and definition of computer science terms

Database Subsystem

The processing subsystem acquires the enhancement resources from the database subsystem. There may be one or more databases, depending on the thematic areas the supported by the enhancement server. The databases hold information such as key terms, definitions, comments, examples or links. The databases may also retain user submitted annotations of concepts. Furthermore, since the information may exist in more than one language, the database subsystem can also afford translation of key terms in other languages.

Implementation – Development

Implementation of the enhancement server is based on an Apache Web Server. To date, we have realised part of the intended functionality. In the current release, users are able to set the enhancement server as their default proxy server and receive enhanced web pages. However, they are not yet able to define personal preferences. Instead, users receive a full set of content enhancements (apart from user annotations).

Two systems have been implemented to assess feasibility and usability in different application areas. The first system addresses the area of computer science – providing computer science key terms translations, definitions and examples in Greek. An illustration from this system is given in Figure 3.

The second system addresses the area of European Union laws with direct links to europa.eu.int legislation. The system recognises patterns that match the format Directive xxxx/yy/EC (in any European language) and includes a link to the relevant law.

Conclusions – Future Work

In this paper we describe on-going work on a system that affords enhanced browsing of web documents. The system is currently under testing to evaluate its potential to support user interaction on the web. This spans from language specific support to subject specific extensions. First results are encouraging, and the next release of the system will allow users to personalise the support information received, both for the resource type and for the presentation style.

References

1. GVU's WWW Surveying Team. "10th WWW User Survey", Georgia Tech, Atlanta, GA.,http://www.cc.gatech.edu/gvu/user_surveys/survey-1998-10/
2. Science Magazine, "Search Engine Effectiveness", April 1998.
3. Eric Digest, "Uncovering the Hidden Web", October 2001, available through http://www.ericit.org/digests/EDO-IR-2001-02.shtml
4. Ben Shneiderman "Supporting Creativity with Advanced Information-Abundant User Interfaces", HCIL Technical Report No. 99-16 (July 1999), http://www.cs.umd.edu/hcil
5. Weir, G.R.S. and Lepouras, G., English Assistant: A Support Strategy for On-Line Second Language Learning, ICALT 2001, IEEE International Conference on Advanced Learning Technologies, Madison, USA, 2001.
6. MySQL group, "Description of MySQL regular expression syntax", available at http://www.mysql.com/documentation/mysql/bychapter/manual_Regexp.html

The Use of Implicit Evidence for Relevance Feedback in Web Retrieval

Ryen W. White [1], Ian Ruthven[2], and Joemon M. Jose[1]

[1] Department of Computing Science
University of Glasgow, Glasgow, G12 8QQ. Scotland
`whiter, jj@dcs.gla.ac.uk`

[2] Department of Computer and Information Sciences
University of Strathclyde, Glasgow G1 1XH. Scotland
`Ian.Ruthven@cis.strath.ac.uk`

Abstract. In this paper we report on the application of two contrasting types of relevance feedback for web retrieval. We compare two systems; one using explicit relevance feedback (where searchers explicitly have to mark documents relevant) and one using implicit relevance feedback (where the system endeavours to estimate relevance by mining the searcher's interaction). The feedback is used to update the display according to the user's interaction. Our research focuses on the degree to which implicit evidence of document relevance can be substituted for explicit evidence. We examine the two variations in terms of both user opinion and search effectiveness.

1 Introduction

The transformation of a user's information need into a search expression, or query, is known as *query formulation*. It is widely regarded as one of the most challenging activities in information seeking, [2]. In particular, problems arise if the user's need is vague [21], and if they lack knowledge about the collection make-up and retrieval environment [19].

The rapid expansion of the Web has led to an increase in the number of casual searchers using Web search engines. Many of these searchers are inexperienced and can have difficulty expressing their information need. For example, Jansen et al. [6] showed that 62% of queries submitted to the Excite web search engine contained only one or two terms. Such short queries can lack very useful search terms, which may detract from the effectiveness of the search [13].

A technique known as *relevance feedback* is designed to overcome the problem of translating an information need into a query. Relevance feedback is an iterative process where users assess the relevance of a number of documents returned in response to an initial, 'tentative' query, [19]. Users peruse the full-text of each document in this set, assess it for relevance and mark those that best meet their information need. The limitations in providing increasingly better ranked results

F. Crestani, M. Girolami, and C.J. van Rijsbergen (Eds.): ECIR 2002, LNCS 2291, pp. 93–109, 2002.
© Springer-Verlag Berlin Heidelberg 2002

based solely on the initial query, and the resultant need for query modification have already been identified [22]. Relevance feedback systems automatically resubmit the initial query, expanding it using terms taken from the documents marked relevant by the user.

In practice, relevance feedback can be very effective but it relies on users assessing the relevance of documents and indicating to the system which documents contain relevant information. In real-life Internet searches, users may be unwilling to browse to web pages to gauge their relevance. Such a task imposes an increased burden and increased cognitive load [20]. Documents may be lengthy or complex, users may have time restrictions or the initial query may have retrieved a poor set of documents. An alternative strategy is to present a query-biased summary of each of the first *n* web pages returned in response to a user's query [23]. The summaries allow users to assess documents for relevance, and give feedback, more quickly.

However the problem of getting the users to *indicate* to the system which documents contain relevant information remains. In this paper, we examine the extent to which *implicit* feedback (where the system attempts to estimate what the user may be interested in) can act as a substitute for *explicit* feedback (where searchers explicitly mark documents relevant). Therefore, we attempt to side-step the problem of getting users to explicitly mark documents relevant by making predictions on relevance through analysing the user's interaction with the system.

Previously, many studies that endeavour through the use of various 'surrogate' measures (links clicked, mouseovers, scrollbar activity, etc.) [11], [7] to unobtrusively monitor user behaviour have been conducted. Through such means, other studies have sought to determine document relevance implicitly [4], [12], [9], [14]. These studies infer relevance from the time spent viewing a document. If a user 'examines' [10] a document for a long time, or if a document suffers a lot of 'read wear' [4] it is assumed to be relevant.

These studies only focus on newsgroup documents and rely on users interaction with the actual document. In this paper we extend these concepts onto web result lists, using document summaries instead of the actual document. Much can be gleaned from a user's ephemeral interactions during a single search session [15]. Our system seeks to capture these and predict relevance based on this interaction.

Specifically, we hypothesised that implicit and explicit feedback were interchangeable as sources of relevance information for relevance feedback. Through developing a system that utilised each type we were able to compare the two approaches from the user's perspective and in terms of search effectiveness.

This paper will describes the system and experiments used to test the viability of interchanging implicit and explicit relevance feedback. The experiments were carried out as part of the TREC-10 interactive track. In this paper we expand on our original analysis of our experiments and provide a deeper insight into our experimental results.

This paper describes the two systems used in section 2, the relevance feedback approaches in section 3, then outlines the experimental methodology employed in section 4. We present the initial results and analyse them in section 5, and conclude in section 6.

2 Systems

In this section we introduce the systems used during our experiments. Our basic experimental system is a generic interface that can connect to any web search engine. In our experiments we use the interface to connect to the Google search engine. The interface is based on a summarisation interface developed for investigating web search behaviour, [23], [24]. The system developed for the experiments in this paper also incorporates a component that displays sentences from the retrieved set of web pages. These sentences are ones that have a high degree of match with the user's query. The set of sentences and the ranking of the sentences automatically updates in the presence of relevance information from the user (relevance feedback). We shall discuss these components in more detail in the following sections. Here, we simply note that the effect of relevance information is presented to the user by the changes in the top-ranking sentence list.

Two interfaces were developed; one which uses explicit feedback and one which uses implicit feedback, Fig. 1. We shall discuss the differences in the two interfaces in section 3.

checkboxes

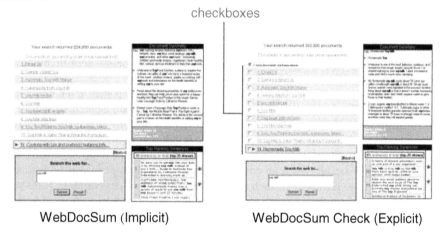

WebDocSum (Implicit)   WebDocSum Check (Explicit)

Fig. 1. System interfaces

Both versions of our basic interface contain four components; query input window (bottom left, Fig. 1), summary (top right, Fig. 1), results list (top left, Fig. 1), top-ranking sentences (bottom right, Fig. 1). We shall discuss each of these in turn.

2.1 Query Input

The query input component displays the current query for quick and easy reformulation by the user. The system supports any syntax that the underlying search engine, Google, supports. However, no participants in the study used anything other than keywords separated by spaces.

Upon submission, the query is sent to Google, where the first 3 result pages are parsed, extracting the titles, web addresses and abstracts of the first 30 documents. A thread is dispatched to each of these pages, the source for each is downloaded and a summary created. All 30 documents are summarised in parallel. The entire process, from query submission to result presentation takes around 7 seconds.

2.2 Summary Window

In [23], [24] it was shown that the presence of document summaries could lead to more interaction with the results of a web search. That is, searchers would assess more documents if they could access document summaries than if they had access to the full-text alone. In this research document summaries were used to facilitate the relevance assessment process.

The summaries are created through a sentence extraction model, presented in [24], in which the web pages are broken up into their component sentences and scored according to how useful they will be in a summary. A number of the highest-scoring sentences are then chosen to compose the summary.

Sentences are scored according to their position (initial introductory sentences are preferred), the words they contain (words that are emphasised by the web page author, e.g. emboldened terms, or words in the document title are treated as important), and the proportion of query terms they contain. The latter component – scoring by query terms – biases the summaries towards the query.

The summary window displays a summary if the mouse passes over either the document title in the results list *or* a sentence in the top ranking sentences list. The window displays the document title, the top four highest ranking sentences and extra document information such as document size and number of outlinks.

The summary window can also display graphical output and provide feedback should a web error occur. Such an error would occur if a web page was unavailable or taking too long to retrieve. In such circumstances the summary window will show the abstract offered by the underlying search engine and an error message detailing the reason for the web error.

2.3 Top Ranking Sentences

Relevance feedback techniques typically either modify a query automatically, [19], or present the user with a set of new terms to allow the user to interactively modify their query, [1]. Automatic relevance feedback techniques can suffer from the fact that users are often not willing to use relevance feedback techniques. In particular this can be because the user does not understand the relation between the relevance assessment and the effect of relevance feedback. Interactive query modification has often been preferred on the grounds that it allows the user more control over their search, [8]. However, searches often do not fully utilise interactive query modification techniques; either because they do not know how to choose good new query terms, [1] of because they do not understand the effect the new terms will have on their search [18].

An alternative, one which we follow in this paper, is not to use relevance feedback to modify the user's query, or to suggest query terms, but to use relevance feedback to suggest new documents to the user. Specifically we use relevance feedback to recommend documents that have been retrieved but have not yet been viewed by the user. We do this by the notion of top-ranking sentences, Fig. 2.

Our summarisation model is basically a sentence extraction model: all retrieved pages are split into their component sentences, ranked and a number are selected to compose the summary. As well as being used to create summaries, these sentences can also be used to indicate to the searcher the sentences in the retrieved set of documents that have the closest match to the query.

The system pools all of the sentences from the documents that it was able to summarise from the first 30 returned by the underlying search engine. It then ranks these initially based on the score assigned by the query-biasing algorithm, section 2.2, and presents the top 25 sentences to the user. Fig. 2 shows the top ranking sentences window.

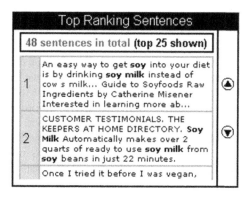

Fig. 2. Top Ranking Sentences window

The top ranking list only contains sentences from summaries that the user has not yet seen. As the user passes over a document title, or in the explicit case, marks a document as relevant, the sentences from the summary associated with that document are removed from the list.

Relevance feedback is used to re-rank the list of sentences. As the user interacts with the system – either through explicit or implicit relevance feedback, section 3, the list of top-ranking sentences is re-ranked. The re-ranking is intended to display the most similar sentences to the user's original query combined with the user's interaction which may show the user's changing information needs. We shall discuss how this is achieved in section 3.

2.4   Results List

Only the title of the document is shown in the result list. When the user moves the mouse over an entry in the result list, the summary window will change to show a summary for that page. If a title is *clicked*, the page will open in a new window. The query form retains the current query for quick and easy reformulation. If the user goes over a sentence in the top ranking sentences list, the document's title to which that sentence belongs is highlighted.

A small window below the main results list displays the title of a document should it fall outside the top 10 documents (i.e. in the range 11 to 30). This is shown in Fig. 3 and comes from Fig. 1, (left hand side).

▶ 19. Cooking with soy and soyfoods featuring tofu,...

[Next>>]

Fig. 3. Document title window

3   Explicit and Implicit Feedback

In the previous section we outlined the details of our interface. We developed two interfaces; one which uses explicit relevance feedback, in the form of check-boxes before the document titles, Fig. 1 (right), and one which uses implicit feedback and has no means for the user to explicitly indicate the relevance of a document, Fig. 1 (left). The main component is the top-ranking sentence list; a list of the sentences that best-match the system's representation of the user's information need. This list updates in the presence of relevance information from the user.

The main difference, therefore, between the two systems lies in how the call is made to re-rank the sentences. In the explicit case, this is made by clicking on a checkbox and hence marking a document relevant. In contrast, the implicit system re-ranks the list when the user moves the mouse over a document title. Through these means the user no longer has to be concerned with marking a document as relevant, the system has mined their interaction and made an educated assumption based on this. That is we assume that viewing a document summary is an indication of a user's interest in the document's contents. Both systems use the same method of re-ranking sentences. That is, the sentences from that document's summary are removed from the top ranking list and the remaining sentences will be re-ranked immediately, in real-time, based on the occurrence of the query expansion terms and query terms within them.

Each time the list of sentences are to be updated, the summaries from the assessed relevant documents (explicit system) or assumed relevant documents (implicit system) are used to generate a list of possible expansion terms. From this listing, the top 6 expansion terms are added to the user's original query. These terms are taken from *all* assumed relevant summaries (i.e. all those that the user had viewed so far).

To rank the possible expansion terms we used the *wpq* algorithm [17] shown in Equation 1. For any term t, where N is the total number of summaries, n is the number of summaries containing t, R is total number of relevant summaries and r is the total number of relevant summaries that contain t. R and r are based on relevance assessments and are therefore prone to increase as users interact with the systems.

Possible expansion terms only come from the document summary generated by the system, and it is assumed that N (i.e. the total number of summaries) is 30.

$$wpq_t = \log\left(\frac{(r+0.5)(N-n-R+0.5)}{(n-r+0.5)(R-r+0.5)}\right) \times \left(\frac{r}{R} - \frac{n-r}{N-R}\right) \qquad (1)$$

The new query representation – the original terms plus the new expansion terms – are then used to re-rank the top-ranking sentence list, assigning a score to each remaining sentence based on term occurrence. The score is calculated based on the term occurrence of the top six query expansion terms. If a sentence contains a query expansion term, its score is incremented by the wpq score for that term. If a sentence contains multiple occurrences of the same term, its score is incremented for each occurrence.

Traditional relevance feedback techniques would reset the sentence scores each feedback iteration, i.e. the sentence score would be recalculated from the wpq values each time. In our application we do not do this: the new score for a sentence is added to the score from the previous iteration. The effect of this is that the *order* in which a user views summaries is important; the same summaries viewed in a different order can give a different ranking of sentences.

Fig. 4 shows how the scores of 5 sentences (s1...s5) change through three iterations of re-ranking. The first sentence shown in the top ranking sentences list after each iteration is the most relevant sentence taken from summaries the user has yet to see, based on the summaries they have viewed so far. Sentences that might have started low in the initial ranking can 'bubble up' (as is the case with s1 in Fig. 4) to the top of the list and present the user with a means of accessing a potentially relevant document based on all previous interaction. A sentence will be removed from the list if it is judged relevant (either implicitly or explicitly). Only sentences from document summaries *not yet viewed* are shown in the list.

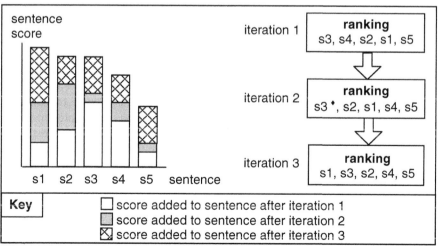

Fig. 4. The cumulative affects of sentence scoring, over three iterations

3.1 Summary

The research question under investigation in this paper is whether implicit indications of relevance can be substituted for explicit assessments of relevance. To test this we developed two interfaces; one that allows users to explicitly mark documents relevant, the other attempts to estimate what the user finds relevant through the user's interaction. The relevance information from both systems is used to alter the user's query using relevance feedback techniques. The modified query is then used to dynamically re-rank a list of sentences that match the modified query. This list of sentences are intended to act as a means of recommending unseen documents to the user. The relevance information is not used to initiate new retrievals, as in standard relevance feedback, but is used to update the information presented to the user. The degree to which the implicitly updated information is as useful as the explicitly updated information is how we measure the degree to which implicit relevance evidence can be substituted for explicit relevance evidence.

4 Experimental Details

The experiments we report in this paper were carried out as part of the TREC-10 interactive track [5].

We used a within-subjects experimental design and in total, 16 subjects participated. Each user attempted 4 web search tasks and used 2 systems. A Greco-Latin square experimental design [16] was used to randomise the tasks and guard against learning effects. Prior to starting the experiment, subjects were given a 15 minute introduction to the system, during which the experimenter walked them through a demonstration task.

4.1 Subjects

In total, 16 subjects participated in our experiments. All subjects were educated to graduate level in a non-computing, non-LIS discipline, with three exceptions, all our subjects were recruited from the Information Technology course at the University of Glasgow. All users, with one exception, used the Internet on a regular basis. Through using a diverse mixture of participants, with a diverse mixture of skills and experiences, the heterogeneous nature of the web populace was better represented.

The average age of the subjects was 24.75 with a range of 11 years. Most users used computers and the Internet frequently – the average time spent online per week was 14 hours. With three exceptions, all users cited Google amongst their favourite search engines.

4.2 Tasks

The tasks were split into four categories: Medical, Buying, Travel and Project. There were 4 tasks in each category – users attempted one task from each. The tasks allocated were randomised to reduce potential learning effects and task bias. Fig. 5 shows the tasks used.

Medical
- Find a website likely to contain reliable information on the effect of second-hand smoke.
- Tell me three categories of people who should or should not get a flu shot and why.
- List two of the generally recommended treatments for stomach ulcers.
- Identify two pros or cons of taking large doses of Vitamin A.

Buying
- Get two price quotes for a new digital camera (3 or more megapixels and 2x or more zoom).
- Find two websites that allow people to buy soy milk online.
- Name three features to consider in buying a new yacht.
- Find two websites that will let me buy a personal CD player online.

Travel
- I want to visit Antarctica. Find a website with information on organized tours/trips there.
- Identify three interesting things to do during a weekend in Kyoto, Japan.
- Identify three interesting places to visit in Thailand.
- I'd like to go on a sailing vacation in Australia, but I don't know how to sail. Tell me where can I get some information about organized sailing cruises in that area.

Project
- Find three articles that a high school student could use in writing a report on the Titanic.
- Tell me the name of a website where I can find material on global warming.
- Find three different information sources that may be useful to a high school student in writing a biography of John F. Kennedy.
- Locate a site with lots of information for a high school report on the history of the Napoleonic wars.

Fig. 5. Tasks used in TREC-10 interactive track experiments

Users were allowed a maximum of 10 minutes for each task. They were asked to use the system presented to them (either implicit or explicit, depending on the particular Greco-Latin square allocation) to search the Internet and attempt to find an answer to the task set. Users were allowed to browse away from the result list to any degree.

4.3 Data Capture

We utilised two different means of collecting data for post-experimental analysis; questionnaires and background system logging. Through these means we could collect data that would allow us to thoroughly test the experimental hypothesis.

We administered two main types of questionnaire during the course of the experiment, five in total. The first gathered both demographic and Internet usage information, and was completed at the start of the experiment. The second made use of Likert Scales and Semantic Differentials to assess the systems and to some extent the tasks, from the perspective of the user. This was completed after each of the four tasks.

The background system logging sought to capture certain aspects of the user's interaction with the system. Information such as the task time, calls for an update of the top ranking sentences list and the query expansion terms used were all logged. Through a detailed analysis of these logs, it was hoped that a complete comparison of the implicit and explicit methods could be carried out.

5   Results & Analysis

In this section, we discuss the results obtained from the experiments. We look at the effectiveness of the searches (number of result pages viewed, task completion and task times) and the users' perceptions of the systems. We also present a subjective evaluation of the usefulness of both the automatic query expansion terms generated by the system and the feedback components.

5.1 Search Effectiveness

Most of the data used to assess search effectiveness came from the logs generated by the system during the experiments.

5.1.1 Number of Result Pages Viewed

The total number of result pages viewed and queries submitted during all the experiments was recorded. Table 1 shows the average results per user obtained.

Table 1. Average result page views and query iterations per user

Variation	Number of result pages	Number of query iterations
Implicit	3.375 *	3.5625
Explicit	2.5 *	2.625

* users occasionally refined query before result page appeared, so result pages ≠ query iterations

These differences are not significant using a Mann-Whitney Test at p ≤ 0.05 (p = 0.234). Our system gave access to the first 30 documents retrieved by the underlying search engine, and in many cases this was sufficient to complete the tasks. This meant that there was no real need for users to browse to the next 30 results (i.e. results 30 to 60 in standard search engines). The lack of a significant difference between the implicit and explicit systems shows that the type of system used does not affect the number of result pages viewed or query iterations needed.

5.1.2 Task Completion

As part of the post-task questionnaire users were asked whether they felt they had successfully completed the task just attempted, it is these results that are presented in Table 2. The choice of whether a task was complete was left up to the user. It was thought that this best reflected real-world retrieval situations. However, the experimenter was occasionally asked to verify the correctness of the results obtained. Table 2 shows these results (out of 64).

Table 2. Number of tasks completed

Variation	Number of tasks completed
Implicit	61
Explicit	57

Again these results are not significant using a Mann-Whitney Test at p ≤ 0.05 (p = 0.361). There is no significant difference between the number of tasks that users completed on the implicit and the explicit systems.

5.1.3 Task Times

The time taken to complete tasks on both systems was measured. When a task was incomplete, a figure of 600 seconds (10 minutes) would be recorded by the system. This was the time limit imposed on each task and users were not allowed to work past this. On no occasion did a user stop before the 10 minute limit had been reached unless they had completed their current task. In Table 3 we can see these results.

Table 3. Average time per task

Variation	Average time per task (secs)
Implicit	372.29
Explicit	437.43

Again these are not significant using a Mann-Whitney Test at p ≤ 0.05 (p = 0.228).

From an analysis of the log files we were able to establish that no significant difference existed between the two variations. This appears to add a little weight to our claim that perhaps the implicit and explicit feedback are at least to some degree substitutable, although factors such as the similarity of the interface design may be important to. If the results obtained were significant we could suggest that one type of system promotes search effectiveness more than the other. In this case, there is no significant difference, and it is safe to assume that some degree of substitutability does indeed exist.

5.2 User Perceptions

As well as assessing the systems in terms of search effectiveness, we also attempted to assess both the systems used and the tasks allocated, from the perspective of the user. By using Likert Scales and Semantic Differentials, subjects could express their feelings with relative ease.

5.2.1 Tasks

Subjects had the opportunity to rate the tasks allocated to them in terms of clarity and difficulty. Each task, or category, was attempted four times in total (twice on each system). Table 4 shows the results obtained.

Table 4. Semantic differential values obtained from user task assessment
(lower = better, range = 1 − 5)

Differential	Implicit	Explicit	Significance [Mann-Whitney]
clear	1.42	1.83	0.5160
easy	2.48	2.42	0.6134

As is apparent from the last column in the table, neither of the two differentials are significant (at $p \leq 0.05$). This test is across all tasks, so any significant value would have pointed to a serious error in our experimental methodology and/or task design. A similar result (i.e. no significance) was obtained when we analysed the fully and partially defined tasks separately.

5.2.2 Systems

Subjects had a chance to rate the systems using both Likert Scales and Semantic Differentials in a similar way as in section 4.2.1. They answered questions relating to the way the top ranking sentences list was updated and its respective usefulness. Table 5 provides an overview of the results obtained.

Table 5. Semantic differential/Likert scale values obtained from system assessment (lower = better, range = 1 – 5)

Differential/Scale	Implicit	Explicit	Significance [Mann-Whitney]
useful (summaries)	2.46	2.16	0.3173
useful (top ranking list)	2.63	2.29	0.4394
see ♦	1.71	1.75	0.244
see o	1.54	1.96	0.00606

♦ potentially relevant sentences from unseen documents helped user decide which to view
o in the user's opinion the top ranking sentences list was updated often enough

There is no significant difference between the first three rows in Table 5 (above) when measuring at $p \leq 0.05$. The way the summaries are produced, the content of the top ranking sentences list and the ability presented to the user to view sentences from unseen documents does not differ from system to system. The averages are less than 2.64 in all cases, with 3 being the middle ('undecided') value. Based on this, we can assume a generally positive response from users to the system in general. Although the significance of this was not tested, it is interesting to note nonetheless and may provide us with some scope for future research.

When users assessed the frequency with which the top ranking sentences list updates, there is a significant difference between the implicit and explicit systems ($p = 0.00606$ using Mann-Whitney at $p \leq 0.05$). It appeared that subjects preferred the top ranking sentences list to update automatically, rather than under their instruction. Users were unwilling to 'instruct' the list to update. This is in accordance with previous research [3, Kons97] that also shows users' apparent unwillingness to provide relevance information explicitly.

5.3 Query Expansion

The query expansion terms were generated automatically by the system each time the list was re-ranked, and were used by the system in this re-ranking only; *the terms were to used to generate a new result set.* The nature and 'usefulness' of query expansion terms is subjective, but a brief evaluation based on how correct they 'appear' to be is possible. The systems we developed utilised automatic query expansion techniques to re-rank the list of top-ranking sentences. Such systems (or variations in our case), by their very nature, hide query expansion terms from the user. We evaluated the terms based on what we thought were 'reasonable', no input from users was utilised.

Overall, the choice of automatic query expansion appeared good, the terms appeared to be a natural expansion of the initial query submitted by the user. Fig. 6 shows an example of how the query expansion terms for the query "effects smoke" changed through three re-ranking iterations. This was taken from the experiments in response to the task: *Find a website likely to contain reliable information on the effect of second-hand smoke.*

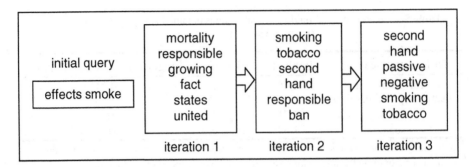

Fig. 6. Changes in automatic query expansion terms (taken from experiments)

As the user views summaries, the terms are modified based on the summaries they view or 'mark' relevant. Fig. 6 shows how this can be an effective means of reformulating a query for web retrieval.

5.4 Use of Feedback Components

In a similar way to the previous subsection, the results reported here are mainly based on observation. One of our main concerns prior to starting the experiments was that users would not make use of the feedback components, namely the top ranking sentences list, the highlighting of the document titles and the checkboxes. Previous research [18] has shown that users often have a reluctance to use such features. Our concerns proved unfounded, as users made use of all components, especially the top ranking sentences (39% of all 'Summary Window' updates came from this source).

The inclusion of checkboxes appealed to some users and not to others; some saw them as a means by which they could retain control over the system's operation whereas others saw them as a hindrance. Overall, just as many users preferred the implicit system as did the explicit one.

5.5 Technical Drawbacks

It is worth mentioning a technical problem observed during our experiments. The implicit system suffered from the effects of accidental 'mouseovers', with users passing over document titles en route to those that interested them. This meant from time to time that sentences were removed from the top ranking list by accident (i.e. the system was interpreting the mouseover as an indication of relevance). A possible solution to this problem would be the introduction of a timing mechanism so that only mouseovers actually meant by the user are taken into account in re-ranking the list.

6   Conclusions

The aim of the research reported in this paper was to test whether implicit relevance feedback was a viable substitute for its explicit counterpart in web retrieval situations. To test this, we developed two interfaces – one that used implicit feedback and another that used explicit feedback. The two systems were then compared in terms of user perception and search effectiveness in a real-life information search environment. We hypothesised that there would be no significant differences in the results of this comparison.

We endeavoured to use techniques previously restricted to the full-text of newsgroup documents and apply them to the result list of a web search interface, using query-biased web page summaries as the means of assessing relevance, instead of the actual document. A list of potentially relevant sentences that evolved, in real-time, to reflect the user's interactions provided users with a 'gateway' to potentially relevant summaries (and hence documents) that they have not yet viewed.

The experiments undertaken to test our hypothesis were as part of the TREC-10 interactive track [5]. The tasks allocated to users appeared to be sufficiently random and exhibited no correlation between search system used and the user's assessment of task difficulty.

Users found the summaries and top ranking sentences useful. There were no significant differences in the comparison of systems, with one exception. The implicit system updated the top ranking sentences list automatically. This was preferred in favour of the explicit system which gives them full control over when the list updates. Users performed equally well on the implicit and explicit systems, which leads us to conclude that perhaps substituting the former for the latter may indeed be feasible. This initial result will be exploited in future research to investigate how implicit evidence is best collected, how it should be used and what are good implicit indicators of relevance.

We assumed that the viewing of a document's summary was an indication of an interest in the relevance of the document's contents. There are several grounds on which this can be criticised; users will view non-relevant summaries, the title rather than the summary was what the user expressed an interest in, and the user may look at all retrieved documents before making real relevance decisions. Nevertheless we felt that our assumption was fair enough to allow an initial investigation into the use of implicit feedback. A future alternative could be to introduce a timing mechanism to eliminate the problems caused by the accidental 'mouseover' of document titles and the unwanted removal of sentences from the top ranking sentences list that follows.

The top ranking sentences proved a useful aid to users, but they were only the means we chose to test the research hypothesis and other alternatives are equally viable. This subject area obviously needs a lot more research, but we hope that we have shown that implicit and explicit relevance feedback can be interchanged in web retrieval.

Acknowledgements

We would like to thank fellow members of the Information Retrieval group for their thoughts and assistance. We would also like to thank those who participated in the experiments, their comments and enthusiasm were greatly appreciated.

References

1. M. Beaulieu. *Experiments on interfaces to support query expansion.* Journal of Documentation 53. 1. (1997) 8-19
2. Cool, C., Park, S., Belkin, N.J., Koenemann, J. and Ng, K.B. *Information seeking behaviour in new searching environment.* CoLIS 2. Copenhagen. (1996) 403-416
3. Grundin, J. *GroupWare and Social Dynamics: Eight Challenges for Developers.* Communications of the ACM 35. (1994) 92-104
4. Hill, W.C., Hollan, J.D., Wrobelwski, D. and McCandless, T. *Read wear and edit wear.* Proceedings of ACM Conference on Human Factors in Computing Systems, (CHI '92) Monterey, California, USA, 3-7 May (1992)
5. Hersh, W. and Over, P. *TREC-10 Interactive Track Report.* NIST Special Publication: 10th Text REtrieval Conference, Gaithersburg, Maryland, USA. 13-16 November (2001)
6. Jansen, B.J., Spink, A. and Saracevic, T. *Real life, real users, and real needs: A study and analysis of users on the web.* Information Processing & Management 36. 2. (2000) 207-227
7. Joachims, T., Freitag, D. and Mitchell, T. *WebWatcher: A Tour Guide for the World Wide Web* Proceedings of the 16th International Joint Conference on Artificial Intelligence (IJCAI '97) Nagoya, Aichi, Japan, 23-29 August (1997)
8. J. Koenemann and N. Belkin. *A Case For Interaction: A Study of Interactive Information Retrieval Behavior and Effectiveness.* Proceedings of the ACM Conference on Computer-Human Interaction (CHI '96). Vancouver. (1996)
9. Konstan, J.A., Miller, B.N, Maltz, D., Herlocker, J.L, Gordon, L.R. and Riedl, J. *GroupLens: Applying Collaborative Filtering to Usenet News.* Communications of the ACM 40. 3. March (1997) 77-87
10. Kim, J., Oard, D.W. and Romanik, K. *Using implicit feedback for user modeling in Internet and Intranet searching.* Technical Report, College of Library and Information Services, University of Maryland at College Park. (2000)
11. Lieberman, H. *Letizia: An Agent That Assists Web Browsing* Proceedings of the 14th International Joint Conference on Artificial Intelligence (IJCAI '95) Montreal, Canada, 20-25 August (1995)
12. Morita, M. and Shinoda, Y. *Information filtering based on user behavior analysis and best match text retrieval.* Proceedings of the 17th Annual International ACM SIGIR Conference on Research and Development in Information Retrieval (SIGIR '94) Dublin, Ireland. 3-6 July (1994)
13. Mitra, M., Singhal, A. and Buckley, C. *Improving Automatic Query Expansion* Proceedings of the 21st Annual International ACM SIGIR Conference on Research and Development in Information Retrieval (SIGIR '98) Melbourne, Australia, 24-28 August (1998)
14. Nichols, D.M. *Implicit ratings and filtering.* Proceedings of the 5th DELOS Workshop on Filtering and Collaborative Filtering (DELOS '97) Budapest, Hungary, 10-12 November (1997)

15. Oard, D. and Kim, J. *Implicit Feedback for Recommender Systems.* Proceedings of the AAAI Workshop on Recommender Systems (AAAI '98) Madison, Wisconsin, 26-30 July (1998)
16. Maxwell, S. E., & Delaney, H. D. *Designing experiments and analyzing data: A model comparison perspective.* Mahwah, NJ: Lawrence Erlbaum Associates. (2000)
17. Robertson, S.E., *On Term Selection for Query Expansion.* Journal of Documentation 46. 4. (1990) 359-364
18. Ruthven, I., Tombros A. and Jose, J. *A study on the use of summaries and summary-based query expansion for a question-answering task.* 23rd BCS European Annual Colloquium on Information Retrieval Research (ECIR 2001). Darmstadt. (2001)
19. Salton, G., and Buckley, C. *Improving retrieval performance by relevance feedback.* Journal of the American Society for Information Science. 41. 4. (1990) 288-297
20. Shavlik, J. and Goecks, J. *Learning users' interests by unobtrusively observing their normal behavior* Proceedings of the 2000 International Conference on Intelligent User Interfaces (IUI '00) New Orleans, USA, 9-12 January (2000)
21. Spink, A., Greisdorf, H., and Bateman, J. *From highly relevant to not relevant: examining different regions of relevance.* Information Processing and Management. 34. 5. (1998) 599-621
22. van Rijsbergen, C.J. *A New Theoretical Framework For Information Retrieval* Proceedings of the 9th Annual International ACM SIGIR Conference on Research and Development in Information Retrieval (SIGIR '86) Pisa, Italy, 8-10 September (1986)
23. White, R., Jose, J.M. and Ruthven, I. *Query-Biased Web Page Summarisation: A Task-Oriented Evaluation.* Poster Paper. Proceedings of the 24th Annual International ACM SIGIR Conference on Research and Development in Information Retrieval (SIGIR '01) New Orleans, USA, 9-13 September (2001)
24. White, R., Ruthven, I. and Jose, J.M. *Web document summarisation: a task-oriented evaluation.* International Workshop on Digital Libraries. Proceedings of the 12th International Database and Expert Systems Applications Conference (DEXA 2001) Munich, Germany, 3-7 September (2001)

Subject Knowledge, Source of Terms, and Term Selection in Query Expansion: An Analytical Study

Pertti Vakkari

Department of Information Studies, FIN-33014 University of Tampere, Finland
Pertti.Vakkari@uta.fi

Abstract. The role of subject and search knowledge in query expansion (QE) is an unmapped terrain in research on information retrieval. It is likely that both have an impact on the process and outcome of QE. In this paper our aim is an analytical study of the connections between subject and search knowledge and term selection in QE based both on thesaurus and relevance feedback. We will also argue analytically how thesaurus, term suggestion in interactive QE and term extraction in automatic QE support users with differing levels of subject knowledge in their pursuit of search concepts and terms. It is suggested that in QE the initial query concepts representing the information need should not be treated as separate entities, but as conceptually interrelated. These interrelations contribute to the meaning of the conceptual construct, which the query represents, and this should be reflected in the terms identified for QE.

1 Introduction

End-users typically formulate short and simple queries and reformulate them using few search tactics. They have difficulties both in expressing their information needs in search terms and in utilizing options provided by the systems. [11], [28] Due to the poor search skills and retrieval effectiveness of the users it has been suggested that searching should be supported by automating term selection and query formulation [8]. Automatic query expansion (AQE) seems to provide a means for overcoming shortcomings in query formulation [9].

Users' ability to articulate their information needs and formulate queries depend crucially on their subject and search knowledge [21], [22], [32], [41], [47]. The level of individuals' subject knowledge regulates their choice of search terms [44], [47]. Search skills (IR knowledge) have an impact on the ability to formulate queries and search tactics [6], [40], [47]. Thus, both subject and search knowledge contribute in the formation of the search outcome. Individuals' subject knowledge also determine their ability to differentiate between relevant and irrelevant documents in the search result [38], [46]. This all has an impact on the success of query expansion (QE): to what extent it is able to produce useful documents for the users' task.

It is plausible that subject and search knowledge also contribute to the articulation and choice of search terms and the use of various means in QE, and consequently to the search results. The findings by [6] and [13] partially support this claim. It is evident that compared to a novice a subject expert is able to formulate a more specific and comprehensive initial query [cf. 44], containing more favorable conditions for

F. Crestani, M. Girolami, and C.J. van Rijsbergen (Eds.): ECIR 2002, LNCS 2291, pp. 110-123, 2002.
© Springer-Verlag Berlin Heidelberg 2002

QE, be it based on search results or knowledge structures. Individuals' ability to choose among relevant and irrelevant items in the search results also differs [38], [46] producing different bases for relevance feedback (RF).

The features of term provision mechanisms probably also have an impact on the identification and selection of search terms for QE depending on the subject and search knowledge of the users. It may be that the structured provision of search terms by thesaurus supports novices in a subject more than a less structured list of suggested terms by RF.

The role of subject and search knowledge in QE is an unmapped terrain in research on information retrieval. "Search knowledge" refers to the understanding that search concepts has to be articulated in terms, which reflect the expressions used in potentially relevant documents. As the arguments above suggest, it is likely that both have an impact on the process and outcome of QE. The role of various term provision mechanisms in supporting concept and term selection in QE has likewise come in for little attention. In this paper our aim is an analytical study of the connections between subject and search knowledge and term selection in QE based both on thesaurus and RF. We will also analytically argue how thesaurus, term suggestion in interactive query expansion (IQE) and term extraction in AQE support users with differing levels of subject knowledge in their search for appropriate search concepts and terms.

In the following we will first analyse the interactive experiments on QE and then focus on analysing the relations between subject and search knowledge in QE. After that we will discuss how the features of a thesaurus compared to AQE and IQE based on RF relate to the users' subject and search knowledge. We will conclude by comparing how these term provision mechanisms support users with various levels of subject knowledge in identifying search concepts and terms.

2 Results of Interactive Studies on QE

In the few interactive studies on QE the research questions vary, producing fragmenting results. There is only a handful studies comparing AQE and IQE. In the following the results from those interactive studies will be presented focusing on the effectiveness of QE, and especially on comparing AQE and IQE.

Most of the studies show that QE benefits users by producing a better retrieval performance [4], [10], [14], [15], [17], [28]. Short and partially matching initial searches seem to gain most from QE [13], [17]. The few comparisons between AQE and IQE suggest that IQE is more efficient [15], [28]. A problem with AQE seems to be the systems' poor ability to recognise facets and structure the query accordingly [cf. 24, 26, 33].

The effectiveness of QE seems also to depend on users' ability to identify search facets (i.e. on the subject knowledge of the users) and on the complexity of the search topic. IQE appears to be more efficient if users' subject knowledge is low and if the search topic is complex. AQE works better if users' knowledge about the topic is high. [7], [13]. It is plausible that the complexity of a search topic as experienced by users reflects their ability to identify search facets. Thus, a major factor leading to differences in search performance between AQE and IQE is the users' ability to articultate search facets and differentiate between relevant and non-relevant documents [cf. 38, 46].

Bias in RF towards non-relevant or marginally relevant documents leads to extraction and selection of non-relevant terms in AQE. Term extraction based on a proportionally high quantity of non-relevant documents generates inappropriate search terms impairing search effectiveness [28]. Blind AQE especially is more sensitive to this bias. IQE performs better probably because users are able to filter out at least the most irrelevant terms provided.

The results also show that users are in favor of controlling the query reformulation process [17], [28].

The quality of the suggested and selected terms had an impact on the success of QE. Difficulty to understand terms provided by Local Context Analysis in IQE caused inconvenience to users in term selection [4]. IQE was successful if the terms suggested seemed to be potentially useful [17] and if the terms selected had clear and central semantic relations to the search topic [28]. Experiments on the effect of structure of the expanded queries on the retrieval effectiveness support the latter finding. Strongly structured queries perform better than weakly structured ones in QE [19], [27]. Highly relevant documents benefit essentially from concept-based QE in ranking than marginally relevant documents [25], [37].

It seems that a strong query structure prevents query drift – the alteration of the search topic caused by improper QE. [33]. A weak query structure does not indicate facet or concept structure with operators as a strong query structure does [26]. An expanded weak query structure does not contain the structural semantic information from the original query, which is then lost [43]. Thus, clear semantic relations between the concepts in the initial query and the expanded ones seem to lead to successful search performance.

3 Subject and Search Knowledge and Term Selection in QE

Next we will analyse mechanisms which connect subject and search knowledge to the term selection in QE, and the consequences of the selection to the structural dimesions of a query plan. The differences argued in query modification and relevance assessments between persons with different degrees of subject knowledge are naturally idealizations.

A search starts with a conceptual analysis of information need. The aim is to conceptualize the need; to identify and articulate the major concepts and their relations representing the need. [18] The conceptual query plan focuses on what information is searched for. Query formulation transforms the conceptual construct into the search terms and query syntax [40]. The query formulation focuses on how information is searched for. It is supposed and also recommended that the search terms represent the expressions used in the potentially relevant documents [18], [30]. Thus, the terms have a dual role. They represent both the concepts of the construct of a person, and the ways these concepts are expressed in the documents.

The structure of a query consists of three dimensions [36]. The exhaustivity of a query consists of the number of facets in the query. A facet is identical with a concept in the query plan. The extent of the query refers to the number of terms used to express a facet. The specificity of the query depends on how specific terms are used to express the facets it contains. [36] Manipulation of the dimensions effects on precision and recall of the result set.

3.1 Subject Knowledge

Two mechanisms connect individuals' subject knowledge to term selection, suggestion, and further to the composition of search results. First, the level of subject knowledge covaries with individuals' ability to articulate information needs, and consequently with the identification of search terms. Secondly, it has an effect on the relevance assessments of documents retrieved, and thus on RF.

Studies [20], [35], [44], [48] refer to the following: The more knowledgeable the individuals are, the more cenral concepts and their relation are they able to articulate; the more variant expressions of a concept they can identify, and the more specific are the terms used. This implies that, by using their larger and more specific vocabulary subject experts are able to generate more exhaustive and specific queries with wider extent than novices.

Based on the results of laboratory experiments [e.g. 36] we tend to predict that the more specific and exhaustive initial queries - like those of the more knowledgeable compared to the less knowledgeable - would produce searches with higher precision and recall. The absolutely and proportionately larger amount of relevant and likely highly relevant documents in the result set (precision) of the former would produce better and more specific conditions for term extraction and suggestion for QE. Thus, automatically expanded queries without the RF of the experts would contain more relevant terms, which represent more closely both the conceptual construct and the relevant expressions of the concepts in the documents. This, in turn, would lead to higher precision or recall or both depending on the search goals.

Relevance assessment is a crucial step for QE in systems using RF. Persons who know more about a subject are able to differentiate more strictly between relevant and irrelevant information [23], [35] and documents [38], [46] than those with less knowledge. As shown above, the former achieve a search result with higher precision and recall, and their superior subject knowledge enables them to select more highly relevant documents for QE. As [37] have shown, the most relevant documents compared to marginal ones tend to contain longer discussion of the topic, deal with several aspects (concepts) of the topic, have more words pertaining to the request, and the authors tend to use multiple expressions of the concepts to avoid tautology. Thus, compared to the selection of the less knowledgeable, the documents selected by the experts for term extraction in QE are likely to contain more aspects of the query as well as more variant and specific terms representing the query and concepts in the information need. This naturally leads to higher precision and recall of the expanded queries by experts. In IQE the experts' ability to differentiate more exactly between relevant and non-relevant terms among the suggested terms compared to that of novices increases the difference in precision and recall between their result sets.

To conclude, the difference in subject knowledge seems to lead to a cumulation of differences in precison and recall in every step of the QE process. Subject expertise creates through QE a Matthew effect on search effectiveness.

3.2 Search Knowledge

AQE does not require much search knowledge from the user after the initial query has been formulated. The system takes care of the selection of terms for QE. IQE is more effective if users understand the connection between the relevant documents identified and the terms suggested for QE [17].

Understanding that in query formulation terms do not only represent subjects' information need, but must also represent the expressions used for the concepts of information need in the potentially useful documents, belongs to the domain of search knowledge [cf. 3]. It is well known that terms used in documents to express a concept vary remarkably, and that a same term may refer to different concepts [2], [5], [42].

The subject knowledge equips the experts with a larger and many-sided vocabulary, which in principle gives them tools for understanding the problems of ambiguous and parallel expressions in documents. However, it is not evident that they understand how to apply this knowledge thoroughly when searching for information in IR systems. Thus, the choice of search terms depends on both the users' subject and search knowledge.

Subject knowledge is more associated with the conceptual analysis of the information need, and search knowledge (indexing knowledge) is associated with the term selection for query formulation. The users' knowledge about the subject is the major resource in structuring the information need and expressing its major concepts and their relations [cf. 20]. Thus, the creation of facets for query formulation depends on the level of subject knowledge. As individuals' subject knowledge grow, they use more facets in their queries [44]. Understanding that concepts can be expressed in various ways does not help in developing the conceptual construct representing the information need. However, this information helps the users in selecting terms for query formulation [3]. When the facets and their relations have been expressed, search knowledge is a crucial resource for selecting terms for facets. Naturally subject knowledge helps in this process. As individuals' subject knowledge grows, they use more terms in expressing facets [44], [47]. However, it does not help as such if the understanding is restricted of how the manipulation of query terms is related to the variation of the search results.

In short, finding facets for a query is more a matter of subject knowledge, articulating them in terms is more a matter of search (indexing) knowledge.

4 Articulation of Information Needs and Semantic Relations between Concepts

In the following we hypothesize how various semantic relations between the concepts may contribute to the articulation of information needs.

When people try to understand a problem or a task, i.e. to articulate an information need, they seek to structure its central concepts and their relations [45], [cf. 34]. Identifying the concepts is not enough, because it is the relations between the concepts which significantly create their meaning. The relations of a concept to other concepts regulate its meaning. [16], [31] What the concepts break down, the theory relates. If the information need is ill-defined, the person is able to express only a couple of vague concepts and relate them in an undetermined way [29], [44]. For constructing a focus, or developing a well-structured problem individuals need to be able at the same time probably to introduce new concepts, refine them and the old ones and relate them to each other in a specific way. Introducing a new concept into the conceptual construct invariably changes the meaning of the concepts it is related to.

The semantic relations of thesaurus terms are typically the following. Synonyms (ST) are terms whose meaning can be regarded as identical. Superordinate terms in a hierarchy are called broader terms (BT), and subordinate terms narrower terms (NT). The associative relationship (RT) covers relations between terms that are mentally associated, but in neither an equivalence nor hierarchical relation. [26]

In articulating an information need it is not likely that terms that are either equivalent or in a hierarchical relation to terms in the conceptual construct will bring a new facet (concept) in it. They do not bring a new aspect (concept) to the request, but may help to modify concepts belonging to it. It seems that mainly RTs could bring new aspects to the information need, because they do not depend hierarchically on the existing concepts.

A well-defined information need includes all the concepts representing it [cf. 22, 34]. NTs and RTs help in modifying and refining these concepts. STs are tautological expressions and thus do not contribute new information in the construct. Refining an information need includes typically entails expressing it more specifically. Broader concepts are not usually suitable for this.

An essential modification of a concept may be its categorization in a way that relates it systematically to one or more concepts in the construct. Categorization depends on what kind of relations we wish to create between concepts. The match between two concepts depends on the categorizations of both. These categorizions produce covariation between the concepts [39]. Constructing covariation is one of the major tools of research, and we may suppose that in many tasks relating concepts systematically contributes towards their accomplishment. Depending on the categorizations of NTs and RTs, they may support in connecting concepts systematically with each other.

5 How Various Sources of Terms in QE Support in Finding Facets and Terms

Subject knowledge has an impact on the articulation of facets and terms in query construction, which in its turn affects the structural dimension of the query, and finally the recall and precision of the search. Both thesaurus and term suggestion based on search results support term selection in query construction. They may support it differently depending on the subject knowledge of the user. Tables 1-3 contain a summary of hypothetical relations between subject knowledge, terminological tool's potential for supporting facet and term articulation, and its impact on query structure and on precision and recall.

5.1 Thesaurus

A thesaurus mainly provides terms with paradigmatic relations to initial query terms. The provision of terms with syntagmatic relations has a minor role. The facets in a query represent syntagmatic relations. [26] Thus, a thesaurus has strong restrictions in providing support for identifying facets. However, it may help in identifying new facets by links to RTs (Table 1). The connections provided by RTs to the original concept are considerably restricted and prescribed. They do not reflect all relevant associative relations the concept may have, especially those created recently by the discourse community of the subject domain. A thesaurus does not provide links to other potentially relevant new concepts in its structure. It is evident that those with more subject knowledge are better able to identify potentially contributing concepts (facets) among RTs than the less informed. Identification of new facets increases the exhaustivity of a query resulting in higher precision.

A thesaurus supports the exhaustive expression of terms within facets by providing STs, NTs, BTs and RTs increasing recall. Users with more advanced subject knowledge are better able to identify relevant alternative expressions for search concepts than those with less knowledge. Their ability to recognize more specific terms is also greater. The former generates a query with greater extent and higher recall, the latter increases specificity and precision [cf. 18]. The more subject knowledge a person has, the greater the extent and specificity of the query, and the greater are recall and precision [cf. 44].

Table 1. Relations between subject knowledge, identification of facets and terms and changes in query structure and search outcome when using thesaurus.

Support	Subject knowledge	
	High	Low
Identifying facets	RTs may provide limited help Exhaustivity + Precision +	Cf. As in high subject knowledge, but the ability to identify facets is lower
Identifying terms facilitates	A richer expression of facets by STs, NTs, BTs and RTs Extent ++ Recall ++ A more specific expression of facets by NTs Specificity ++ Precision ++	A richer expression of facets by STs, NTs, BTs and RTs Extent + Recall + A more specific expression of facets by NTs Specificity + Precision +

Legend: ++ = large increase; + = small increase

It is evident that if expert searchers do not know much about the subject, a thesaurus or any other term provision tool will not help them identifying new facets (concepts) for the query plan. However, structured term provision mechanisms like thesauri indicating links between terms are powerful tools in IQE in the hands of skilled searchers to support the expression of facets in search terms [cf. 12].

In term selection subject and search (indexing) knowledge interact. Indexing knowledge supports both those having more and those having less knowledge in expressing facets by using more terms. It is difficult to suggest without empirical evidence which of these two groups would benefit most from term provision by thesaurus. Given the information need, compared to the novices the subject experts would be able 1) to identify in the initial query more facets articulating the information need more exhaustively and 2) probably also more specifically, and 3) possibly expressing the facets with more terms, thereby increasing the extent of the query. They may also be better able 4) to locate in the thesaurus matching terms for their facets, and 5) select more pertinent terms for expressing facets among terms that are linked with these matching terms. Thus, there are at least five factors which may cause variation in the number and quality of the new facets and terms identified, and consequently in the structure of queries, and in the quantity and quality of relevant items retrieved. Although it is impossible to predict the relative gain, if both groups have equal search knowledge, tone mat predict that the subject experts would construct the most optimal queries, and produce the best search results.

5.2 Automatic Query Expansion

In query modification AQE does not provide means of identifying new facets, although it is possible when checking the final search results (Table 2).

The initial query of experts produce a better set of results for automatic term extraction than that of novices.. The set contains more facets and terms, and more specific terms generating a query with more exhaustivity, extent and specificity, and thus a higher precision and recall [cf. 44].

If the system is based on RF, the experts tend to select more highly relevant documents [38], [46] producing more good terms for QE than novices with the results in query structure and search outcome mentioned above.

Table 2. Relations between subject knowledge, identification of facets and terms and changes in query structure and in search outcome in AQE.

Support	Subject knowledge	
	High	Low
Identifying facets	No help Exhaustivity o Precision o	No help Exhaustivity o Precision o
Identifying terms	Initial query contains more facets, terms and more specific terms resulting in a search result with more exhaustivity, extent and specificity, RF produces highly relevant documents generating good terms Extent ++ Recall ++ Specificity ++ Precision ++	Initial query contains fewer facets, terms and less specific terms resulting in a search result with less exhaustivity, extent, and specificity, RF produces fewer highly relevant documents generating less good terms, and prehaps query drift Extent + Recall + Specificity + Precision +

Legend: ++ = large increase; + = small increase; o = no changes

It seems that in AQE those who have less subject knowledge are in greater danger of generating query drift by inferior choice of search terms in the initial query. If RF is provided, their poorer relevance judgements may contribute towards biased query reformulation.

In AQE search knowledge may have an effect on the quantity and quality of terms used in the initial query. The number of terms expressing facets depends both on the indexing and subject knowledge of the users. If the search knowledge is advanced, the initial queries of those knowing more about the subject compared to those knowing less contain more terms per facet, and are thus more exhaustive.

5.3 Interactive Query Expansion

The candidate terms generated by the RF may contain terms which users may identify as new facets (Table 3). Their provision is not structured showing links between the original concepts and RTs as in a thesaurus. However, it is likely that some of the terms in the list will reflect the central thematizations in the subject domain. These terms express the major aspects (concepts) in the domain. We may also suppose that implicit relations between some terms on the list reflect the shared conceptual constructs in the subject domain, which are incorporated into the documents retrieved. It depends on the users' subject knowledge if they identify connections between their original conceptual construct and the potential facets in the term list. The subject experts have a more advanced ability to recognize patterns based on meager information and also conclude beyond the information given compared to novices [23], [36]. This suggests that they also have a greater ability to construct new facets from the terms given.

In IQE based on RF the possible facets form a broader range of options than RTs in a thesaurus with their predifined relations.

Subject knowledge has a significant role in IQE. A high knowledge level leads to a more optimal initial query and more pertinent RF with highly relevant items. As [37] show, highly relevant documents deal with several aspects (concepts) of the topic. Thus, the list of candidate terms is likely to contain not only more pertinent concepts, but also to focus more on meaningful implicit relations between the concepts, i.e. it provides a few meaningful constructs reflecting the information need. We suppose that the term list reflects implicitly conceptual constructs shared by the discourse community of the subject domain and expressed in the documents retrieved. The stricter relevance criteria of the experts filter out from the RF documents containing non-relevant constructs, which do not contain pertinent concepts, and, more importantly, meaningful relations between the concepts. Thus, the list of candidate tems produced by subject experts is likely to include terms that represent the central conceptual constructs in the topic. Although the list does not explicitly reflect the relations between the concepts, it is likely that it will include fewer irrelevant terms and thus, facilitate better the identification of new facets. By providing a more closed range of implicit central constructs, the term list of an expert steers towards selecting new concepts, which have meaningful relations to the conceptual construct of the user.

Table 3. Relations between subject knowledge, identification of facets and terms and changes in query structure and in search outcome in IQE.

Support	Subject knowledge	
	High	Low
Identifying facets	May provide unrestricted help Exhaustivity + Precision +	Cf. As in high subject knowledge, but the ability to identify facets is lower
Identifying terms	Initial query contains more facets, terms and more specific terms resulting in a search result with more exhaustivity, extent, and specificity, RF produces highly relevant documents generating good candidate terms, Term selection contains more pertinent and more specific terms Extent ++ Recall ++ Specificity ++ Precision ++	Initial query contains fewer facets, terms and less specific terms resulting in a search result with less exhaustivity, extent, and specificity, RF produces fewer highly relevant documents generating fewer good candidate terms, Term selection contains less pertinent and less specific terms Extent + Recall + Specificity + Precision +

Legend: ++ = large increase; + = small increase

In IQE subject and search knowledge also interact. *Mutatis mutandis* the argumention concerning the interaction of these factors in using thesaurus is also valid here.

6 Relevance Feedback and Subject Knowledge

The problem with the less knowledgeables' RF is that due to their inferior initial queries and their looser relevance criteria, the selected documents contain fewer highly relevant and more marginally relevant items. They produce more mixed and less pertinent concepts providing fewer meaningful and more marginal and accidentally implicit conceptual constructs. The terms suggested are therefore less relevant and more diffuse. [cf. 1, 33] It is likely that they do not contain as structured implicit conceptual constructs as the term list of the experts. The relations between the terms suggested are more haphazaed and meaningless, producing a great potential for alternative, but pointless combinations of concepts. It opens the way to query drift. This reduces the options of the less knowledgeable to identify and construct new facets, especially due to their inferior ability to recognize patterns.

RF by novices in a subject domain evidently generates a set of terms that contains both relevant and irrelevant terms. Relevant terms are those representing concepts (facets) in the information need correctly and having meaningful interrelations forming a meaningful construct representing the need. Irrelevant terms do not represent the facets and their interrelations correctly. The problem with AQE and partly with IQE based on low subject knowledge is that they generate queries which a) confuse relevant and irrelevant terms, and b) more importantly, confuse facets and terms. The algorithm typically breaks the connections, i.e. meanings, between the concepts (facets) in the initial query, and cannot distinquish between the concepts and the terms representing these concepts neither in the initial query nor in the documents retrieved.

Structuring the initial query and the expanded queries by facet-term distinction is a means for producing more pertinent term lists, which also contain meaningful implicit constructs reflecting more accurately the information need. Expanded structured queries have been shown to perform better than unstructured ones in experiments [27], [33]. It is probable that they also do so in real search situations.

Providing users in IQE with a list of terms grouped according to the facets of the initial query would help them in expressing the facets more richly and also possibly to refine the query [cf. 1]. However, this would not solve the problem of identifying new facets for articulating the information need more clearly. If the system could indicate the degree of dependencies between each initial concept (facet) and the suggested terms grouped under concepts (facets), these dependence indicators would steer users to construct new facets. The weighted links between the old facets and the potential new ones would bridge the gap between the initial conceptual construct and the new one under construction. The links with strong weights would act as suggestions for concepts, which might make sense if connected to the initial conceptual construct. Such a linking mechanism would support the users in restructuring their prior knowledge by providing cues to potentially enriching new aspects (concepts) of their subject.

7 Conclusion: Aids for QE and the Subject Knowledge

It is evident that the effectiveness of QE depends on the concepts and terms identified for query reformulation. The meaning of the concepts and the corresponding terms representing an information need depends on the relations of these concepts. Consequently, it is important that term provision mechanisms in QE treat concepts as interrelated constructs, not as separate entities. The experiments show that structured, concept-based queries perform better than unstructured queries in QE [26], [33] and that highly relevant documents benefit essentially from structured queries [26], [37]. Treating the initial query as representing the interrelated concepts of a construct opens up a way to develop a mechanism for term identification from documents, thereby generating terms that correspond appropriately to the concepts, and more importanty, to the construct in the initial query. This would also support users in selecting appropriate terms reflecting their conceptual construct (information need), not only separate concepts.

It seems that those knowing most about a subject are likely to generate the best process and product performance independent of the type of mechanisms for QE compared to those knowing less. However, analytical reasoning like this does not indicate the volume of changes in precision and recall on various levels of subject knowledge brought about by term selection be it based on RF or a thesaurus. It may be that the increase in performance is greater among those who know less about a subject than among the more knowledgeable. Experiments show that short queries gain more from QE, and that searches which result in a partial match initially are more likely to benefit from IQE than those which match exactly in the first place [17], [26]. If we suppose that a short query and initial partial match are indications of low subject knowledge, we may conclude that queries based on low subject knowledge gain most from the QE. What is however evident, is that the initial and reformulated queries of those who have most subject knowledge produce the best performance, although the improvement of the performance by QE may be greater among those who know less about the subject. Answering these questions requires empirical research.

Comparisons between the mechanisms for the QE in relation to subject knowledge is difficult based on analytical arguments. The reasoning above suggests that, independent of the subject knowledge, IQE based on RF provides more support for identifying facets than AQE because humans are able to filter out at least the most irrelevant documents and meaningless terms. However, the few empirical findings suggest that the effectiveness of the QE depends on the user's ability to identify search facets (i.e. subject knowledge of the user) as well as on the complexity of the search topic. IQE appears to be more efficient than AQE if users' subject knowledge is low and if the search topic is complex [7], [13].

Based on these analytical arguments our next step is to study empirically how the level of subject knowledge affects the query formulation process and the search outcome in AQE and IQE based on RF.

References

1. Anick, P. & Tiperneni, S. The paraphrase search assistant: terminological feedback for iterative information seeking. In Proceedings of the SIGIR´99. ACM, New York (1999) 153-159
2. Bates, M. Subject access to online catologs: A design model. Journal of the American Society for Information Science 37 (6) (1986) 357-376
3. Bates, M. Indexing and access for digital libraries and the internet: Human, database, and domain factors. Journal of the American Society for Information Science. 49 (13) (1998) 1185-1205
4. Belkin, N. & Cool, C. & Head, J. & Jeng, J. Kelly, D. & al., Relevance Feedback versus Local Context Analysis as term suggestion devices: Rutgers' TREC-8 interactive track experience. In: Proceedings of TREC-8. Available from: (2000)
5. Blair, D. & Maron, M. An evaluation of retrieval effectiveness for a full-text document retrieval system. Communications of the ACM. 28 (3) (1985) 289-299
6. Borgman, C. Why are online catologs still hard to use? Journal of the American Society for Information Science. 47 (1996) 493-503.
7. Brajnik, G., Mizzaro, S. & Tasso, C. Evaluating user interfaces to information retrieval systems. A case study. In Proceedings of the SIGIR'96. ACM, New York (1996) 128-136
8. Croft, B. & Das, R. Experiment with query acquisition and use in document retrieval systems. In: Proceedings of the SIGIR´90. Springer, Berlin (1990) 368-376
9. Eftimiadis, E. Query expansion. In: M.E. Williams (ed), Annual review of information science and technology, vol 31. N.J.: Information Today, Medford (1996) 121-187
10. Eftimiadis, E. Interactive query expansion: A user-based evaluation in relevance feedback environment. Journal of the American Society for Information Science. 51 (11) (2000) 989-1003
11. Fenichel, C. The process of searching online bibliographic databases. Library Research 2 (1981) 107-127
12. Fidel, R. Searchers' selection of search keys: III searching styles. Journal of the American Society for Information Science, 42 (1991) 515-527

13. Fowkes, H., & Beaulieu, M. Interactive searching behavior: Okapi experiment for TREC-8. In Proceedings of the BCS-IRSG: 22nd Annual Colloquium on Information Retrieval Research. Cambridge (2000)
14. Greenberg, J. Automatic query expansion via lexical-semantic relationships. Journal of the American Society for Information Science, 52 (2) (2001a) 402-415
15. Greenberg, J. Optimal query expansion processing methods with semantically encoded structured thesauri terminology. Journal of the American Society for Information Science, 52 (6) (2001b) 487-498
16. Hahn, U., & Chater, N. Concepts and similarity. In K. Lamberts, & D. Shanks (Eds.), Knowledge, concepts and categories. Psychology Press, Hove (1997) 43-92
17. Hancock-Beaulieu, M. & Fieldhouse, M. & Do, T. An evaluation of interactive query expansion in an online library catalogue with graphical user interface. Journal of Documentation. 51 (3) (1995) 225-243
18. Harter, S. Online information retrieval. Academic Press, Orlando (1986)
19. Hawking, D. & Thistlewaite, P. & Bailey, B. ANU/ACSys TREC-5 experiments. In: E. Voorhees & D. Harman (eds), Information technology: The fifth text retrieval conference (TREC-5). MD, Gaithersburg (1997) 359-375
20. Heit, E. Knowledge and concept learning. In K. Lamberts, & D. Shanks (Eds.), Knowledge, Concepts and Categories. Psychology Press, Hove (1997) 7-41
21. Hsieh-Yee, I. Effects of search experience and subject knowledge on the search tactics of novice and experienced searchers. Journal of the American Society for Information Science. 44 (1993) 161-174
22. Ingwersen, P. Information retrieval interaction. Taylor Graham, London (1992)
23. Isenberg, D. Thinking and managing: a verbal protocol analysis of managerial problem solving. Academy of Management Journal. 20 (1986) 775-788.
24. Jones, S & Gatford, M. & Robertson, S. & Hancock-Beaulieu, M. & Secker, J. Interactive thesaurus navigation: Intelligence rules OK? Journal of the American Society for Information Science. 46 (1) (1995) 52-59
25. Järvelin, K. & Kekäläinen, J., IR evaluayion methods for highly relevant documents. Proceedings of the SIGIR'00. ACM, New York (2000) 41-48
26. Kekäläinen, J. The effects of query complexity, expansion and structure on retrieval performance in probabilistic text retrieval. Doctoral Dissertation. Tampere University Press, Tampere (1999)
27. Kekäläinen, J. & Järvelin, K. The impact of query structure and query extension on retrieval performance. In: Proceedings of the SIGIR´98. ACM, New York (1998) 130-137
28. Koenemann, J. & Belkin, N. A case for interaction: A study of interactive information retrieval behavior and effectiveness. In: Proceedings of the Human Factors in Computing Systems Conference (CHI'96). ACM Press, New York (1996) 205-212
29. Kuhlthau, C. Seeking Meaning. Norwood, N.J. Ablex (1993)
30. Lancaster, W & Warner, A. Information retrieval today. VA: Information Resources Press, Arlington (1993)
31. Lormand, E. How to be a meaning holist. The Journal of Philosophy. 93 (1996)
32. Marchionini, G. Information seeking in electronic environments. Cambridge University Press (1995)
33. Mitra, M.. & Singhal, A. & Buckley, C. Improving automatic query expansion. In Proceedings of the SIGIR´98. ACM, New York (1998) 206-214
34. Partridge, D., & Hussain K. Knowledge based information-systems. McGraw-Hill, London (1995)
35. Patel, V. & Ramoni, M. Cognitive models of directional inference in expert medical reasoning. In P. Feltovich, & K. Ford, & R. Hoffman (Eds.), Expertise in context: human and machine. AAAI Press, Menlo Park (Calif.) (1997) 67-99
36. Sormunen, E. A method of measuring wide range performance of Boolean queries in full-text databases. Acta Universitatis Tamperensis 748. Doctoral Dissertation. Tampere University Press, Tampere (2000)

37. Sormunen, E. & Kekäläinen, J. & Koivisto, J. Järvelin, K. Document text characteristics affect the ranking of the most relevant documents by expanded structured queries. Journal of Documentation. 57 (3) (2001) 358-376.

38. Spink, A., Greisdorf, R., & Bateman, J. From highly relevant to non-relevant: examining different regions of relevance. Information Processing & Management. 34 (1998) 599-622

39. Stinchcombe, A. Constructing Social Theories. University of Chicago Press, Chicago (1987)

40. Sutcliffe, A., & Ennis, M. Towards a cognitive theory of IR. Interacting with Computers. 10 (1998) 321-351

41. Sutcliffe, A., Ennis, M., & Watkinson, S. Empirical studies of end-user information searching. Journal of the American Society for Information Science. 51 (2000) 1211-1231

42. Swanson, D. Historical note: Information retrieval and the future of an illusion. Journal of the American Society for Information Science. 39 (4) (1988) 92-98

43. Turtle, H. & Croft, W. Evaluation of inference network-based retrieval model. ACM transactions on information systems. 9 (3) (1991) 187-222

44. Vakkari, P. Cognition and changes of search terms and tactics during task performance. Proceedings of the RIAO´2000 Conference Paris: C.I.D. (2000) 894-907. Also: http://www.info.uta.fi/informaatio/vakkari/Vakkari_Tactics_RIAO2000.html

45. Vakkari, P. A Theory of the Task-based Information Retrieval. Journal of Documentation. 57 (1) (2001) 44-60

46. Vakkari, P., & Hakala, N. Changes in relevance criteria and problem stages in task performance. Journal of Documentation. 56 (2000) 540-562

47. Vakkari, P. & Pennanen, M. & Serola, S. Changes of search terms and tactics while writing a research proposal: A longitudinal case study. Submitted for publication (2002)

48. Wang, P. User's information needs at different stages of a research project: a cognitive view. In P. Vakkari, R. Savolainen, & B., Dervin (Eds.), Information Seeking in Context. Taylor, London & Los Angeles (1997) 307-318

Automatic Profile Reformulation Using a Local Document Analysis

Anis Benammar[1], Gilles Hubert[1], and Josiane Mothe[1,2]

[1] Institut de recherche en informatique de Toulouse
118 Route de Narbonne, 31066 Toulouse Cedex, FRANCE
{benammar, hubert, mothe}@irit.fr
[2] Institut universitaire de formation des maîtres
http://www.irit.fr/ACTIVITES/EQ_SIG/personnes/mothe/

Abstract. User profiles are more and more used in information retrieval system in order to assist users in finding relevant information. Profiles are continuously updated to evolve at the same time the user information need does. In this paper we present a reformulation strategy used to automatically update the profile content. In a first stage, a local document set is computed from the search results. In a second stage, the local set is analyzed to select the terms to add to the profile expression. Experiments have been performed on an extract from the OHSUMED database to evaluate the effectiveness of the adaptation process.

1 Introduction

In information retrieval, a profile is a constant user information need [13], [3]. A simple profile looks like a query that can be periodically run. It consists of a set of weighted key terms [3]. The weights represent the importance of the terms. Profiles are more and more employed by servers and intelligent agents in order to overcome the associated problems with [8]:
- Broad spaces of data. Because the mass of handled information increases, the user '*feels lost*' in the information space. A profile is used to remove information that does not match the user information need, so that the user can focus on relevant information.
- Language variations. Documents are written in different languages. A profile can be used to overcome mismatches in languages.
- Word mismatches. Users often use different words to describe a same information need. They also have some difficulties to find the keywords that express exactly their information need. When the user inputs a query, the retrieval process uses the profile to modify the query as to be more consistent with the user information need.
The aim of our study is to set up a system of profiles that corresponds to the third type of problem. The final goal is to provide users with personalised profiles that can assist them during the information retrieval process. The profile acts as a query to best match the user information need and improve the retrieval results.

F. Crestani, M. Girolami, and C.J. van Rijsbergen (Eds.): ECIR 2002, LNCS 2291, pp. 124-134, 2002.

A profile in our system is composed of a *user profile* and of different *query profiles*. The user profile memorises information on the user himself (user-id, affiliation, …), whereas a query profile corresponds to the description of an information need (set of terms that represent the user interest). Two levels of query profiles have been defined as follows (Fig. 1-1): a short-term query profile is associated to the current retrieval session (same user and same information need) and a long-term query profile is built over different sessions (same information need). Initially, the short-term query profile corresponds to the user query. Alternatively, it can correspond to a long-term query profile built over previous search sessions. In the latter case, the user chooses to use an existing profile to start his search.

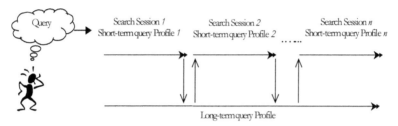

Fig. 1-1. Short-term and long-term query profiles

In the remainder of the paper, the short-term query profile will be referred to as query profile.

During the retrieval process, a query profile must regularly be adapted to follow the user information need. Query reformulation is usually used to achieve this task. In this paper, we focus on the reformulation strategies used to update the query profile content. Query reformulation involves the following goals:

- Expanding the query with new terms from relevant documents [5], [12],[17],
- Re-weighting the terms in the expanded query [17].

Several kinds of query reformulation methods have been studied in the literature. We are interested in methods that use the feedback from top-ranked documents in the search result. The method is called *pseudo-relevance feedback* [12], [11] as the relevance is not given by the user. The improvement of the results, when applying pseudo-relevance feedback, depends on the quality of the top ranked documents [9]. Generally, irrelevant documents are retrieved among the top ranked ones. In this case, the query reformulation may be less efficient since the reformulation information is extracted from irrelevant documents.

In this paper, we present a reformulation strategy to update the query profile content. It is carried out through a two step process. In the first stage, we use document similarities to build a *local set of documents* from the initial retrieved documents. This local set contains the documents that best fit the user information need. It is a re-ranking step which goal is to improve the quality of the documents to be used for the query profile reformulation. The local set is then analysed in order to extract the best terms to be added to the query profile. Experiments have been performed to evaluate the adaptation process performance and the importance of the re-ranking step. The experiments are carried out on the OHSUMED 1987 collection.

The paper is organised as follows: section 2 presents the related works on the query reformulation methods. Section 3 details the reformulation process we define to automatically update query profiles. Finally, section 4 presents the framework of the experiments and results.

2 Related Work

Query reformulation approaches through query expansion are generally used to create a new query expression according to the associated retrieval result. Query expansion methods consists in adding new terms to the initial query. These approaches can be grouped in three categories [2]:

➢ User relevance feedback approaches: they are based on the use of user feedback. In these approaches, the user is asked to mark the documents he considers as relevant. An automatic analysis allows the system to select the terms that are representative of the relevant documents and add them in the new query formulation [17].

➢ Global techniques: these approaches are based on the analysis of the entire document collection. They are typically based on the association hypothesis [20]. One of the earliest global techniques is term clustering [18] which groups related terms into clusters based on their co-occurrence in the corpus. The terms that are most correlated with the query terms are then added to the query. Global techniques use concepts (single noun, two adjacent nouns or three adjacent nouns in the texts) instead of simple words and passages (a window of fixed size) instead of entire documents. Concepts are used to overcome the problem of term ambiguity. On the other hand, passages are used in order to focus the analysis on the relevant parts of documents [1], [2].

➢ Pseudo-relevance feedback and local techniques: these approaches are based on the set of initially retrieved documents. They are generally fully automatic and do not require the assistance of the user. There are mainly two local strategies: the local relevance feedback [1] and the local context analysis [11]. With regard to the local relevance feedback strategy, the main idea is to build global structures such as an association matrices that quantifies term correlations. The more correlated terms are then used to expand the query. The local context analysis (LCA) is a more recent local technique; it inherits the notions of global approach (use of the passages and concepts) and applies it to a local set of documents. The concepts are selected from the top ranked documents or passages based on their co-occurrence with the query.

A problem that always raises with the pseudo-relevance feedback concerns the 'quality' of the documents used for the feedback [7], [9], [12]. In several cases, irrelevant documents appear among the top ranked ones. Using these documents to achieve the reformulation degrades the retrieval performance.

The approach we develop to adapt the query profile deals with the document quality problem. It integrates the following aspects:

The documents that are used for the query profile modification are the retrieved ones. In that sense, our approach is similar to the local relevance feedback for which the modification is based only on the retrieved documents. However, we use an additional step that consists in re-ranking the initial retrieved documents [15]. The goal of this step is to improve the quality of the documents to be analysed in order to select the best terms. The more relevant these documents are (or closer to the retrieval context), the better the modification result will be. The re-ranking step is based on a similarity analysis between the top ranked documents in the search result and the current query profile.

The document analysis is based on co-occurrence measures. The co-occurrences between the terms from the documents and the whole query profile are computed to deduce the terms to be added to the query profile.

In the following sections, we present in details the reformulation process.

3 Query Profile Reformulation

Throughout a search session the query profile acts as a query and it is automatically adapted according to the search results and to the relevance feedback information. The following figure (Fig. 2-1) illustrates the different steps of the reformulation process.

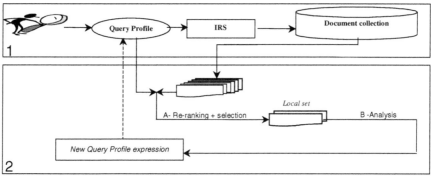

Fig. 2-1. Reformulation process

A classical retrieval process is firstly employed to retrieve the documents in response to the initial request. The results are then used to reformulate the query profile expression. The reformulation process uses an alternative approach compared to the usual local relevance feedback. The major difference with the other local relevance feedback approaches is the use of a preliminary step consisting in the construction of a local set of documents from the search result. In the second step of the process, a co-occurrence analysis is performed on the documents of the local set. This analysis consists in measuring the correlation between the terms of the local set and the query profile. The most correlated terms are then used for the expansion. In the following sections we detail the adaptation process steps.

3.1 Document Re-ranking

Pseudo-relevance feedback techniques use the top-ranked retrieved documents from the initial query to create a new query expression [2], [14]. The quality of the modifications depends on the relevance of these documents. However, the top ranked documents are not always relevant. In some cases, among the 20 top-ranked documents, only 3 documents are relevant. Experiments in TREC have shown that the performances of the techniques that use the first documents from the search result are irregular [9]. To improve the quality of the set of documents that is used to modify the query profile expression, we employ an additional stage in the process. This stage consists in building a local set of documents from the search result. This set gathers the documents that correspond best to the search context. It is computed by re-ranking the documents that have initially been retrieved (100 top ranked documents). Indeed, instead of directly using the top documents in the retrieved set as it is usually done, we re-rank the first 100 documents according to the current query profile and we select the new top ranked documents. The goal is to try to get in the top list relevant documents that were initially ranked in a lower position. Documents reordering is done by computing the similarity between the documents and the query profile. We have experimented several similarity measures (inner product, cosine and logical metrics).

The documents are represented as vectors in the term space [19]. To each term is associated a weight computed as follows:

$$w(t_d) = \log_{10}\left(\frac{N}{N_{t_d}}\right). \tag{1}$$

Where t_d is a term from the document d, N is the number of documents from the collection and N_{td} is the number of documents from the collection that contain the term t_d. The query profiles are also represented in a vector space but a different formula (2) is used to compute a term weight in the profile:

$$w(t_p) = \frac{tf(t_p)}{tf_{max}}. \tag{2}$$

Where $tf(t_p)$ is the term frequency in the query profile and tf_{max} is the highest frequency in the query profile.

The similarity value between a document vector $\overrightarrow{D}$ and a query profile vector $\overrightarrow{P}$ using, for example, the *Cosine* measure is computed as follows:

$$Sim(D,P) = Cos(\overrightarrow{D}, \overrightarrow{P}) = \frac{\sum_{i=1}^{n} wt(td_i) wt(tp_i)}{\sqrt{\left(\sum_{i=1}^{n} w(td_i)\right)^2} \times \sqrt{\left(\sum_{i=1}^{n} w(tp_i)\right)^2}} \tag{3}$$

Where n is the number of documents in the local set.

The documents that are most correlated to the query profile constitute the local document set that is used to perform the cooccurrence analysis.

3.2 Analysis of the Local Documents Set

The analysis is carried out on the basis of the local set of documents as built in the first step. The goal of this analysis is to automatically extract the correlations that exist between the terms from the documents and the query profile. Then, the most correlated terms from the local documents set are used to expand the query profile. The term correlations are computed using term co-occurrence as follows:

$$Correlation(t_i, P) = \sum_{j \in P} co-occurrence(t_i, p_j) \cdot \tag{4}$$

Where t_i is a term from a document in the local set and p_j is a term from the query profile P.
The co-occurrence degree between a term from a document and a term from the query profile is expressed as in [11]:

$$\tag{5}$$

$$co-occurrence \ (t_i, p_j) = \log_{10}(Co-occ \ (t_i, p_j) + 1) \ idf \ (t_i)/\log_{10}(n)$$
$$Co-occ \ (t_i, p_j) = \sum_{dinS} tf \ (t_i, d) \, tf \ (p_j, d)$$

- $tf(t_i, d)$ and $tf(p_j, d)$ are the frequencies of the terms t_i and p_j in the document d,
- n is the number of documents in the local set,
- N is the number of documents in the whole collection,
- N_{t_i} is the number of documents in the collection that contain the term t_i.
- $idf(t_i) = \log_{10}(N / N_{t_i})$

Several parameters in these formulas such as the number of documents in the local set are evaluated in the experimentation section. The goal is to determine the optimal values of the different parameters.

4 Experiments

The experiments were conducted according to the following axes:
- Evaluate the capacity of the reformulation process to improve the retrieval performance,
- Evaluate the importance of the re-ranking step: we compare the search result when applying the entire reformulation process and the result when directly using the top ranked documents as it is usually done in the literature (without re-ranking step). Our goal is to evaluate the importance of the re-ranking step in the adaptation process.

The adaptation process can be summarised as follows:

1. Perform an initial search. The initial query profile corresponds to the user query or to an existing profile built over previous sessions. The search engine we use to perform the retrieval is Mercure [6]. It is an information retrieval system based on the combination of the neural network approach and the vector model.
2. Re-rank the 100 first retrieved documents in the initial result. The top ranked ones constitute the local document set. A threshold value is also used to take only the most similar documents to the query profile.
3. Perform an analysis on the local set of documents to deduce the terms to add to the query profile expression. The number of terms depends on the number of documents used to perform the analysis.
4. Add the best n terms to the query profile and start again the retrieval process.

The experiments were carried out on the medical database OHSUMED 1987. The following table summarises the database characteristics.

Table 1. Characteristics of the OHSUMED 1987 collection

OHSUMED 1987 corpus	
Corpus size	54 710 documents
Number of terms	46 095 terms
Average document length	Approximately 130 terms

We used a set of 63 queries (topics) defined in the filtering track in TREC9 [16]. Relevance judgements are associated to this test collection and are used to evaluate the results. In these experiments, we compare the performance of the search when using the original query profile and when applying the adaptation process. We also evaluate the importance of the re-ranking step.
The *Trec_Eval* program was used to evaluate the search results. The precision was measured on several levels: p5, p10, p15, p20, p30 and p100, which respectively represents the number of relevant documents among the 5, 10, 15, 20, 30 and the 100 top ranked documents. The *average precision* (AvgPr) over all retrieved documents was also considered as well as the *Exact precision* (ExactPr) value that represents the precision computed for the nth first retrieved documents, where n is the total number of relevant documents. Several parameters have been evaluated in the experiments:
- Number of documents in the local set to be used in the analysis,
- Number of terms to add to the query profile expression,
- Measure used to evaluate the similarities between the documents and the query profile when re-ranking the top ranked documents (cosine, inner product or logical measures).

Preliminary experiments have been done to choose the optimal parameter values. Several tests were performed to deduce the optimal local set size. Finally, we set it at 5 documents. The inner product proved to be the best measure when searching similar documents to the query profile. We also used a threshold value when building the local set of documents. Indeed, only the documents for which the similarity with the profile exceeds the threshold value were included in the local set. The threshold eliminates including documents that do not correspond exactly to the retrieval context. The number of terms (n) to add to the query profile expression depends on the number of documents in the local set. We did several evaluations to set this parameter (number of terms to add), the best results were obtained using the formula (6) defined in [4]: let n be the number of terms to add to the query profile and i the number of documents in the local set, n is computed as follows:

$$n = 5 * i + 5 . \tag{6}$$

4.1 Results

Over the 63 queries used during the experiments, some queries (approximately 23%) have no results in the initial search (no relevant document is retrieved). In these particular cases, we can not improve the search performance using our technique. Because the initially retrieved documents are not relevant, the added terms will probably be irrelevant as well. For that reason, we focused only on the remaining queries (48) to evaluate the adaptation process.

The following table summarises the results. The results are evaluated according to the precision (at 10, 15 and 20 documents), the average precision and the exact precision. The first row represents the first retrieved results. The second row presents the results when applying the cooccurrence analysis on the top ranked documents. The third row describes the obtained results when applying the full process including the re-ranking and the cooccurrence analysis. The last row presents the improvement percentage when applying the reformulation process (initial results VS Reformulation results using full process).

Table 2. Results

	P10	P15	P20	AvgPr	ExactPr
Initial Result	0.387	0.326	0.276	0.3946	0.3893
Reformulation results: No re-ranking	0.427	0.342	0.290	0.4171	0.4180
Reformulation results: Full process	0.427	0.361	0.305	0.4187	0.4234
Improvement percentage	10.3%	10.7%	10.5%	6.1%	8.75%

4.1.1 Adaptation Process VS Initial Search

When using the adaptation process, the search results were improved in 26 cases over 48. In 10 cases, the results remain invariant. The average values over the 48 queries show an improvement of 6.1% for the *Average Precision* value and 8.75% for the *Exact Precision* value. The elementary precision at 10, 15 and 20 documents are also improved.

4.1.2 Documents Re-ranking

The experiments show that the adaptation process using the re-ranking step improves the results better than the adaptation process using directly the top ranked documents.

In 63% of the cases, the reformulation process is more effective when using the re-ranking. In fact the re-ranking improves the quality of the local set used in the analysis by including more relevant documents. In some cases, even if the re-ranking step does not include more relevant documents in the local set, the retrieval performance increases. In this latter case, the documents are not relevant, but they are close enough to the search context so that the results are also improved. The re-ranking step shows the importance of the quality of the documents used to achieve the relevance feedback. In these cases, the analysis performs better because the added terms are relevant since they are extracted from relevant documents.

An additional experiments confirm the last conclusions: when the local set is manually constructed by choosing the relevant documents, the retrieval results are always improved.

4.2   Conclusions on the Experiments

The experiments carried out on the OHSUMED database brought us to the following conclusions:
- The adaptation process improves the search results,
- The re-ranking step is an important stage in the adaptation process. The experiments show that using the re-ranking step improves the results more than the adaptation process using directly the top ranked documents in the initial result.

5   General Conclusion

In this paper, we present a reformulation process used to update the short-term query profile. The reformulation process is based on a co-occurrence analysis performed over a subset of the initially retrieved documents. It is a similar approach to the local relevance feedback. The major problem with such a technique is the quality of the top-ranked documents. Indeed, the reformulation results can be seriously degraded if some irrelevant documents are classified among the first retrieved ones. To overcome this problem, we induce a preliminary re-ranking step based on similarity measurements. The goal of this step is to construct a local set that will contain the documents that best fit the user information need. The local set is then analysed to select the terms to be added to the query profile. Several experiments have been carried out on the OHSUMED 1987 database. Different criteria have been studied (number of documents in the local set, number of terms to be added to the query profile per modification, …). The reformulation process proves to be suitable for query profile reformulation. In fact, evaluations show that elementary as well as average and exact precision are enhanced when applying the reformulation process. The re-ranking step used to construct the initial local document set also proves to be important. Indeed, it improves the quality of the documents used during the analysis.

Our future study will continue within the same objective of improving the retrieval performance using new re-ranking methods. Indeed, the adaptation process we employ always improves the retrieval results when the local set quality is good. We will also extend our study to deal with the network structure of a hyperlinked environment as a special document type. Indeed, the link structure is a rich source of information that can be exploited to enhance the quality of the local document set.

Acknowledgement. Research outlined in this paper is part of the IRAIA project supported by the European Commission under the fifth Framework Programme (IST – 1999 – 10602). However views expressed herein are ours and do not necessarily correspond to the IRAIA consortium.

References

1. Attar R., Frankel A. S, Local feedback in Full-Text Retrieval Systems. Journal of associations for Computing Machinery, 24 (3), 397-417, 1977.
2. Baeza-Yates R., Ribeiro-Neto B. Modern Information Retrieval, Addison-Wesley Ed., ISBN 0-201-39829-X, 1999.
3. Belkin N. J., Croft W.B. Information retrieval and information Filtering: two sides of the same coin, CACM, Pages 29-38, 1992.
4. Belkin N. J. Relevance Feedback versus Local Context Analysis as term suggestion devices, Rutger's TREC-8 Interactive Track Experience, Proceedings of Trec-8, Pages 565-574, November 16-19, 1999
5. Buckley C., Salton G., Allan J. The effect of adding information in a relevance feedback Environment, Conference on Research and development in Information Retrieval (SIGIR), 1994
6. Boughanem M., Dkaki T., Mothe J., Soulé-Dupuy C. Mercure at Trec-7. 7th International Conference on Text REtrieval TREC7, Harman D.K. (Ed.) SP 500-236, November 11-17, NIST Gaithersburg, 1998.
7. Boughanem M., Chrisment C., Soulé-Dupuy C. Query modification based on relevance back-propagation in ad hoc environment, Information Processing & Management 35 (1999) 121-139.
8. Gurthet A., http://www.biermans.com/culminating/fall_1999.html, 1999.
9. Croft W.B., Xu J. Query Expansion using local and global document analysis. Proceeding of the 19th Annual International ACM SIGIR Conference on research and development in Information retrieval (SIGIR 96', Zurich, Switzerland, August 18-22,)1996.
10. Croft W.B., Jing, Y. Corpus-Based Stemming Using Co-occurrence of Word Variants. Transactions On Information Systems Volume 16, number 1 pp 61-81, 1998.
11. Croft W.B., Xu J. Improving Effectiveness of information retrieval with local context analysis. ACM Transaction on Information systems Volume 18, Number 1, January 2000, Pages 79 – 112
12. Koji EGUCHI. Incremental Query expansion Using local information of clusters, Proceedings of the 4th World Multiconference on systemics, Cybernetics and informatics (SCI 2000), Vol.2, pp310-316, 2000.
13. Korfhage R. Information storage and retrieval. Wiley Computer Publishing 0-471-14-338 3, 1997.
14. Kwok K. L. TREC-6 English and chinese retrieval experiments using PIRCS. In: D. K. Harman, NIST SP, 6th International Conference on Text Retrieval, Gaithersburg, MD.

15. Mothe J. Correspondance analysis method applied to document re-ranking, Rapport interne IRIT/00-22 R, 2000
16. Robertson S., Hull D. The TREC-9 filtering track final report, TREC-9, 2000
17. Rocchio J. J. Relevance feedback in information retrieval, In G. Salton, editor, The Smart retrieval System, Experiments in Automatic Document processing,. Prentice Hall Inc., Engelwoods Cliffs, NJ, 1971.
18. Sparck J. Automatic Keywords Classification for Information Retrieval, Buterworths, London, 1971.
19. Salton G. The SMART retrieval system, Experiments in automatic document processin, Prentice Hall Inc., Englewood Cliffs, NJ, 1971.
20. Yonggang Q., Frei H. F. Concept based query expansion. In proceedings of the 16th ACM SIGIR Conference on Research and development in information retrieval, pages 160-169, Pittsburgh, PA, USA, 1993.

A Study on Using Genetic Niching for Query Optimisation in Document Retrieval

Mohand Boughanem[1] and Lynda Tamine[2]

[1] IRIT SIG Université de Toulouse III, 118 Route de Narbonne, 31062 Toulouse, France
bougha@irit.fr
[2] ISYCOM/ GRIMM Université de Toulouse II, 5 Allées A. Machado, 31058 Toulouse Cedex, France
tamine@univ-tlse2.fr

Abstract. This paper presents a new genetic approach for query optimisation in document retrieval. The main contribution of the paper is to show the effectiveness of the genetic niching technique to reach multiple relevant regions of the document space. Moreover, suitable merging procedures have been proposed in order to improve the retrieval evaluation. Experimental results obtained using a TREC sub-collection indicate that the proposed approach is promising for applications.

Keywords: Information retrieval , multiple query evaluation, genetic algorithm, niching

1. Introduction

The web is becoming a universal repository of human knowledge, which has allowed unprecedent sharing of ideas and information in a very large scale. As an immediate consequence, the area of information retrieval has grown well beyond its primary goal of indexing text and searching for useful document in a collection. Nowadays, research in information retrieval includes modelling, system architecture, data visualisation, etc.

 The focus of our study is on the retrieval process of an information retrieval system using query operations. In fact, as observed with web search engines, the users might need to reformulate their queries in the hope of retrieving additional useful documents. Several approaches for improving the user query formulation have been proposed in information retrieval area. The approaches are grouped into two main categories. In the first category, relevance feedback methods are used for query expansion and term reweighting [22], [24] ,[21].

In the second category, the global approach is based on information derived from the context of the document retrieved. Two main strategies have been proposed: local clustering [1], [28] and global analysis [20] [25] or a combination of both local and global context [18].

F. Crestani, M. Girolami, and C.J. van Rijsbergen (Eds.): ECIR 2002, LNCS 2291, pp. 135-149, 2002.
© Springer-Verlag Berlin Heidelberg 2002

In this work, we propose a strategy for multiple query reformulation using both relevance feedback techniques and context query improvement methods. More precisely, we exploit genetic techniques to handle the process of query optimisation.

Genetic Algorithms (GA) can be viewed as search procedures that try to find in a solution search space S, a solution s[*] that maximise a function f called the fitness function. GA use some principle of natural selection and genetics [13]. The GA processes a population of individuals that evolve according to crossover and mutation operators.

Genetic techniques processing query optimisation have been proposed by several authors.

Gordon [12] adopted a GA to derive better descriptions of documents. Each document is assigned N descriptions represented by a set of indexing terms. Genetic operators and relevance judgement are applied to the descriptions in order to build the best document descriptions. The author showed that the GA produces better document descriptions than the ones generated by the probabilistic model. Redescription improved the relative density of co-relevant documents by 39,74% after twenty generations and 56,61% after forty generations.

Yang & Korfhage [29] proposed a GA for query optimisation by reweighting the query term indexing without query expansion. They used a selection operator based on a stochastic sample, a blind crossover at two crossing points, and a classical mutation to renew the population of queries.

The experiments showed that the queries converge to their relevant documents after six generations.

Kraft & al [16] apply GA programming in order to improve the weighted Boolean query formulations. Their first experiments showed that the GA programming is a viable method for deriving good queries.

Horng & Yeh [15] propose a novel approach to automatically retrieve keywords and then uses genetic techniques to tune the keywords weights. The effectiveness of the approach is demonstrated by comparing the results obtained to those using a PAT-tree based approach.

These diffrent works show that the genetic approach is suitable for query optimisation. However, there is still some open questions:

- How to elleviate the genetic query drift in order to reach multiple relevant regions of the document space?
- How to define the optimal strategy of combination results?

In this work, we address these questions. Indeed, our goal is to exploit a suitable genetic technique for solving multimodal problems, named niching [11], [17]. Rather than processing a traditional GA which finally generates a unique optimal query corresponding to similar descriptors of assumed relevant documents, the integration of the niching method will tune the genetic exploration in direction of the multiple relevant documents. Furthermore, we propose some utilities to perform the merging of evaluation results.

The remaining of the paper is organised as follows. Section 2 gives an introduction of genetic niching techniques. Section 3 gives the main principles of our approach for query optimisation. Section 4 presents the results and discussion of experiments carried out on a sub-collection of TREC.

2. Multiomodal Optimisation Using Genetic Niching

GA is stochastic optimisation methods based on principles of evolution and heredity [13]. A GA maintains a population of potential solutions to a given optimisation problem. Each individual is defined using a genotype corresponding to its structure characteristics and also a phenotype corresponding to it's meaning representation in the context of the current optimisation problem. The population of individuals is renewed at each generation using both a fitness measure to evaluate the individuals quality and genetic transformations to reproduce the fittest ones. The children of each generation are produced using selection, crossover and mutation operators. At the termination of the process, a classical GA produces a unique optimal solution corresponding to the fittest individual produced at the last generation.

However, the goal of a multimodal optimisation process is to find multiple and diverse optima across the search space of a given problem. Convergence may occur to some degree within local regions but diversity must prevail across the most prominent regions. But, it is well known in GA theory that the selection pressure causes the phenomena of *genetic drift* which corresponds to the convergence in local regions. Thus, various techniques for reducing the selection pressure have been proposed [2], [11], [9] but are not overly selective as they generally enable to reach geographically close solutions.

Dejong [8] has proposed another technique based on an iterative execution of the GA.Using the assumption that the probabilities of reaching the multiple optima are equal, the number of executions required is computed using the following formula:

$$p * \sum_{i=1}^{p} \frac{1}{i} \cong p * (\alpha + \log p)$$

p : number of optima
$\alpha = 0.577$, Euler constant

However, this method gives bad results in real life applications [26].

In this study, we restrict our efforts on niching techniques. Various other techniques for promoting genetic diversity are presented in [17], [14]. A niching method is based on the formation of subpopulations which explore different regions of the search space.We present in the following, the most common approaches.

2.1. Sequential Niching

The approach is based on a sequential location of multiple niches using an iterative run of a traditional GA.Beasly & al [3] present a sophisticated strategy where at the end of each run, the algorithm proposed depresses the fitness function at all points with a certain radius of the fittest solutions. This transformation encourages the optimisation process to explore other area of the search space.

2.2. Ecological Niching

This approach is based on the creation and exploitation of multiple environments of evolution. The basic theory of the ecological niching approach propose a simultaneously coevolution of subpopulations of individuals which are implicitly able to use food resources. Individuals that are unable to properly use resources die. Thus, the environment varies over time in its distribution of food resources, but individuals that are geographically close tend to experience the same environment [17]. The sharing [10] and clearing techniques [19] presented below are based on this ecological inspiration.

2.2.1. Sharing Technique. Goldberg & Richardson [10] presented an implementation of the concept known as the *sharing method*. In this study, each individual in a niche can consume a fraction of the available resources: the greater the population size of the niche, the smaller the fraction. This leads towards a steady state in which subpopulation sizes are proportional to the amount of the corresponding available resources. The general formula of sharing fitness function is the following [10]:

$$f'(x) = \frac{f(x)}{\sum_{y \in Pop} sh(dist(x, y))}$$

x,y : individuals of the population Pop
f(x) : initial fitness function
sh(dist(x,y)) : sharing function

The sharing function depends on the distance between two individuals of the population. The simplified version is the following form [10]:

$$sh(dist(x, y)) = \begin{cases} 1 - \left(\dfrac{dist(x, y)}{\delta_{sh}} \right)^{\alpha} & \text{if } dist(x, y) < \delta_{sh} \\ 0 & otherwise \end{cases}$$

α : constant
δ_{sh} : dissimilarity threshold

The distance function can be defined in the genotypic or phenotypic space search [9] or their combination [14].
Mahfoud [17] applied the principle of perfect discrimination of the niches which has two main consequences:
-    each individual in a given niche, regardless of the distance measure , is always closer to every individual of its own niche than to any individual of another niche,
-    the difference measure is able to determine whether two individuals are members of the same niche.

The author concludes that the sharing technique is most effective in cases of no overlap niches.

2.2.2. Clearing Technique. The clearing technique [19] is a niching method based on the sharing ecological inspiration. It is applied after evaluating the fitness of individuals and before applying the selection operator.Like the sharing method, the clearing algorithm uses a dissimilarity measure between individuals to determinate if they belong to the same subpopulation or not. In contrast, the clearing procedure fully attributes the whole resource of a niche to a single individual: the winner. The winner takes all rather than sharing resources with the other individuals of the same niche. Comparatively to the sharing technique, the complexity of the clearing procedure is lower and is more compatible with elitist strategies [19].

3. Our Approach: Genetic Niching for Query Optimisation

The retrieval process as shown in figure 1, is based on an iterative feedback evaluation of query niches. A niche represents a set of individual queries exploring a specific region of the document space according to their evaluation results. The genotype representation of an individual query is of the form Q_u (q_{u1}, q_{u2}, ..., q_{uT}).

T : Total number of stemmed terms automatically extracted from the documents
q_{ui} : weight of the term i in Q_u

The phenotype of an individual query is traduced by its evaluation results in the IRS. The general query optimisation process is done as follows:

```
Begin
    Submit the initial query and do the search
    Judge the top thousand documents
    Build the initial population
    Repeat
        For each niche of the population
        do the search
        build the local list of documents
        Endfor
    Build a merged list
    Renew the niches
    Judge the top fifteen documents
    Compute the fitness of each individual query
    For each niche N^(s) of the population
        Repeat
        parent1= Selection (N^(s))
        parent2= Selection (N^(s))
        Crossover (Pc , parent1, parent2,son)
        Mutation (Pm , son, sonmut)
        Add_Niche (sonmut,N^(s+1)
        Until Niche_size (N^(s+1)) = Niche_size (N^(s))
    Endfor
    Until a fixed number of feedback iterations
End
```

3.1. The Niching Method

In the current study, we applied the sharing technique to build the niches. Our choice is motivated by the fact that we attempt to explore widely the document space.We hope that the analysis of our first experiments using this technique will give us suitable utilities in order to exploit in the future, other niching techniques like the clearing one.

Regardless of the niching method used, the fitness function must be correlated with the standard goodness measure in IR that is average and precision. Considering this characteristic,we propose two distinct fitness function formulations. Each one is related to a specific strategy of formation of the niches.

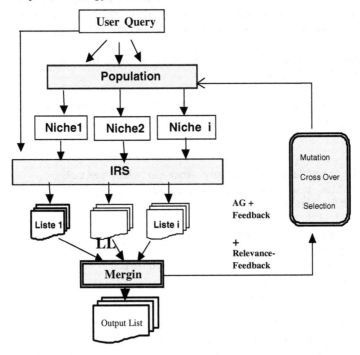

Fig. 1. The genetic retrieval process

3.1.1. Niching Using Genotypic Sharing.
In this case, a niche is a set of individual queries having closed genotypes. The sharing function is the following:

$$sh(dist(Q_u^{(s)}, Q_v^{(s)})) = \begin{cases} 1 & \text{if } dist(Q_u^{(s)}, Q_v^{(s)}) < \delta \\ 0 & \text{otherwise} \end{cases}$$

$Q_u^{(s)}$: individual query at the generation s of the GA
dist : Euclidian distance
δ : niching threshold ($\delta > 0$)

The function has the following properties:

1. $0 \le sh(dist(Q_u^{(s)}, Q_v^{(s)})) \le 1$

2. $sh(0) = 1$

3. $\lim\limits_{dist(Q_u^{(s)}, Q_v^{(s)}) \to \infty} sh(dist(Q_u^{(s)}, Q_v^{(s)})) = 0$

Furthermore, the niches are perfectly distinct.
The fitness function is computed using the formula:

$$Fitness(Q_u^{(s)}) = \frac{QFitness(Q_u^{(s)})}{\sum\limits_{Q_v^{(s)} \in Pop} sh(dist(Q_u^{(s)}, Q_v^{(s)}))}$$

where :

$$QFitness(Q_u^{(s)}) = \frac{\dfrac{1}{|Dr|} * \Sigma_{dr \in Dr} J(dr, Q_u^{(s)})}{\dfrac{1}{|Dnr|} * \Sigma_{dnr Dnr} J(dnr, Q_u^{(s)})}$$

dr: relevant document
dnr: irrelevant document
Dr: set of relevant documents retrieved across the GA generations
Dr: set of irrelevant documents retrieved across the GA generations
J(D$_j$, Q$_u$$^{(s)}$): Jaccard measure

3.1.2. Niching Using Phenotypic Sharing. In this case, the formation of the niches is based on the results (the documents retrieved) of their individual query members rather on their genotypic similarity. The niche structure is defined according to the coniche operators as following:

$$(Q_u^{(s)} \equiv_N Q_v^{(s)}) \Leftrightarrow (|(Ds(Q_u^{(s)}, L)) \cap (Ds(Q_v^{(s)}, L)|) > Coniche\_Limit)$$

Q$_u$$^{(s)}$: indivudial query at generation (s) of the GA
Ds(Q$_u$$^{(s)}$,L): the L top documents retrieved by Q$_u$$^{(s)}$
Coniche _ Limit: the min number of common documents retrieved by queries of the same niche

In order to maintain distinct niches, we assume to affect an individual query once, to the niche of lower capacity. The fitness function is computed using a formula built on the Guttaman model:

$$\sum_{dr\in Dr^{(s)},dnr\in Dnr^{(s)}} J(Q_u^{(s)},dr)-J(Q_u^{(s)},dnr)$$

$$Fitness(Q_u^{(s)})=1+\frac{\sum_{dr\in Dr^{(s)},dnr\in Dnr^{(s)}} J(Q_u^{(s)},dr)-J(Q_u^{(s)},dnr)}{\left|\sum_{dr\in Dr^{(s)},dnr\in Dnr^{(s)}} J(Q_u^{(s)},dr)-J(Q_u^{(s)},dnr)\right|}$$

J: Jaccard measure
$Dr^{(s)}$: set of relevant documents retrieved at the generation(s) of the GA
$Dnr^{(s)}$: set of non relevant documents retrieved at the generation(s) of the GA
dr: relevant document
dnr: irrelevant document

3.2. Genetic Operators

The genetic operators defined in our approach [27] are not classical ones as they are not based on the basic structure proposed in GA theory [11]. They have been adopted to take advantage of techniques developed in IR. Thus, we qualify them as knowledge based operators. Adding to this, they are restrictively applied to the niches in order to focus the search in the corresponding directions of the document space. The selection procedure is based on a roulette wheel selection. Crossover and mutation perform a query reformulation using both feedback technique and local context information. The crossover is applied to a pair of individuals that are selected in the same niche, according to the crossover probability Pc. The mutation is applied to an individual query according to a mutation Pm. It consists essentially of reweighting a query term using a relevance measure formula.

3.3. Merging Method

At each generation of the GA, the system presents to the user a limited list of new documents. These documents are selected from the whole ones retrieved by all the individual queries of the population, using a specific merging method.
Indeed, we investigate two main methods for building the merged list according to two different rank formula.

3.3.1. Full Merging. This merging method runs in two steps.
Step 1:
A ranked list of documents is obtained from each niche of the population by computing the following relevance measure:

$$Rel_{Ni}^{(s)}(dj)=\frac{1}{|Ni|}\sum_{Q_u^{(s)}\in Ni} RSV(Q_u^{(s)},dj)$$

$RSV(Q_u^{(s)},d)$: RSV (Retrieval Status Value) of the document at the generation (s) of the GA
N_i : ith niche at the current generation of the GA

Step 2:
The local lists of the documents corresponding to the different niches of the population are merged into a single list using the rank formula:

$$Rel^{(s)}(dj) = \sum_{i=1}^{Nb\_Niche^{(s)}} Average\_Fit(N_i) * Rel_{Ni}^{(s)}(dj)$$

$$Average\_Fit(N_i) = \frac{1}{|N_i|} \sum_{Q_u^{(s)} \in N_i} Fitness(Q_u^{(s)})$$

Nb_Niche$^{(s)}$: number of niches at the generation s of the GA

The main feature of this relevance measure formula is the use of the fitness value of the niches in order to adjust the global ranking value of the output list of documents. Thus, ranking order given by the fittest niches is more considered when building the outcome list of documents.

3.3.2. Selective Merging. This method runs in a single step. Rather than considering the fittest niches, we consider in this case the fittest individual queries and perform a global merging of the corresponding documents retrieved using the rank formula:

$$Rel^{(s)}(dj) = \sum_{Nj \in Pop^{(s)}} \sum_{Q_u^{(s)} \in N_j^{(s)}} Fitness(Q_u^{(s)^{**}}) x RSV(Q_u^{(s)}, dj)$$

Pop$^{(s)}$: population at the generation (s) of the GA
*$Q_u^{(S)}$ ** : individual queries characterised by a fitness value higher than the average fitness of Pop$^{(s)}$*

The main characteristic of this merging method is the use of the real fitness value of the fittest individual queries rather than the average fitness of the corresponding niches. Thus, we may reduce the error on the relevance assumption of the documents issued from their evaluation.

4. Experiments and Results

The experiments were carried out on a sub-collection of TREC-4 corpus. The documents we used are the AP88 newswire. We used 24 queries of TREC-4 (query numbered 1-24). The experiments were run using the Mercure IRS [4] that process the spreading activation technique. Because of the multiple iteration aspect of the search and the use of relevance judgements,the results reported in the paper are based on a residual ranking evaluation [7].

Prior experiments [5] allowed us to evaluate the main parameters of the GA: crossover and mutation probability. The best performances have been reached for respectively the following values: 0.7, 0.07 and then were chosen for all the remaining experiments presented in this paper.

4.1. Effect of the Genetic Query Optimisation

At this level, we address the question of how well our genetic combination performs relative to a single query evaluation. For this aim, we compare the performance results issued from two distinct runs:

-   the first one based on a genetic combination of multiple query evaluation results as described above
-   the second one is based on a classic single query evaluation as performed in Mercure IRS

In order to make sens to our comparative evaluation, we consider that an iterative single query evaluation process may be based on the scanning of the overall output list, beginning from the top in direction of the bottom, using sub-lists presented to the user. This means that we analyze at each iteration, the following sub-list of documents (a sub-list is composed of 15 documents in the case of our experiments) ordered after the above list presented to the user according to the output list.

Finally, we compare the retrieval performance of residual lists issued from the same iteration of both single query evaluation and genetic combination process.

Table 1 presents the details of the evaluation results (measured by average precision (Avg Prec), precision at 15 documents cutoff (Prec @ 15) and number of relevant documents retrieved (Rel. Doc)) of the two runs using the merging methods previously presented.

Table 1. Retrieval performances

Single Query Evaluation				
	Iter1	Iter2	Iter3	Iter4	Iter5
Avg Prec	0.12	0.07	0.05	0.03	0.02
Prec @ 15	0.30	0.25	0.22	0.18	0.17
Rel. Doc	110(110)	92(203)	82(285)	65(351)	61(412)
Genetic Multiple Query Evaluation				
Full merging				
	Iter1	Iter2	Iter3	Iter4	Iter5
Avg Prec	0.21	0.04	0.07	0.05	0.03
Prec @ 15	0.5	0.18	0.20	0.20	0.19
Rel. Doc	180(180)	65(245)	86(331)	74(406)	69(475)
Selective merging				
	Iter1	Iter2	Iter3	Iter4	Iter5
Avg Prec	0.21	0.10	0.07	0.05	0.03
Prec @ 15	0.5	0.31	0.24	0.20	0.19
Rel. Doc	180(180)	88(266)	97(366)	75(442)	78(520)

Table 2 provides a summary of the performance due to our proposed approach measured by the improvement achieved comparatively to the single query evaluation method.

Table 2. Improvements of the genetic approach

Genetic Multiple Query Evaluation					
Full Merging					
	Iter1	**Iter2**	**Iter3**	**Iter4**	**Iter5**
Avg Prec	75%	-43%	40%	67%	50%
Prec @ 15	67%	-28%	-9%	11%	12%
Rel. Doc	63%	20%	16%	15%	15%
Selective merging					
	Iter1	**Iter2**	**Iter3**	**Iter4**	**Iter5**
Avg Prec	75%	43%	40%	67%	50%
Prec @ 15	67%	24%	9%	11%	12%
Rel. Doc	63%	32%	28%	25%	26%

As the tables illustrate,the genetic multiple query evaluation approach yields large improvements in average precision, precision at 15 documents cutoff and number of relevant documents, for both merging methods. We note however that the improvements obtained by using the selective merging method are better than those obtained using the full one. In light of these results, it would seem that the query fitness value is more significant than the niches average fitness when merging the evaluation results. This might be due to the probable variation of the performances of the individual queries belonging to the same niche.Furthermore, the results suggest that we should perform a prior selection of the individual queries before merging the corresponding results.

According to these results, we choose the selective merging method to perform the remaining experiments.

4.2. Comparative Evaluation of the Sharing Techniques

This experiment compares the sharing techniques proposed. We report in table 3 the number of relevant documents in top 15 retrieved at each iteration of the GA and cumulative number of relevant documents retrieved at that point, using both genotypic sharing and phenotypic sharing.

Table 3. Comparative evaluation of the sharing techniques

	Iter1	**Iter2**	**Iter3**	**Iter4**	**Iter5**
Genotypic sharing	177(177)	114(291)	93(384)	69(453)	56(510)
Improvement	38%	41%	24%	25%	22%
Phenotypic sharing	180(180)	88(268)	97(366)	75(442)	78(520)
Improvement	63%	32%	28%	25%	26%

Table 3 reveals that the phenotypic sharing technique is more effective than the genotypic one. More precisely, the cumulative number of relevant documents retrieved at the fifth generation of the GA is 510 using the genotypic sharing and 520 using the phenotypic sharing. The number of relevant documents retrieved by iteration is also generally higher in the case of using the phenotypic sharing.

These results are according with previous analyses presented in (Mahfoud, 1995) (Talbi, 1999) on the goodness of the phenotypic sharing technique. The main reason might be due to *the meaning distance* between the genotypic individual representation and its significant phenotypic one.

4.3. Effect of the Niching Technique

The main goal of using niching technique is to reach different optima for a specific optimisation problem. In the context of our study, niching would allow to recall relevant documents with quite different descriptors. In order to evaluate its precise effect on the search results, we have organised the query collection test into bins. Each bin is characterised by a corresponding average similarity value between relevant documents in fixed intervals: [20 25[, [25 30[, [30 35[.

Table 4 shows, for each bin, the cumulative number of relevant documents retrieved at the fifth generation of the GA.

Table 4. Effect of the niching technique

	[20 25[	[25 30[	[30 35[
No niching	19	263	226
With niching	27	275	219
Improvement	42%	45%	-3%

It can be seen that niching technique improves the results for the first and the second bin with respectively 42% and 45% comparatively to the baseline. In contrast, the performances decrease in the case of the third bin. This might be due to the fact that because of the related quite important distance between relevant documents, the convergence of the GA becomes slow.

Considering this assumption, we have developed this experimentation by running the 6th iteration of the GA for especially the third bin of queries. Table 5 shows the effect of the niching technique on the cumulative number in the top 15 retrieved at this iteration.

Table 5. Effect of niching at the 6th iteration of the GA

Query number	No niching	With niching
22	64	83
11	41	40
25	14	14
10	40	40
16	6	9
12	37	33
21	9	10
17	55	53
14	16	14
	282	296

We notice clearly that the results are better when using niching technique at the following iteration of the GA (4,9 % of improvement). This suggests that in order to increase the convergence of the GA, it might be interesting to use more suitable combination between the coniche operator definition and prior user relevance judgements.

5 Conclusion

In this paper, we have described a genetic approach for query optimisation in information retrieval. This approach takes into account the relevance multimodality problem in document retrieval by using an interactive retrieval process based on niching technique.

Prior experiments have been performed on TREC6 comparing genetic query evaluation and single pass search equivalent to Rocchio type search (Boughanem & al, 2000). The results have shown that the genetic approach is more effective particularly to improve recall.

We have showed in this study, that adding niching technique associated with suitable merging formula improves the exploration of the document space. Indeed, the approach has been applied to a sub-collection of TREC4 with success.

Additional work is certainly necessary to analyze the evolution of the niches structure across the GA generations in order to improve the merging procedures.

Finally, we believe that genetic niching provide interesting possibilities to solve the issue of relevance optimisation multimodality in document retrieval.

References

1. A. Attar & S. Franenckel (1977). Local Feedback in Full Text Retrieval Systems. Journal of the ACM, 397-417, 1977
2. J E.Baker (1985). Adaptive Selection Methods for Genetic Algorithm, in Proceedings of the first International Conference on Genetic Algorithm (ICGA) pp 101-111
3. D. Beasly, D.R Bull & R. R Martin (1993). A sequential niche technique for multimodal function optimization, Evolutionary Computation, 1(2) : pp 101-125
4. M. Boughanem (1997). Query modification based on relevance backpropagation, In Proceedings of the 5th International Conference on Computer Assisted Information Searching on Internet (RIAO'97), Montreal pp 469-487
5. M. Boughanem, C. Chrisment & L.Tamine (1999). Genetic Approach to Query Space Exploration. Information Retrieval Journal volume 1 N°3 , pp175-192
6. M. Boughanem, C. Chrisment, J. Mothe, C. Soule-Dupuy & L. Tamine (2000). Chapter in Connectionist and Genetic Approaches to perform IR, Soft Computing, Techniques and Application, Crestani & Pasi Eds, pp 173-196
7. Chang Y K, Cirillo G C and Razon J (1971). Evaluation of feedback retrieval using modified freezing, residual collections and test and control groups. In: the Smart retrieval system: Experiments in automatic document processig, Prentice Hall Inc, chap 17, pp 355-370

8.   K. A Dejong (1975). An analysis of the behavior of a class of genetic adaptive systems, Doctocal dissertation University of Michigan,. Dissertation abstracts International 36 (10), 5140B. University Microfilms N°76-9381

9.   C.M Fonseca & P. J Fleming (1995). Multi-objective genetic algorithms made easy: selection, sharing and mating restrictions, In IEEE International Conference in Engineering Systems: Innovations and Application, pp 45-52, Sheffield, UK

10. Goldberg D.E & Richardson (1987). Genetic algorithms with sharing for multimodal function optimization, in Proceedings of the second International Conference on Genetic Algorithm (ICGA) , pp 41-49

11. Goldberg D.E (1989) : Genetic Algorithms in Search, Optimisation and Machine Learning, Edition Addison Wesley 1989

12. M. Gordon (1988) . Probabilistic and genetic algorithms for document retrieval, Communications of the ACM pp 1208-1218

13. Holland J. (1962). Concerning Efficicent Adaptive Systems.In M.C Yovits, G.T Jacobi, &G.D Goldstein(Eds) Self Organizing Systems pp 215-230 Washinton : Spartan Books, 1962

14. J. Horn (1997). The nature of niching : Genetic algorithms and the evolution of optimal cooperative populations, PhD thesis, university of Illinois at Urbana, Champaign

15. Horng J.T & Yeh C.C (2000). Applying genetic algorithms to query optimisation in document retrieval, In Information Processing and Management 36(2000) pp 737-759

16. Kraft DH, Petry FE, Buckles BP and Sadisavan T (1995). Applying genetic algorithms to information retrieval system via relevance feedback, In Bosc and Kacprzyk J Eds, Fuzziness in Database Management Systems Studies in Fuzziness Series, Physica Verlag, Heidelberg, Germany pp 330-344

17. Mahfoud S. W (1995). Niching methods for genetic algorithms, PhD thesis, university of Illinois at Urbana, Champaign, 1995

18. R. Mandala, T. Tokunaga & H. Takana. Combining multiple evidence from different types of thesaurus for query expansion, In Proceedings of the 22 th Annual International ACM SIGIR, Conference on research and development in information retrieval, August 1999, Buckley USA

19. Petrowski A. (1997) . A clearing procedure as a niching method for genetic algorithms. In the Proceedings of the IEE International Conference on Evolutionary Computation (ICEC), Nagoya, Japan

20. Y. Qiu & H.P. Frei, (1993). Concept Based Query Expansion. In Proceedings of the 16th ACM SIGIR Conference on Research and Development in Information Retrieval, 160-169, Pittsburg, USA 1993

21. S. Robertson, S. Walker & M.M Hnackock Beaulieu (1995): Large test collection experiments on an operational interactive system: Okapi at TREC, in Informatio Processing and Management (IPM) journal, pp 260-345.

22. Rocchio(1971). Relevance Feedback in Information Retrieval, in The Smart System Experiments in Automatic Document Processing, G.Salton, Editor, Prentice-Hall, Inc., Englewood Cliffs, NJ, pp 313-23, 1971

23. G. Salton (1968). Automatic Information and Retrieval, Mcgrawhill Book Company, N. Y., 1968

24. G. Salton & C.Buckley (1990). Improving Retrieval Performance By Relevance Feedback, Journal of The American Society for Information Science, Vol. 41, N°4, pp 288-297, 1990

25. Schutze H.& Pedersen J. (1997). A Cooccurrence- Based Thesaurus and two Applications to Information Retrieval, Information Processing & Management, 33(3) : pp 307-318, 1997

26. E.G Talbi (1999). Métaheuristiques pour l'optimisation combinatoire multi-objectifs : Etat de l'art, Rapport CNET (France Telecom) Octobre 1999

27. L. Tamine & M. Boughanem (20001). Un algorithme génétique spécifique à une évaluation multi-requêtes dans un système de recherche d'information, journal Information Intelligence et Interaction, volume 1 n°=1, september 2001

28. J. Xu & W.B. Croft (1996). Query Expansion Using Local and Global Document Analysis. In Proc. ACM SIGIR Annual Conference on Research and Development, Zurich, 1996

29. J.J Yang & R.R Korfhage (1993). Query optimisation in information retrieval using genetic Algorithms, in Proceedings of the fifth International Conference on Genetic Algorithms (ICGA), pp 603-611, Urbana, IL

Concept Based Adaptive IR Model Using FCA-BAM Combination for Concept Representation and Encoding

R.K. Rajapakse and M. Denham

Centre for Neural and Adaptive Systems, University of Plymouth, UK
rohan/mike@soc.plym.ac.uk

Abstract. The model described here is based on the theory of Formal Concept Analysis (FCA). Each document is represented in a Concept Lattice: a structured organisation of concepts according to a subsumption relation and is encoded in a Bidirectional Associative Memory (BAM): a two-layer heterogeneous neural network architecture. The document retrieval process is viewed as a continuous conversation between queries and documents, during which documents are allowed to learn a consistent set of significant concepts to help its retrieval. A reinforcement learning strategy based on relevance feedback information makes the similarity of relevant documents stronger and nonrelevant documents weaker for each query.

1. Introduction

The primary objective of our research is to improve the effectiveness of the document retrieval. Our approach is two-fold:

1. investigate for a better scheme for document (and query) representation. We attempt to make use of the FCA-BAM combination to achieve this goal.

2. attempt to make use of a reinforcement learning strategy based on relevance feedback information for learning well representative set of concepts for document representation.

Almost all the existing IR models make use of either single terms (keywords) or phrases (two or more adjoining terms) to represent the basic unit of matching: a *concept* [17]. Exceptional to these are the network models that try to learn the implicit relations between keywords to build a form of implicit concepts to assist the IR task and the Knowledge based techniques in which additional (related) keywords are incorporated with the keywords extracted from the text to enhance the query or document(s). Most of these approaches do not extract concepts and their relationships explicitly straight from the text and also do not store them in a hierarchical structure representing specificity-generality relationships between concepts which we suppose is important for deciding the relevancy of a document. In addition the said hierarchical structure must support efficient access to those specific-generic concepts as desired.

F. Crestani, M. Girolami, and C.J. van Rijsbergen (Eds.): ECIR 2002, LNCS 2291, pp. 150–168, 2002.

In our work, great deal of effort was extended to the direct extraction of meaningful ideas/concepts from text and their representation in a formal framework to assist the IR task. The major contribution of our work is the investigation of the applicability of concept lattices, that are based on the theory of the formal concept analysis and lattice theory, to the representation of concepts/ideas expressed in natural language (English) text, and encoding such concept lattices in Bidirectional Associative Memories (BAMs) in order to effectively and efficiently manipulate the concepts captured to support Information Retrieval. An interesting feature of concept lattices is that the concepts are hierarchically organized according to a subsumption order relation, that defines a specificity-generality relationship between concepts. BAMs have been recognised as a simple neural network that is able to learn a concept lattice in its two-layered architecture. Once a concept lattice is encoded in a BAM, it can directly give the most specific or most generic concept of the concept lattice it has learnt for a given set of interested objects or attributes, by presenting them to the corresponding layer(s) of the BAM. This avoids the complex searching and traversing otherwise required for accessing concepts.

Our model views the document retrieval process as a continuous conversation between queries and documents. Through these conversations, it attempts to learn a consistent set of significant concepts for each document resulting queries similar to already seen ones to retrieve the documents that were retrieved for those similar queries and judged as relevant in the past (improves recall) and conversely queries similar to already seen ones not to retrieve the documents that were retrieved for those similar queries but judged as not relevant (improves precision). This is achieved through a reinforcement learning strategy based on relevance feedback, in which the document representation is improved to make the similarity between a query and a retrieved relevant document stronger and that between a query and a retrieved nonrelevant document weaker.

We present the theoretical background for the techniques used (FCA & BAM) and discuss the suitability of such a representation scheme for Information Retrieval. The analogy between the representation of formal concepts in a structured manner in a concept lattice and the representation of ideas/concepts in human brain in the process of human understanding is briefed. The IR process, including what is (what concepts) matched with what (concepts) in the document, how a similarity value is computed and how the relevance feedback is used for reinforcement learning are detailed.

The work reported here is ongoing research work. Preliminary results using the proposed model and reinforcement learning process are encouraging. Future work will include making further improvements to the proposed model and finally evaluating its performances by comparing its results with published results on public document collections.

2. Formal Concept Analysis (FCA)

Formal Concept Analysis was first proposed by Rudolf Wille in 1982 [19,11] as a mathematical framework for performing data analysis. It provides a conceptual analytical tool for investigating and processing given information explicitly. Such data is be structured into units, which are formal abstractions of "*concepts*" of human thought allowing meaningful and comprehensible interpretation. FCA models the world as being composed of *objects* and *attributes*. It is assumed that an incident relation connects objects to attributes. The choice of what is an object and what is an attribute is dependent on the domain in which FCA is applied. Information about a domain is captured in a "formal context". A formal context is merely a formalization that encodes only a small portion of what is usually referred to as a "*context*".

A *Formal Context* $K = (G,M,I)$ consists of two sets G (set of objects) and M (set of attributes) and a relation I between G and M. A *Formal Concept* is defined on a Formal Context as a pair of sets (A,B) where A is a set of objects and B is a set of attributes, in which attributes in A are maximally possessed by the set of objects in B and the objects in A are the maximal set of objects possessing the set of attributes in B. A formal definition is given below.

A pair (A,B) of sets where $A \subseteq G$ and $B \subseteq M$ is a formal concept if :
$$A' = B \text{ and } B' = A ; \quad \text{(This is called the completeness constraint)} \tag{1}$$

where, $A' = \{ m \in M \mid gIm \text{ for all } g \in A \}$ (i.e. the set of attributes common to all the objects in A)   **AND** $B' = \{ g \in G \mid gIm \text{ for all } m \in B \}$ (i.e. the set of objects which have all attributes in B). gIm means "g is related to m" (e.g. a binary relation).

The set of all concepts of a context (G,M,I) which consists of all pairs (A,B) where $A \subseteq G$ and $B \subseteq M$ s.t. $A = B'$ and $B = A'$ is denoted by $B(G,M,I)$.

FCA models the specificity and generality relationships between two related concepts by means of sub-super relationship, which is formally defined as:

If (A_1,B_1) and (A_2,B_2) are concepts of a context, then (A_1,B_1) is called a subconcept of (A_2,B_2), if $A_1 \subseteq A_2$ (equivalently $B_1 \supseteq B_2$). In this case (A_2,B_2) is a superconcept of (A_1,B_1) and this sub-super concept relation is written as $(\mathbf{A_1,B_1}) \leq (\mathbf{A_2,B_2})$, i.e. a subconcept is a concept with less objects than any of its superconcepts (equivalently, a subconcept is a concept with more attributes than any of its superconcepts).

2.1 Concept Lattice

A set of all concepts of the context (G,M,I) (denoted by $B(G,M,I)$) when ordered with the order relation $\leq$ (a subsumption relation) defined above forms a *concept lattice* of the context and is denoted by $\underline{B}(G,M,I)$ [11].

A lattice is an ordered set V with an order relation in which for any given two elements x and y, the supremum and the infimum elements always exist in V [11]. Furthermore, such a lattice is called a *complete lattice* if supremum and infimum elements exist for any subset X of V [19,11]. The fundamental theorem of FCA states that the set of formal concepts of a formal context forms a complete lattice [11,9,19]. This complete lattice, which is composed of *formal concepts* is called a *concept lattice*.

Join/Meet Concepts

A Concept lattice can be visualized as a graph with nodes and edges/links (fig 1). Concepts at the nodes from which two or more lines run up are called *meet* concepts (i.e. nodes with more than one parent) and concepts at the nodes from which two or more lines run down are called *join* concepts (i.e. nodes with more than one child). An interesting feature of concept lattices is that we do not need to know explicitly all of these meet and join concepts to build the complete lattice, as they can be inferred from other concepts. A join (parent) node is inferred given all of its child nodes and a meet (child) node is inferred given all of its parent nodes. (See figure 1)

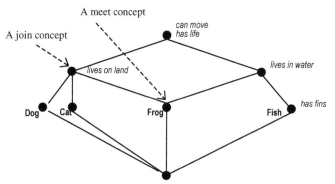

Fig. 1. Example concept lattice to illustrate join and meet concepts

A Join concept groups objects sharing the same attributes and a meet concept separate out objects that have combined attributes from different parents (groups of objects). Each of these join and meet concepts creates a new sub- or super- category or class of a concept.

3. Bidirectional Associative Memories (BAMs)

Based on the early associative memory models [1,14], Kosko [15,16] proposed a bi-directional associative neural network called Bidirectional Associative Memory (BAM). A BAM consists of two layers of neurones. The states (activities) of the neurons in the first Layer (X) are denoted by x_i $(i=1,...,k)$ and in the second layer (Y) by y_j $(j=1,...,l)$ where k and l are the number of neurons in the layers. The states x_i and y_j can be encoded either a binary (0 or 1) or a bipolar (+1 or -1) encoding. Each (i^{th}) neuron of the first layer is connected to each (j^{th}) neuron of the second layer, by a connection weight. A number of different weighting schemes can be found in the literature for setting the connection weights. Amongst are the one proposed by Kosko[15], the originator of BAMs and that proposed by Radim Bělohlávek [2].

A real threshold θ_i^x (θ_j^y) is assigned to the ith neuron of the first layer and the jth neuron of the second layer, respectively.

3.1 Dynamics of BAMs

Given a pair $<X,Y> = <<x_1,...,x_k>,<y_1,...y_l>> \in \{0,1\}^k \times \{0,1\}^l$ of patterns of signals, the signal X is fed to the first layer to obtain a new pair $<X,Y'>$, then Y' to the second layer to obtain $<X',Y'>$, and so on. The dynamics is given by the formulas:

$$y'_i = \begin{cases} 1 & for \quad \sum_{i=1}^{k} w_{ij}x'_i > \theta_j^y \\ y_j & for \quad \sum_{i=1}^{k} w_{ij}x'_i = \theta_j^y \\ 0 & for \quad \sum_{i=1}^{k} w_{ij}x'_i < \theta_j^y \end{cases} \quad x'_i = \begin{cases} 1 & for \quad \sum_{j=1}^{l} w_{ij}y'_j > \theta_i^x \\ x_i & for \quad \sum_{j=1}^{l} w_{ij}y'_j = \theta_i^x \\ 0 & for \quad \sum_{j=1}^{l} w_{ij}y'_j < \theta_i^x \end{cases} \quad (2)$$

The pair of patterns <X,Y> is called a stable point if the states of neurones, when set to <X,Y>, do not change under the above defined dynamics. Using appropriate energy function, Kosko [16] proved that such a network is stable for any weights w_{ij} and any thresholds θ_p^x, θ_j^y. Stability means that given any initial pattern <X,Y> of signals, the network eventually stops after a finite number of steps (feeding signal from layer to layer back and forth).

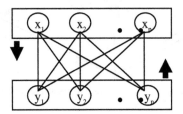

Fig. 2. Structure of a BAM

The aim of learning in the context of associative memories is to set the parameters of the network so that a prescribed training set of patterns is related in some way to the set of all stable points. Usually all training patterns have to become stable points (this is not always the case with learning concept lattices). Kosko proposed a kind of Hebbian learning, by which the weights w_{ij} are determined from the training set T = $\{<X_p,Y_p>|p \in P\}$ by

$$w_{ij} = \sum_{p \in P} bip(x_i^p).bip(y_j^p) \quad \text{where } bip() \text{ maps } 1 \text{ to } 1 \text{ and } 0 \text{ to } -1, \text{ i.e. changing}$$

the binary encoding to a bipolar one and P = {1,2,3....no.of patterns in T}. Thresholds are set to 0 [6].

3.2 BAMs for Storing Concept Lattices

In [2] Radim Belohlávek showed that BAMs can learn concept lattices. He observed that there are BAM stable points that cannot be interpreted as concepts. This raised the most important question "*weather there is a BAM corresponding to each concept lattice B(G,M,I) such that the set of all concepts of B(G,M,I) is precisely the set of all the stable points of the BAM ?*". Using the weight computation given below, Bělohlávek proved that there is a BAM, given by the weights W and thresholds θ such that Stab(W, θ)={<A,B>| <A,B> $\in B(G,M,I)$}, corresponding to the concept lattice given by the context <G,M,I> with G and M finite.

Bělohlávek 's weight computation formula is given by

$$w_{ij} = \begin{cases} 1 & if <g_i, m_j> \in I \\ -q & if <g_i, m_j> \notin I \end{cases} \qquad \text{For } i=1,\dots,k, \ j=1,\dots l \qquad (3)$$

where $q = \max\{k,l\}+1$. All the thresholds are set to $-1/2$.

We use this weighting scheme in our implementations described below to train BAMs with concepts lattices.

A Training Set for a BAM to Learn a Concept Lattice

A training set T consists of a set of concepts in the form (A,B), where elements of A comes from the set of objects G and elements of B from the set of attributes M of the context (G,M,I). Here the set G contains all the objects necessary to define the extents (A) of the concepts (A,B) in the training set and M contains all the attributes necessary to define the intents in the training set. This means that the elements in T are defined on (G,M,I). A conceptually consistent training set however needs its training patterns to obey the fundamental rule (completeness constraint) of the formal concept: $A'=B$ & $B'=A$ which ensures that the set of formal concepts in the training set are storable in the BAM.

Any given set of arbitrary concepts (a Training set T) which satisfies the above condition defines a concept lattice on the context (G,M,I) formed by all the objects and attributes of the concepts in T. This training set is a subset of $B(G,M,I)$ (set of all the concepts of the context (G,M,I)).   It also is a subset of the concept lattice $\underline{B}(G,M,I)$ of the context (G,M,I) .

What Actually a BAM Learns and Returns?

Given a set of training pairs of objects and attributes that satisfy the completeness constraint (i.e. they are formal concepts in a given context), a BAM learns the underlying concept lattice. As mentioned before, join and meet concepts that are inferred by the patterns in the training set are automatically detected and learnt by the BAM. For example, given four training patterns, one for each object: dog, cat, frog and fish (with all of their corresponding attributes) the concept lattice given in fig.1 is derived.

Unlike purely feed-forward neural network architectures, BAMs can accept input patterns from either layer. We can present a pattern with objects to the first layer (referred to as the object layer) or a pattern with attributes to the second layer (referred to as the attribute layer). The BAM returns the most specific concept containing all the objects of the input pattern in the first case and the most generic concept containing all the attributes of the input pattern in the second case. We use this interesting property during the extraction of candidate concepts from query and documents BAMs to match between concepts (as described in section 5.2).

Stable Points

An arbitrary pair consisting of a set of objects and a set of attributes extracted from text is not necessarily a stable point in a BAM. Also an actual training pattern used for training a BAM with a concept lattice does not necessarily become a stable point in the BAM. This is because:

1. A set of objects and set of attributes initially extracted from text might not be a formal concept as it might not comply to the completeness constraint (1).
2. A given input to a BAM may lead to retrieving an inferred *Join* or *Meet* concept instead of a concept(s) in the training set that contributed to infer the join or the meet concept.

4. Towards Concepts/Ideas Expressed in Natural Language

A number of questions have to be addressed before employing these techniques into IR tasks. These include: what is an object; what is an attribute; what is a concept/idea; how can we extract objects, attributes and concepts from textual material; what is the analogy between the order relationship defined for formal concepts and the ideas/concepts extracted from textual documents; what is the role of join/meet concepts in human understanding of natural language text etc. This section attempts to answer these questions.

4.1 Abstracting Ideas/Concepts in Human Understanding

The theory of concept lattices has been founded [11,19] based on a traditional understanding of concepts by which a concept is determined by its extent and intent. The extent of a concept (e.g. *DOG*) is the collection of all objects covered by the concept (the collection of all *dogs*), while the intent is the collection of all attributes (e.g. *to bark, to be a mammal*) covered by the concept. This interpretation of a concept can be directly employed in representing concepts expressed in natural language. The formation of an idea or a concept in the human mind during the understanding of natural language text is initially triggered by the objects (physical or conceptual) and attributes (properties of objects) in the text followed by the overall context of the subject being read and the reader's background knowledge of the subject.

The Two Entities: *Objects* and *Attributes*
In general, an object corresponds to the subject of the context, and attributes modify the meaning of the object to express the context in which the object is being used. For instance, a particular set of attributes of the object *DOG* may support the context of say *eating patterns of dogs,* while certain other set of attributes may support say the *sleeping patterns of dogs.* FCA captures these two important aspects/features, the *subject* and the *context* in its two entities *objects* and *attributes* to formulate an idea/concept. This makes FCA suitable for formulating and manipulating "human thoughts" (concepts) within computer systems.

4.2 Similarity of Super-Sub Order Relationship in Formal Concepts and Natural Ideas/Concepts

A sub-concept in FCA, defined as a concept with less objects and more attributes than its superconcept(s) means we need more attributes to define something specific compared to the less attributes needed to define something generic. Ideas/concepts stored in human mind may be structured in a similar manner, whereby we need more detail to learn a more specific idea/concept. For instance to define a *bird* we need to say it *can fly* and it *has a beak*, in addition to the information necessary to say that its an *animal*. However the frequently used generic attributes (in this case the attributes to specify bird is a living animal) are not usually used to express an idea during normal human conversations and writing. They are implicit. In general human brain has gained the necessary background knowledge in understanding frequently used common ideas when expressed just by the main object(s) of the subject. For instance, we never try to define what an animal is during conversations, instead we simply use the term *"animal"*. At some point during our learning process (implicit or explicit), we have absorbed all the necessary attributes to understand what an animal is. It is obvious however that encoding concepts/ideas in a computer requires all the information necessary to distinctly identify a particular idea/concept to be explicitly specified. These background general ideas/concepts are analogous to the superconcepts and the specific sub-categories/concepts of them are analogous to the subconcepts defined in the FCA formalization.

4.3 The Role of Join & Meet Concepts in Human Understanding

Categorising common objects (or ideas) together is a natural phenomenon in the human understanding. If you are asked to name few animals you can give a vast number of different animals as examples for animals. If you are then asked to name few animals which are carnivorous, you certainly have no problem of naming a set of animals who eat meat. You may have given names of some of these carnivorous animals as examples for animals for the first question as well. This means your brain knows how to categorise the same set of objects depending on the context (depending on the attributes that each object possesses). It is the same phenomenon that the *meet* and *join* concepts model in FCA.

These similarities between the formalization of concepts in FCA and ideas/concepts of human understanding/thought process mentioned above suggest that the way the humans formulate concepts, structure them and use them in the process of understanding and expressing ideas is analogous to the way concepts are formulated in FCM and are structured in a Concept Lattice.

5. The Model

The proposed model has 3 major components:

1. Preprocessor
2. Matcher
3. User feedback processor

Structure of the model is illustrated in the following diagram.

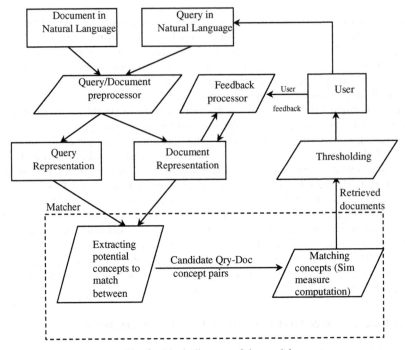

Fig. 3. Block diagram of the model

5.1 The Preprocessor

The most important component of all is the preprocessor. It is responsible for extracting concepts (objects, attributes & their relationships) from natural language text material (queries or documents), constructing a training set of concepts/patterns for the BAM, transforming the initial set of training concepts into a consistent set of formal concepts that can be represented in a concept lattice structure, and encoding the underlying concept lattice structure in a BAM.

Extracting Concepts

Extracting objects and their attributes from natural language text is partly a natural language understanding problem that has not yet been very successful, especially for unrestricted text. Even though the large amount of unrestricted text makes extracting desired features more difficult for IR, the fact that a deep and complete understanding of the text may not be necessary for IR makes a shallow and partial representation of the content of text sufficient [11]. We use a set of conventional natural language processing techniques such as part-of-speech tagging (POS) and syntactic chunking (of sentences into noun and verb phrases). The results of tagging and chunking together with a selected set of prepositions (in English language) such as *of, in, at* etc that appears as connecting words between noun groups are used to extract a shallow, but sufficiently representative set of objects and (their) attributes from documents (and also from queries) to form concepts to represent the text.

Noun-Phrase analysis has been used by a number of researchers for extracting features for document indexing for IR and has proved to be superior to full text indexing [11]. The way we use noun phrases, however is different to the way they are used in phrase-based document indexing. Each noun and verb group detected is assigned an identification label and a string representing the syntactic structure is constructed for each sentence using these labels. Note that text that does not belong to a noun or verb group is left unlabelled and used as it is. For example, the syntactic structure of the sentence *"[The dog] (chased) [the cat] away"* would looks like: $NG_1|VB_1|NG_2|away$, where NG_1 is the label for the first noun group (in this case *[The dog]*), NG_2 is the label for the second noun group and VB_1 is the label for the first verb group. | is the separator character.

The syntactic structures of the sentences thus constructed and their individual components are then further analysed for the identification of objects and attributes. We use a few rules that were developed after analysing the empirical results of POS tagging and chunking of textual material for this purpose.

Prepositions (Connectors) between Two Chunks

Use of Noun phrases for document indexing in general do not capture the relationships between noun groups. We capture the relationships between those noun groups that are connected by the prepositional connectors *in, on, of, with, to, into* and *from.* The relationships between noun groups inferred by these connectors can be interpreted as *object-attribute* relationships. It should be noted here that unlike in conceptual graphs, concept lattices do not keep relationship types (e.g. is_a, part-of etc). It only needs to know whether there is a object-attribute relationship between two terms/phrases. The set of connectors/prepositions mentioned were selected after analysing experimental results on the syntactic structure of sentences. This list is not complete by any means, but consists of the most frequent and useful connectors.

Syntactic Structure of Noun Groups

In most of the cases, noun groups contain several noun words and adjectives/modifiers within them. These words within a noun group have important relationships between them and therefore will be useful if extracted to form meaningful concepts. The POS tags attached to each word is helpful to analyse the syntactic structure within each noun group in order to detect useful object-attribute relationships between the words within the group. We make use of a number of rules developed after analysing experimental results on the syntactic structures of noun groups for this purpose (that are not detailed here).

For example, if the syntactic structure of a noun group is DT|JJ|NN   or JJ|NN (e.g. *"The*_DT *fat*_JJ *man*_NN") then a concept is formed as NN $\rightarrow$ JJ (i.e. *man* $\rightarrow$ *fat*). Here *"fat"* is an attribute of the object *"man"*. Here the tag _DT stands for a determinant, _JJ for an adjective and _NN for a noun.

Some noun groups were found to contain only noun words (no adjectives). (E.g. [*compute*_NN *keyboard*_NN]). In such cases it is difficult to determine which word(s) to be taken as the attribute and which word(s) as object(s). For such noun groups, concepts are formed taking each noun word in the group as an object as well as an attribute. For the example [*computer*_NN *keyboard*_NN], two concepts are formed one as *computer* → *keyboard* and the other as *keyboard* → *computer*. In the first case *computer* is regarded as the main subject in which case *keyboard* is an attribute of the computer. In the second case, *keyboard* is considered as the main topic in which case *computer* is an attribute of the keyboard. This specifies that the context of the topic "keyboards" is computers (not typewriter keyboards).

In addition to the above, possessive relationships between two noun terms within noun groups denoted by a trailing '*s* or '*s* are also detected and used. These are correctly identified by taggers and tagged by most taggers (e.g. LtChunk tags them with the tag _*POS*), e.g. [*The*_DT *man*_NN*'s*_POS *hair*_NN].These possessive relationships are also captured and processed separately to form concepts containing all the words in the noun group up to " ' " as the object and the words after the tag POS as the attribute. i.e.   *Man* → *hair*   for the above example. Note that determinants (like *A*, *The*) are always ignored.

The above-mentioned methods/rules, though not perfect, have shown to extract a reasonably well representative set of concepts from a given text. Additionally, they happen to deal with certain verbal groups as well, e.g. both *"Man's hair"* and the *"Hair of the man"* gives the same concept *Man* → *hair* (can be interpreted as *"man has hair"*)

The set of objects and their attributes thus extracted makes up the initial training set for training a BAM. A consistent set of storable training patterns is then constructed from the extracted set of concepts (by applying the completeness constraint $A' = B$ and $B' = A$) and a BAM is trained (weights are set according to the equation (3) given in section 3.2). BAMs formed as described above for each document/query represents that document/query in our model in its subsequent stages of the IR process.

Importance of Concepts and Keywords

A given document generally consists of more than one simple concept (of the kind we extract from text). Some of these may be more generic concepts that might not be very important to distinctly identify the document (by a query) while some others may be much more important. This importance of a concept in a document is modelled by means of a weight. More important concepts are expected to gain bigger weights compared to the less important ones as a result of the online learning process describe below. In the proposed model, we use weights for:

1. each related object-attribute pair present in each document representation (we call such a pair a *unit concept*) and
2. each keyword/keyphrase in each document

The weights of unit concepts model the importance of their object-attribute pairs with respect to the individual documents, within which the concepts are present, while the weights of the keywords/keyphrases model the importance of keywords/keyphrases in the documents. Note that we distinguish between unit concepts and keywords as we are more interested in concept matching rather than keyword matching. For us a unit concept (i.e. an object and a related attribute) makes more sense than a single keyword/keyphrase, as it describes a topic and its context.

We also consider it important to maintain the importance of concepts/keywords with respect to each individual document. A concept which is important to identify and retrieve one document may not be important to identify another document, which also contains the same concept. The presence of the said concept in the second document should not miss-recognize the second document as relevant to a query that contains the said unit concept. Most centralised document indexing schemes for IR have this drawback as they assign a single weight for each index term with respect to the whole document collection. Instead maintaining weights separately with respect to each individual document allows the same object-attribute pair (unit concept) or the same keyword/keyphrase to have different importance weights in different documents. It should be noted here that we do not weight concepts or keywords in the query.

The weights of all the unit concepts and keywords of document representations are initialised to a pre-decided value and are then continuously updated during the subsequent query sessions depending on the user feedback. It is these updated document representations that represent the documents at the subsequent query sessions.

5.2 The Matcher

Once queries and documents are represented in concept lattices (encoded in BAMs), the next step is to match a given query with the documents and compute similarity measures (known as the RSV: Retrieval Status Value) for each query-document pair. These RSV values are then subject to threshold in order to decide what documents should be presented to the user. This whole process involves three subtasks.

Obtaining Candidate Concepts to Match between (from the Document and the Query Representations)

Not all the concepts in a given pair of a query and a document lattices match each other. Therefore attempting to compare each and every concept in the query lattice with each and every concept in the document lattice is not worth the effort. In addition such a matching strategy fails to make use of the important knowledge of the order relationship structure, which has already been captured and encoded in the document/query representations (in BAMs). This is where the importance of using BAMs matters. Instead of using conventional traversing and searching, we make use of the BAM's properties to get most specific (and most generic) concept for a given set of objects (and attributes) respectively. Our strategy is based on the *object concepts* and *attribute concepts* defined by each object and attribute in the query. An *object concept* (*attribute concept*) is the concept returned by a BAM when a pattern containing only one object (attribute) is presented to its object (attribute) layer. The goal here is to extract the most specific concepts (wherever possible) to match between, as we are interested in matching the most specific ideas/concepts between queries and documents whenever such information is available.

For instance, the word *dog* may appear in many documents in different contexts. A given user may be interested in (say) *dog races*. In this case, we need to look for the more specific context (*dog races*) of the object *dog*.

For obtaining candidate concepts to match between a query and a document, we first look for the presence of query objects and attributes in the document representation. For each object and attribute common to the document and the Query, Object and attribute concepts (respectively) are extracted from both the query and the document BAMs. Such object and attribute concept pairs are the candidate concept pairs to match between the query and the document. During this process, we make sure to extract the most specific concepts wherever possible and also not to extract the same concept pair more than once. Also we avoid extracting document (query) concepts that are general (in the general-specific hierarchy in the concept lattice) to any of the already extracted document (query) concepts to match with the same query (document) concept.

Notice that, in case of an object or attribute in the query appearing as both object and attribute in the document representation, we check whether there is any order relation (in the concept hierarchy) between them in order to avoid matching two related document concepts with the same query concept. In case of such related document concepts, only the most specific concept is considered for matching. In some cases we find the same term (word or phrase) appears both as an object and as an attribute in document representations, but they represent two different ideas/concepts (i.e. they are not related in the concept hierarchy). In this case, the attribute concept given by the query BAM is also taken in to account as a candidate concept to matched with the object concept given by the query BAM, in addition to the object concept given by the document BAM.

The following are the eight different cases identified and taken into account in the development of the algorithm that extracts candidate concepts to match between queries and documents in our implementation.

1. Query object is present ONLY in the document object set
2. Query object is present ONLY in the document attribute set
3. Query object is present in both (document object & attribute) sets and they are related (i.e. the query object plays both object and attribute roles in the document and they are present in the same concept or in different concepts of which one is a super/sub concept of the other.)
4. Query object is present in both (document object & attribute) sets and they are not related
5. Query attribute is present ONLY in the document object set
6. Query attribute is present ONLY in the document attribute set
7. Query attribute is present in both (document object & attribute) sets and they are related
8. Query attribute is present in both (document object & attribute) sets and they are not related

Computing a Similarity Measure (RSV Value)

Each candidate query and document concept pair extracted to match between is then examined for the presence of common unit concepts and keyword/keyphrases. Presence of matching unit concepts between a candidate query and a document concept pair leads to a concept match. The more unit concept matches is the better, as it means the two concepts are more similar. The presence of a common object or an attribute that do not participate in a matching unit concept leads to a keyword matching (see the following illustration).

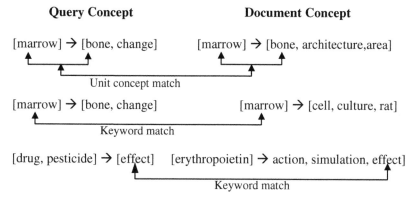

A similarity measure for each candidate query-document concept pair considered is computed as the sum of the weights of matching unit concepts and keywords. The final RSV value for a query-document pair is the sum of the similarity measures of all the candidate query-document concept pairs considered between the query and the document.

Thresholding

The RSV values computed for each query-document pair are then subject to thresholding in order to decide which documents are to be presented to the user as the retrieved set of documents. We use a kind of dynamic thresholding strategy by taking into account the total number of unit concepts available in all the candidate query concepts considered for comparing with document concepts (i.e. the total number of unit concepts we are looking for in the candidate document concepts) to compensate the varied sizes (size of a query is determined by the number of unit concepts in its representation) of queries. This value is multiplied by a predefined base threshold value. Use of a base threshold value allows us to experiment on the best thresholding value to be used by varying the base threshold.

$$\text{(Base Threshold)} \times \left(\begin{array}{l} \text{No. of unit concepts in all the candidate query concepts} \\ \text{considered for matching between a given query-document pair} \end{array} \right)$$

5.3 Feedback Processor

The task of feedback processor is to accept the user feedback in the form of *yes* or *no* (i.e. accepts a document as relevant or reject it as irrelevant) and accordingly modify the document representation.

Unlike most other models, we use the user feedback to modify the document representation rather than the query representation. The traditional approach, which uses user feedback for query reformulation, though it has shown about 20% improvements on recall and precision, does not lead however to a learning system, because the important user decisions are used only within one query session for searching for one information need. The result gained by relevance feedback at one query session is usually not available for the subsequent query sessions, as they are not learned by the system. A separate learning mechanism is required to make the systems adaptive.

In our model, the document representations are updated instead, and the modifications made are retained for later use. We expect the document representations to converge to a well representative set of concepts (for each document) over a period of time. Such a set of concepts, in fact, will become more customized to the vocabulary and the writing style of the end user, as it is the concepts of the user formulated queries that are appended into relevant document representations. Our reinforcement learning process works as follows:

If user says a particular (retrieved) document is relevant to a given query, all the unit concepts of the query are amended to the document representation. In case that a particular unit concept of the query is already present in the document, we consider it as an important unit concept (because it has made some contribution for the document's retrieval in the first place) and therefore its weight is increased by a pre-decided amount. Unit query concepts not present in the document are simply added to the document representation with an initial weight value. This may result in unnecessary unit concepts getting into the document's representation, but we expect such concepts to end up with low weights in the long run. It is important to note that we strictly maintain the roles of the terms during this document updating process. Also, we apply the completeness constraint after adding new unit concepts to a document representation in order to combine the new unit concept(s) with appropriate concepts and place them at the appropriate positions in the concept hierarchy.

On the other hand, if a user says a particular (retrieved) document is not relevant to the query then we examine the unit concepts and keywords that are common to the query-document pair (i.e. those matching unit concepts and keywords that contributed for the document's retrieval) and their weights are decreased (by a pre-decided value) to say that those unit concepts and keywords, though common to both the query and the document, are not very important to decide the relevancy of the document to the query.

6. Related Work

Concept lattices have been used for information retrieval by a number of researchers including Godin et al., [12,13,5]; Carpineto and Romano, [3,4]; Cole and Eklund [7]; Cole at al [8]. Most of these researchers have employed FCA to support user interface design, to help the user navigate through the concept lattice to locate desired documents. Almost all of them formulate a concept as a set of documents as the objects and their keywords as the attributes, and represent the entire document collection in a single large concept lattice. In contrast, we attempt to capture concepts as an analogue of how the human cognitive brain process might work. The most related work to that which we describe here is the Lattice-based data structure proposed by Merwe and Kourie [18]. Their data structure is very much similar to our representation scheme in the sense that we both define "a concept" in the same way and embed lattice structures in two layered data structures. However, Merwe's paper lacks a retrieval process to compare with ours.

7. Discussion

We expect that in the long run, when used on a given collection of documents with a good representative set of natural language queries, the system should stabilise on a better set of representative concepts for each document in the collection, through which a better recall and precision can be achieved. We expect our system to perform better than the traditional models in terms of effectiveness, given representative query and document concept lattices.

Several advantages and disadvantages of the proposed model have been identified in comparison to the well known IR models.

Advantages
1. Performs explicit concept matching
2. Adaptive - the system continuously learns as it is used making it suitable for more customised/personalised type of IR applications. However, it is possible to provide an option to remove the knowledge learnt by the system over its lifetime, leaving it with only the initial knowledge/original concepts extracted initially from the documents. This would reset the system back to its starting point.
3. Improves recall through use. Documents that were not picked up for a particular query at an early attempt will be picked up later (for the same or similar query) as a result of upgrading the representations of those documents by other queries. This is very useful and one of the most important features of our model. A collection of documents and queries that has more than one query relevant to each document is required for exploiting the potential of this feature.
4. Improves precision through use. Because of the degrading of weights of matching unit concepts and keywords between a query and documents that are retrieved but judged as not relevant, the RSV values of such documents for the same or similar query at later trials will be smaller, and as such the likelihood of retrieving them at later trials for similar queries is less.

5. The number of terms used/stored may be less (Inverted index indexes all the terms)
6. Nothing is central (each document is represented independently) and so is suitable for an agent-based retrieval on documents distributed over a computer network.
7. Used only information local to a given document and therefore can be applied on collections, which are not restricted to a particular domain.

Disadvantages

1. The document representation process may be computationally expensive especially because the system needs to build BAMs for each document at each query session.
2. Extracting concepts from queries and documents to match between may also be expensive especially when the documents are lengthy (and so have more concepts in the representation). This process has two stages (1) to check the presence of each object/attribute of the query representation in the document representation and (2) presenting the object/attribute concepts made up of the matching object/attribute into the corresponding layers of the query and Document BAMs to extract the concepts to match between.
3. Only local information is used. Therefore the matching process does not have any idea of the global document collection (the problem space).
4. At present, no query reformulation mechanism is used. Short queries are adversely affected.
5. At present the implemented model does not support pure keyword-queries, i.e. queries formulated with few isolated keywords.
6. The concept extraction process is not perfect in the sense that some important concepts will not be extracted, especially because of the distant special locations the participating components appear in the sentences. Also, some useless concepts get into the representations, leading to the retrieval of irrelevant documents. A better object and attribute extraction for the document/query representation will improve the performance of the model.

At present, we are at the stage of conducting preliminary testing for improving our model. Due to the long training process, we have been working on a small document collection with 236 documents and 177 queries. This is a subset of the Cranfield collection. Since our model works best if each document is relevant to many queries (this allows the document representations to learn), we have created the above mentioned document collection by choosing documents/queries from the Cranfield collection which are judged as relevant to three or more queries. Preliminary results are promising with 5.1 average precision over all 177 queries. Following are the precisions at various points.

Retrieval points	Avg. Precision
5 documents	0.37
10 documents	0.270
20 documents	0.168

It should be noted that, due to less number of relevant documents for queries in the document collection used, number of (actual) recall points for queries are less. This might have affected the value of the average precision to have a high value. Also the less number of relevant documents for queries makes the precision values shown in the table (above) smaller down the retrieval points. However, the value of precision at 5 seems an interesting figure that shows how good the performance (precision) is within the top 5 documents retrieved.

We have no information (at present) to comment on the storage requirements over a long period of time as the document representations tend to grow over the time. But, we expect the system to converge to a fixed document representation. Keeping track of the less-used or never-used unit concepts, and thus perceived unimportant concepts in document representations and removing such less useful concepts from the documents will help making the model efficient in terms of retrieval speed, and also reduce the storage requirements of the system.

An important future enhancement to the model for better performance will be to incorporate a query enhancement/reformulation mechanism. At present, the model does not have a query reformulation component to enhance the initial user queries with additional related concepts/keywords.

References

1. Amari, S. (1972). Learning patterns and pattern sequences by self-organizing nets of thresholding elements. IEEE Trans. On Computers, 21(11), 461-482.
2. Bělohlávek, R (2000): Representation of Concept Lattices by Bidirectional Associative Memories, Neural Computation Vol 12 N.10 October 2000. Pp 2279-2290
3. Carpineto, C., & Romano, G. (1996): A Lattice Conceptual Clustering System and its Application to Browsing Retrieval. Machine Learning, 24, 1-28.
4. Carpineto, C., & Romano, G. (1996) : Information retrieval through hybrid navigation of lattice representations. International Journal of Human-Computer Studies, 45, 553-578.
5. Carpineto, C. & Romano, G. (2000): Order-theoretical ranking, JASIS vol51 No. 7 587-601 (2000).
6. Cole, R and Eklund, P.W. (1993): Scalability of Formal Concept Analysis, Computational Intelligence, Vol 2, No. 5, 1993 http://www.int.gu.edu.au/kvo/papers/
7. Cole, R.J. and Eklund, P.K. (1996): Application of Formal Concept Analysis to Information Retrieval using a Hierarchically Structured Thesaurus, http://www.int.gu.edu.au/kvo/papers/ International Conference on Conceptual Graphs, ICCS '96, Sydney, 1996, pp. 1-12, University of New South Wales, 1996.
8. Cole, R.J. Eklund, P.K. Stumme, G.: CEM-A Program for Visualization and Discovery in Email, http://www.int.gu.edu.au/kvo/papers/ In D.A. Zighed, J. Komorowski, J. Zytkow (Eds), Proc. of PKDD 2000, LNAI 1910, pp. 367-374, Springer-Verlag, Berlin, 2000.
9. Darmstadt University of Technology: Formal Concept Analysis S/W, http://www.mathematik.tu-darmstadt.de/ags/ag1/Software/software_en.html
10. Evans, D.A. and Zhai, C. (1996): Noun-Phrase Analysis in Unrestricted Text for Information Retrieval, Proceedings, 34th Annual Meeting of the Association for Computational Linguistics (ACL'96), pages 17--24, Santa Cruz, CA.
11. Ganter, B. Wille, R. (1999) : Formal Concept Analysis : Mathematical Foundations, ISBN 3-540-627771-5 Springer-Verlag Berlin Heidelberg 1999
12. Godin, R., Gecsei, J., & Pichet, C. (1989): Design of a browsing interface for information retrieval. Proceedings of the 12th International Conference on Research and Development in Information Retrieval(ACM SIGIR'89), pp.32-39. Cambridge, MA, ACM.

13. Godin, R., Missaoui, R., April, A. (1993): Experimental comparison of navigation in a Galois lattice with conventional information retrieval methods. International Journal of Man-machine Studies, 38, 747-767.
14. Hopfield, J.J.(1984) : Neurons with graded response have collective computational properties like those of two-state neurons. Proc. Natl. Acad. Sci. U.S.A., 81, 3088-3092.
15. Kosko, B. (1987) : Adaptive bidirectional associative memory. Applied Optics, 26(23), 4947-4960.
16. Kosko, B. (1988) : Bidirectional associative memory. IEEE Trans. Systems, Man and Cybernetics, 18(1), 49-60.
17. Lewis, D. (1992): Feature Selection and Feature Extraction for Text Categorization, Proceedings of Speech and Natural Language Workshop, 1992
18. van der Merwe, F.J. & Kourie, D.G. (2001): A Lattice-Based Data Structure for Information Retrieval and Machine Learning, ICCS'01 International workshop on Concept Lattices-based KDD.
19. Wille. R. (1997): Conceptual Graphs and Formal Concept Analysis. In: Lukose, D. et. al. (eds.): Conceptual Structures: Fulfilling Peirce's Dream, Proceedings of the ICCS'97. Springer, Berlin--New York (1997) 290--303 16

A Layered Bayesian Network Model for Document Retrieval

Luis M. de Campos[1], Juan M. Fernández-Luna[2], and Juan F. Huete[1]

[1] Dpto. de Ciencias de la Computación e Inteligencia Artificial, E.T.S.I. Informática,
Universidad de Granada, 18071 – Granada, Spain
{lci,jhg}@decsai.ugr.es
[2] Departamento de Informática, Escuela Politécnica Superior
Universidad de Jaén, 23071 – Jaén, Spain
jmfluna@ujaen.es

Abstract. We propose a probabilistic document retrieval model based
on Bayesian networks. The network is used to compute the posterior
probabilities of relevance of the documents in the collection given a query.
These computations can be carried out efficiently, because of the specific
network topology and conditional probability tables being considered,
which allow the use of a fast and exact probabilities propagation algorithm. In the initial model, only direct relationships between the terms in
the glossary and the documents that contain them are considered, giving
rise to a Bayesian network with two layers. Next, we consider an extended
model that also includes direct relationships between documents, using
a network topology with three layers. We also report the results of a set
of experiments with the two models, using several standard document
collections.

1 Introduction

Information Retrieval (IR) is the field that deals with the automated storage
and retrieval of information. In our case, the pieces of information considered
will always be texts (the textual representations of any objects), referred to as
documents. An *IR model* is a specification about how to represent documents
and queries (formal statements of user's information needs), and how to compare them, whereas an *IR system* is the computer software that implements a
model. Probabilistic IR models [4,9,12] use probability theory to deal with the
intrinsic uncertainty with which IR is pervaded [3]. Also founded on probabilistic methods, *Bayesian networks* [5] have been proven to be a good model to
manage uncertainty, even in the IR environment, where they have already been
successfully applied as an extension of probabilistic IR models [13,14,7].

In this paper we introduce new IR models based on Bayesian networks. The
retrieval engine of our first model is composed of a Bayesian network with two
layers of nodes, representing the documents and the terms in the document
collection and the relationships among each other. The second model extends

F. Crestani, M. Girolami, and C.J. van Rijsbergen (Eds.): ECIR 2002, LNCS 2291, pp. 169–182, 2002.

the first one by including a third layer, also composed by documents, with the aim of capturing some relationships between documents.

The rest of the paper is organized as follows: we begin in Section 2 with the preliminaries. In Section 3 we introduce the basic model, the assumptions that determine the network topology being considered, the details about probability distributions stored in the network, and the way in which we can efficiently use the network model for retrieval, by performing probabilistic inference. In Section 4 we study the extended model. In Section 5 we discuss the similarities and differences between our models and other retrieval models also based on Bayesian networks. Section 6 shows the experimental results obtained with the two models, using several standard document collections. Finally, Section 7 contains the concluding remarks and some proposals for future research.

2   Preliminaries

Many IR models usually represent documents and queries by means of vectors of *terms* or *keywords*, which try to characterize their information content. Because these terms are not equally important, they are usually weighted to highlight their importance in the documents they belong to, as well as in the whole collection. The most common weighting schemes are the *term frequency*, tf_{ij}, i.e, the number of times that the ith term appears in the jth document, and the *inverse document frequency*, idf_i, of the ith term in the collection, $idf_i = \lg(N/n_i) + 1$, where N is the number of documents in the collection, and n_i is the number of documents that contain the ith term. The combination of both weights, $\text{tf}_{ij} \cdot idf_i$, is also a common weighting scheme.

The evaluation of the retrieval performance of an IR system is usually carried out by means of two complementary measures: *recall* and *precision* [10]. The first one measures the ability of the IR system to present all the relevant documents (number of relevant documents retrieved / number of relevant documents). The second one, precision, measures its ability to present only the relevant documents (number of relevant documents retrieved / number of documents retrieved). By computing the precision for a number of fixed points of recall (the average precision values for all the queries being processed), the recall-precision curves are obtained. If a single value of performance is desired, the average precision, for all the points of recall considered, may be used.

A Bayesian network $G = (V, E)$ is a *Directed Acyclic Graph* (DAG), where the nodes in V represent the variables from the problem we want to solve, and the arcs in E represent the dependence relationships among the variables. In that kind of graph, the knowledge is represented in two ways [5]: *(a)* Qualitatively, showing the (in)dependencies between the variables, and *(b)* Quantitatively, by means of conditional probability distributions which shape the relationships. For each variable $X_i \in V$, we have a family of conditional probability distributions $P(X_i|Pa(x_i))$, where $Pa(X_i)$ represents the parent set of the variable X_i in G. From these conditional distributions we can recover the joint distribution over V:

$$P(X_1, X_2, \ldots, X_n) = \prod_{i=1}^{n} P(X_i | Pa(X_i)) \tag{1}$$

This expression represents a decomposition of the joint distribution (which gives rise to important savings in storage requirements). The dependence/independence relationships which make possible this decomposition are graphically encoded (through the d-separation criterion [5]) by means of the presence or absence of direct connections between pairs of variables. Bayesian networks can perform efficiently reasoning tasks: the independencies represented in the graph reduce changes in the state of knowledge to local computations. There are several algorithms [5] that exploit this property to perform probabilistic inference (propagation), i.e., to compute the posterior probability for any variable given some evidence about the values of other variables in the graph.

3   A Bayesian Network Model with Two Layers

In IR problems we can distinguish between two different sets of variables (nodes in the graph): The set $\mathcal{T}$ of the M terms, T_i, in the glossary from a given collection, and the set $\mathcal{D}$ of the N documents, D_j, that compose the collection. Each term, T_i, consists on a binary random variable taking values in the set $\{\bar{t}_i, t_i\}$, where $\bar{t}_i$ stands for 'the term T_i is not relevant', and t_i represents 'the term T_i is relevant'[1]. Similarly, a variable referring to a document D_j has its domain in the set $\{\bar{d}_j, d_j\}$, where in this case, $\bar{d}_j$ and d_j respectively mean 'the document D_j is not relevant for a given query', and 'the document D_j is relevant for a given query'[2].

Focusing on the structure of the network, the following guidelines have been considered to determine the topology of the graph [2]:

- For each term that has been used to index a document, there is a link between the node representing that keyword and each node associated with a document it belongs to.
- The relationships between documents only occur through the terms included in these documents.
- Documents are conditionally independent given the terms that they contain. Thus, if we know the relevance (or irrelevance) values for all the terms indexing document D_i then our belief about the relevance of D_i is not affected by knowing that another document D_j is relevant or irrelevant.

These assumptions partially determine the structure of the network: On one hand, links joining terms and documents must be directed from term nodes to

---

[1] We speak about the relevance of a term in the sense that the user explicitly employs this term when formulating a query. Similarly, a term is not relevant when the user also explicitly employs it, but in this case in a negative sense: he/she is not interested in documents containing this term.

[2] In this case a document is relevant if it satisfies the user's information need.

document nodes and, on the other hand, there are not links between document nodes. The parent set of any document node D_j is then the set of term nodes that belong to D_j, i.e., $Pa(D_j) = \{T_i \in \mathcal{T} \,|\, T_i \in D_j\}$. To completely determine the network topology, we include an additional assumption: the terms are marginally independent among each other, which implies that there are not links between terms nodes (all of them are root nodes). In this way, we get a network composed of two simple layers, the term and document subnetworks, with arcs only going from nodes in the first subnetwork to nodes in the second one (see Figure 1).

Term subnetwork

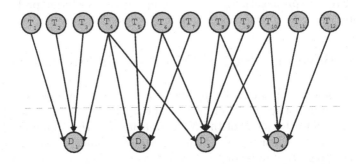

Document subnetwork

Fig. 1. Two-layered Bayesian network.

The final step to completely specify a Bayesian network is to estimate the probability distributions stored in each node. Two different cases have to be considered:

• Term nodes: In this case we store marginal distributions, estimated as follows:

$$p(t_i) = \frac{1}{M} \quad \text{and} \quad p(\bar{t}_i) = \frac{M-1}{M} \tag{2}$$

M being the number of terms in a given collection.

• Document nodes: In this case, the estimation of the conditional probabilities $p(D_j|Pa(D_j))$ is more problematic because of the huge number of parents that a document node has. For example, if a document has been indexed by 30 terms, we need to estimate and store 2^{30} probabilities. Therefore, instead of explicitly computing these probabilities, we use a *probability function*, also called a canonical model of multicausal interaction [5], which returns a conditional probability value when it is called during the inference stage, each time that a conditional probability is required. We have developed a new general canonical model: for any configuration $pa(D_j)$ of $Pa(D_j)$ (i.e., any assignment of values to all the term variables in D_j), we define the conditional probability of relevance of D_j as follows:

$$p(d_j|pa(D_j)) = \sum_{\substack{T_i \in D_j \\ t_i \in pa(D_j)}} w_{ij} \qquad (3)$$

where the weights w_{ij} have to verify $0 \le w_{ij}$ and $\sum_{T_i \in D_j} w_{ij} \le 1$. So, the more terms are relevant in $pa(D_j)$ the greater is the probability of relevance of D_j.

Given a query Q submitted to our system, the retrieval process starts placing the evidences, i.e., the terms T_Q belonging to Q, in the term subnetwork by setting their states to t_Q (relevant). The inference process is run, obtaining for each document its probability of relevance given that the terms in the query are also relevant, $p(d_j|Q)$. Then, the documents are sorted by their posterior probability to carry out the evaluation process.

Taking into account the number of nodes in the Bayesian network and the fact that, although the network topology seems relatively simple, it contains cycles and nodes with a great number of parents, general purpose inference algorithms cannot be applied due to efficiency considerations, even for small document collections. To solve this problem, we have designed a specific inference process that takes advantage of both the topology of the network and the kind of probability function used for document nodes, eq. (3): the propagation process is substituted by a single evaluation for each document node, but ensuring that the results are the same that the ones obtained using exact propagation in the entire network [2]:

$$p(d_j|Q) = \sum_{T_i \in D_j} w_{ij} \, p(t_i|Q) \qquad (4)$$

Moreover, as terms nodes are marginally independent, we know, using eq. (2), that

$$p(t_i|Q) = \begin{cases} 1 & \text{if } T_i \in Q \\ \frac{1}{M} & \text{if } T_i \notin Q \end{cases} \qquad (5)$$

Therefore, the computation of $p(d_j|Q)$ can be carried out as follows:

$$p(d_j|Q) = \sum_{T_i \in D_j \cap Q} w_{ij} + \frac{1}{M} \sum_{T_i \in D_j \setminus Q} w_{ij} \qquad (6)$$

A simple modification of this model is to include the information about the frequency of the terms in the query Q, qf_i, with the aim of giving more importance to the terms more frequently used (as is usual in other IR models). This can be done by duplicating qf_i times in the network each term T_i appearing in the query. Then, eq. (6) is transformed in

$$p(d_j|Q) = \sum_{T_i \in D_j \cap Q} w_{ij} \, qf_i + \frac{1}{M} \sum_{T_i \in D_j \setminus Q} w_{ij} \qquad (7)$$

4   A Bayesian Network Model with Three Layers

In the previous model, document nodes are related only through terms in common. This fact makes almost impossible to retrieve a document that does not contain any of the terms used to formulate the query, even in the case that these terms are related (in some way) to the ones indexing the document. One approach to deal with this situation could be to include arcs in the term subnetwork modeling direct relationships between terms [1]. Using these relationships, the instantiation of the query terms would increase the probability of relevance of other terms, which in turn would increase the probability of relevance of some documents containing them. A different approach, which is the one considered in this paper, is to directly include in the model relationships between documents. These relationships will play in our model a role similar to the clustering techniques used in other IR models [8,10].

In the absence of information about direct and obvious relationships between documents in the form of, for example, citations or common references, these relationships in our model will be based on measuring (asymmetric) similarities between documents, by means of the estimation of the conditional probabilities of relevance of every document given that another document is relevant. These probabilities will be computed using the Bayesian network with two layers described previously.

So, given any document D_j, if we compute the probabilities $p(d_j|d_i) \ \forall D_i \in \mathcal{D}$, then the documents giving rise to the greatest values of $p(d_j|d_i)$ are the ones which are more closely related with D_j (in the sense that D_j has a high probability of being relevant when we know that D_i is relevant for a given query). Let $R_c(D_j)$ be the set of the c documents more related with D_j[3]. These relationships would be represented in the document subnetwork as arcs going from the documents $D_i \in R_c(D_j)$ to document D_j.

However, instead of using a document subnetwork with one layer, we will use two layers: we duplicate each document node D_k in the original layer to obtain another document node D_k', thus forming a new document layer, and the arcs connecting the two layers go from $D_i \in R_c(D_j)$ to D_j' (i.e., $Pa(D_j') = R_c(D_j)$). In this way we obtain a new Bayesian network with three layers (see Figure 2). We use this topology for two reasons: (1) the network with two layers used so far is maintained without changes as a subnetwork of the extended network, and therefore we do not have to redefine the conditional probabilities associated to the document nodes (eq. 3); (2) the new topology contains three simple layers, without connections between the nodes in the same layer, and this fact will redound to the efficiency of the inference process.

Now, we have to define the conditional probabilities $p(D_j'|pa(D_j'))$ for the documents in the second document layer. We use a probability function of the type defined in eq. (3), more precisely:

---

[3] Note that D_j will always belong to $R_c(D_j)$.

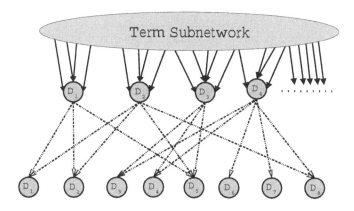

Document Subnetwork

Fig. 2. Three-layered Bayesian network.

$$p(d'_j|pa(D'_j)) = \frac{1}{S_j} \sum_{\substack{D_i \in Pa(D'_j) \\ d_i \in pa(D'_j)}} p(d_j|d_i) \tag{8}$$

where $S_j = \sum_{D_k \in Pa(D'_j)} p(d_j|d_k)$, and the values $p(d_j|d_i)$ are obtained, using the network with two layers, during the building process of the network with three layers.

To compute $p(d'_j|Q)$, we can again take advantage of both the layered topology and eq. (8) to replace the propagation process in the whole network by the following evaluation [2]:

$$p(d'_j|Q) = \frac{1}{S_j} \sum_{D_i \in Pa(D'_j)} p(d_j|d_i)p(d_i|Q) \tag{9}$$

where the probabilities $p(d_i|Q)$ are computed according to equations (6) or (7). Note that the value $p(d'_j|Q)$ measures the relevance of a document by combining the contribution of the query, $p(d_i|Q) \; \forall D_i \in R_c(D_j)$ (using the probabilities computed for the two layered network), and the document relationships, $p(d_j|d_i)$.

To completely specify the Bayesian network model with three layers, we need to explain how to calculate the values $p(d_j|d_i)$ and how to select the documents D_i that will be the parents of D'_j. Although the derivation is somewhat more involved, it can be proven that $p(d_j|d_i)$ can be calculated (without propagation) by means of

$$p(d_j|d_i) = \frac{1}{M} \left(\sum_{T_k \in D_j} w_{kj} \right) + \frac{M-1}{M} \left(\frac{\sum_{T_k \in D_j \cap D_i} w_{kj}w_{ki}}{\sum_{T_h \in D_i} w_{hi}} \right) \tag{10}$$

Using eq. (10), given a document D_j, to select the c parents of its copy D'_j in the second document layer, we only have to select the c documents D_i with the greatest values of

$$\frac{\sum_{T_k \in D_j \cap D_i} w_{kj} w_{ki}}{\sum_{T_h \in D_i} w_{hi}} \tag{11}$$

Eq. (11) says that the more terms have the documents D_j and D_i in common, the more related (similar) is D_i with D_j, which seems us quite natural. At the same time, the more terms D_i contains (which may indicate that D_i is a document related with many topics), the degree of similarity of D_i with any document D_j decreases.

5   Related Work

In this section we will briefly describe the two main retrieval models based on Bayesian networks, comparing them with our model and establishing the main differences.

The first model was developed by Croft and Turtle [13,15,16], the *Inference Network Model*, which is composed, in its simplified form, by two networks: the document and query networks. The former represents the document collection and contains two kinds of nodes: the document nodes, representing the documents, and the concept nodes, symbolizing the index terms contained in the documents. The arcs go from each document node to each concept node used to index it. The document network is fixed for a given collection. However, the query network is dynamic, in the sense that it is specific for each query, and is composed by three types of nodes: The Information Need node (inn), that represents the user's generic information need; a set of intermediate query nodes, used in case of having multiple query representations, and, finally, the query concept nodes (in the simplified form, they are just the concept nodes in the document network, and represent the connection between the two networks). The arcs in the query network go from query concept nodes to query nodes, and from query nodes to the Information Need node.

Each type of node stores a probability matrix, called link matrix in their notation, that in certain cases, depends on the type of query being formulated (boolean or probabilistic).

The retrieval is carried out by instantiating a single document node D_j each time, and computing the probability that the Information Need is satisfied given that this document has been observed, $p(inn|d_j)$. Actually, Turtle and Croft precompute the intermediate probabilities $p(t_i|d_j)$ in the document network, and, later, use closed-form expressions to evaluate $p(inn|d_j)$ as a function of the probabilities $p(t_i|d_j)$, for those terms T_i appearing in the query submitted by the user.

A first difference with our approach is that we do not have a query network. A second distinction, also topological, is that the arcs in our model are directed in the opposite way (from term nodes to document nodes). We think that is more intuitive to speak about the probability that a document is relevant given a query than the opposite. Therefore, our choice implies to instantiate the query, or specifically, the terms that it contains, and propagate towards document nodes. This fact means that we only have to propagate once, unlike Turtle and Croft's model in which they have to run one propagation per document. With respect to propagation, our inference method allows us to propagate in the whole network by only estimating prior probabilities and evaluating probability functions.

The Ribeiro and Reis' model [7,6,11] is designed to simulate the Vector Space, Boolean and Probabilistic models. Their network is composed of three types of nodes: document nodes, concept nodes, and the query node. The arcs go from concept nodes to the document nodes where they occur, and from the concept nodes (appearing in the query) to the query node. In this model, the probabilities of interest are $p(d_j|Q)$, which could be computed as

$$p(d_j|Q) = \alpha^{-1} \sum_\tau p(d_j|\tau)p(Q|\tau)p(\tau), \tag{12}$$

where τ represents any of the 2^M assignments of values to all the terms in the collection. This computation is obviously unfeasible. So, depending on the model to be simulated, the probabilities $p(Q|\tau)$ and $p(\tau)$ are defined in such a way that all the terms in the previous addition except one (corresponding to a given configuration τ_Q) are always equal to zero. Thus, the computation in eq. (12) becomes straightforward: the inference is reduced to evaluate a function $(p(d_j|\tau_Q))$ in the only non-zero configuration.

The network topologies of this model and ours are very similar, except by the fact that we do not consider a query node. The main differences appear in the conditional probability distributions considered, in our case these distributions are not 'degenerated' and do not depend on the query, and we truly perform probabilities propagation.

Another important difference between these two models ans ours is that we include direct relationships between documents, thus obtaining a more expressive model.

6 Experimental Results

To test the performance of the two retrieval models explained in the previous sections, we have used four well-known document collections: ADI, CISI, CRAN-FIELD and MEDLARS. The main characteristics of these collections with respect to number of documents, terms and queries are (in this ordering): ADI (82, 828, 35), CISI (1460, 4985, 76), CRANFIELD (1398, 3857, 225) and MEDLARS (1033, 7170, 30). The results obtained by our models will be compared with the ones obtained by two different IR systems: SMART [10][4] and the Inference Network model[5]. The performance measure that we have used is the average precision for the *eleven* standard values of recall (denoted AP-11).

---

[4] We used the implementation of this IR system available at the Computer Science Department of Cornell University, using the *ntc* weighting scheme.

[5] In this case we have built our own implementation, and we used the configuration parameters proposed by Turtle in [13]: $p(t_i|d_j = \text{true}) = 0.4 + 0.6 * \text{tf} * \text{idf}$ and $p(t_i|\text{all parents false}) = 0.3$.

In the experiments, the specific weights w_{ij}, for each document D_j and each term $T_i \in D_j$, used by our models (see eq. 3) are:

$$w_{ij} = \alpha^{-1} \frac{\mathrm{tf}_{ij} \cdot \mathrm{idf}_i^2}{\sqrt{\sum_{T_k \in D_j} \mathrm{tf}_{kj} \cdot \mathrm{idf}_k^2}} \tag{13}$$

where α is a normalizing constant (to assure that $\sum_{T_i \in D_j} w_{ij} \leq 1 \ \forall D_j \in \mathcal{D}$).

The AP-11 values obtained by SMART and the Inference Network are shown in Table 1.

Table 1. AP-11 values for SMART and Inference Network.

	ADI	CISI	CRAN	MED
SMART	0.4706	0.2459	0.4294	0.5446
Inf. Network	0.4612	0.2498	0.4367	0.5534

The results for the experiments with the Bayesian network with two (BN-2) and three (BN-3) layers are displayed in Tables 2 and 3, respectively. The columns of the experiments that use eq. (6) are labeled with '1' and the ones that use eq. (7) are labeled with 'qf'. The rows labeled with '%SM' and '%IN' show the percentage of change of the performance measure obtained by our methods with respect to SMART and the Inference Network, respectively. For the Bayesian network with three layers, we have carried out experiments with three different values for the number, c, of document nodes in the first document layer that are parents of the document nodes in the second document layer ($c = 5, 10, 15$).

Table 2. Experiments with the two-layered Bayesian network.

	ADI		CISI		CRAN		MED	
	BN-2 1	BN-2 qf	BN-2 1	BN-2 qf	BN-2 1	BN-2 qf	BN-2 1	BN-2 qf
AP-11	0.4707	0.4709	0.2206	0.2642	0.4323	0.4309	0.5552	0.5458
%SM	+0.02	+0.06	-10.29	+7.44	+0.68	+0.35	+1.95	+0.22
%IN	+2.06	+2.10	-11.69	+5.76	-1.01	-1.33	+0.33	-1.37

Several conclusions may be drawn from these experiments: First, with respect to the use of eq. (7), i.e., the frequency qf of the terms in the query, instead of eq. (6), none of the two methods is clearly preferable to the other: For two collections (CRANFIELD and MEDLARS), the best results are obtained without using qf, whereas for the other two collections (ADI and CISI), the use of qf improves the results. Anyway, the differences between the two methods are rather

Table 3. Experiments with the three-layered Bayesian network.

		ADI		CISI		CRAN		MED	
		BN-3 1	BN-3 qf	BN-3 1	BN-3 qf	BN-3 1	BN-3 qf	BN-3 1	BN-3 qf
$c = 5$	AP-11	0.4724	0.4728	0.2211	0.2639	0.4331	0.4318	0.5651	0.5551
	%SM	+0.38	+0.47	-10.09	+7.32	+0.86	+0.56	+3.95	+1.93
	%IN	+2.43	+2.52	-11.49	+5.64	-0.82	-1.12	+2.29	+0.55
$c = 10$	AP-11	0.4717	0.4719	0.2221	0.2650	0.4333	0.4321	0.5687	0.5580
	%SM	+0.23	+0.28	-9.68	+7.77	+0.91	+0.63	+4.43	+2.46
	%IN	+2.28	+2.32	-11.09	+6.08	-0.78	-1.05	+2.76	+0.83
$c = 15$	AP-11	0.4715	0.4716	0.2223	0.2651	0.4332	0.4323	0.5708	0.5598
	%SM	+0.19	+0.21	-9.60	+7.81	+0.89	+0.68	+4.81	+2.79
	%IN	+2.23	+2.26	-11.01	+6.12	-0.80	-1.01	+3.14	+1.16

small, except in the case of CISI, where the results are remarkably better using qf (perhaps the explanation may be that the qf values for CISI are considerably larger than for the other collections).

Second, the results in Tables 1 and 2 show that BN-2 can compete with SMART and the Inference Network: in general, BN-2 obtains better AP-11 values, although the percentages of change are very low, except in the case of CISI.

Third, looking at Tables 2 and 3, we can see that the extended network BN-3 systematically improves the results of BN-2, showing that taking into account document interrelationships may be a good idea. It can also be observed that, except in the case of ADI, the AP-11 values obtained by BN-3 increase as the parameter c increases. However, the differences between BN-2 and BN-3 are so small, that it could be questioned the usefulness of increasing the complexity of the Bayesian network retrieval model by including the new document layer (which implies the necessity of precomputing the probabilities $p(d_j|d_i)$). After analysing, for each document D_j, the values $p(d_j|d_i)$, we realized that even the greatest values of $p(d_j|d_i) \forall i \neq j$ are extremely low compared with $p(d_j|d_j) = 1$ (typically $p(d_j|d_i) \approx 0.0025$). This fact may be the cause of the scarce improvement produced by BN-3 with respect to BN-2, since the value $p(d_j|Q) = p(d_j|d_j)p(d_j|Q)$ dominates completely the other components in eq. (9), $\sum_{D_i \in Pa(D'_j), D_i \neq D_j} p(d_j|d_i)p(d_i|Q)$, and therefore the ranking of documents obtained by using eq. (9) would be almost the same that the one obtained by the BN-2 model (which only uses $p(d_j|Q)$).

In order to test the truthfulness of this conjecture and, if possible, overcome the problem, we have modified the probability function defined in eq. (8) to reduce the importance of the term $p(d_j|Q)$ in the computation of $p(d'_j|Q)$. The new probability function $p(d'_j|pa(D'_j))$, also of the type defined in eq. (3), is the following:

$$p(d'_j|pa(D'_j)) = \begin{cases} \frac{1-\beta}{S_j-1} \sum\limits_{\substack{D_i \in Pa(D'_j) \\ d_i \in pa(D'_j) \\ D_i \neq D_j}} p(d_j|d_i) & \text{if } d_j \notin pa(D'_j) \\ \\ \frac{1-\beta}{S_j-1} \sum\limits_{\substack{D_i \in Pa(D'_j) \\ d_i \in pa(D'_j) \\ D_i \neq D_j}} p(d_j|d_i) + \beta & \text{if } d_j \in pa(D'_j) \end{cases} \tag{14}$$

where the parameter β will control the importance of the contribution of the document relationships being considered for document D_j to its final degree of relevance. Once again taking advantage of the layered topology, we can compute $p(d'_j|Q)$ as follows:

$$p(d'_j|Q) = \frac{1-\beta}{S_j-1} \sum_{\substack{D_i \in Pa(D'_j) \\ D_i \neq D_j}} p(d_j|d_i)p(d_i|Q) + \beta p(d_j|Q) \tag{15}$$

The results obtained by using eq. (15) instead of eq. (9), with a value $\beta = 0.3$, are displayed in Table 4.

Table 4. Experiments with the BN-3 model using eq. (15) and $\beta = 0.3$.

		ADI		CISI		CRAN		MED	
		BN-3 1	BN-3 qf	BN-3 1	BN-3 qf	BN-3 1	BN-3 qf	BN-3 1	BN-3 qf
	AP-11	0.4732	0.4787	0.2301	0.2575	0.4477	0.4453	0.6640	0.6480
$c = 5$	%SM	+0.55	+1.72	-6.43	+4.72	+4.26	+3.70	+21.92	+18.99
	%IN	+2.60	+3.79	-7.89	+3.08	+2.52	+1.97	+19.99	+17.09
	AP-11	0.4757	0.4822	0.2413	0.2754	0.4591	0.4554	0.6878	0.6734
$c = 10$	%SM	+1.08	+2.46	-1.87	+12.00	+6.92	+6.05	+26.29	+23.65
	%IN	+3.14	+4.55	-3.40	+10.25	+5.13	+4.28	+24.29	+21.68
	AP-11	0.4783	0.4825	0.2424	0.2787	0.4630	0.4577	0.6999	0.6847
$c = 15$	%SM	+1.64	+2.53	-1.42	+13.34	+7.82	+6.59	+28.52	+25.73
	%IN	+3.71	+4.62	-2.96	+11.57	+6.02	+4.81	+26.47	+23.73

The results obtained in Table 4 clearly represent a remarkable improvement with respect to the ones in Table 3, thus showing that the use of the document relationships is quite useful, provided that the weights measuring the strength of these relationships are set appropriately. In this case the best results are always obtained using $c = 15$ parents for each document node in the second document layer. We have also carried out some other experiments with different values for the parameter β and, in general, the results are quite similar to the ones displayed in Table 4, for values $\beta \leq 0.5$, whereas the performance decreases for higher values of β.

7   Concluding Remarks

In this paper we have presented two new IR models based on Bayesian networks. The first model, BN-2, is composed of a layer of term nodes and a layer of document nodes, joining each term node to the document nodes representing the documents indexed by this term. This model has been endowed with an inference mechanism that allows us performing exact propagation in the whole network efficiently. The experimental results obtained with four collections show that this model is competitive with respect to SMART and the Inference Network Model.

This initial model has been enriched, establishing the most important relationships among documents, thus increasing the expressiveness of BN-2 and giving rise to the model with three layers, BN-3. In this second approach, we have shown the mechanism by which the document relationships are captured. The new inference method, also exact, is composed of two stages: a propagation in the original network, and the combination of this information with that one stored in the second document layer, updating the probability of relevance of each document given a query with the strength of the relationships among the documents. The empirical results show an improvement of the performance of the BN-3 model, revealing the suitability of the document layer extension.

As future works, we plan to design another method to establish the parents of each document node by using, instead of the values $p(d_j|d_i)$, the values $p(d_j|pa(D_i))$ (i.e., instantiating, instead of each document D_i, the individual terms it contains). We want to test whether there is any difference in the results, and determine which method would perform better. A second research line will be the development of new probability functions in the second document layer, to more accurately combine the information about the relevance of the documents given the query and the strength of the document relationships. We are also planning to extend our model to cope with boolean queries.

On the other hand, we have tested our models with some standard test collections, whose sizes are smaller than actual collections. Our objective has been just to determine the validity of the proposed models for IR, focusing our attention only in modelling aspects. Experimentation with TREC collections will be one of the most important points in which we are going to center our future research. The basic next objective will be to determine the efficiency and effectiveness of our models with these collections. This task could suggest some modifications or refinements in our models, related to the propagation and construction of the second document layer.

Acknowledgments. This work has been supported by the Spanish Comisión Interministerial de Ciencia y Tecnología (CICYT), under Project TIC2000-1351.

References

1. L.M. de Campos, J.M. Fernández-Luna, and J.F. Huete. Building Bayesian network-based information retrieval systems. In 2nd *Workshop on Logical and Uncertainty Models for Information Systems (LUMIS)*, 543–552, 2000.
2. J.M. Fernández-Luna. Modelos de Recuperación de Información Basados en Redes de Creencia (in Spanish). Ph.D. Thesis, Universidad de Granada, 2001.
3. R. Fung and B.D. Favero. Applying Bayesian networks to information retrieval. *Communications of the ACM*, 38(2):42–57, 1995.
4. M.E. Maron and J.L. Kuhns. On relevance, probabilistic indexing and information retrieval. *Journal of the ACM*, 7:216–244, 1960.
5. J. Pearl. *Probabilistic Reasoning in Intelligent Systems: Networks of Plausible Inference*. Morgan and Kaufmann, San Mateo, 1988.
6. I. Reis Silva. Bayesian Networks for Information Retrieval Systems. Ph.D. Thesis, Universidad Federal de Minas Gerais, 2000.
7. B.A. Ribeiro-Neto and R.R. Muntz. A belief network model for IR. In *Proceedings of the 19th ACM–SIGIR Conference*, H. Frei, D. Harman, P. Schäble and R. Wilkinson, eds., 253–260, 1996.
8. C.J. van Rijsbergen. *Information Retrieval. Second Edition*. Butter Worths, London, 1979.
9. S.E. Robertson and K. Sparck Jones. Relevance weighting of search terms. *Journal of the American Society for Information Science*, 27:129–146, 1976.
10. G. Salton and M.J. McGill. *Introduction to Modern Information Retrieval*. McGraw-Hill, Inc., 1983.
11. I. Silva, B. Ribeiro-Neto, P. Calado, E. Moura, and N. Ziviani. Link-based and content-based evidential information in a belief network model. In *Proceedings of the 23th ACM–SIGIR Conference*, 96–103, 2000.
12. K. Sparck Jones, S. Walker, and S.E. Robertson. A probabilistic model of information retrieval: development and comparative experiments Part 1. *Information Processing and Management*, 36:779–808, 2000.
13. H.R. Turtle, Inference Networks for Document Retrieval, Ph.D. Thesis, Computer and Information Science Dpt., University of Massachusetts, 1990.
14. H.R. Turtle and W.B. Croft. Inference networks for document retrieval. In *Proceedings of the 13th ACM–SIGIR Conference*, J.-L. Vidick, ed., 1–24, 1990.
15. H.R. Turtle and W.B. Croft. Efficient probabilistic inference for text retrieval. In *Proceedings of the RIAO'91 Conference*, 644–661, 1991.
16. H. R. Turtle and W. B. Croft. Evaluation of an inference network-based retrieval model. *Information Systems*, 9(3):187–222, 1991.

Term Frequency Normalization via Pareto Distributions

Gianni Amati[1,2] and Cornelis Joost van Rijsbergen[2]

[1] Fondazione Ugo Bordoni,
v. B. Castiglione 59, 00142 Roma, Italy
gba@fub.it
[2] Computing Science Department, University of Glasgow,
17 Lilybank Gardens, G12 8QQ Glasgow, Scotland
keith@dcs.gla.ac.uk

Abstract. We exploit the Feller-Pareto characterization of the classical Pareto distribution to derive a law relating the probability of a given term frequency in a document and its the length. A similar law was derived by Mandelbrot. We exploit the paretian distribution to obtain a term frequency normalization to substitute for the actual term frequency in the probabilistic models of Information Retrieval recently introduced in TREC-10. Preliminary results show that the unique parameter of the framework can be eliminated in favour of the the term frequency normalization derived by the Paretian law.

1 Introduction

A new framework [2] for deriving models of Information Retrieval was introduced in TREC-10[1]. One of these models, $B_E L$, together with Kullback-Leibler query expansion technique[4], performed very well in topic relevance WEB track.

The term weighting model $B_E L$ is based on the Bose-Einstein statistics and is defined as follows

$$\frac{1}{tfn+1} \cdot \left(-\log_2 \left(\frac{1}{1+\lambda} \right) - tfn \cdot \log_2 \left(\frac{\lambda}{1+\lambda} \right) \right) \tag{1}$$

$$tfn = tf \cdot \log_2 \left(1 + \frac{c \cdot avg\_l}{l} \right)$$

where

- λ is the mean of the term frequency in the collection,
- tf the actual term frequency in the observed document
- l, the document length and
- avg_l is the average document length

For the WT10g collection (containing about 10Gbytes of real WEB pages) the unique parameter c of the model was set to 7. This value was derived by using the relevance assessments on the collection. The definition of the term frequency

F. Crestani, M. Girolami, and C.J. van Rijsbergen (Eds.): ECIR 2002, LNCS 2291, pp. 183–192, 2002.

normalization tfn of Formula 1 is formally obtained by supposing that the density of the term frequency $\frac{tf}{l}$ is not constant but a function of the length l.

In this paper we we will test an alternative way of deriving the function tfn. The objective is to eliminate the only parameter c. In substitution of c, we introduce another parameter which does not need to be learned from the relevance assessments, but directly from the collection. The advantage of obtaining such a result would be extremely important in pratical applications, since we will obtain the first example of a robust Information Retrieval model which does not need to be trained by relevance data.

We will derive two laws from Pareto-Feller distributions. The first (see Equation 14) relates the probability of a given term frequency in a document with its the length, the second (see Equation 16) relates the probability of a given term frequency in a document with the size of the vocabulary (the number of unique terms used in the document). Similar laws were derived by Mandelbrot[12] by using the Zipf distribution (see Equation 24). We exploit these results to obtain a new term frequency normalization function tfn wich will be substituted for the actual term frequency in Formula 1.

The paper is organized as follows:

- We first introduce the Pareto-Feller distribution and derives the classical Pareto distribution [3].
- We formally derive the two main relations between term frequencies and size of the sample and between size of the sample and size of the vocabulary.
- We exploit both these two relations to derive Relation 17 and the value for A as defined in Formula 19 respectively.
- Finally, experiments will show the soundness of the approach.

2   Fat–Tailed Distributions

Fat–tailed (or heavy-tailed) distributions are encountered in many different linguistic, sociological, biological and economic settings, such as distributions of word frequencies, cities by population, biological genera by numbers of species, scientists by number of published papers, income by size and, recently, files by size [6,10]. Among fat-tailed distributions there are the family of Pareto's distributions [3], which were originally introduced for income distributions, Champernowne's lognormal distribution [5], the Waring distribution [11], the Yule distribution [15], the generalized inverse Gaussian distribution [14,13].

In the context of linguistic applications, Estoup, Willis and Zipf[7,16,17] introduced an empirical relationship between the frequency and the rank of the words which are used in the ordinary discourse. Such an empirical law is commonly known as Zipf's law. The distribution used by Zipf's law is the discrete analogue of the Pareto distribution.

An alternative frequency word distribution law was due to Champernowne who used the lognormal distribution (the normal distribution of the logarithmic values of the random variable). The use of Champernowne's distribution was strongly criticised by Mandelbrot [12] in favour of Simon's proposal [15] which endeavoured to use the Yule distribution, a generalization of the Zipf distribution, as a unified model to derive many fat–tailed distributions. He applied the Yule distribution to the word distribution in prose sample. Though Pareto's distributions and the Yule distributions both generalize Zipf's law, they differ significantly. Feller[9] has proposed an interesting characterization of fat-tailed distributions known as Feller-Pareto distributions. Classical and standard Pareto distributions can be derived from Feller-Pareto's family by introducing the generalized Pareto distributions. According to this representation a generalized Pareto distribution can be seen as a linear combination of a power of the inverse of the Beta distribution[3].

3   Preliminaries: Feller-Pareto Distributions

Let $U = Y^{-1} - 1$ be a random variable where Y has the beta distribution with parameters $\alpha > 0$ and $\beta > 0$. U is said to have a *Feller-Pareto distribution*. With the Feller-Pareto distributions we are able to introduce the generalized, the classical and the standard Pareto distributions. The standard Pareto distribution is the continuous analogue of the standard discrete Zipf distribution.

The Feller-Pareto probability density function derives from 22[see appendix] by substituting $y = (1 + u)^{-1}$

$$f_U(u) = \frac{\Gamma(\alpha + \beta)}{\Gamma(\alpha)\Gamma(\beta)} \left(\frac{1}{u+1}\right)^{\alpha-1} \left(\frac{u}{u+1}\right)^{\beta-1} (u+1)^{-2}$$

$$= \frac{\Gamma(\alpha + \beta)}{\Gamma(\alpha)\Gamma(\beta)} (u+1)^{-(\alpha+\beta)} u^{\beta-1} \tag{2}$$

$$\text{with } u > 0$$

Equation 2 follows from $\dfrac{dY}{dU} = -(U+1)^{-2}$ and from that U is a decreasing function with respect to Y.

The generalized Pareto distribution. The *generalized Pareto distribution* of a random variable W is obtained by a linear combination of a power of U, where U has the Feller-Pareto distribution, as follows:

$$W(\mu, \sigma, \gamma, \alpha, \beta) = \mu + \sigma U^\gamma \tag{3}$$

$$P(W > w) = P(\mu + \sigma U^\gamma > w) = P\left(U > \left(\tfrac{w-\mu}{\sigma}\right)^{\frac{1}{\gamma}}\right)$$

$$\text{with } w > \mu$$

From $U = \left(\dfrac{W - \mu}{\sigma}\right)^{\frac{1}{\gamma}}$, $\dfrac{dU}{dW} = \dfrac{1}{\gamma\sigma}\left(\dfrac{W - \mu}{\sigma}\right)^{\frac{1}{\gamma}-1}$ and Equation 2 we derive the probability density function of the generalized Pareto distribution:

$$f_W(w) = \frac{\Gamma(\alpha + \beta)}{\Gamma(\alpha)\Gamma(\beta)} \left(\left(\frac{w - \mu}{\sigma}\right)^{\frac{1}{\gamma}} + 1\right)^{-(\alpha+\beta)} .$$

$$\cdot \left(\frac{w - \mu}{\sigma}\right)^{\frac{\beta - 1}{\gamma}} \frac{1}{\gamma\sigma} \left(\frac{w - \mu}{\sigma}\right)^{\frac{1}{\gamma} - 1}$$

$$= \frac{\Gamma(\alpha + \beta)}{\Gamma(\alpha)\Gamma(\beta)\gamma\sigma} \left(\left(\frac{w - \mu}{\sigma}\right)^{\frac{1}{\gamma}} + 1\right)^{-(\alpha + \beta)} \left(\frac{w - \mu}{\sigma}\right)^{\frac{\beta}{\gamma} - 1}$$

$$\text{with } w > \mu \tag{4}$$

3.1   The Classical Pareto Distribution

The *classical Pareto distribution* is obtained from the generalized Pareto distribution with $W(\sigma, \sigma, 1, \alpha, 1)$ whose probability density function is:

$$f_W(w) = \frac{\Gamma(\alpha + 1)}{\Gamma(\alpha)\sigma} \left(\frac{w}{\sigma}\right)^{-(\alpha + 1)} \text{ with } w > \sigma$$

$$= \frac{\alpha}{\sigma} \left(\frac{w}{\sigma}\right)^{-(\alpha + 1)} \qquad \text{with } w > \sigma \tag{5}$$

The classical Pareto distribution is then

$$P(W > x) = \int_\sigma^x \frac{\alpha}{\sigma} \left(\frac{w}{\sigma}\right)^{-(\alpha + 1)} dw = 1 - \left(\frac{x}{\sigma}\right)^{-\alpha}$$

The discrete analogue of classical Pareto distribution: Zipf's law. Suppose that the random variable X receives the discrete values $0, 1, 2, \ldots$ or $1, 2, \ldots$ and that X has a fat-tailed distribution. Consider a sample made up of n observations. Suppose that there are V possible outcomes and that their frequency is such that $p(r + 1) = P(X = r + 1) \leq p(r) = P(X = r)$. According to [3] Zipf distributions are discretized Pareto distributions. The discrete analogous of Formula 4 is

$$P(X \geq r) = \left(1 + \left(\frac{r - r_0}{\sigma}\right)^{\frac{1}{\gamma}}\right)^{-\alpha} \quad r \geq r_0 \tag{6}$$

For $\gamma = \alpha = \sigma = 1$ and $r_0 = 0$ we obtain the standard Zipf distribution:

$$P(X \geq r) = (1 + r)^{-1} \ r \geq 0 \tag{7}$$

For $\gamma = 1$ we obtain the Zipf distributions which are the discrete analogues of the classical Pareto distributions:

$$P(X \geq r) = \left(1 + \frac{r - r_0}{\sigma}\right)^{-\alpha} r \geq r_0 \tag{8}$$

The standard Pareto distribution. The *standard Pareto distribution* of a random variable Z is obtained from the generalized Pareto distribution $W(0, 1, 1, 1, 1)$. Its probability density function is:

$$f_Z(z) = (1 + z)^{-2} \text{ with } z > 0 \tag{9}$$

4   Term Frequency Normalization Based on the Classical Pareto Distribution

Let d be a document of length l and let V be the set of all terms contained in the collection. The probability that a given term t_r occurs i times in the document is according to the binomial law:

$$p(i|l, t_r) = \binom{l}{i} p_r^i (1 - p_r)^{l-i} \quad \text{where} p_r = P(X = r) \tag{10}$$

The probability $p(i|l)$ that *any* term occurs i times in the documents is given by the sum of $p(i|l, t_r)$ over all terms. If we use the classical Pareto density function to obtain the sum then $p = p(r)$ and r ranges from 0 to ∞:

$$p(i|l) = \int_0^\infty \binom{l}{i} p^i (1 - p)^{l-i} dr \tag{11}$$

We have to express the ranking variable r as function of its probability p by using Equation 5, namely

$$r = \sigma \left(p \frac{\sigma}{\alpha} \right)^{-\frac{1}{\alpha+1}}$$

hence

$$\frac{dr}{dp} = -\frac{1}{\alpha(\alpha+1)} \sigma^2 \left(p \frac{\sigma}{\alpha} \right)^{-\frac{1}{(\alpha+1)} - 1}$$

$$= -\frac{\sigma}{(\alpha+1)} \left(\frac{\sigma}{\alpha} \right)^{-\frac{1}{(\alpha+1)}} \cdot p^{-\frac{\alpha+2}{\alpha+1}}$$

Let

$$C = \frac{\sigma}{(\alpha+1)} \left(\frac{\sigma}{\alpha \cdot l} \right)^{-\frac{1}{\alpha+1}} \tag{12}$$

and $\lambda = pl$. We approximate the binomial by the Poisson, thus Equation 11 becomes for l large:

$$p(i|l) = C \int_0^1 l^{-\frac{1}{\alpha+1}} \binom{l}{i} p^i (1 - p)^{l-i} p^{-\frac{\alpha+2}{\alpha+1}} dp$$

$$= C \int_0^\infty \frac{e^{-\lambda}}{i!} \lambda^{i - \frac{1}{\alpha+1} - 1} d\lambda$$

$$= \frac{C}{i!} \Gamma \left(i - \frac{1}{\alpha+1} \right)$$

$$= C \frac{\Gamma \left(i - \frac{1}{\alpha+1} \right)}{\Gamma(i+1)} \tag{13}$$

By using the approximation formula of the gamma function [8, page 66]

$$\Gamma(x) \sim \sqrt{2\pi} e^{-x} x^{x-0.5}$$

and by using the Stirling formula for the approximation of the factorial

$$n! \sim \sqrt{2\pi} e^{-n} n^{n+0.5}$$

Equation 13 becomes with $A = (\alpha + 1)^{-1}$

$$p(i|l) = \frac{C\sqrt{2\pi} e^{-i+A} (i-A)^{i-A-0.5}}{\sqrt{2\pi} e^{-i} i^{i+0.5}}$$

$$= C \frac{e^A \left(\dfrac{i-A}{i}\right)^{i-A-0.5}}{i^{A+1}}$$

When i is large, $\left(\dfrac{i-A}{i}\right)^{i-A-0.5} \sim e^{-A}$, therefore:

$$p(i|l) = C \cdot i^{-(A+1)}$$

$$= A\sigma \left(\frac{\sigma}{\alpha \cdot l}\right)^{-A} i^{-(A+1)}$$

$$p(i|l) = A\sigma^{1-A} (A^{-1} - 1)^A l^A i^{-(A+1)} \tag{14}$$

$$i \text{ large and } A = (1 + \alpha)^{-1}$$

4.1   The Relationship between the Vocabulary and the Length of the Document

Let t be the r-th term with probability $p(r)$ of occurring at a given place in the document d of length l. Its probability of occurring in the document is thus $p(t_r) = 1 - (1 - p(r))^l = 1 - e^{-\lambda(r)}$ where $\lambda(r) = p(r)l$. Suppose that l is large. The expected number of different words which will appear in the sample of l words is

$$V(l) = \sum_r p(t_r)$$

By setting $A = (1 + \alpha)^{-1}$ and

$$C_0 = A\sigma^{1-A} \left(A^{-1} - 1\right)^A$$

then

$$\frac{dr}{dp} = C_0 \cdot p^{-A-1}$$

By computing

$$V(l+1) - V(l) = \sum_r p(r)(1 - p(r))^l = \sum_r p(r) \left(1 - e^{-\lambda(r)}\right)$$

By using the classical Pareto distribution

$$
\begin{aligned}
V(l+1) - V(l) &= C_0 \int_0^1 e^{-\lambda(r)} p^{-A} dp \\
&= C_0 \int_0^1 e^{-\lambda(r)} p^{-A} dp \\
&= C_0 l^{A-1} \int_0^\infty e^{-\lambda} \lambda^{-A} d\lambda \\
&= C_0 l^{A-1} \Gamma(1-A)
\end{aligned}
\tag{15}
$$

Equation 15 can be considered the variation of the function V with respect to the length. Hence its integral in the interval $[0, l]$ is

$$
\begin{aligned}
V(l) &= \frac{C_0}{A} l^A \Gamma(1-A) \\
&= \sigma^{1-A} \left(\frac{1-A}{A}\right)^A l^A \Gamma(1-A)
\end{aligned}
\tag{16}
$$

4.2 Application to the WT10g Collection

Let us exploit relation 16 in order to derive suitable values for A for the collection WT10g. According to our indexing process we have determined a number V of $293,484$ unique words with length $L = 469,493,061$. If $\sigma = 230$ is the number of most frequent words used in the stop list, then the value for α (A) in Equation 16 relating σ, V and L is 0.82 (0.55). This value for α (A) will be used in the term frequency normalization in Section 4.3.

4.3 The *tfn* Formula

We can use formula 14 to obtain the relation

$$
\frac{p(tf|l)}{p(tfn|avg\_l)} = \frac{l^A tf^{-(A+1)}}{avg\_l^A tfn^{-(A+1)}}
$$

If we suppose that $p(tf|l) = p(tfn|avg\_l)$ we derive

$$
tfn = tf \cdot \left(\frac{avg\_l}{l}\right)^{\frac{A}{A+1}}
\tag{17}
$$

Since A is related to the value $\alpha > 0$ by relation 14, A ranges in the interval $(0, 1]$ and thus $Z = \frac{A}{A+1}$ ranges in the interval $(0, 0.5]$. As for the collection WT10g we get

$$
Z = \frac{A}{A+1} = 0.35
\tag{18}
$$

Therefore, we obtain the following relation

$$
tfn = tf \cdot \left(\frac{avg\_l}{l}\right)^{0.35}
\tag{19}
$$

Table 1. Comparison of performance of B_EL and term frequency normalizations.

Method	Parameter	AvPrec	Prec-at-10	Prec-at-20	Prec-at-30
	Model performance without query expansion				
B_EL	c=7	0.1788	0.3180	0.2730	0.2413
B_EL	Zipf Z =0.30	0.1824	0.3180	0.2700	0.2393
B_EL	Zipf Z =0.35	0.1813	0.3200	0.2590	0.2393
B_EL	Zipf Z =0.40	0.1817	0.3240	0.2670	0.2393

5   Experiments

It is quite surprising to verify that the value 0.35 in Equation 19 is indeed in the range of to the best matching values for retrieval $(0.30 - 0.40)$ with the set of queries of TREC-10 as reported in Table 1. Moreover, the performance of the model B_EL without query expansion is slightly superior to that used in TREC–10 without query expansion (first line of the Table 1.

6   Conclusions

This paper shows how to define an information retrieval model which does not make use of parameters to be learned by training the system with relevance assessment data. The model uses as basic model the Bose-Einstein statistics, whilst the Pareto-distribution is used to derive the normalization of the term frequency. Experiments with a large collection corroborates the theory. Indeed the basic model B_EL used in TREC-10 which, together with the query expansion, has produced an excellent performance in the WEB topic relevance track has improved its performance with this new normalization.

7   Appendix

The Gamma function is defined by

$$\Gamma(x) = \int_0^\infty t^{x-1}e^{-t}dt \ (\text{ where } x > 0) \tag{20}$$

A random variable X has a Gamma distribution with parameters α and β $(\alpha > 0$ and $\beta > 0)$ if X has the probability density function defined by

$$\frac{\beta^\alpha}{\Gamma(\alpha)}x^{\alpha-1}e^{-\beta x} \ (\text{ where } x > 0) \tag{21}$$

The Beta distribution function of a random variable Y with parameters α and β is defined by the probability density function:

$$f_Y(y, \alpha, \beta) = \frac{\Gamma(\alpha+\beta)}{\Gamma(\alpha)\Gamma(\beta)}y^{\alpha-1}(1-y)^{\beta-1} \ (0 < y < 1) \tag{22}$$

Mandelbrot's probability density function of rank-word frequency is:

$$p(r) = (B - 1)V^{B-1}(r + V)^{-B} \qquad (23)$$

The following distribution is the Zipf distribution and was claimed to be experimentally an excellent approximation of the Equation 23 by Mandelbrot:

$$p(r) = P \cdot r^{-B} \text{ where } P^{-1} = \sum_{r=1}^{\infty}(r + V)^{-B} \qquad (24)$$

The *Yule distribution* is:

$$p(r) = C \cdot B(r, \rho + 1) \text{ where } B(.,.) \text{ is the Beta function} \qquad (25)$$

Acknowledments. We would like to thank Giovanni Romano to have produced the runs on TREC-10 data reported in this paper.

References

1. Gianni Amati, Claudio Carpineto, and Giovanni Romano. FUB at TREC 10 web track: a probabilistic framework for topic relevance term weighting. In *In Proceedings of the 10th Text Retrieval Conference (TREC-10)*, Gaithersburg, MD, 2001.
2. Gianni Amati and Cornelis Joost van Rijsbergen. Probabilistic models of information retrieval based on measuring divergence from randomness. *Submitted to TOIS*, 2001.
3. Barry C. Arnold. *Pareto distributions.* International Co-operative Publishing House, Fairland, Md., 1983.
4. C. Carpineto, R. De Mori, G. Romano, and B. Bigi. An information theoretic approach to automatic query expansion. *ACM Transactions on Information Systems*, 19(1):1–27, 2001.
5. D.G. Champernowne. The theory of income distribution. *Econometrica*, 5:379–381, 1937.
6. Mark E. Crovella, Murad S. Taqqu, and Azer Bestavros. Heavy–tailed probability distributions in the world wide web. In R.J. Adler, R.E. Feldman, and M.S. Taqqu, editors, *A practical guide to heavy tails*. Birkhauser, Boston, Basel and Berlin, 1998.
7. J.B. Estoup. *Gammes Stenographiques.* 4th edition, Paris, 1916.
8. William Feller. *An introduction to probability theory and its applications. Vol. I.* John Wiley & Sons Inc., New York, third edition, 1968.
9. William Feller. *An Introduction to Probability Theory and Its Applications*, volume II. John Wiley & Sons, New York, second edition, 1971.
10. D Hawking. Overview of the trec-9 web track. In *In Proceedings of the 9th Text Retrieval Conference (TREC-9)*, Gaithersburg, MD, 2001.
11. G. Herdan. *Quantitative Linguistics.* Butterworths, 1964.
12. Benoit Mandelbrot. On the theory of word frequencies and on related markovian models of discourse. In *Proceedings of Symposia in Applied Mathematics. Vol. XII: Structure of language and its mathematical aspects*, pages 190–219. American Mathematical Society, Providence, R.I., 1961. Roman Jakobson, editor.
13. H. S. Sichel. Parameter estimation for a word frequency distribution based on occupancy theory. *Comm. Statist. A—Theory Methods*, 15(3):935–949, 1986.

14. H. S. Sichel. Word frequency distributions and type-token characteristics. *Math. Sci.*, 11(1):45–72, 1986.
15. Herbert A. Simon. On a class of skew distribution functions. *Biometrika*, 42:425–440, 1955.
16. J.C. Willis. *Age and area*. Cambridge University Press, London and New York, 1922.
17. G.K. Zipf. *Human behavior and the principle of least effort*. Addison-Wesley Press, Reading, Massachusetts, 1949.

Optimal Mixture Models in IR

Victor Lavrenko

Center for Intelligent Information Retrieval
Department of Comupter Science
University of Massachusetts, Amherst, MA 01003,
lavrenko@cs.umass.edu

Abstract. We explore the use of Optimal Mixture Models to represent topics. We analyze two broad classes of mixture models: set-based and weighted. We provide an original proof that estimation of set-based models is NP-hard, and therefore not feasible. We argue that weighted models are superior to set-based models, and the solution can be estimated by a simple gradient descent technique. We demonstrate that Optimal Mixture Models can be successfully applied to the task of document retrieval. Our experiments show that weighted mixtures outperform a simple language modeling baseline. We also observe that weighted mixtures are more robust than other approaches of estimating topical models.

1 Introduction

Statistical Language Modeling approaches have been steadily gaining popularity in the field of Information Retrieval. They were first introduced by Ponte and Croft [18], and were expanded upon in a number of following publications [4,15,24,8,9,11,14]. These approaches have proven to be very effective in a number of applications, including ad-hoc retrieval [18,4,15], topic detection and tracking [26,10], summarization [5], question answering [3], text segmentation [2], and other tasks. The main strength of Language Modeling techniques lies in very careful estimation of word probabilities, something that has been done in a heuristic fashion in prior research on Information Retrieval [21, 19,20,25].

A common theme in Language Modeling approaches is that natural language is viewed as a result of repeated sampling from some underlying probability distribution over the vocabulary. If one accepts that model of text generation, many Information Retrieval problems can be re-cast in terms of estimating the probability of observing a given sample of text from a particular distribution. For example, if we knew a distribution of words in a certain topic of interest, we could estimate the probability that a given document is relevant to that topic, as was done in [26,21,14]. Alternatively, we could associate a probability distribution with every document in a large collection, and calculate the probability that a question or a query was a sample from that document [18,4,15].

1.1 Mixture Models

Mixture models represent a very popular estimation technique in the field of Language Modeling. A mixture model is simply a linear combination of several different distributions. Mixture models, in one shape or another, have been employed in every major

F. Crestani, M. Girolami, and C.J. van Rijsbergen (Eds.): ECIR 2002, LNCS 2291, pp. 193–212, 2002.
© Springer-Verlag Berlin Heidelberg 2002

Language Modeling publication to date. For example, *smoothing* [6,12,17], a critical component of any language model, can be interpreted as a *mixture* of a topic model with a background model, as highlighted in [15,13,16].

This paper will be primarily concerned with the use of mixtures to represent semantic topic models. For the scope of this paper, a topic model will be defined as a distribution, which gives the probability of observing any given word in documents that discuss some particular topic. A popular way to estimate the topic model is by mixing word probabilities from the documents that are believed to be related to that topic. In the next section we will briefly survey a number of publications exploring the use of mixture models to represent topical content.

1.2   Related Work on Mixture Models

Hoffman [9] described the use of latent semantic variables to represent different topical aspects of documents. Hoffman assumed that there exist a fixed number of latent topical distributions and represented documents as weighted mixtures of those distributions. Hoffman used an expectation-maximization algorithm to automatically induce topical distributions by maximizing the likelihood of the entire training set. It is worthwhile to point out that the nature of the estimation algorithm used by Hoffman also allows one to re-express these latent aspect distributions as mixtures of individual document models.

Berger and Lafferty [4] introduced an approach to Information Retrieval that was based on ideas from Statistical Machine Translation. The authors estimated a semantic model of the document as a weighted mixture of translation vectors. While this model does not involve mixing document models, it is still an example of a mixture model.

In the context of Topic Detection and Tracking [1], several researchers used un-weighted mixtures of training documents to represent event-based topics. Specifically, Jin et.al. [10] trained a Markov model from positive examples, and Yamron et.al. [26] used clustering techniques to represent background topics in the dataset (a topic was represented as a mixture of the documents in the cluster).

Lavrenko [13] considered topical mixture models as a way to improve the effectiveness of smoothing. Recall that smoothing is usually done by combining the sparse topic model (obtained by counting words in some sample of text) with the background model. Lavrenko hypothesized that by using a *zone* of closely related text samples he could achieve semantic smoothing, where words that are closely related to the original topic would get higher probabilities. Lavrenko used an unweighted mixture model, similar to the one we will describe in section 3.1. The main drawback of the approach was that performance was extremely sensitive to the size of the subset he called the *zone*. A similar problem was encountered by Ogilvie [16] when he attempted to smooth document models with models of their nearest neighbors.

In two very recent publications, both Lafferty and Zhai [11], and Lavrenko and Croft [14] proposed using a weighted mixture of top-ranked documents from the query to represent a topic model. The process of assigning the weights to the documents is quite different in the two publications. Lafferty and Zhai describe an iterative procedure, formalized as a Markov chain on the inverted indexes. Lavrenko and Croft estimate a joint probability of observing the query words together with any possible word in the vocabulary. Both approaches can be expressed as mixtures of document models, and in both cases the authors pointed out that performance of their methods was strongly dependent on the number of top-ranked documents over which they estimated the probabilities.

1.3 Overview

The remainder of this paper is structured as follows. In section 2 we formally define the problem of finding an *Optimal Mixture Model* (OMM) for a given observation. We also describe a lower bound on solutions to any OMM problem. Section 3 describes unweighted optimal mixture models and proves that finding such models is computationally infeasible. Section 4.1 defines weighted mixture models, and discusses a gradient descent technique for approximating them. Section 5 describes a set of retrieval experiments we carried out to test the empirical performance of Optimal Mixture Models.

2 Optimal Mixture Models

As we pointed out in section 1.2, a number of researchers [13,16,11,14] who employed mixture models observed that the quality of the model is strongly dependent on the subset of documents that are used to estimate the model. In most cases the researchers used a fixed number of top-ranked documents, retrieved in response to the query. The number of documents turns out to be an important parameter that has a strong effect on performance and varies from query to query and from dataset to dataset. The desire to select this parameter automatically is the primary motivation behind the present paper. We would like to find the optimal subset of documents and form an *Optimal Mixture Model*. Optimality can be defined in a number of different ways, for instance it could mean best retrieval performance with respect to some particular metric, like precision or recall. However, optimizing to such metrics requires the knowledge of relevance judgments, which are not always available at the time when we want to form our mixture model. In this paper we take a very simple criterion for optimality. Suppose we have a sample observation: $W_1 \ldots W_k$, which could be a user's query, or an example document. The optimal mixture model M_{opt} is a model which assigns the highest probability to our observation.

2.1 Formal Problem Statement

Suppose $W = \{1 \ldots n\}$ is our vocabulary, and $W_1 \ldots W_k$ is a string over that vocabulary. Let $I\!P$ be the simplex of all probability distributions over W, that is $I\!P = \{x \in I\!R^n : x \geq 0, |x| = 1\}$. In most cases we will not be interested in the whole simplex $I\!P$, but only in a small subset $I\!P' \subset I\!P$, which corresponds to the set of all possible mixture models. Exact construction of $I\!P'$ is different for different types of mixture models, and will be detailed later. The optimal model M_{opt} is the element of $I\!P'$ that gives the maximum likelihood to the observation $W_1 \ldots W_k$:

$$M_{opt} = \arg \max_{M \in I\!P'} P(W_1 \ldots W_k | M) \qquad (1)$$

In Information Retrieval research, it is common to assume that words $W_1 \ldots W_k$ are mutually independent of each other, once we fix a model M. Equivalently, we can say that each model M is a *unigram* model, and W_i represent repeated random samples from M. This allows us to compute the joint probability $P(W_1 \ldots W_k | M)$ as the product of the marginals:

$$M_{opt} = \arg \max_{M \in I\!P'} \prod_{i=1}^{k} P(W_i | M) \tag{2}$$

Now we can make another assumption common in Information Retrieval: we declare that $W_1 \ldots W_k$ are identically distributed according to M, that is for every word w we have $P(W_1 = w | M) = \ldots = P(W_k = w | M)$. Assuming W_i are identically distributed allows us to re-arrange the terms in the product above, and group together all terms that share the same w:

$$M_{opt} = \arg \max_{M \in I\!P'} \prod_{w \in W} P(w | M)^{\#w(W_1 \ldots W_k)} \tag{3}$$

Here the product goes over all the words w in our vocabulary, and $\#w(W_1 \ldots W_k)$ is just the number of times w was observed in our sample $W_1 \ldots W_k$. If we let $T_w = \frac{\#w(W_1 \ldots W_k)}{k}$, use a shorthand M_w for $P(w|M)$, and take a logarithm of the objective (which does not affect maximization), we can re-express M_{opt} as follows:

$$M_{opt} = \arg \max_{M \in I\!P'} \sum_{w \in W} T_w \log M_w \tag{4}$$

Note that by definition, T is also a distribution over the vocabulary, i.e. T is a member of $I\!P$, although it may not be a member of our subset $I\!P'$. We can think of T as an *empirical* distribution of the observation $W_1 \ldots W_k$. Now, since both M and T are distributions, maximization of the above summation is equivalent to minimizing the cross-entropy of distributions T and M:

$$M_{opt} = \arg \min_{M \in I\!P'} H(T|M) \tag{5}$$

Equation (5) will be used as our objective for forming optimal mixture models in all the remaining sections of this paper. The main differences will be in the composition of the subset $I\!P'$, but the objective will remain unchanged.

2.2   Lower Bound on OMM Solutions

Suppose we allowed $I\!P'$ to include all possible distributions over our vocabulary, that is we make $I\!P' = I\!P$. Then we can prove that T itself is the unique optimal solution of equation (5). The proof is detailed in section A.1 of the Appendix.

This observation serves as a very important step in analyzing the computational complexity of finding the optimal model M out of the set $I\!P'$. We proved that any solution M will be no better than T itself. This implies that for every set $I\!P'$, determining whether $T \in I\!P'$ is no more difficult than finding an optimal mixture model from that same set

$I\!P'$. The reduction is very simple: given $I\!P'$ and T, let M be the solution of equation (5). Then, according to section A.1, $T \in I\!P'$ if and only if $M = T$. Testing whether $M = T$ can be done in linear time (with respect to the size of our vocabulary), so we have a polynomial-time reduction from testing whether T is a member of $I\!P'$ to solving equation (5) and finding an optimal mixture model.

This result will be used in the remainder of this paper to prove that for certain sets $I\!P'$, solving equation (5) is NP-hard. In all cases we will show that testing whether $T \in I\!P'$ is NP-hard, and use the polynomial-time reduction from this section to assert that solving equation (5) for that particular $I\!P'$ is NP-hard as well.

3   Set-Based Mixture Models

The most simple and intuitive type of mixture models is a set-based mixture. In this section we describe two simple ways of constructing a mixture model if we are given a set of documents. One is based on concatenating the documents in the set, the other – on averaging the document models. Very similar models were considered by Lavrenko [13] and Ogilvie [16] in their attempts to create unweighted mixture models. Estimating either of these models from a given set of documents is trivial. However, if we try to look for the *optimal* set of documents, the problem becomes infeasible, as we show in section 3.3.

3.1   Pooled Optimal Mixture Models

First we define a restricted class of mixture models that can be formed by "concatenating" several pieces of text and taking the empirical distribution of the result. To make this more formal, suppose we are given a large collection $\mathcal{C}$ of text samples of varying length. In this paper we will only consider finite sets $\mathcal{C}$. For Information Retrieval applications $\mathcal{C}$ will be a collection of documents. For every text sample $\mathcal{T} \in \mathcal{C}$ we can construct its empirical distribution by setting $\mathcal{T}_w = \frac{\#w(\mathcal{T})}{|\mathcal{T}|}$, just as we did in section 2.1. Here, $|\mathcal{T}|$ denotes the total number of words in $\mathcal{T}$. Similarly, for every subset $S \subset \mathcal{C}$, we can construct its empirical distribution by concatenating together all elements $\mathcal{T} \in S$, and constructing the distribution of the resulting text. In that case, the probability mass on the word w would be:

$$S_w = \frac{\sum_{\mathcal{T} \in S} \#w(\mathcal{T})}{\sum_{\mathcal{T} \in S} |\mathcal{T}|} \tag{6}$$

Now, for a given collection of samples $\mathcal{C}$, we define the pooled mixture set $I\!P_{\mathcal{C},pool}$ to be the set of empirical distributions of all the subsets S of $\mathcal{C}$, where probabilities are computed according to equation (6). We define the *Pooled Optimal Mixture Model* (POMM) problem to be the task of solving equation (5) over the set $I\!P_{\mathcal{C},pool}$, i.e. finding the element $M \in I\!P_{\mathcal{C},pool}$, which minimizes the cross-entropy $H(T|M)$ with a given target distribution T.

3.2   Averaged Optimal Mixture Models

Next we consider another class of mixture models, similar to pooled models described in the last section. These models are also based on a collection $\mathcal{C}$ of text samples, and can be formed by "averaging" word frequencies across several pieces of text. To make this formal, let $\mathcal{C}$ be a finite collection of text samples. Let $\mathcal{M}$ be the corresponding collection of empirical distributions, that is for each observation $\mathcal{T}_j \in \mathcal{C}$, there exists a corresponding distribution $M_j \in \mathcal{M}$, such that $M_{j,w} = \frac{\#w(\mathcal{T})}{|\mathcal{T}|}$. For a subset $S' \subset \mathcal{C}$, we can construct its distribution by averaging together the empirical distributions of elements in S'. Let S' be a set of text samples, let S be the set of corresponding empirical models, and let $\#(S)$ denote the number of elements in S. The probability mass on the word w is:

$$S_w = \frac{1}{\#(S)} \sum_{M_j \in S} M_{j,w} \tag{7}$$

For a given collection of samples $\mathcal{C}$, we define the averaged mixture model set $\mathbb{P}_{\mathcal{C},avg}$ to be the set of averaged distributions of all subsets S' of $\mathcal{C}$, with probabilities computed according to equation (7). We define the *Averaged Optimal Mixture Model* (AOMM) problem to be the task of solving equation (5) over the set $\mathbb{P}_{\mathcal{C},avg}$.

3.3   Finding the Optimal Subset Is Infeasible

We outlined two possible ways for estimating a mixture model if we are given a set of documents. Now suppose we were given a target distribution T and a collection $\mathcal{C}$, and wanted to find a subset $S \subset \mathcal{C}$ which produces an optimal mixture model with respect to T. It turns out that this problem is computationally infeasible. Intuitively, this problem involves searching over an exponential number of possible subsets of $\mathcal{C}$. In section A.3 of the Appendix we prove that finding an optimal subset for pooled models is NP-hard. In section A.4 we show the same for averaged models. In both proofs we start by using the result of section 2.2 and converting the optimization problem to a decision problem over the same space of distributions. Then we describe a polynomial-time reduction from 3SAT to the corresponding decision problem. 3SAT (described in A.2) is a well-known NP-hard problem, and reducing it to finding an optimal subset of documents proves our searching problem to be NP-hard as well.

It is interesting to point out that we were not able to demonstrate that finding an optimal subset can actually be solved by a nondeterministic machine in polynomial time. It is easy to show that the *decision* problems corresponding to POMM and AOMM are in the NP class, but the original *optimization* problems appear to be more difficult.

4   Weighted Mixture Models

Now we turn our attention to another, more complex class of Optimal Mixture Models. For set-based models of section 3, the probabilities were completely determined by which documents belonged to the set, and no weighting on documents was allowed. Now we consider the kinds of models where in addition to selecting the subset, we also allow putting different weights on the documents in that subset. This flavor of mixture models was used by Hoffman [9], Lafferty and Zhai [11], and Lavrenko and Croft [14] in their research.

4.1   Weighted Optimal Mixture Models

Now if we want to find an optimal mixture model for some observation we not only need to find the subset of documents to use, but also need to estimate the optimal weights to place on those documents. At first glance it appears that allowing weights on documents will only aggravate the fact that finding optimal models is infeasible (section 3.3), since we just added more degrees of freedom to the problem. In reality, allowing weights to be placed on documents actually makes the problem solvable, as it paves the way for numerical approximations. Recall that both POMM and AOMM are essentially combinatorial problems, in both cases we attempt to reduce cross-entropy (equation (5)) over a finite set of distributions: $\mathbb{P}_{C,pool}$ for POMM, and $\mathbb{P}_{C,avg}$ for AOMM. Both sets are exponentially large with respect to C, but are finite and therefore full of discontinuities. In order to use numerical techniques we must have a continuous space $\mathbb{P}'$. In this section we describe how we can extend $\mathbb{P}_{C,pool}$ or equivalently $\mathbb{P}_{C,avg}$ to a continuous simplex $\mathbb{P}_{C,\lambda}$. We define the *Weighted Optimal Mixture Model* problem (WOMM) to be the optimization of equation (5) over the simplex $\mathbb{P}_{C,\lambda}$. We argue that a WOMM solution will always be no worse than the solution of a POMM or AOMM for a given C, although that solution may not necessarily lie in $\mathbb{P}_{C,pool}$ or $\mathbb{P}_{C,avg}$. We look at a simple gradient descent technique for solving WOMM. The technique is not guaranteed to find a globally optimal solution, but in practice converges quite rapidly and exhibits good performance.

WOMM Definition. Let C be our set of text samples and let $\mathcal{M}_C$ be the corresponding set of of empirical models $M_{\mathcal{T}}$ for each sample $\mathcal{T} \in C$. For an arbitrary set of weights $\lambda \in \mathbb{R}^{\#(C)}$ we can define the corresponding model M_λ to be the average of all the models in $\mathcal{M}_C$, weighted by λ:

$$M_{\lambda,w} = \sum_{\mathcal{T} \in C} \lambda_{\mathcal{T}} M_{\mathcal{T},w} \qquad (8)$$

It is easy to verify that equation (8) defines a valid distribution, as long as $|\lambda| = 1$. Now we can define $\mathbb{P}_{C,\lambda}$ to be the set of all possible linear combinations of models in $\mathcal{M}_C$, i.e. $\mathbb{P}_{C,\lambda} = \{M_\lambda : \lambda \geq 0, |\lambda| = 1\}$. WOMM is defined as solving equation (5) over $\mathbb{P}_{C,\lambda}$.

Relationship to Set-based Models. It is important to realize that there is a strong connection between WOMM and set-based models from section 3. The simplex $\mathbb{P}_{C,\lambda}$ includes both sets $\mathbb{P}_{C,pool}$ and $\mathbb{P}_{C,avg}$, since:

(i) equations (7) and (8) imply that an AOMM model of a set S is the same thing as a WOMM model M_λ where $\lambda_{\mathcal{T}} = \frac{1}{\#(S)}$ when $\mathcal{T} \in S$, and $\lambda_{\mathcal{T}} = 0$ for $T \notin S$

(ii) equations (6) and (8) imply that a POMM model of a set S is equivalent to a WOMM model M_λ where $\lambda_T = \frac{|T|}{\sum_{T \in S} |T|}$ when $T \in S$, and $\lambda_T = 0$ for $T \notin S$

This implies that every element of either $\mathbb{P}_{C,avg}$ or $\mathbb{P}_{C,pool}$ is also an element of $\mathbb{P}_{C,\lambda}$. Therefore, a weighted optimal mixture model will be as good, or better than any set-based mixture model, as long as we are dealing with the same collection C.

4.2   Iterative Gradient Solution

Since $\mathbb{P}_{C,\lambda}$ is a continuous simplex, we can employ numerical techniques, to iteratively approach a solution. We describe a gradient descent approach, similar to the one advocated by Yamron et.al. [26]. Recall that our objective is to minimize the cross-entropy (equation (5) of the target distribution T over the simplex $\mathbb{P}_{C,\lambda}$. For a given collection C, every element of $\mathbb{P}_{C,\lambda}$ can be expressed in terms of λ, the vector of mixing weights, according to equation (8). We rewrite the objective function in terms of the mixing vector λ:

$$H_\lambda(T|\{M_T\}) \tag{9}$$
$$= -\sum_w T_w \log \sum_T (\lambda_T / \Sigma_T \lambda_T) M_{T,w}$$
$$= -\sum_w T_w \log \sum_T \lambda_T M_{T,w} + \log \sum_T \lambda_T$$

Note that in equation (10), we used the expression $\frac{\lambda_T}{\Sigma_T \lambda_T}$ instead of λ_T. Doing this allows us to enforce the constraint that the mixing weights should sum to one without using Lagrange multipliers or other machinery of constrained optimization. In other words, once we made this change to the objective function, we can perform unconstrained minimization over λ. In order to find the maximum of equation (10) we take the derivative with respect to the mixing weight of each element k:

$$\frac{\partial H_\lambda}{\partial \lambda_k} = -\sum_w \frac{T_w M_{k,w}}{\Sigma_T \lambda_T M_{T,w}} + \frac{1}{\Sigma_T \lambda_T} \tag{10}$$

After setting the derivative equal to zero, and re-arranging the terms, we see that the extremum is achieved when for every $k \in C$ we have:

$$1 = \sum_w \frac{T_w M_{k,w}}{\Sigma_T (\lambda_T / \Sigma_T \lambda_T) M_{T,w}} \tag{11}$$

We can take this equation and turn it into an incremental update rule. Suppose λ_k^n is the mixing weight of element k after n iterations of the algorithm. Then at the next iteration the weight should become:

$$\lambda_k^{n+1} \leftarrow \sum_w \frac{T_w M_{k,w} \lambda_k^n}{\Sigma_T (\lambda_T / \Sigma_T \lambda_T) M_{T,w}} \tag{12}$$

It is easy to see that when the extremum is achieved, equation (11) holds, and the value λ_k will not change from one iteration to another, so the procedure is convergent. In practice, it is sufficient to run the procedure for just a few iterations, as it converges rapidly. Every iteration of update (12) requires on the order of $(\#(\mathcal{C}) \times \#(W))$, and the number of iterations can be held at a constant.

Local Minima. It is important to realize that the iterative update in equation (12) is not guaranteed to converge to the global minimum of equation (10). The reason for that is that the objective function is not convex everywhere. We can see that clearly when we take the second derivative of the objective with respect to the mixture weights:

$$\frac{\partial^2 H_\lambda}{\partial \lambda_k \partial \lambda_l} = \sum_w \frac{T_w M_{k,w} M_{l,w}}{\left(\sum_j \lambda_j M_{j,w}\right)^2} - \frac{1}{\left(\sum_j \lambda_j\right)^2} \tag{13}$$

It is not obvious whether left-hand side of the equation above is positive or negative, so we cannot conclude whether the function is globally convex, or whether it has local minima. In practice we found that the incremental algorithm converges quite rapidly.

5   Experimental Results

In this section we discuss an application of Optimal Mixture Models to the problem of estimating a topic model from a small sample. The experiments were carried out in the following setting. Our collection $\mathcal{C}$ is a collection of approximately 60,000 newswire and broadcast news stories from the TDT2 corpus [7]. For this dataset, we have a collection of 96 event-centered topics. Every topic is defined by the set $R \subset \mathcal{C}$ of stories that are relevant to it. The relevance assessments were carried out by LDC [7] and are exhaustive.

For every topic, our goal is to estimate M_R, the distribution of words in the documents relevant to that topic. We assume that the relevant set R is unknown, but we have a single example document $\mathcal{T} \in R$. The goal is to approximate the topic model M_R as closely as possible using only $\mathcal{T}$ and $\mathcal{C}$. We formulate the problem as finding the optimal weighted mixture model, and use the iterative update detailed in section 4.2 to estimate the optimal mixture. Since we do not know R, we cannot optimize equation (5) for M_R directly. We hypothesize that optimizing for $T = M_{\mathcal{T}}$ is a good alternative. This hypothesis is similar to the assumptions made in [14]. Note that this assumption may be problematic, since effectively $\mathcal{T}$ is an element of $\mathcal{C}$. This means that our gradient solution will eventually converge to $M_{\mathcal{T}}$, which is not what we want, since we want to converge to M_R. However, we hope that running the gradient method for just a few iterations will result in a reasonable mixture model.

We carry out three types of experiments. First we demonstrate that the gradient procedure described in section 4.2 indeed converges to the target. Second we look at how well the resulting mixture model approximates the real topic model M_R. Finally, we perform a set of *ad-hoc* retrieval experiments to demonstrate that our mixture model can be used to produce effective document rankings.

5.1   Convergence to Target

Figure 1 shows how quickly the weighted mixture model converges to the target distribution $M_{\mathcal{T}}$. On the y-axis we plotted the relative entropy (equation (14) in the Appendix) between the mixture model and the target model, as a function of a number of gradient updates. Relative entropy is averaged over all 96 topics. The solid line shows the mean value, while the bars indicate one standard deviation around the mean. We observe that relative entropy rapidly converges to zero, which is understandable, since $\mathcal{T} \in \mathcal{C}$. Eventually, the iterative procedure will force the mixing vector λ to have zeros in all places except $\lambda_{\mathcal{T}}$, which would be driven to one.

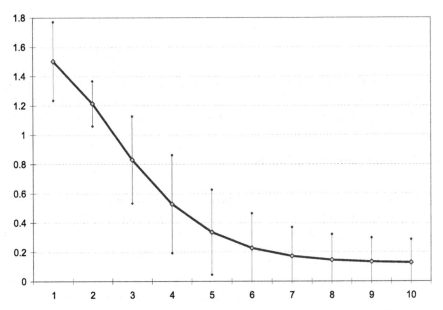

Fig. 1. Convergence of the Weighted Optimal Mixture Model to the target distribution. Target is a single document discussing the topic of interest. Mixture Model estimated using iterative gradient updates.

5.2   Convergence to True Topic Model

In the next set of experiments, we measure relative entropy of our mixture model with respect to M_R, which is the true topic model. M_R is estimated as an averaged mixture model from R, the set of documents known to be relevant to the topic. Note that since the solutions were optimized towards $M_{\mathcal{T}}$ and not towards M_R, we cannot expect relative entropy to continue decreasing with more and more iterations. In fact, once the solution is very close to $M_{\mathcal{T}}$, we expect it to be "far" from M_R. What we hope for is that after a few (but not too many) iterations, the solution will be sufficiently close to M_R. Figure 2 shows the performance with respect to M_R for 0, 1, 2 and 5 iterations. We show relative entropy as a function of how many documents we include in our collection $\mathcal{C}$. The documents are ranked using $\mathcal{T}$ as query, and then some number n of top-ranked documents is used. This is done to highlight the fact that even with gradient optimization, the model shows strong dependency on how many top-ranked documents are used to estimate the probabilities. For comparison, we show the lower bound, which is what we would obtain if we used n documents that are known to be in R.

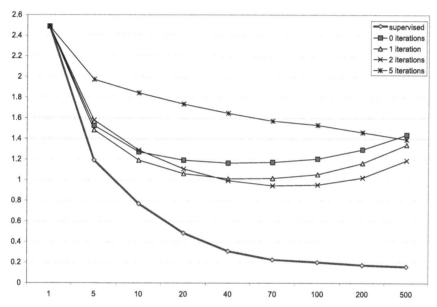

Fig. 2. Convergence of the mixture model to the true topic model: running the gradient update for two iterations is promising.

We observe that running the gradient algorithm for two iterations moves the solution closer to M_R, but doing more iterations actually hurts the performance. Running it for five iterations results in higher relative entropy than not running it at all. We also note that with more iterations, performance becomes less sensitive to the number of documents in $\mathcal{C}$. Overall, we can conclude that running the gradient algorithm for very few iterations is promising.

5.3   Retrieval Experiments

Finally, we consider an application of Optimal Mixture Models to the problem of document retrieval. We start with a single relevant example and estimate a mixture model as was described above. Then, for every document in our dataset we compute the relative entropy (equation (14) in the Appendix) between the model of that document and the estimated mixture model. The documents are then ranked in increasing order of relative entropy. This type of ranking was first proposed by Lafferty and Zhai [11] and was found to be quite successful in conjunction with *Query Models* [11] and *Relevance Models* [14].

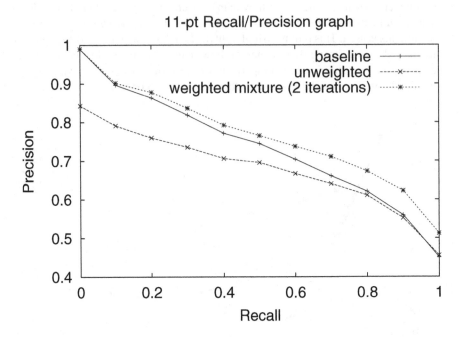

Fig. 3. Document retrieval: mixture model (top) outperforms a baseline of single training example (middle). Mixture model used 10 documents for two iterations.

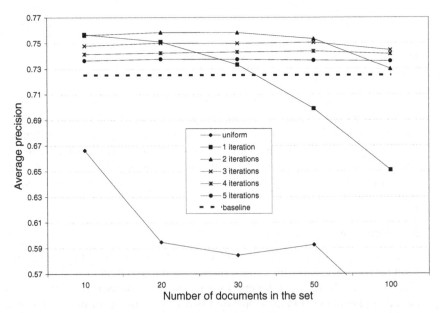

Fig. 4. Optimal Mixture Models exhibit less dependency on the number of top-ranked documents used in the estimation. Two or more iterations with any number of documents outperforms the baseline.

Figure 3 shows the retrieval performance when a mixture model is estimated over a set of 10 top-ranked documents using two iterations of the gradient update. To provide a baseline, we replace the estimated mixture model by the model of the single training example, and perform retrieval using the same ranking function. For comparison we also show the performance unweighted mixture model formed from the same set of 10 top-ranked documents.

We observe that our weighted mixture noticeably outperforms the baseline at all levels of recall. The improvement is statistically significant at all levels of recall, except at zero. Significance was determined by performing the sign test with a p value of 0.05. The magnitude of the improvement is not very large, partly due to the fact that the baseline performance is already very high. Baseline has non-interpolated average precision of 0.7250, which is very high by TREC standards. Such high performance is common in TDT, where topic definitions are much more precise than in TREC. Weighted mixture model yields average precision of 0.7583, an improvement of 5%. Note that unweighted mixture model constructed from the same set of documents as the weighted model performs significantly worse, resulting in a 9% drop from the baseline. This means that document weighting is a very important aspect of estimating a good topic model.

Finally, we re-visit the issue that motivated this work, the issue of sensitivity to the number of top-ranked documents used in the estimation. We repeated the retrieval experiment shown in Figure 3, but with varying numbers of top-ranked documents. The results are summarized in Figure 4. We observe that Weighted Optimal Mixture Model with two or more iterations of training is fairly insensitive to the number of top-ranked documents that are used in the estimation. The performance is always above the single-document baseline. In contrast to that, we see that unweighted models (uniform weights) perform significantly worse than the baseline, and furthermore their performance varies widely with the number of top-ranked documents used. We believe these results to be extremely encouraging, since they show that weighted mixture models are considerably more stable than unweighted models.

6   Conclusions and Future Work

In this paper we explored using Optimal Mixture Models to estimate topical models. We defined optimality in terms of assigning maximum likelihood to a given sample of text, and looked at two types of mixture models: set-based and weighted. We presented an original proof that it is not feasible to compute set-based optimal mixture models. We then showed that weighted mixture models are superior to set-based models, and suggested a gradient descent procedure for estimating weighted mixture models. Our experiments show weighted mixtures outperforming the baseline on a simple retrieval task, and, perhaps more importantly, demonstrate that weighted mixtures are relatively insensitive to the number of top-ranked documents used in the estimation.

In the course of this work we encountered a number of new questions that warrant further exploration. We would like to analyze in detail the relationship between Optimal Mixture Models proposed in this paper and other methods of estimating a topic model from a small sample. The two obvious candidates for this comparison are query models [11] and relevance models [14]. Both are very effective at estimating accurate topic models starting with a very short (2-3 word) sample. Optimal Mixture Models appear to be more effective with a slightly longer sample (200-300 words). Another question we would like to explore is the use of tempered or annealed gradient descent to prevent over-fitting to the target sample. Finally, we would like to explore in detail the impact of the length of the training sample on the quality of the resulting model.

Acknowledgments. The author would like to thank Micah Adler and W. Bruce Croft for numerous discussions which led to this work. This work was supported in part by the Center for Intelligent Information Retrieval, in part by the National Science Foundation under grant number EIA-9820309, and in part by SPAWARSYSCEN-SD grant number N66001-99-1-8912. Any opinions, findings and conclusions or recommendations expressed in this material are the authors and do not necessarily reflect those of the sponsors.

References

1. J. Allan, J.Carbonell, G.Doddington, J.Yamron, and Y.Yang. Topic detection and tracking pilot study: Final report. In *Proceedings of DARPA Broadcast News Transcription and Understanding Workshop, pp194-218*, 1998.
2. D. Beeferman, A. Berger, and J. Lafferty. Statistical models for text segmentation. In *Machine Learning, vol.34*, pages 1–34, 1999.
3. A. Berger, R. Caruana, D.Cohn, D. Freitag, and V. Mittal. Bridging the lexical chasm: Statistical approaches to answer-finding. In *Proceedings of SIGIR*, pages 192–199, 2000.
4. A. Berger and J. Lafferty. Information retrieval as statistical translation. In *Proceedings on the 22nd annual international ACM SIGIR conference*, pages 222–229, 1999.
5. A. Berger and V. Mittal. OCELOT: a system for summarizing web pages. In *Proceedings of SIGIR*, pages 144–151, 2000.
6. S. F. Chen and J. T. Goodman. An empirical study of smoothing techniques for language modeling. In *Proceedings of the 34th Annual Meeting of the ACL*, 1996.
7. C. Cieri, D.Graff, M.Liberman, N.Martey, and S.Strassel. The TDT-2 text and speech corpus. In *Proceedings of the DARPA Broadcast News Workshop, pp 57-60*, 1999.
8. D. Hiemstra. Using language models for information retrieval. In *PhD Thesis, University of Twente*, 2001.
9. T. Hoffmann. Probabilistic latent semantic indexing. In *Proceedings on the 22nd annual international ACM SIGIR conference*, pages 50–57, 1999.
10. H. Jin, R. Schwartz, S. Sista, and F. Walls. Topic tracking for radio, TV broadcast and newswire. In *Proceedings of DARPA Broadcast News Workshop, pp 199-204*, 1999.
11. J. Lafferty and C. Zhai. Document language models, query models and risk minimization for information retrieval. In *Proceedings on the 24th annual international ACM SIGIR conference*, pages 111–119, 2001.
12. J. Lafferty and C. Zhai. A study of smoothing methods for language models applied to ad hoc information retrieval. In *Proceedings on the 24th annual international ACM SIGIR conference*, pages 111–119, 2001.
13. V. Lavrenko. Localized smoothing of multinomial language models. In *CIIR Technical Report IR-222*, 2000.
14. V. Lavrenko and W.B.Croft. Relevance-based language models. In *Proceedings on the 24th annual international ACM SIGIR conference*, pages 120–127, 2001.

15. D. Miller, T. Leek, and R. Schwartz. A hidden markov model information retrieval system. In *Proceedings on the 22nd annual international ACM SIGIR conference*, pages 214–221, 1999.
16. P. Ogilvie. Nearest neighbor smoothing of language models in ir. In *unpublished*, 2000.
17. J. Ponte. Is information retrieval anything more than smoothing? In *Proceedings of the Workshop on Language Modeling and Information Retrieval*, pages 37–41, 2001.
18. J. Ponte and W. B. Croft. A language modeling approach to information retrieval. In *Proceedings on the 21st annual international ACM SIGIR conference*, pages 275–281, 1998.
19. S. Robertson and K. S. Jones. Relevance weighting of search terms. In *Journal of the American Society for Information Science, vol.27*, 1977.
20. S. Robertson and S. Walker. Some simple effective approximations to the 2-poisson model for probabilistic weighted retrieval. In *Proceedings of the 17th annual international ACM SIGIR conference*, pages 232–241, 1996.
21. S. E. Robertson. *The Probability Ranking Principle in IR*, pages 281–286. Morgan Kaufmann Publishers, Inc., San Francisco, California, 1997.
22. M. Sipser. *Time Complexity: The Cook-Levin Theorem*, pages 254–260. PWS Publishing Company, Boston, 1997.
23. M. Sipser. *Time Complexity: The Subset Sum Problem*, pages 268–271. PWS Publishing Company, Boston, 1997.
24. F. Song and W. B. Croft. A general language model for information retrieval. In *Proceedings on the 22nd annual international ACM SIGIR conference*, pages 279–280, 1999.
25. H. Turtle and W. B. Croft. Efficient probabilistic inference for text retrieval. In *Proceedings of RIAO 3*, pages 644–651, 1991.
26. J. Yamron, I. Carp, L. Gillick, S.Lowe, and P. van Mulbregt. Topic tracking in a news stream. In *Proceedings of DARPA Broadcast News Workshop, pp 133-136*, 1999.

A Appendix

A.1 Lower Bound on Cross-Entropy

In this section we prove that T itself is the unique optimal solution of equation (5). The proof is rudimentary and can be found in many Information Theory textbooks, but is included in this paper for completeness. Assuming T is in $I\!P$, we have to show that:

(i) for every $M \in I\!P$ we have $H(T|T) \leq H(T|M)$
(ii) if $H(T|T) = H(T|M)$ then $M = T$.

To prove the first assertion we need to show that the difference in cross-entropies $H(T|M) - H(T|T)$ is non-negative. This difference is sometimes referred to as *relative entropy* or *Kullback-Leibler divergence*. By definition of cross-entropy:

$$H(T|M) - H(T|T) = -\sum_w T_w \log \frac{M_w}{T_w} \qquad (14)$$

By Jensen's inequality, for any concave function $f(x)$ we have $E[f(x)] \leq f(E[x])$. Since logarithm is a concave function, we obtain:

$$-\sum_w T_w \log \frac{M_w}{T_w} \geq -\log \sum_w T_w \frac{M_w}{T_w} \qquad (15)$$

Now we note that right-hand side of the above equation is zero, which proves **(i)**. In order to prove **(ii)** we recall that Jensen's inequality becomes an equality if and only if $f(x)$ is linear in x. The only way $\log \frac{M_w}{T_w}$ can be linear in $\frac{M_w}{T_w}$ is when $M_w = kT_w$, for some constant k. But since M and T are both in $I\!P$, we must have:

$$1 = \sum_w T_w = \sum_w M_w = \sum_w kT_w = k\sum_w T_w$$

Hence $k = 1$, and therefore $M = T$, which proves **(ii)**.

A.2   3SAT Definition

3SAT is a problem of determining satisfiability of a logical expression. An instance of 3SAT is a logical formula F in conjunctive normal form, with clauses limited to contain three primitives. The formula is a conjunction (an AND) of m clauses, each of which is a disjunction (an OR) of three variables from the set $\{x_1...x_n\}$, or their negations $\{\neg x_1...\neg x_n\}$. An example of such formula may be: $F = (\neg x_1 \vee x_2 \vee x_3) \wedge (\neg x_1 \vee \neg x_2 \vee \neg x_4)$. Every formula of propositional calculus can be represented as a 3SAT formula. The task is to determine whether F is satisfiable. The formula is satisfiable if there exists an assignment of true/false values to the variables $x_1...x_n$, which makes the whole formula true. In the given example, setting $x_1 = False$ and all other variables to $True$ satisfies the formula.

A.3   POMM Is NP-Hard

In this section we will show that solving Pooled Optimal Mixture Model problem is NP-hard. In order to do that, we define a corresponding decision problem EXACT-POMM, prove EXACT-POMM to be NP-hard, and use the results in section 2.2 to assert that POMM itself is NP-hard.

In a nutshell, EXACT-POMM is a problem of testing whether a target distribution T is a member of the pooled mixture model set $I\!P_{C,pool}$ induced by some collection C of text samples. Let M denote the collection of integer-valued *count vectors* corresponding to each text sample in C. Each element of M is a vector M_j that specifies how many times every word w occurs in T_j, the corresponding text sample in C, i.e. $M_{j,w} = \#w(T_j)$. The task is to determine whether there exists a subset $S \subset M$, such that vectors in S, when added up, form the same distribution as T:

$$T_w = \frac{\sum_{M_j \in S} M_{j,w}}{\sum_w \sum_{M_j \in S} M_{j,w}} \quad for \ all \ w \in W \tag{16}$$

We will prove that EXACT-POMM is NP-hard by reduction from 3SAT, a well-known problem of the NP-complete class [22]. We describe a polynomial time reduction that converts an instance of 3SAT into an instance of EXACT-POMM, such that 3SAT instance is satisfiable if and only if EXACT-POMM instance has a positive answer. The reduction we describe is very similar to the one commonly used to prove that SUBSET-SUM problem is NP-hard. We are given a formula in conjunctive normal form: $F = (p_{1,1} \vee p_{1,2} \vee p_{1,3}) \wedge ... \wedge (p_{m,1} \vee p_{m,2} \vee p_{m,3})$, where each proposition

$p_{j,k}$ is either some variable x_i or its negation $\neg x_i$. We want to construct a collection of vectors $\mathcal{M}$ and a target distribution T such that F is satisfiable if and only if there exists a subset $S \subset \mathcal{M}$ of vectors which satisfies equation (16). Let $\mathcal{M}$ be the set of rows of the matrix in Figure 5, let T' be the target row at the bottom, and set the target distribution $T_w = T'_w / \sum_w T'_w$ for all w.

$I_{n \times n}$	$POS_{n \times m}$
$I_{n \times n}$	$NEG_{n \times m}$
$0_{2m \times n}$	$I_{m \times m}$
	$I_{m \times m}$

$1 \cdots 1$	$3 \cdots 3$

Fig. 5. Matrix used in the proof that 3SAT is reducible to EXACT-POMM

In Figure 5, $I_{n \times n}$ denotes a n by n identity matrix. $POS_{n \times m}$ is a n by m positive variable-clause adjacency matrix, that is $POS_{i,j} = 1$ when clause j contains x_i, and $POS_{i,j} = 0$ otherwise. Similarly, $NEG_{n \times m}$ is a n by m negative variable-clause adjacency matrix: $NEG_{i,j}$ is 1 if clause j contains $\neg x_i$, and 0 if it does not. $0_{2m \times n}$ is just a $2m$ by n all-zero matrix.

Note that the matrix is identical to the one that is used to prove that the SUBSET-SUM problem [23] is NP-hard by reduction from 3SAT. In line with the SUBSET-SUM argument, it is easy to see that the formula F is satisfiable if and only if there exists a subset $S \subset \mathcal{M}$ of the rows such that $T'_w = \sum_{M_j \in S} M_{j,w}$ for all w. The first n components of target $(T'_1 \ldots T'_n)$ ensure that for every variable i either x_i is true or $\neg x_i$ is true, but not both. The last m components $(T'_{n+1} \ldots T'_{n+m})$ ensure that every clause has at least one proposition set to true.

To demonstrate that satisfiability of F reduces to EXACT-POMM, we just need to show that:

$$\left[T'_w = \sum_{M_j \in S} M_{j,w} \right] \Leftrightarrow \left[T_w = \frac{\sum_{M_j \in S} M_{j,w}}{\sum_w \sum_{M_j \in S} M_{j,w}} \right] \tag{17}$$

The forward implication is trivial, since $T'_w = \sum_{M_j \in S} M_{j,w}$ clearly implies that $\sum_w T'_w = \sum_w \sum_{M_j \in S} M_{j,w}$, and therefore

$$T_w = \frac{T'_w}{\sum_w T'_w} = \frac{\sum_{M_j \in S} M_{j,w}}{\sum_w \sum_{M_j \in S} M_{j,w}} \tag{18}$$

The converse is not obvious, since the equality of two ratios in equation (18) does not by itself guarantee that their numerators are equal, we have to prove that their denominators are equal as well. The proof is as follows. Assume equation (18) holds. Let k be a (constant) ratio of the denominators:

$$k = \frac{\sum_w \sum_{M_j \in S} M_{j,w}}{\sum_w T'_w} \tag{19}$$

Then we can re-write equation (18) as follows:

$$kT'_w = \sum_{M_j \in S} M_{j,w}, \quad for \ all \ w \tag{20}$$

Now, for the left side of the matrix in Figure 5 ($w = 1 \ldots n$), we have $T_w = 1$, and $\sum_w M_{j,w}$ can be 0, 1 or 2. Therefore it must be that k is either 1 or 2, otherwise we cannot satisfy equation (20). Similarly, for the right side of the matrix ($w = n + 1 \ldots n + m$) we have $T_w = 3$, and $\sum_w M_{j,w}$ can be 0, 1, 2, 3, 4 or 5. Therefore, to satisfy equation (20), k must take a value in the set $\{\frac{1}{3}, \frac{2}{3}, \frac{3}{3}, \frac{4}{3}, \frac{5}{3}\}$. Since equation (20) must be satisfied for all w, k must take a value in the intersection $\{1, 2\} \cap \{\frac{1}{3}, \frac{2}{3}, \frac{3}{3}, \frac{4}{3}, \frac{5}{3}\}$. Therefore $k = 1$, which means that the denominators in equation (18) are equal, and the converse implication holds.

The matrix in Figure 5 is of size $(2n+2m)$ by $n+m$, therefore we have a polynomial-time reduction from an instance of 3SAT to an instance of EXACT-POMM, such that a 3SAT formula is satisfiable if and only if a corresponding instance of EXACT-POMM is satisfiable. Accordingly, if a polynomial-time algorithm exists for solving EXACT-POMM problems, this algorithm could be used to solve 3SAT in polynomial time. Thus EXACT-POMM is NP-hard.

We have just demonstrated that EXACT-POMM is NP-hard. In section 2.2 we demonstrated a reduction from decision problems (like EXACT-POMM) to optimization problems (like POMM). Therefore POMM is NP-hard.

A.4   AOMM Is NP-Hard

In this section we will prove that solving AOMM problem is NP-hard. The proof follows the same outline as the proof in section A.3. We define a corresponding decision problem EXACT-AOMM, prove it to be NP-hard by reduction from 3SAT, then use the result of section 2.2 to assert that AOMM is NP-hard.

AOMM is defined as an optimization problem over $I\!\!P_{\mathcal{C},avg}$ with respect to a given target T. Correspondingly, EXACT-AOMM is a problem of determining whether T itself is an element of $I\!\!P_{\mathcal{C},avg}$. An instance of EXACT-AOMM is a target distribution $T \in I\!\!P$, and a finite collection of empirical distributions $\mathcal{M} = \{M_j \in I\!\!P\}$ corresponding to a set of text samples $\mathcal{C}$. The task is to determine whether there exists a subset $S \in \mathcal{M}$, such that the average of elements in $M_j \in S$ is exactly the same as T:

$$T_w = \frac{1}{\#(S)} \sum_{M_j \in S} M_{j,w} \quad for \ all \ w \in W \tag{21}$$

We now present a reduction from 3SAT to EXACT-AOMM. We are given F, an instance of 3SAT, and want to construct a set of distributions $\mathcal{M}$ together with a target T, such that F is satisfiable if and only if there exists a subset $S \in \mathcal{M}$ which satisfies equation (21). The construction of EXACT-AOMM is similar to EXACT-POMM, but the proof is complicated by the fact that we are now dealing with distributions, rather than count vectors. We cannot directly use the matrix constructed in Section A.3 (Figure 5), because the rows may have varying numbers of non-zero entries, and if we normalize them to lie in $I\!\!P$, the proof might fail. For example, suppose we normalize the rows of the matrix in Figure 5. Then a 1 in a row from the upper half of that matrix becomes $1/m$ (where m is the the number of non-zero entries in that row, which will be greater than 1 for any variable x_i that occurs in any of the clauses in F). At the same time, a 1 in the lower half of the matrix remains a 1, since every row in the lower half contains exactly one non-zero entry. To alleviate this problem, we augment the matrix from Figure 5 in such a way that every row has the same number of non-zero entries. This is non-trivial, since we have to augment the matrix in such a way that satisfiability of 3SAT is not violated.

$I_{n \times n}$	$POS_{n \times m}$	$\neg POS_{n \times m}$	0	
$I_{n \times n}$	$NEG_{n \times m}$	$\neg NEG_{n \times m}$		
	$I_{m \times m}$	0		
	$I_{m \times m}$			
0		$I_{m \times m}$	m	
	0	$I_{m \times m}$		
		$I_{m \times m}$		
$1 \cdots 1$	$3 \cdots 3$	$n \cdots n$	$3m^2$	

Fig. 6. Matrix used in the proof that 3SAT is reducible to EXACT-AOMM

Let $\mathcal{M}'$ be the set of rows of the matrix in Figure 6, and let T' be the target (bottom) row. Here sub-matrices I, 0, POS and NEG have the same meaning as in Section A.3. In addition, $\neg POS$ is a logical negation of POS, i.e. $\neg POS_{i,j} = 1$ whenever $POS_{i,j} = 0$, and vice-versa. Similarly, $\neg NEG$ is a negation of NEG. The last column of the matrix contains zeros in the top $2n$ rows and m in the bottom $3m$ rows. Note that the new matrix contains the tableau constructed in Section A.3 as a sub-matrix in the upper-left corner. The columns to the right of the original tableau ensure that the sum of every row in the matrix is exactly $m + 1$. The first $n + m$ positions of the target row are also identical to the target row for the POMM problem.

We define a corresponding instance of EXACT-AOMM by setting $T = T'/(n + 3m + nm + 3m^2)$, and $\mathcal{M} = \{M'_j/(m + 1) : M'_j \in \mathcal{M}'\}$, dividing each row by the sum of its elements to ensure that the result is in $\mathbb{P}$. Now we want to prove that F is satisfiable if and only there exists a subset $S \subset \mathcal{M}$ which satisfies equation (21).

Let $S \subset \mathcal{M}$ be the subset that satisfies equation (21). We assert that $\#(S)$, the size of S, must be $(n + 3m)$. The proof is as follows:

(i) The sum of the first column over S can be either $\frac{1}{m+1}$ or $\frac{2}{m+1}$, and the target is $T_1 = \frac{1}{(n+3m)(m+1)}$. Therefore $\#(S)$ can be either $(n + 3m)$ or $2(n + 3m)$.

(ii) The sum of the last column over S can be any one of $\frac{m}{m+1} \times \{1, 2, 3, \ldots, m, \ldots, 5m\}$, while the target is $\frac{3m^2}{(n+3m)(m+1)}$. Therefore $\#(S)$ can be any one of $\frac{n+3m}{3m} \times \{1, 2, 3, \ldots, m, \ldots, 5m\}$.

Since S must satisfy equation (21) for all w, we must have $\#(S)$ satisfy both (i) and (ii), and therefore it must be that $\#(S) = (n + 3m)$. Now, since by definition $M_{j,w} = \frac{M'_{j,w}}{m+1}$ and $T_w = \frac{T'_w}{(n+3m)(m+1)}$, we can claim that:

$$\left[T_w = \frac{1}{\#(S)}\sum_{M_j \in S} M_{j,w}\right] \Leftrightarrow \left[T'_w = \sum_{M'_j \in S'} M'_{j,w}\right] \qquad (22)$$

Here S' is a subset of the rows that corresponds to S. It remains to show that F (an instance of 3SAT) is satisfiable if and only if there exists a subset $S' \in \mathcal{M}'$ which satisfies the right hand side of equation (22).

($\Leftarrow$) If such S' exists, columns $\{1 \ldots n\}$ of $\mathcal{M}'$ guarantee that we have a proper truth assignment, and columns $\{n + 1 \ldots n + m\}$ guarantee that every clause of F has at least one true proposition, thus F is satisfied.

($\Rightarrow$) If F is satisfiable, it is clear that right hand side of equation (22) holds for columns $\{1 \ldots n+m\}$ (e.g. by the the SUBSET-SUM argument). Each one of the columns $\{n + 1 \ldots n + m\}$ contained 1, 2, or 3 non-zero entries (in the first $2n$ rows), and therefore required 2, 1 or 0 "helper" variables to add up to 3. Because columns $\{n+m+1 \ldots n+m+m\}$ represent a logical negation of columns $\{n+1 \ldots n+m\}$, they will contain $(n-1)$, $(n-2)$ or $(n-3)$ non-zero entries respectively and may require 1, 2, or 3 "helper" variables to sum to n. Finally, the last column will reflect the total number of "helpers" used for each of the m clauses, which will always be 3 for every clause: either $(2+1)$, or $(1+2)$, or $(0+3)$. Since there are m clauses, the last column will sum up to $3m \times m$.

This proves that F is satisfiable if and only if the right hand side of equation (22) is satisfiable, which in turn holds if and only if left-hand side (EXACT-AOMM) is satisfiable. The matrix in Figure 6 is of size $(2n + 5m)$ by $(n + 2m + 1)$, thus we have a polynomial-time reduction from an instance of 3SAT to an instance of EXACT-AOMM. Thus EXACT-AOMM is NP-hard, and by the result in section 2.2, AOMM is NP-hard as well.

Text Categorization: An Experiment Using Phrases

Madhusudhan Kongovi, Juan Carlos Guzman, and Venu Dasigi

Southern Polytechnic State University
1100 S. Marietta Parkway
Marietta, GA 30060
mkongovi@lucent.com
jguzman@spsu.edu
vdasigi@spsu.edu

Abstract. Typical text classifiers learn from example and training documents that have been manually categorized. In this research, our experiment dealt with the classification of news wire articles using category profiles. We built these profiles by selecting feature words and phrases from the training documents. For our experiments we decided on using the text corpus Reuters-21578. We used precision and recall to measure the effectiveness of our classifier. Though our experiments with words yielded good results, we found instances where the phrase-based approach produced more effectiveness. This could be due to the fact that when a word along with its adjoining word – a phrase – is considered towards building a category profile, it could be a good discriminator. This tight packaging of word pairs could bring in some semantic value. The packing of word pairs also filters out words occurring frequently in isolation that do not bear much weight towards characterizing that category.

1. Introduction

Categorization is a problem that cognitive psychologists have dealt with for many years [1]. There are two general and basic principles for creating categories: *cognitive economy* and *perceived world structure* [12]. The principle of cognitive economy means that the function of categories is to provide maximum information with the least cognitive effort. The principle of perceived world structure means that the perceived world is not an unstructured set of arbitrary or unpredictable attributes. The attributes that an individual will perceive, and thus use for categorization, are determined by the needs of the individual. These needs change over time and with the physical and social environment. In other words, a system for automatic text categorization should in some way "know" both the type of text and the type of user. The maximum information with least cognitive effort is achieved if categories map the perceived world structure as closely as possible (*ibid*). Coding by category is fundamental to mental life because it greatly reduces the demands on perceptual processes, storage space, and reasoning processes, all of which are known to be limited [13]. Psychologists agree that *similarity* plays a central role in placing

F. Crestani, M. Girolami, and C.J. van Rijsbergen (Eds.): ECIR 2002, LNCS 2291, pp. 213–228, 2002.
© Springer-Verlag Berlin Heidelberg 2002

different items into a single category. Furthermore, people want to maximize within-category similarity while minimizing between-category similarity (*ibid*).

In the process of categorization of electronic documents, categories are typically used as a means of organizing and getting an overview of the information in a collection of several documents. *Folders* in electronic mail (e-mail) and *topics* in Usenet News are a couple of concrete examples of categories in computer-mediated communication.Text categorization is, in this paper, defined as an information retrieval task in which one category label is assigned to a document [11]. Techniques for automatically deriving representations of categories ("category profile extraction") and performing classification have been developed within the area of text categorization [9], a discipline at the crossroads between information retrieval and machine learning. Alternatively, a document can be compared to previously classified documents and placed in the category of the closest such documents [6], avoiding the need for category profiles. All these categorization approaches perform *categorization by content* [14], since information for categorizing a document is extracted from the document itself.

Our work primarily focuses on building a category profile of words and phrases as a vocabulary for a category and using that to perform a match, to categorize.

Terms & Definitions

Feature Words – Representative words that describe a given information category. Words that occur more regularly and more frequently than others in documents of a category are good candidates for topic words. These words are different from *stop words*, which are defined below.

Stop words are words with little or no indexing value and would comprise conjunctions, prepositions, adverbs, articles, some verbs, pronouns and some proper names. Although we have tried to come up with a standard, there is some unavoidable subjectivity.

Phrases – two adjoining words in the text with zero word distance, eliminating all the stop words in between.

The retrieval activity divides the collection into four parts, consisting of relevant retrieved items (a), relevant not retrieved (d), non-relevant retrieved (b) and non-relevant not retrieved (c).

True Positive (a_i) **TP** - This represents the total number of relevant documents retrieved for a particular category (i).

False Positive (b_i) **FP** - This represents the total number of non-relevant documents retrieved for a particular category (i).

True Negative (c_i) **TN** - This represents the number of non-relevant documents not retrieved for a particular category (i).

False Negative (d_i) **FN** - This represents the total number of relevant documents not retrieved for a particular category (i).

We can define precision for that category (i) as follows:
Precision$_i$ = a_i /(a_i +b_i)
Recall$_i$ = a_i /(a_i +d_i)

The overall performance measures for a collection having C categories can be defined [Dasigi et al, 2001] as follows:
Macro precision = $\sum_i$ Precision$_i$ / C

Macro recall = $\sum_i$ Recall$_i$ / C

Micro precision = $\sum_i a_i / \sum_i (a_i + b_i)$

Micro recall = $\sum_i a_i / \sum_i (a_i + d_i)$

Typicality is a measure of how typical or how representative a document is of a particular category. Suppose we identify 15 phrases or words that characterize a particular category. And we decide that a document needs to have all the 15 phrases or words to be 100% representative of that category and if a document **A** contains 12 phrases or words, its typicality is 12/15 or 0.8 or it is 80% typical of that document. And the **semantic distance** of the two documents, in that category, is measured by the difference of their typicalities in that category.

2. Previous Related Research

The basic approach of Verma and Dasigi [3] was to first come up with a pattern of words (called category profiles) defining a given information category, and then apply classification algorithms that make use of these profiles to classify test documents. David Lewis's primary research area is information retrieval, including the categorization, retrieval, routing, filtering, clustering, linking, etc. of text. His [7, 8] research focuses on the application of statistical and machine learning techniques in information retrieval (IR). Automatic text categorization is an important research area in Katholieke Universiteit Leuven, Belgium. Marie-Francine Moens and Jos Dumortier have worked on applying text categorization techniques in new areas of text routing and filtering. Their research discusses the categorization of magazine articles with broad subject descriptors. They especially focus upon the following aspects of text classification: effective selection of feature words and proper names that reflect the main topics of the text, and training of text classifiers. Fabrizio Sebastiani of Instituto di Elaborazione dell'Informazione [5], Pisa, Italy, investigates a novel technique for automatic categorization, which is dubbed *categorization by context*, since it exploits the context surrounding a link in an HTML document to extract useful information for categorizing the document referred by the link. Neural networks have proven very effective for tasks involving pattern recognition since text classification, in essence, is a pattern recognition problem. Some researches [2] have used neural networks in conjunction with the latent semantic indexing model [4] to classify text data.

3. Text Corpus

As our work was motivated by a previous research [3] in text classification using the corpus Reuters-21578, we decided to use the same source for our experiment so that we could compare results and determine if our work added any value to the existing body of research literature. For our experiments we decided on working with five categories – GRAIN, CRUDE, METAL, MONEY-FX and SHIP. As we set out with the idea that our experiments – categorization task – should result in categorizing test documents in just one category, we decided on using stories – both for training and testing – that had less chance of falling into more than one category.

4. Empirical Work: An Attempt to Automate Classification Based on Phrases

Our empirical research consisted of developing an automatic text classifier. Considering the scope of the experiment, the following assumptions were made:

i.   The training and test documents would only come from the corpus Reuters-21578. No other source of data would be used. The documents would distinctly fall under just one category.

ii.   We would use a much larger set to train the classifier as compared to testing the classifier.

iii. We define a phrase as two adjoining words in the text with zero word distance, eliminating all the stop words.

iv.   Stop words would comprise conjunctions, prepositions, adverbs, articles, some verbs, pronouns and some proper names. Although we have tried to come up with a standard, there is some unavoidable subjectivity.

v.   Lastly, as this is an experimental prototype, we did not spend much time on writing efficient programs using sophisticated software tools and utilities.

Programs

Since our work environment was UNIX, we used a lot of tools and utilities available in the UNIX world. The core programs were written in the C language. The lexical analyzer was written using the tool LEX. The computation of results and manipulation were done using the AWK and SHELL programming languages. The final analysis and plotting of graphs were done using EXCEL. As the Reuters-21578 data is in SGML format, a program had to be written to filter out the SGML tags and extract the text along with the topic names for the training document set. We had decided on using five categories for the experiment – GRAIN, CRUDE, MONEY-FX, METAL and SHIP. After extraction, the training documents were put in separate directories. Table 1 shows the number of test and training documents for each category.

Table 1. Subject categories and number of test and training documents

Category	Category Description	# Test Docs	# Train Docs
Grain	All topics that include grain	58	324
Crude	Oil Prices, Production & Distribution	226	2619
Money-Fx	Money Market & Exchange	47	501
Ship	Shipping	58	154
Metal	All topics that include Metal	60	64

We came up with a list of stop words – words that do not add value towards categorization – consisting of adverbs, verbs, conjunctions, prepositions, adjectives, pronouns and some proper names. The primary task involved extracting the phrases from the training documents. The lex program generated the tokens (phrases) based on the rules – stop words, sentence beginnings and categories – we had provided. The phrases across all the training documents, specific to the categories, were collected. This resulted in five buckets – categories – of unsorted phrases. The next step was to compute the frequencies of the phrases. The phrase lists were further processed based on the relative frequencies of the phrases and probabilities. The list was ordered highest to the lowest frequency. The last step involved maintaining a column of cumulative probabilities in the ordered list. Thus the final ordered phrases list per category contained five columns comprising **phrase, frequency, relative frequency, probability** and **cumulative probability**. These lists gleaned from the training documents formed the phrases-vocabulary for the classifier. The classifier would look up these lists to find phrase matches in the test documents in the process of classifying. The category with the highest match is what the test document would belong to. A document would not be categorized (**No Cat**) if it got equal score in more than one category or did not get the minimum score in any.

Experiments

Since there was no clear picture of how many phrases would fairly represent a category, we decided to conduct a series of experiments using the programs mentioned in the previous section.

Absolute Cut-off

We used an absolute number of phrases per category from their respective phrase list to start with. Of the list of the phrases – by frequency – we picked the top 15 from each category and used that as the look up table. Figure 1 shows the precision and recall values for this experiment. Recall is poor as quite a big number of documents did not get categorized, resulting in no category (**No CAT**).

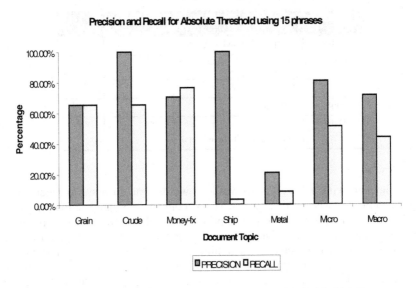

Fig. 1. Precision and recall values for an absolute threshold of 15 phrases

Relative Cut-off

For each category, with the phrases sorted in decreasing order of probability, the cumulative probability for the top ranked phrases down to each ranked position is kept track of. When this cumulative probability is reached at a certain chosen threshold point, we cut off the selection of phrases for that category. For the first experiment we used top ranked phrases until the cumulative probability (**CP**) totaled up to **0.08** as the cut-off. We had varied number of phrases across different categories. Table 2 shows the results of this run.

Table 2. Results of the 0.08CP run

Category	# Test Docs	TP	FP	No CAT	FN
Grain	58	49	16	5	4
Crude	226	163	0	31	32
Money-Fx	47	45	13	1	1
Ship	58	36	13	17	5
Metal	60	20	17	24	16

For the next experiment we raised the cumulative probability threshold to **0.1** as the cut-off. The number of phrases naturally went up as shown in Table 3.

Table 3. Results of the 0.1CP run

Category	# Test Docs	TP	FP	No CAT	FN
Grain	58	49	12	4	5
Crude	226	201	3	15	10
Money-Fx	47	46	7	1	0
Ship	58	37	11	14	7
Metal	60	22	7	24	14

For the next experiment we raised the cut-off threshold to **0.13** cumulative probability as shown in Table 4.

Table 4. Results of the 0.13CP run

Category	# Test Docs	TP	FP	No CAT	FN
Grain	58	50	19	3	5
Crude	226	180	0	20	26
Money-Fx	47	44	19	1	2
Ship	58	39	8	12	7
Metal	60	37	10	11	12

The results of the experiment using a **0.18** cumulative probability threshold as the cut-off are shown in Table 5.

Table 5. Results of the 0.18CP run

Category	# Test Docs	TP	FP	No CAT	FN
Grain	58	53	32	1	4
Crude	226	157	0	18	51
Money-Fx	47	46	27	0	1
Ship	58	39	7	10	9
Metal	60	33	16	13	14

For the final experiment we had raised the cut-off threshold to **0.25** cumulative probability as shown in Table 6.

Table 6. Results of the 0.25CP run

Category	# Test Docs	TP	FP	No CAT	FN
Grain	58	53	29	2	3
Crude	226	182	0	15	29
Money-Fx	47	47	23	0	0
Ship	58	38	6	9	11
Metal	60	30	7	11	19

Table 7. Number of phrases that qualified for different runs

Category	# of phrases	# of distinct phrases	0.08CP	0.1CP	0.18 CP	0.25 CP
Grain	34544	25514	142	229	787	1661
Crude	148416	69328	14	24	47	143
Money-Fx	58708	35349	80	133	522	1239
Ship	15125	11979	179	250	696	1225
Metal	7152	5995	104	153	414	664

Results

The analysis of the various experiments conducted shows a pattern. Table 7 shows the number of phrases that were used in different runs. The absolute cut-off threshold has the least acceptable *precision and recall*. As we start experimenting with relative cut-off thresholds, we begin to see better results. Using thresholds based on cumulative probability (CP) cut-offs gives a better weight to the phrases in a category's context. A 0.1 cumulative probability gives a better weight across all categories as shown in Table 8 and Table 9

Table 8. Precision at various thresholds

Precision						
Category	Absolute	0.08CP	0.1CP	0.13CP	0.18CP	0.25CP
Grain	65.52%	75.38%	80.33%	72.46%	62.35%	64.63%
Crude	100.00%	100.00%	98.53%	100.00%	100.00%	100.00%
Money-Fx	70.59%	77.59%	86.79%	69.84%	63.01%	67.14%
Ship	100.00%	73.47%	77.08%	82.98%	84.78%	86.36%
Metal	20.83%	54.05%	75.86%	78.72%	67.35%	81.08%
Micro	80.92%	84.14%	89.87%	86.21%	80.00%	84.34%
Macro	71.39%	76.10%	83.72%	80.80%	75.50%	79.84%

Table 9. Recall at various thresholds

Recall						
Category	Absolute	0.08CP	0.1CP	0.13CP	0.18CP	0.25CP
Grain	65.52%	84.48%	84.48%	86.21%	91.38%	91.38%
Crude	65.49%	72.12%	88.94%	79.65%	69.47%	80.53%
Money-Fx	76.60%	95.74%	97.87%	93.62%	97.87%	100.00%
Ship	3.45%	62.07%	63.79%	67.24%	67.24%	65.52%
Metal	8.33%	33.33%	36.67%	61.67%	55.00%	50.00%
Micro	51.00%	69.71%	79.06%	77.95%	73.05%	77.95%
Macro	43.88%	69.55%	74.35%	77.68%	76.19%	77.49%

We notice that as we start using cumulative probabilities as thresholds, we begin to see an improvement in *precision and recall*. The effectiveness of the classifier improves with relative thresholds. As the cumulative probability increases, the number of words characterizing a category increases too. We begin to see a bigger measure of typicality in each document. The adverse effect of this is the reduction in semantic distances between the documents. Thus we see in later experiments a larger number of documents being classified under "**No Cat**", as the hit rates are equal in more than one category.

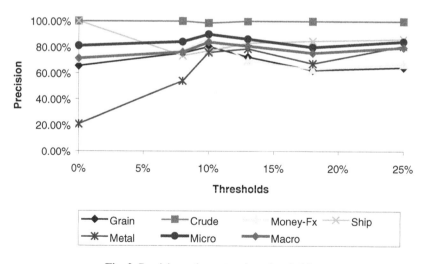

Precision at various thresholds

Fig. 2. Precision values at various thresholds

From Figure 2 and Figure 3 we also notice the values of *precision and recall* changing with the experiments. *Recall* seems to improve with increase in cumulative probability cut-off, whereas *precision* seems to work the other way. We notice also that an optimum value of *precision and recall* results at a cumulative probability of 0.1.

We notice the measurements are lower for the categories METAL and SHIP. This could be because of the smaller training set. The bigger the training set, the better the phrasal descriptors that can be extracted.

Another interesting inference drawn is that this classifier works well in the context of the Reuters-21578 corpus. As the phrases are drawn from this corpus, the jargons, acronyms and phrases local to Reuters are picked up as the descriptors. But a more generic classifier can be designed if the local expressions – jargons, acronyms, phrases, short-forms – are identified from this corpus and added to the stop list.

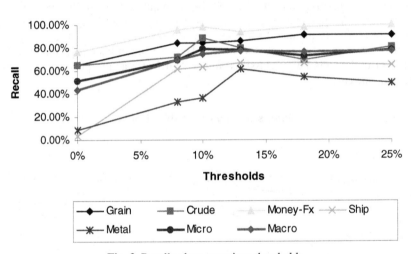

Fig. 3. Recall values at various thresholds

Suppose

T = Total number of test documents

N= Number of documents that cannot be categorized

Then effective decision ED = (T-N)/T

%ED = (T − N)/T * 100

This new measurement of effective decisions, as seen in Figure 4, seems to give a better perspective of the classifier's effectiveness. Again, we notice that all the graphs are flat after a cumulative probability threshold of 0.1.

Experiment with *Words*

To compare the phrase-based approach to a word-based approach, we conducted experiments using a similar classifier, with words constituting the category profile, instead of phrases.

Our initial attempts were not too successful, as certain words in most of the categories made up more than three percent of the total profile. For example, the word "vs" in the CRUDE category made up more than 5% of the total words that described the category. We had to eliminate this word. On the other hand, "vs" along with its adjoining word formed a meaningful phrase in the experiment with phrases. So we had to come up with more stop words to stem out these spurious words that did not contribute towards characterizing the category.

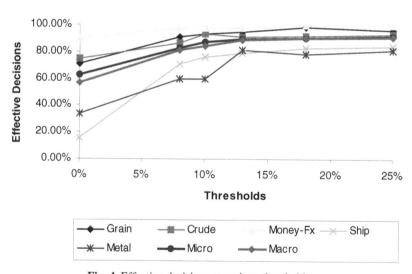

Fig. 4. Effective decisions at various thresholds

We conducted six experiments using the same thresholds as the ones we had used for the phrases.

For the first run, we used an absolute number of words across all the categories – 15 words. The results of the runs are shown in Figure 5.

The next five runs were based on relative thresholds of 0.08, 0.1, 0.13, 0.18 and 0.25 cumulative probabilities as the cut-off. The results of the runs from relative thresholds are shown in Figure 6 and Figure 7.

Though the results from the two runs – phrases-based and words-based – are not really comparable, as the stop words for the words-based experiment had to be increased to stem out high frequency low descriptive (of the category) words, it definitely can be studied closely to make some valid deductions. The results from the words-based experiment definitely seem to have better precision and recall with absolute thresholds. But with relative thresholds we see a better precision with phrases at lower thresholds and then the value holds steadily. Recall seems to peak with phrases with a relative threshold between 0.1 and 0.13CP, unlike with words where the recall steadily climbs up at higher thresholds.

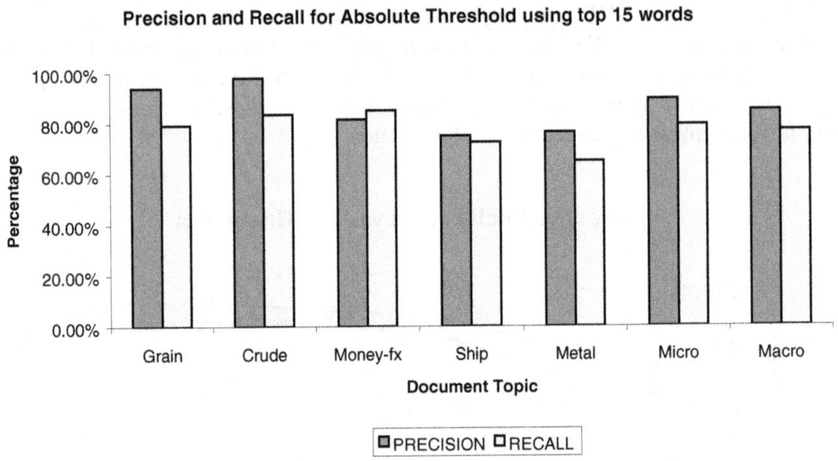

Fig. 5. Results of the words-based experiment using absolute threshold

5. Conclusions

Words and phrases are the salient features involved in classifying magazine articles. The number of different features in a corpus of magazine articles is enormous. Because the text classes regard the main topics of the texts, it is important to identify content terms that relate to the main topics and to discard terms that do not bear upon content or treat only marginal topics in training and test corpuses. The results of the empirical work conducted clearly emphasize the importance of phrases in classifying texts. Though our experiments with words yielded good results, we found instances and situations where the phrase-based approach produced more effectiveness. This could be due to the fact that when a word along with its adjoining word – a phrase – is considered towards building a category profile, it could be a good discriminator. This tight packaging of two words could bring in some semantic value. The packing of two words also filters out words occurring frequently in isolation that do not bear much weight towards characterization of the category.

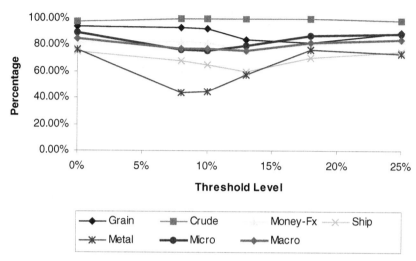

Fig. 6. Precision for the words-based experiment

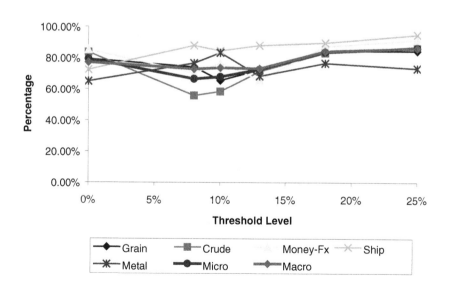

Fig. 7. Recall for the words-based experiment

Seemingly the graphs contradict this inference, as the macro recall and macro precision for the words are, at the least, as good as the ones for phrases if not better. The macro averages for the phrases have been weighed down by the categories SHIP and METAL. These categories' poor phrasal descriptors, resulting from small training sets, have lowered the measurements. Our conclusions are better substantiated by the graphs of GRAIN, CRUDE and MONEY-FX.

Our results seem more promising than the results of Lewis's[8] and Dasigi's[2] text categorization works based on the usage of phrases, for more than one reason. Both their works dealt with quite a big number of topics/categories employing techniques like *clustering*, *neural networks* and *Vector Space Modeling*, as opposed to our five categories of smaller test set and a straightforward method of category profile match-score. Another important distinction was that Dasigi's category profiles were entirely made up of single words. Their use of phrases was in the phrase-document matrix to which LSA [4] was applied. Our use of phrases is simply in the category profiles and therefore constitutes a somewhat different kind of use for phrases. We also found that our definition of a phrase gained better relevance in the context of Reuters-21578 corpus because the frequent use of phrases like "billion dlrs", "mln stg", "mln dlrs", "mln tonnes", "dlrs per", "mln acres", "mln vs", "cts vs", "shrs cts", "pct pay", etc, in the corpus helped us build a good set of category profiles for phrases rather than for words, with a better chance of profile matches. A complete list of phrases and words generated per topic as a part of this experiment is documented in the thesis report, which is at the Southern Polytechnic State University library.

The empirical research reveals a gray area of distinct classification – the ambiguity of a story falling into any one category because of high typicality values in more than one category. This always happens in the real world. Text classification by humans will always be subjective to a certain degree. We can try to refine the extraction or the classification process to reduce the ambiguity. The results of this experiment are definitely encouraging and pave the way for future research in the area of phrases based approach for text classification.

Limitations of the Research

As the experiments were conducted using just five categories and a small test set, the results – precision and recall – might appear more significant than they really are. To get more substantial results we need to expand our text corpus to comprise a higher – say at least 15 – number of categories with a much bigger set of test documents per category. The results of the empirical work can always be extrapolated to wider contexts.

Where Do We Go from Here?

Our goal in this research was to determine how meaningful it is to use phrases as discriminators, in categorizing documents. Although our experiment indicated effectiveness for phrases, we still need to expand the scope of this research to establish conclusively that phrases are indeed effective.

Future researchers do not need to restrict themselves to just one data corpus. With more data sources, researchers can come up with a better word or phrase profiling, as the source will not be parochial. We realized in our analysis of phrases that the Reuters-21578 corpus does contain a lot of words, jargons, phrases, acronyms and a lot of other language inflections that are very familiar to their domain.

Our empirical experiment classified a big number of articles under "No Category", as there was no clear-cut score for the article to fall under any one category. Future research work could focus on refining the algorithm to reduce this ambiguity of "No Category". Another experiment that could be conducted is to follow a two-pass approach in classification, where the first pass involves classification by words and the second pass could further refine the experiment using phrases or synonyms.

References

1. Cañas, A.J., F. R. Safayeni, D. W. Conrath, *A Conceptual Model and Experiments on How People Classify and Retrieve Documents.* Department of Management Sciences, University of Waterloo, Ontario, Canada, 1985.
2. Dasigi. V, Mann C. Reinhold, Protopopescu A. Vladimir, "Information fusion for text classification – an experimental comparison", in *The Journal of The Pattern Recognition Society,* 34(Sept 2001) 2413-2425.
3. Dasigi, V. and N. Verma: Automatic Generation of Category Profiles and their Evaluation through Text Classification, Proc.2nd International Conference on Intelligent Technologies, November, 2001, pp. 421-427.
4. Deerwester, Scott, Susan T. Dumais, George W. Furnas, Thomas K. Landauer and Richard Harshman, "Indexing by latent semantic analysis", in *Journal of the American Society for Information Science,* 41(6), 391-407, 1990.
5. Sebestiani, Fabrizio. Attardi, Guiseppe , "Theseus: Categorization by context", Giuseppe Attardi Dipartimento di Informatica Universit di Pisa, Italy...(1999).
6. Fuhr, Norbert, Stephen Hartman, Gerhard Lustig, Michael Schwanter, Konstadinos Tzeres and Gerhard Knorz, "Air/X-- a rule based multistage indexing system for large subject fields, In *RIAO 91 Conference Proceedings: Intelligent Text and Image Handling,* 606-623, 1991.
7. Lewis, David D., "Representation and Learning in Information Retrieval" Ph.D. thesis, Department of Computer Science; University of Massachusetts; Amherst, MA, 1992.
8. Lewis, David D., "An Evaluation of Phrasal and Clustered Representations on a Text Categorization Task", *Fifteenth Annual International Association for Computing Machinery SIGIR Conference on Research and Development in Information Retrieval,* Copenhagen, 1992, 37-50.
9. Ittner, D.D., Lewis, D.D., Ahn, D., "Text categorization of low quality images". In *Proceedings of SDAIR-95, 4th Annual Symposium on Document Analysis and Information Retrieval,* Las Vegas, US, 1995, 301–315.
10. Moens, M.-F. and Dumortier, J., *Automatic Categorization of Magazine Articles,* Katholieke Universiteit Leuven, BelgiumInterdisciplinary Centre for Law & IT (ICRI).
11. Riloff, E., W. Lehnert, "Information Extraction as a Basis for High-Precision Text Classification," *ACM Transactions on Information Systems,* 12 (3), 1994, 296--333.

12. Rosch, E., "Principles of Categorization," in *Cognition and Categorization*, E. Rosch, B. B. Lloyd (Eds.), (Hillsdale, New Jersey: Lawrence Erlbaum Associates, 1978), 27--48.
13. Smith, E.E., "Categorization," in *An invitation to Cognitive Science, Vol. 3, Thinking*, D. N. Osherson, E. E. Smith (Eds), The MIT Press, 1990, 33--53.
14. Yang, Y., An Evaluation of Statistical Approaches to Text Categorization, Technical Report CMU-CS-97-127, Computer Science Department, Carnegie Mellon University, 1999.

A Hierarchical Model for Clustering and Categorising Documents

E. Gaussier[1], C. Goutte[1], K. Popat[2], and F. Chen[2]

[1] Xerox Research Center Europe, 6 Ch. de Maupertuis, F–38240 Meylan, France
Eric.Gaussier,Cyril.Goutte@xrce.xerox.com
[2] Xerox PARC, 3333 Coyote Hill Rd, Palo Alto, CA94304, USA
popat,fchen@parc.xerox.com

Abstract. We propose a new hierarchical generative model for textual data, where words may be generated by topic specific distributions at any level in the hierarchy. This model is naturally well-suited to clustering documents in preset or automatically generated hierarchies, as well as categorising new documents in an existing hierarchy. Training algorithms are derived for both cases, and illustrated on real data by clustering news stories and categorising newsgroup messages. Finally, the generative model may be used to derive a Fisher kernel expressing similarity between documents.

1 Overview

Many IR tasks, such as clustering, filtering or categorisation, rely on *models* of documents. The basic approach to document modelling considers that each document is an (independent) observation, with words used as features and word frequencies, combined with various normalisation schemes, are the feature values. This so-called *bag of word* approach is exemplified by the Naïve Bayes method [24] and hierarchical extensions [14,19], where the features are modelled using multinomial distributions. Other related techniques rely eg on Gaussian mixture models[18], fuzzy k-means, etc.

In the following, we adopt a different standpoint, using the concept of co-occurrence [10]. In this approach, one basic observation is the co-occurrence of a word in a document. There is no numerical feature, only the absence or presence of co-occurrences and associated counts. A document (and thus a document collection) arises as an assortment of such co-occurrences.

In this article we address the problem of clustering and categorising documents, using probabilistic models. Clustering and categorisation can be seen as two sides of the same coin, and differ by the fact that categorisation is a supervised task, ie labels identifying categories are provided for a set of documents (the training set), whereas, in the case of clustering the aim is to automatically organise unlabelled documents into clusters, in an unsupervised way. Popular document categorisation methods include nearest neighbours, Naïve Bayes [24] or support vector machines [12], while document clustering has been tackled with

F. Crestani, M. Girolami, and C.J. van Rijsbergen (Eds.): ECIR 2002, LNCS 2291, pp. 229–247, 2002.

eg k-means, latent semantic indexing [3] or hierarchical agglomerative methods [23,21]. Even though clustering and categorisation can be studied independently of each other, we propose a general model that can be used for both tasks. One strength of our model lies in its capacity to deal with hierarchies of categories/clusters, based on soft assignments while maintaining a distinction between document and word structures. This has to be contrasted with traditional approaches which result in hard partitions of documents.

In the next section, we will give a detailed presentation of the generative hierarchical probabilistic model for co-occurrences that we will use for performing clustering and categorisation of documents. One interesting feature of this model is that it generalises several well-known probabilistic models used for document processing. We then describe the motivations behind our model (section 3), then give further details on the implementation of clustering (section 4) and categorisation (section 5) using it. After presenting some encouraging experimental results (section 6), we discuss in section 7 some technical and methodological aspects, and in particular we show how our model can be used to obtain a measure of similarity between documents using Fisher kernels [11].

2   Modelling Documents

In this contribution we address the problem of modelling documents as an assortment of co-occurrence data [10]. Rather than considering each document as a vector of word frequency (bag-of-word), we model the term-document matrix as the result of a large number of co-occurrences of words in documents. In that setting, the data can be viewed as a set of triples $(i(r), j(r), r)$, where $r = 1 \ldots L$ is an index over the triples, each triple indicating the occurrence of word $j(r)$ in document $i(r)$. Note that a word can occur several times in a document. For example, the fact that word "line" (with number $i = 23$) occurs twice (for $r = 6$ and $r = 9$) in document #1 will correspond to two triples: $(1, 23, 6)$ and $(1, 23, 9)$, ie $i(6) = i(9) = 1$ and $j(6) = j(9) = 23$. An alternative representation is (i, j, n_{ij}) indicating that word j occurs n_{ij} times in document i (leading to $(1, 23, 2)$ in the previous example). Note that the index is then over i and j, with several instances of $n_{ij} = 0$.

In order to structure the data, we adopt a generative probabilistic approach, where we assume it was generated from a hierarchical model. Some early attempts at defining such models are Hofmann's Hierarchical Asymmetric Clustering Model (HACM) [10] or Hierarchical Shrinkage [14]. In this paper we propose a new model which has some additional flexibility. In our model the data are generated by the following process:

1. Pick a document class α with probability $P(\alpha)$,
2. Choose document i using the class-conditional probability $P(i|\alpha)$,
3. Sample a word topic ν with the class-conditional probability $P(\nu|\alpha)$,
4. Generate word j using the topic-conditional distribution $P(j|\nu)$.

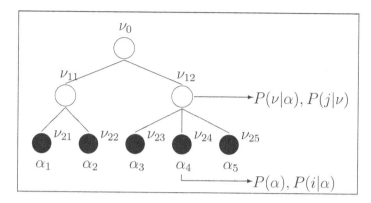

Fig. 1. An example hierarchical model with classes at the leaves: document classes $\alpha_1 \ldots \alpha_5$ are indicated by filled circles, topics $\nu_0 \ldots \nu_{25}$ are indicated by circles (accordingly, classes are also topics). Sampling of a co-occurrence is done by first sampling a class (ie selecting the fourth leaf here) and a document from the class-conditional $P(i|\alpha)$, then sampling a topic from the class conditional $P(\nu|\alpha)$ (second topic at the second level here) and a word from the topic-conditional $P(j|\nu)$.

Here we use the term of (document) class α to denote a group of documents sharing some common thematic feature (for example they all deal with "computer graphics"). We use the term of (word) topic to denote a homogeneous semantic field described by a specific word distribution. One document may be partly relevant to different topics, and several documents from different classes may share common, higher level topics. For example, a document on "computer graphics" and a document on "algorithmics" may have parts relevant to the more general "computer science" topic.

In a typical hierarchy, we may for example assign documents to classes at the leaves of the hierarchy, while words are sampled from topics which are any node in the hierarchy (figure 1). This therefore allows classes to be linguistically related by sharing some common ancestors/topics, as exemplified in our previous example. In a more general hierarchy, documents could be assigned to classes at any node of the hierarchy, like in Yahoo! or Google directories. In all cases, topics ν will here be restricted to the set of ancestors of a class α, a fact that we note $\nu \uparrow \alpha$. This can also be achieved by setting $P(\nu|\alpha) = 0$ whenever $\nu \not\uparrow \alpha$.

According to this model, the probability of a given co-occurrence (i, j) is:

$$P(i,j) = \sum_{\alpha} P(\alpha)P(i|\alpha) \sum_{\nu \uparrow \alpha} P(\nu|\alpha)P(j|\nu) \tag{1}$$

where we have used the conditional independence of documents and words given the class α. The parameters of the model are the discrete probabilities $P(\alpha)$, $P(i|\alpha)$, $P(\nu|\alpha)$ and $P(j|\nu)$. One interesting feature of this model is that several known models can be written as special cases of ours. For example:

- $P(i|\alpha) = P(i), \forall \alpha$ (documents independent of class) yields the HACM [10];
- Dropping $P(\alpha)$ and $P(i|\alpha)$ (or imposing uniform probabilities on these quantities) yields a hierarchical version of the Naïve Bayes model;[1]
- Flat (ie non-hierarchical) models are naturally represented using $P(\nu|\alpha) = 1$ iff $\nu = \alpha$ (ie one topic per class), yielding $P(i,j) = \sum_\alpha P(\alpha)P(i|\alpha)P(j|\alpha)$, aka Probabilistic Latent Semantic Analysis (PLSA, [8]).
- A flat model with a uniform distribution over classes α and documents i reduces to the (flat) Naïve Bayes model [24].

Our general model does not account eg for the "hierarchical" model described in [22], where probabilities for classes α are directly conditioned on the parent node $Pa(\alpha)$. The co-occurrence model in this framework is, at each level l in the hierarchy: $P(i,j) \propto \sum_{\alpha \in l} P(\alpha|Pa(\alpha))P(i|\alpha)P(j|\alpha)$. In this framework, however, the parent node mainly serves as a pooling set for its children, whereas in our model (eq. 1), the whole hierarchical structure is used and co-occurrences are generated by a single class-topic combination. In contrast, the model in [22] leads in fact to a series of flat clustering distributing all data across the nodes at each level, a strategy that we do not consider fully hierarchical in the context of this paper.

In addition, we will see in the Discussion (section 7) that the document similarity induced by the Fisher kernel [11] gives similar contribution for the model in [22] and for (flat) PLSA [9], whereas fully hierarchical models introduce a new contribution from the hierarchy.

Because our model can be seen as a hierarchical extension to PLSA, where both documents and words may belong to different clusters, we will refer to our hierarchical model as HPLSA, ie Hierarchical Probabilistic Latent Semantic Analysis, in the case of clustering (unsupervised classification). In the context of categorisation (supervised classification), we will call it HPLC, ie Hierarchical Probabilistic Latent Categoriser, or PLC when no hierarchy is used.

3   Motivations behind Our Model

Depending on the meaning we may give to i and j, different problems can be addressed with our model. Generally, we can view i and j as representing any pairs of co-occurring objects. In the preceding section, we have focused on modelling documents, with i objects representing documents, and j objects representing words. Within the general framework of clustering a large collection of unlabelled documents,[2] an important application we envisage is topic detection, where the goal is to *automatically* identify topics covered by a set of documents. In such a case, a cluster can be interpreted as a topic defined by the word probability

---

[1] Several models implement hierarchical extensions to Naïve Bayes, eg Hierarchical Shrinkage [14], Hierarchical Mixture Model [19], and the unpublished [1]. One key difference between these models lie in the estimation procedures.

[2] This contrasts with the task of categorising documents in pre-defined classes induced by a corpus of labelled documents.

distributions, $P(j|\nu)$. Our soft hierarchical model takes into account several important aspects of to this task: 1) a document can cover (or be explained by) several themes (soft assignment of i objects provided by $P(i|\alpha)$), 2) a theme is described by a set of words, which may belong to different topics due to polysemy and specialisation (soft assignment of j objects provided by $P(j|\nu)$), and 3) topics are in many instances hierarchically organized, which corresponds to the hierarchy we induce over clusters. Moreover, our use of a general probabilistic model for hierarchies allows us to deal with document collections in which topics cannot be hierarchically organized. In that case, probabilities $P(\nu|\alpha)$ are concentrated on $\nu = \alpha$, inducing a flat set of topics rather than a hierarchy. We obtained such a result on an internal, highly heterogeneous, collection.

Another important application we envisage for our model is knowledge structuring (see for example [5]), where it is important first to recognize the different realisations (ie terms and their variants) of the main concepts used in a domain, and secondly to organize them into ontologies.[3] A common feature of all ways of organizing terms in taxonomies is the central role of the "generalisation/specialisation" relation. Traditional approaches [6,17] induce hierarchies by repeatedly clustering terms into nested classes, each identified with a concept. Such clustering relies on some measure of similarity of the contexts in which terms occur as (inverse) distance between terms themselves.[4] Different kinds of contexts can be considered, from local ones, such as direct syntactic relations, or small windows centered on the term under consideration, to global ones, such as sentences, or paragraphs. However, problems in such clustering approaches arise from the following:

- Terms may be polysemous, and thus may belong to several classes;
- Contexts (eg a verb of which the term of interest is the direct object) may be ambiguous, suggesting the inclusion of similar context in different classes.

The collocation "hot line" illustrates the above two points: the meaning of the (polysemous) head "line" is determined by the collocate "hot", the meaning of which in the complete expression differs from its usual, daily one. We thus should be able to assign both "line" and "hot" to different clusters.

Polysemy of words, whether regarded as terms under focus or contexts of terms, and polytopicality of textual units, at various levels of granularity (from sentences to complete documents), thus call for models able to induce hierarchies of clusters while assigning objects to different clusters. The additional flexibility provided by our model over previously proposed ones exactly amounts to the ability of soft clustering both objects in the hierarchy instead of one.

---

[3] Here ontologies are the taxonomies structuring concepts of a domain.

[4] This approach is reminiscent of Harris' distributionalism, where classes of linguistic units are identified by the different contexts they share [7].

4   Soft Hierarchical Document Clustering

We first consider the task of automatically organising unlabelled documents, given as an i.i.d. collection of co-occurrences $\mathcal{D} = \{(i(r), j(r), r)\}_{r=1...L}$. The class membership of the documents (and co-occurrences) is unknown and must be inferred from the unlabelled data alone. The likelihood of the parameters can be expressed (using the independence assumption) as the product of the individual likelihoods (1) as $P(\mathcal{D}) = \prod_r P(i(r), j(r))$. Due to the presence of the multiple sums under the product of examples, the log-likelihood

$$\log P(\mathcal{D}) = \sum_{r=1}^{L} \log \left(\sum_{\alpha} P(\alpha) P(i(r)|\alpha) \sum_{\nu} P(\nu|\alpha) P(j(r)|\nu) \right) \qquad (2)$$

must in general be maximised numerically. This is elegantly done using the Expectation-Maximisation (EM) algorithm [4] by introducing the unobserved (binary) indicator variables specifying the class and topic choices for each observed co-occurrence.

Unfortunately, the iterative EM method is often sensitive to initial conditions. As a remedy, we used deterministic annealing [16,20] in conjunction with the EM iterations. Deterministic annealing EM is also called tempered EM in a statistical physics analogy, as it corresponds to introducing a temperature which is used to "heat" and "cool" the likelihood, in order to obtain a better and less sensitive maximum. Deterministic annealing has two interesting features: first it has been shown empirically [20,8] to yield solutions that are more stable with respect to parameter initialisation; second, it provides a natural way to grow the hierarchy (cf. [15] and below).

Tempered EM iteratively estimates the maximum likelihood parameters for the model using the completed likelihood, ie the likelihood of the data plus unobserved indicator variables. Let us note $C_\alpha(r)$ the (binary) class indicator for observation r, such that $C_\alpha(r) = 1$ iff document $i(r)$ is sampled from class α ($C_\alpha(r) = 0$ otherwise), and $T_{\alpha\nu}(r)$ the (binary) topic indicator such that $T_{\alpha\nu}(r) = 1$ iff $(i(r), j(r))$ is sampled from class α and topic ν ($T_{\alpha\nu}(r) = 0$ otherwise). Noting C (resp. T) the indicator vector (resp. matrix) of all C_α (resp. $T_{\alpha\nu}$), the likelihood of a generic completed observation consisting of (i, j, C, T) is:

$$P(i, j, C, T) = \sum_{\alpha} C_\alpha \, P(\alpha) \, P(i|\alpha) \sum_{\nu} T_{\alpha\nu} \, P(\nu|\alpha) \, P(j|\nu) \qquad (3)$$

Again, the (completed) log-likelihood over the entire dataset is expressed by combining (3) for all observations as $\sum_r \log P(i(r), j(r), C(r), T(r))$. At each EM iteration t, we first take the expectation of the completed log-likelihood over a "tempered" version (using temperature β) of the posterior probability of the indicator variables:

$$Q_\beta^{(t)} = \sum_{C,T} \left[\sum_r \log P^{(t)}(i(r), j(r), C(r), T(r)) \frac{P^{(t)}(i(r), j(r), C(r), T(r))^\beta}{\sum_{C,T} P^{(t)}(i(r), j(r), C, T)^\beta} \right] \qquad (4)$$

For $\beta = 0$, the tempered distribution is uniform, and for $\beta = 1$, we retrieve the posterior at iteration t, $P^{(t)}(C(r), T(r)|i(r), j(r))$. $Q_\beta^{(t)}$ can be conveniently expressed using two quantities:

$$\langle C_\alpha(r) \rangle_\beta^{(t)} = \frac{P(\alpha)^\beta P(i(r)|\alpha)^\beta \sum_\nu P(\nu|\alpha)^\beta P(j(r)|\nu)^\beta}{\sum_\alpha P(\alpha)^\beta P(i(r)|\alpha)^\beta \sum_\nu P(\nu|\alpha)^\beta P(j(r)|\nu)^\beta} \tag{5}$$

$$\langle T_{\alpha\nu}(r) \rangle_\beta^{(t)} = \frac{P(\alpha)^\beta P(i(r)|\alpha)^\beta P(\nu|\alpha)^\beta P(j(r)|\nu)^\beta}{\sum_\alpha P(\alpha)^\beta P(i(r)|\alpha)^\beta \sum_\nu P(\nu|\alpha)^\beta P(j(r)|\nu)^\beta} \tag{6}$$

also known as the E-step formula. Note that all probabilities on the right-hand sides of (5) and (6) are estimates at iteration t (not indicated for notational convenience). The iterated values for the model parameters are obtained by maximising $Q_\beta^{(t)}$ with respect to these parameters, leading to:

$$P^{(t+1)}(\alpha) = \frac{1}{L} \sum_r \langle C_\alpha(r) \rangle_\beta^{(t)} \qquad P^{(t+1)}(i|\alpha) = \frac{\sum\limits_{r, i(r)=i} \langle C_\alpha(r) \rangle_\beta^{(t)}}{\sum\limits_r \langle C_\alpha(r) \rangle_\beta^{(t)}} \tag{7}$$

$$P^{(t+1)}(\nu|\alpha) = \frac{\sum\limits_r \langle T_{\alpha\nu}(r) \rangle_\beta^{(t)}}{\sum\limits_r \sum\limits_\nu \langle T_{\alpha\nu}(r) \rangle_\beta^{(t)}} \qquad P^{(t+1)}(j|\nu) = \frac{\sum\limits_{r, j(r)=j} \sum\limits_\alpha \langle T_{\alpha\nu}(r) \rangle_\beta^{(t)}}{\sum\limits_r \sum\limits_\alpha \langle T_{\alpha\nu}(r) \rangle_\beta^{(t)}} \tag{8}$$

also known as the M-step formulas. At each value of β, iterating the E-step and M-step formulas is guaranteed to converge to a local maximum.

Tempered EM has an additional advantage in connection to hierarchical clustering, as increasing the "temperature" parameter β provides a natural way to grow a hierarchy. Starting with $\beta = 0$, only one class exists. As β increases, classes start to differentiate by splitting in two or more (typically one class will split into two). In the statistical physics analogy, this is the result of "phase transitions" in the system. Ideally, we could track the generalisation abilities (using eg held-out data or cross-validation) while β increases, and retain the hierarchy which gives the lowest estimated generalisation error. However, we have not implemented this complete process currently, and we use the following annealing schedule instead. Starting from $\beta = 0.3$, we iterate the E-step and M-step with one class only. β is then increased by increments of 0.1 (until $\beta = 0.8$) and 0.05 (above 0.8). At each increment of β, we track phase transitions by duplicating the classes, perturbing them slightly and running the EM iterations. We then check whether class duplicates have diverged, and if so, replace the former class by the new ones, while if duplicates of a class haven't diverged, we return to the original class. This process continues until a pre-specified number of classes is reached. Note that only the number of classes, not the hierarchy, is specified, such that the resulting hierarchy need not be a balanced tree.

In order to schematically represent the relationships between the parameters and the observed and latent variables, we present in figure 2 the graphical models

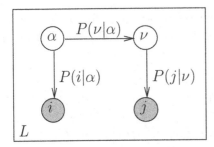 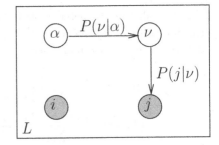

Fig. 2. Graphical models for the Hierarchical Probabilistic Latent Semantic Analysis, or HPLSA, model (left) discussed in this paper (equation 1) and the Hierarchical Asymmetric Clustering Model (HACM) from [10]. Gray-filled circles indicate observed variables.

corresponding to our clustering model (on the left). Note the difference with the HACM presented on the right: the generation of the document depends on the class which introduces extra flexibility. If we force i to be independent of α, the rightmost downward arrow in our model disappears, which reduces to the HACM, as mentioned earlier.

5   Hierarchical Document Categorisation

We will now consider the supervised counterpart of the previous problem, where the goal is to categorise, ie assign labels to, incoming document, based on the information provided by a dataset of labelled documents. Each document $i(r)$ now has a category label $c(r)$,[5] so the training data is $\mathcal{D} = \{(i(r), j(r), c(r), r)\}_{r=1...L}$, recording the category label associated with each co-occurrence. The purpose of the categorisation task is to assign a category to a new document d expressed as a set of co-occurrences $(d, j(s), s)$, where s runs across the number L_d of co-occurrences in document d (or alternatively (d, j, n_{dj})).

   We will further assume that each document category c corresponds to a single class α, such that $\forall r, \exists! \alpha, c(r) = \alpha$.

   In the training phase, the model parameters are obtained again by maximising the likelihood. Note that the category/class labels actually give additional information, and the only remaining latent variable is the choice of the topic. For the full hierarchical model:

$$P(i, j, c = \alpha) = P(\alpha)P(i|\alpha) \sum_{\nu} P(\nu|\alpha)P(j|\nu) \qquad (9)$$

   The (log-)likelihood may be maximised analytically over both $P(\alpha)$ and $P(i|\alpha)$, leading to estimates which are actually the empirical training set frequencies. Noting $\#\alpha$ the number of examples with category $c(r) = \alpha$ in the

---

[5] We assume that each example is assigned to a single category. Examples assigned to multiple categories are replicated such that each replication has only one.

training set (ie $\#\alpha = \#\{r|c(r) = \alpha\}$), and $\#(i, \alpha)$ the number of examples from document i and category $c = \alpha$,[6] the maximum likelihood estimates are:

$$P(\alpha) = \frac{\#\alpha}{L} \quad \text{and} \quad P(i|\alpha) = \frac{\#(i, \alpha)}{\#\alpha} \tag{10}$$

Due to the presence of the sum on ν in (9), the remaining parameters cannot be obtained analytically[7] and we again use an iterative (tempered) EM algorithm. The re-estimation formula are identical to (6) for the E-step and (8) for the M-step. The only difference with the unsupervised case is that the expressions of $P(\alpha)$ and $P(i|\alpha)$ are known and fixed from eq. 10. Note also that as the ML estimate for $P(i|\alpha)$ (eq. 10) is 0 for all documents i not in class α, the expression for the E-step (6) will simplify, and most notably, $\langle T_{\alpha\nu}(r)\rangle$ is 0 for all examples r not in class α. As a consequence, the re-estimation formulas are identical to those of the Hierarchical Mixture Model (equations (5-7) of [19]). The difference between both models lies in the additional use of $P(\alpha)$ and $P(i|\alpha)$ (10) in the training phase and our use of EM in the categorisation step (in addition to training, see below), as opposed to the approach presented in [19].

Categorisation of a new document is carried out based on the posterior class probability $P(\alpha|d) \propto P(d|\alpha)P(\alpha)$. The class probability $P(\alpha)$ are known from the training phase, and $P(d|\alpha)$ must again be estimated iteratively using EM to maximise the log-likelihood of the document to categorise:

$$\mathcal{L}(d) = \sum_s \log\left(\sum_\alpha P(\alpha)P(d|\alpha)\sum_\nu P(\nu|\alpha)P(j(s)|\nu)\right) \tag{11}$$

$\mathcal{L}(d)$ will be maximised wrt $P(d|\alpha)$ using the following EM steps, for $s = 1\ldots L_d$:

E-step: $$\langle C_\alpha(s)\rangle^{(t)} = \frac{P(\alpha)P^{(t)}(d|\alpha)\sum_\nu P(\nu|\alpha)P(j(s)|\nu)}{\sum_\alpha P(\alpha)P^{(t)}(d|\alpha)\sum_\nu P(\nu|\alpha)P(j(s)|\nu)} \tag{12}$$

M-step: $$P^{(t+1)}(d|\alpha) = \frac{\sum_s \langle C_\alpha(s)\rangle^{(t)}}{\#\alpha + \sum_s \langle C_\alpha(s)\rangle^{(t)}} \tag{13}$$

Notice that this is usually much faster than the training phase, as only $P(d|\alpha)$ (for all α) are calculated and all other probabilities are kept fixed to their training values. Once $P(d|\alpha)$ are obtained for all values of α, document d may be assigned to the class α_d for which the class posterior $P(\alpha|d)$ is maximised.

Note that as mentioned above, only $P(d|\alpha)$ is estimated, although clearly one may decide to benefit from the additional (unsupervised) information given by document d to update the class, topic and word distributions using a full EM. However we have decided not to implement this feature in order to classify all incoming documents on the same grounds.

---

[6] As document i is assigned to one category only, $\#(i, \alpha)$ will be zero for all but one class α, for which it will be equal to the number of co-occurrences in document i.

[7] For the flat model the ML estimate of $P(j|\alpha)$ is obtained directly as in (10).

For categorisation, the following tables present a summary of different models. In the tables, we indicate the model parameters, and whether parameter estimation or categorisation of a new example is performed directly or using an EM-type iterative algorithm.

Flat models		
Naïve Bayes	Parameters	$P(j|\alpha), P(\alpha)$
	Estimation	Direct
	Categorisation	Direct
PLSA[8]	Parameters	$P(j|\alpha), P(i|\alpha), P(\alpha)$
	Estimation	EM
	Categorisation	EM
PLC	Parameters	$P(j|\alpha), P(i|\alpha), P(\alpha)$
	Estimation	Direct
	Categorisation	EM for $P(d|\alpha)$

Hierarchical models		
Hierarchical Naïve Bayes[8]	Parameters	$P(j|\nu), P(\nu|\alpha), P(\alpha)$
	Estimation	EM
	Categorisation	Direct
HACM[10]	Parameters	$P(j|\nu), P(\nu|\alpha), P(i), P(\alpha)$
	Estimation	EM
	Categorisation	Direct
HPLC	Parameters	$P(j|\nu), P(\nu|\alpha), P(i|\alpha), P(\alpha)$
	Estimation	EM
	Categorisation	EM for $P(d|\alpha)$

where PLC stands for Probabilistic Latent Categorisation and HPLC for Hierarchical PLC. Notice that by using class labels efficiently, PLC estimates its parameters directly. In contrast standard PLSA implementations such as [19] apply a standard EM for both estimation and categorisation.

6   Experiments

6.1   Clustering

For evaluating our model in the context of document clustering, we used as a test collection the labeled documents in TDT-1. TDT-1 is a collection of documents provided by the Linguistic Data Consortium for the Topic Detection and Tracking project, consisting of news articles from CNN and Reuters, and covering various topics such as Oklahoma City Bombing, Kobe earthquake, etc.

The labeled portion of the TDT-1 collection was manually labeled with the main topic of each document as one of twenty-two topics. We randomly selected a subset of sixteen topics with the corresponding documents, obtaining

---

[8] This is valid for several variants related to the hierarchical structure and/or estimation procedure [1,14,19].

700 documents with 12700 different words. We then removed the labels from the documents and clustered the obtained collection with our model. For easy comparison, we used a binary tree with 16 leaves as hierarchy (corresponding to 15 cluster splits in tempered EM), where documents are assigned to the leaves of the induced hierarchy. We followed the same methodology using a version of Hierarchical Shrinkage described in [14,1], which we will refer to as HS, and PLSA, a flat model we retained to test the influence of the induced hierarchy (note that the original document collection is not hierarchically organized).

To measure the adequacy between obtained clusters and manual labels, we used the average, over the labels and over the clusters, of the Gini function, defined as:

$$G_l = \frac{1}{L} \sum_l \sum_\alpha \sum_{\alpha' \neq \alpha} P(\alpha|l)P(\alpha'|l)$$

$$G_\alpha = \frac{1}{\Lambda} \sum_\alpha \sum_l \sum_{l' \neq l} P(l|\alpha)P(l'|\alpha)$$

where L is the number of different labels and Λ the number of different clusters ($L = \Lambda = 16$ here). G_l measures the impurity of the obtained clusters α with respect to the labels l, and reciprocally for G_α. Smaller values of these functions indicate better results since clusters and labels are in closer correspondence, ie if the "data clusters" and "label clusters" contain the same documents with the same weights, the Gini index is 0. Furthermore, these functions have an upper bound of 1. Our choice for the Gini index was motivated by the fact that it is more fine-grained, and therefore more informative, than the direct misclassification cost in many instances.

The results we obtained are summarized in the following table:

	G_l	G_α
PLSA	0.34	0.30
HS	0.40	0.45
HPLSA	0.20	0.16

We thus see that PLSA, which is a flat model, ranks between the two hierarchical models we tested. HS, which results in most cases in a hard assignment of documents to clusters, is significantly worse than the other two models, which result in a soft assignment. Furthermore, our hierarchical model significantly outperforms the flat model. This last result is interesting since we assigned documents to the leaves of the hierarchy only, so, except for the words, the documents are assigned in the same manner as in a flat model. However, by making use of the hierarchy for words, we have better results than a flat model for both words and documents (even though we do not display the results here, experiments, eg [10], show that a standard approach to flat clustering, like K-means, yields results similar to, if not worse than, PLSA).

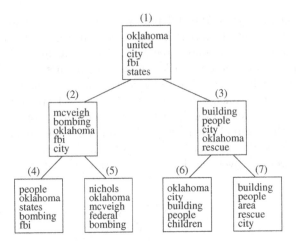

Fig. 3. Cluster hierarchy for Oklahoma City Bombing

As an example, we present the hierarchy we obtained on the 273 documents related to Oklahoma City Bombing. These documents contain 7684 different non-empty words (empty words, such as determiners, prepositions, etc., were removed using a stop list). An experiment, conducted with a flat model on the same data, revealed that the documents were best explained with three topics/clusters. We have chosen to cluster the data with a binary tree containing 4 leaves and 7 nodes. Figure 3 shows the hierarchy obtained with our model. For each node, we provide the first five words associated with the node, ie the five words for which $p(j|\nu)$ is the highest.

We can see that the data is first separated into two topics/clusters, respectively related to the investigation and the description of the event itself (nodes (2) and (3)). Node (2) is then divided into two parts, the investigation itself (node (4)) and the trial (node (5)), whereas node (3) is split between the description of the bombing and casualties (node (6)) and the work of the rescue teams (node (7)). Note also that despite our use of upper nodes to describe a given topic (through $P(\nu|\alpha)$ and $P(j|\nu)$), certain words, eg *Oklahoma*, appear in different nodes of the hierarchy. This is due to the fact that these words appear frequently in all documents. Our data is thus best explained by assigning these words to different topics/clusters.

6.2   Categorisation

In order to illustrate the behaviour of the hierarchical categorisation method, we address the task of categorising messages from 15 different newsgroups organised in a simple two-level hierarchy ([19] and figure 4). The data is taken from the benchmark "20 newsgroups" dataset.[9] The only pre-processing we perform on

---

[9] http://www.ai.mit.edu/~jrennie/20_newsgroups/

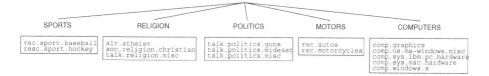

Fig. 4. The newsgroup hierarchy. There are 15 newsgroups at the leaves, organised with 5 mid-level topics and a root topic.

the data is that all tokens that do not contain at least one alphabetic character are removed. In particular, we do not filter out words or tokens with very low frequency.

We consider several sample sizes, using from 7 to 134 messages per class for training, and 3 to 66 messages for testing, such as the total amount of data varies from 10 to 200. For each sample size, we average results over ten replications of the same size.

We consider 4 categorisation methods:

- Naïve Bayes, with smoothed[10] class-conditional word distributions;
- Probabilistic Latent Categorisation (PLC) with 15 classes, no hierarchy;
- Hierarchical Mixture [19] with uniform conditional topic distributions $P(\nu|\alpha)$;
- Hierarchical PLC where the conditional topic distributions are estimated using maximum likelihood implemented with EM (HPLC).

The choice of uniform class-conditional topic distributions is due to a tendency to overfit, especially with small samples. This will be discussed in more details below.

Results are displayed in figure 5. Somewhat surprisingly, Naïve Bayes performs quite badly on our data, with some 10 to 20 percent lower classification rate compared to results published in [19] on similar data (as each document belongs to and is assigned a single category, the micro-averaged $F1$ reported in table 5 is equal to the percentage of correct class assignment). We blame the preprocessing for this somewhat dismal performance: as we retain all tokens which contain at least one alphabetic character, we introduce a high level of noise in the estimation of the topic-conditional word distributions by including many words which occur only once or twice in the entire collection.

The performance of both the flat and hierarchical PLC models with our noisy data is close to that reported by [19] for their hierarchical mixture model with cleaner pre-processed data. Although it uses a hierarchy to constrain the classes, HiMi doesn't manage to outperform the non-hierarchical PLC in our experiments. This is due to 2 factors. Firstly, HiMi is a hierarchical version

---

[10] We used a particular version of Lidstone smoothing [13] with $\lambda = 0.5$, which corresponds to the MAP estimate for a multinomial with a non-informative Dirichlet(1/2) prior on the parameters.

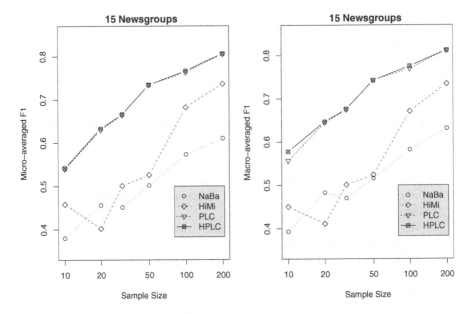

Fig. 5. Categorisation results for Naïve Bayes and PLC (both flat models) and for hierarchical mixture (HiMi) using uniform class-conditional topic distributions and hierarchical PLC (HPLC) using maximum likelihood class-conditional topic distributions trained by EM. The plots give the micro-averaged (left) and macro-averaged (right) $F1$ for sample sizes ranging from 10 to 200.

of Naïve Bayes, such that the increased noise level mentioned above will also hurt HiMi significantly. Secondly, the estimates of the class-conditional topic distributions are different here and in [19]. As the ML estimates of $P(\nu|\alpha)$ will tend to overfit, we need to somehow address this problem. Typical solutions include using held-out data to estimate $P(\nu|\alpha)$ in EM, or using a resampling strategy [14,19] to leverage available data more efficiently. We have chosen here to use a uniform distribution on topics instead, meaning that words can be sampled in equal parts from either the class or one of its ancestors. Although sub-optimal, this solution performs much better than the degenerate ML solution, which is equivalent to (flat) Naïve Bayes.

HPLC also suffers from this overfitting problem for small sample sizes, which explains why the performance of HPLC in table 5 is not significantly better than PLC's, suggesting that the hierarchy is not used to its full extent. In the case of HPLC, using a uniform distribution on the class-conditional topic distributions does not improve (or harm) performance. Although there is clearly room for improvement here, we take this as an indication that HPLC is not overly sensitive to these parameters, in particular when overfitting is concerned.

7   Discussion

Other EM variants. The co-occurrence model discussed here is a mixture model and relies on the EM algorithm for estimating the maximum likelihood parameters in cases where no analytical solution exist. Problems with the EM algorithm are the stability of the obtained solution and the convergence speed. The use of deterministic annealing [20,8] addresses the first problem in a satisfactory way, at the expense of the second, as typically more iterations will be needed during the annealing procedure than for a typical standard EM run. Although the gain in stability of the solution partially offsets this problem, by requiring only a single EM run, training times can still be problematic for large scale problems. With Gaussian mixture models, several strategies have been proposed, such as classification EM (CEM) or stochastic EM (SEM) [2]. Classification EM consists in assigning at every iteration each example r to the most likely class and topic, ie the α and ν with the highest values of $\langle C_\alpha(r)\rangle_\beta$ and $\langle T_{\alpha\nu}(r)\rangle_\beta$. The well-known K-means algorithm is an instance of CEM in the context of a uniform mixture of isotropic Gaussian distributions. CEM has been observed to operate quite fast, usually reaching a stable partition of the data in very few iterations. Similarly, stochastic EM assigns examples to classes and topics at random with probabilities given by $\langle C_\alpha(r)\rangle_\beta$ and $\langle T_{\alpha\nu}(r)\rangle_\beta$, rather than averaging over those values as standard EM does.

Fisher Kernels. Probabilistic models may be used to derive a model-based measure of similarity between examples, using the so-called Fisher kernel [11, 9]. Fisher kernels are defined using the gradient (wrt parameters) of the log-likelihood of a document d, $\nabla_\theta \ell(d)$, aka Fisher score, and the Fisher information matrix. The Fisher information matrix is $\mathbf{I} = \mathsf{E}\left(\nabla_\theta \ell(d) \, \nabla_\theta \ell(d)^\top\right)$, where the expectation is taken over $P(d|\theta)$. With this notation, the similarity between two documents d_i and d_n induced by the Fisher kernel is:

$$k(d_i, d_n) = \nabla_\theta \ell(d)^\top \, \mathbf{I}^{-1} \, \nabla_\theta \ell(d) \approx \nabla_\theta \ell(d)^\top \, \nabla_\theta \ell(d) \tag{14}$$

using the standard approximation that the Fisher information $\mathbf{I}$ is approximately the unit matrix. Notice that the original expression (including $\mathbf{I}$) is independent of the parameterisation. However, this is clearly not true for the simplified expression. It is therefore very relevant to use the parameterisation for which the approximation is best. In particular, we will here follow [9] and use a square root parameterisation for the multinomial parameters in our model.

Previous works [11,9,22] have shown how to make efficient use of unlabelled data into discriminative classifiers using Fisher kernels. Even though we have not experimented with Fisher kernels, we want to give here their forms for the different models, since we believe it sheds some light on the models.

For HPLSA, the likelihood of a document d, normalised by document length, is:

$$\ell(d) = \sum_j \widehat{P}(j|d) \log \left(\sum_\alpha P(\alpha)P(d|\alpha) \sum_\nu P(\nu|\alpha)P(j|\nu) \right) \tag{15}$$

where $\widehat{P}(j|d)$ is the empirical word frequency for word j in document d. The relevant derivatives are:

$$\frac{\partial \ell(d)}{\partial P(\alpha)} = \frac{P(\alpha|d)}{P(\alpha)} \sum_j \frac{\widehat{P}(j|d)}{P(j|d)} P(j|\alpha) \approx \frac{P(\alpha|d)}{P(\alpha)} \tag{16}$$

$$\frac{\partial \ell(d)}{\partial P(\nu|\alpha)} = P(\alpha|d) \sum_j \frac{\widehat{P}(j|d)}{P(j|d)} P(j|\nu) \approx P(\alpha|d) \tag{17}$$

$$\frac{\partial \ell(d)}{\partial P(j|\nu)} = \frac{\widehat{P}(j|d) \, P(\nu|d,j))}{P(j|d)} \tag{18}$$

where we have used the approximation $\widehat{P}(j|d) \approx P(j|d)$. Using this and the square root parameterisation, the similarity between two documents d_i and d_n is evaluated by Fisher kernel as the following expression:

$$k(d_i, d_n) = k_1(d_i, d_n) + k_2(d_i, d_n) + k_3(d_i, d_n)$$

$$k_1(d_i, d_n) = \sum_\alpha \frac{P(\alpha|d_i) \, P(\alpha|d_n)}{P(\alpha)} \tag{19}$$

$$k_2(d_i, d_n) = \sum_j \widehat{P}(j|d_i) \, \widehat{P}(j|d_n) \sum_\nu \frac{P(\nu|j, d_i) \, P(\nu|j, d_n)}{P(j|\nu)} \tag{20}$$

$$k_3(d_i, d_n) = \sum_\alpha P(\alpha|d_i) \, P(\alpha|d_n) \tag{21}$$

Contributions k_1 and k_3 can be summed up in a single contribution, involving the (weighted) inner product of the document mixing weights. This captures, up to a certain point, synonymy between words. Contribution k_2 performs a weighted inner product between the empirical distributions of words in the document, with a weight depending on whether the words have similar conditional topic distributions over the whole hierarchy. This distinguishes words used with different meanings in different contexts (polysems). Similar contributions can also be found in the kernel expressions of PLSA [9] and in [22].

Interestingly, under the above assumption, the contribution from parameters $P(\nu|\alpha)$ vanishes in the kernel function. This suggests that the values obtained for these parameters do not play a direct role in computing the similarity between documents, or, in other words, if the other parameters are fixed, varying the parameters $P(\nu|\alpha)$ does not impact the similarity function. The same is not true for hierarchical versions of Naïve Bayes, since the partial derivative of the log-likelihood function with respect to the $p(\nu|\alpha)$ parameters is given by (for brevity, we omit the details of the derivation):

$$\frac{\partial l(d)}{\partial P(\nu|\alpha)} = P(\alpha|d) \sum_j \widehat{P}(j|d) \frac{P(j|\nu)}{P(j|\alpha)} \tag{22}$$

leading to the following contribution to the kernel function:

$$k_3^{NB}(d_i, d_n) = \sum_\alpha P(\alpha|d_i) P(\alpha|d_n) \times$$

$$\sum_{\nu} \left(\sum_{j} \widehat{P}(j|d_i) \frac{P(j|\nu)}{P(j|\alpha)} \right) \left(\sum_{j} \widehat{P}(j|d_n) \frac{P(j|\nu)}{P(j|\alpha)} \right) \quad (23)$$

Thus, in this case, varying the parameters $P(\nu|\alpha)$ yields different similarities.

Although a more complete study of the relations between the Fisher kernel and the Maximum Likelihood estimates is needed, we believe this explains our observation that HPLC does not seem overly sensitive to the parameters $P(\nu|\alpha)$, whereas HiMi (a hierarchical version of Naïve Bayes) is. Future work should focus on working out the exact conclusions one can draw from the above facts.

Model selection. One of the objectives of this paper was to propose a very flexible model (1) which encompasses a number of previously proposed methods [8,14,19,24]. In addition to shedding some light on the assumptions built in the different models, this opens a possibility for using standard tools for performing model selection. Indeed, we have shown that we have a family of embedded models of increasing complexity, where we could select a model, typically using arguments based on generalisation relying on eg algebraic estimators or cross-validation. Note however that typically we would expect more flexible models to perform worse for small sample sizes. The results we have reported suggest that the most flexible model (HPLC) actually does quite well even for small sample sizes.

8   Conclusion

In this paper, we proposed a unifying model for hierarchical clustering and categorisation of co-occurrence data, with particular application to organising documents. This generative mixture model encompasses several other models, both hierarchical and flat, already proposed in the literature. We gave details on how to perform parameter estimation, either using a tempered version of the EM algorithm, or using direct formula when applicable.

The use of this model is illustrated on two task: clustering incoming news articles and categorising newsgroup messages. In both cases, the proposed model was compared to competing alternatives. Although there is certainly room for improvement on several fronts, we note that the combined use of the hierarchy and soft class assignment yields performance that is at least as good (and in most cases better) as previously proposed generative models. We also presented the Fisher kernels associated with the model and discussed how they relate to its behaviour.

Acknowledgements. We wish to thank Nicola Cancedda and Jean-Michel Renders for useful discussions on several aspects of this paper, and the anonymous reviewers for their helpful and constructive comments.

References

1. L. Douglas Baker, Thomas Hofmann, Andrew McCallum, and Yiming Yang. A hierarchical probabilistic model for novelty detection in text. http://www-2.cs.cmu.edu/ mccallum/papers/tdt-nips99s.ps.gz.

2. Gilles Celeux and Gérard Govaert. A Classification EM algorithm for clustering and two stochastic versions. *Computational Statistics and Data Analysis*, 14:315–332, 1992.

3. S. Deerwester, S. T. Dumais, G. W. Furnas, T. K. Landauer, and R. Harshman. Indexing by latent semantic analysis. *Journal of the American Society for Information Science*, 41(6):391–407, 1990.

4. A. P. Dempster, N. M. Laird, and D. B. Rubin. Maximum likelihood from incomplete data via the EM algorithm. *Journal of the Royal Statistical Society, Series B*, 39(1):1–38, 1977.

5. E. Gaussier and N. Cancedda. Probabilistic models for terminology extraction and knowleddge structuring from documents. In *Proceedings of the 2001 IEEE International Conference on Systems, Man & Cybernetics*, 2001.

6. G. Grefenstette. *Explorations in Automatic Thesaurus Construction*. Kluwer Academic Publishers, 1994.

7. Z. S. Harris. Distributional structure. *Word*, 10:146–162, 1954.

8. Thomas Hofmann. Probabilistic latent semantic analysis. In *Proceedings of the Fifteenth Conference on Uncertainty in Artificial Intelligence*, pages 289–296. Morgan Kaufmann, 1999. http://www2.sis.pitt.edu/ dsl/UAI/uai99.html.

9. Thomas Hofmann. Learning the similarity of documents: An information-geometric approach to document retrieval and categorization. In *Advances in Neural Information Processing Systems 12*, page 914. MIT Press, 2000.

10. Thomas Hofmann and Jan Puzicha. Statistical models for co-occurence data. A.I. Memo 1625, A.I. Laboratory, February 1998.

11. Tommi S. Jaakkola and David Haussler. Exploiting generative models in discriminative classifiers. In *Advances in Neural Information Processing Systems 11*, pages 487–493, 1999.

12. Thorsten Joachims. Text categorization with support vector machines: Learning with many relevant features. In *Proceedings of the European Conference on Machine Learning (ECML98)*, number 1398 in Lecture Notes in Computer Science, pages 137–142. Springer Verlag, 1998.

13. Christopher D. Manning and Hinrich Schütze. *Foundations of Statistical Natural Language Processing*. MIT Press, Cambridge, MA, 1999.

14. Andrew McCallum, Ronald Rosenfeld, Tom Mitchell, and Andrew Y. Ng. Improving text classification by shrinkage in a hierarchy of classes. In *Proceedings of the Fifteenth International Conference on Machine Learning*, pages 359–367, 1998.

15. Fernando Pereira, Naftali Tishby, and Lillian Lee. Distributional clustering of english words. In *Proceedings of the International Conference of the Association for Computational Linguistics*, 1993.

16. K. Rose, E. Gurewitz, and G. Fox. Statistical mechanics and phase transitions in clustering. *Physical Review Letters*, 65(8):945–848, 1990.

17. G. Salton. *Automatic Thesaurus Construction for Information Retrieval*. North Holland Publishing, 1972.

18. D. M. Titterington, A. F. Smith, and U. E. Makov. *Statistical Analysis of Finite Mixture Distribution*. John Wiley & Sons, San Diego, 1985.

19. Kristina Toutanova, Francine Chen, Kris Popat, and Thomas Hofmann. Text classification in a hierarchical mixture model for small training sets. In *Proceedings of the ACM Conference on Information and Knowledge Management*, 2001.
20. Naonori Ueda and Ryohei Nakano. Deterministic annealing variant of the EM algorithm. In Gerry Tesauro, David Touretzky, and Todd Leen, editors, *Advances in Neural Information Processing Systems 7*, pages 545–552. MIT Press, 1995.
21. C. J. van Rijsbergen. *Information Retrieval*. Butterworth, 2nd edition edition, 1979.
22. Alexei Vinokourov and Mark Girolami. A probabilistic framework for the hierarchic organisation and classification of document collections. *Journal of Intelligent Information Systems*, 18(2–3):153–172, 2002.
23. Peter Willett. Recent trends in hierarchical document clustering: A critical review. *Information Processing & Management*, 24(5):577–597, 1988.
24. Yiming Yang and Xin Liu. A re-examination of text categorization methods. In *Proceedings of the 22nd ACM SIGIR Conference on Research and Development in Information Retrieval*, pages 42–49, 1999.

Uncertainty-Based Noise Reduction and Term Selection in Text Categorization

C. Peters and C.H.A. Koster

Department of Computer Science,
University of Nijmegen, The Netherlands
{kees,charlesp}@cs.kun.nl

Abstract. This paper introduces a new criterium for term selection, which is based on the notion of Uncertainty. Term selection according to this criterium is performed by the elimination of noisy terms on a class-by-class basis, rather than by selecting the most significant ones. Uncertainty-based term selection (UC) is compared to a number of other criteria like Information Gain (IG), simplified χ^2 (SX), Term Frequency (TF) and Document Frequency (DF) in a Text Categorization setting. Experiments on data sets with different properties (Reuters-21578, patent abstracts and patent applications) and with two different algorithms (Winnow and Rocchio) show that UC-based term selection is not the most aggressive term selection criterium, but that its effect is quite stable across data sets and algorithms. This makes it a good candidate for a general "install-and-forget" term selection mechanism. We also describe and evaluate a hybrid Term Selection technique, first applying UC to eliminate noisy terms and then using another criterium to select the best terms.

1 Introduction

In this article we first provide a short introduction to measurement theory and then demonstrate its relevance to Information Retrieval by deriving a new technique for Term Selection. We describe a new uncertainty-based term selection algorithm and a hybrid algorithm combining the uncertainty-based elimination of noisy terms with a term selection method which tries to find the "best" terms.

By means of experiments using the Rocchio and Winnow Algorithms to classify a collection of large documents (patent applications) and two collections of small documents (newspaper items, patent abstracts) we shall compare the effectiveness of uncertainty-based term selection with that of other methods.

1.1 Term Selection

The automatic classification of documents presents a form of machine learning where features abound. By far the most of these have no value for the classification and should be eliminated. Even though some learning algorithms are more robust against spurious features than others, the performance of the algorithms

F. Crestani, M. Girolami, and C.J. van Rijsbergen (Eds.): ECIR 2002, LNCS 2291, pp. 248–267, 2002.

deteriorates with larger numbers of features. That is why term selection is an important issue in many Information Retrieval applications.

For the further development of the Linguistic Classification System LCS in the PEKING project[1] a term selection technique is needed which is applicable to linguistic phrases as well as to single keywords.

We can not use a conventional stop list, because a list of stop phrases makes little sense. Furthermore, for performance reasons we need the term selection to make a drastic reduction in the number of terms that have to be considered by the classification algorithm, without any loss in precision. The fewer the terms, the lower the cost of classification in time and memory.

After some earlier experiments with absolute term frequency as a criterium [12], we have implemented a large battery of criteria mentioned in the literature (see section 3.1) but found that they all involved the choice of parameters (in particular, the number of terms to select) whose effect depends on the corpus and is difficult to predict. The uncertainty-based term selection criterium, described in the following sections, is controlled by a single parameter which is corpus-independent.

1.2   Measuring Scores

Most Information Retrieval applications are based on some form of scoring, in particular Text Categorisation (TC; for an overview see [14]), where documents are to be assigned to those categories for which they obtain the highest score by a categorization algorithm. The score is usually some real number, representing the degree of its similarity to other documents in that category rather than a true probability. This makes it hard to compare scores given by different algorithms. Furthermore, usually no variance in the score is computed, neither is any other indication of the reliability of that score.

This is in great contrast to other fields like Physics, which have long relied on the adage "to measure is to know", but have recently come to realize that it is also important to quantify how much you do not know [4].

It is our conviction that measurements made in Information Retrieval can benefit greatly by embracing the notion of *Uncertainty* as it is used in modern measurement theory [1].

2   Measurement and Uncertainty

Every measurement represents essentially an estimate. Consequently, a measurement process should give as its result not only the measured value, an estimate v of the "real" value, but also an uncertainty $u(v)$ in this value. The uncertainty delimits, together with the measured value, the interval in which the "real" value is expected to lie. From an information-theoretic point of view, the measurement value represents the information gained about the object under investigation and

---

[1] **http://www.cs.kun.nl/peking**

the uncertainty represents the missing information about the object. This interpretation is best illustrated by looking at the entropy (the amount of missing information) of the normal distribution:

$$-\frac{\int_{-\infty}^{\infty} \left(-\frac{(x-v)^2}{2\,u^2(v)} - \log u\,(v) - \frac{\log \pi}{2} - \frac{\log 2}{2}\right) e^{-\frac{(x-v)^2}{2\,u^2(v)}}\,dx}{\sqrt{2}\,\sqrt{\pi}\,u\,(v)}$$

$$= \frac{2\,\log u\,(v) + \log \pi + \log 2 + 1}{2}$$

This is clearly only dependent on the uncertainty. In general, however, for real world measurements, the use of the normal distribution is not appropriate since important boundary conditions may exist on the possible values of the measurand. The most common of these are: strict positiveness of the measurand or boundedness of the measurand between a minimal and a maximal value. Such constraints provide important additional information, making other distributions than the normal distribution more appropriate.

For the associated probability distribution, representing the measurement result in the presence of such boundary conditions, the worst case distribution should be taken for the situation under investigation. This worst case distribution is determined by demanding stationarity of the entropy of the distribution under the given information and the constraints. The normal distribution is appropriate when no boundary conditions are given, and furthermore serves as an interesting case for illustrative purposes.

In case only the mean and standard deviation are given, with no additional constraints, two cases can be distinguished:

1. **TYPE A** – it is certain that the measured value is single valued (for example a mass). In this case the standard deviation itself is taken as the uncertainty and the corresponding normal distribution is taken as the representation. In this case the measurement result is given by the estimated value (the mean) and the uncertainty in this estimate.
2. **TYPE B** – it is known that the measurand has some natural variability and the measurement result is a mean value with a standard deviation. In this case the uncertainty is two times the statistical reliability in the mean. The worst case distribution is then given by a normal distribution with a standard deviation equal to the estimated uncertainty. This distribution can be interpreted as the probability density for the real mean of the measurement. The measurement result then comprises: the estimated mean, the estimated uncertainty in the mean and the estimated standard deviation.

In both these cases, the two-times-the-uncertainty interval is the 95% confidence interval in which the estimated value is expected to lie. For this reason the uncertainty is often stated with a so called k-factor of two [1]. For general distributions however it is not true that the 95% interval is given by two standard distributions; in most cases it is less. So in this case it makes no sense to use a k-factor of two. In some cases a k-factor of two is not even valid, because it would imply that the specified interval can cross the boundary conditions, implying that there are real values possible lying outside the boundaries, which was stated to be impossible.

2.1   An Example from Physics

Constraints on measurands are mostly implied by the measurement method. To give an obvious example from Physics, the length of a rod is dependent on temperature. So for measuring its length, its temperature has to be measured and controlled. The measurement of the temperature implies an uncertainty in the temperature. Its contribution to the uncertainty in the length of the rod has to be taken into account in the uncertainty in the measurement result of the length of the rod.

The fact that the rod's length l certainly is greater than zero, $l > 0$, implies for the worst case distribution a second constraint. The associated worst case distribution is the so called *Pierson III distribution*. However, modern length measurement techniques may be so accurate (with relative uncertainties in the order of $\frac{u(l)}{l} = 10^{-6} - 10^{-12}$) that the normal distribution is a nearly perfect approximation, and the boundary conditions give hardly any additional information.

2.2   Uncertainty in Text Categorization

At the first sight, all of this has little to do with text categorization, in which the relevant quantified terms like Term Frequency and Document Frequency (see later) are obtained by counting occurrences of terms in documents and categories from the training set. We shall show how to estimate the uncertainties in these quantities. Furthermore, we shall use constraints on the quantified information obtained from a training set to provide additional information, based on the estimation of the statistical uncertainties.

2.3   Term Frequency Measurement

Let the *relative term frequency* of term k in document i be given by

$$f_{ki} = \frac{n_{ki}}{N_i} \qquad (1)$$

in which n_{ki} stands for the number of occurrences of term t_k in document d_i and N_i for the total number of terms in document d_i. Both of these quantities are natural numbers. The category-dependent *term frequency* for term k in category j is given by the mean

$$TF_{jk} = \frac{1}{C_j} \sum_{d_i \in T_j} f_{ki} \qquad (2)$$

in which T_j is the set of training documents for category j and C_j the total number of documents in this train set. Since the document term frequency has a natural variability, it has a standard deviation around this mean which is given by

$$s_{jk} = \sqrt{\frac{1}{C_j} \sum_{d_i \in T_j} (f_{ki} - TF_{jk})^2} \tag{3}$$

Usually, the uncertainty is chosen to be based on two times the standard deviation equivalent. However, since in this paper the distribution function representation approach is used, the standard deviation itself will be used as the base of the uncertainty. The uncertainty in the mean is then estimated by the reliability in the estimated mean, i.e.

$$u(TF_{jk}) = \frac{s_{jk}}{\sqrt{C_j - 1}} \tag{4}$$

The measurement result is now given by the set of associations

$$TM_j = \{[t_k \mid [TF_{jk}, u(TF_{jk})]]\}$$

for category j. The total information over all categories is given by the set

$$TM^\star = \{\{TM_j\}\}$$

.

2.4 Document Frequency Measurement

Defining the *document frequency* of term t_k as the fraction of documents in T_j which contain term t_k, it is clear that another approach has to be taken to estimate the uncertainty in this fraction. We want to estimate the reliability of the estimated document frequency as a representative value of the "real" document frequency from the training set T_j, where by the "real" value we mean the exact value of the document frequency for the entire category. Let DF_{jk} be the estimated document frequency, which is defined as

$$DF_{jk} = \frac{D_{jk}}{C_j} \tag{5}$$

with D_{jk} the number of documents in T_j containing t_k, i.e. the documents in the set $\{d_i \mid (d_i \in T_j) \wedge (t_k \in d_i)\}$, and C_j as defined above. Usually the estimated frequency is obtained by simply counting over the training set. In this case, however, the estimated as well as the "real" value are exact and have no variability. Thus, from this simple counting process no information is available concerning the uncertainty in this estimate. Since the estimation is done by an exact counting procedure, there clearly is no standard deviation defined.

The only fact which can be stated about this "measurement" result is:

The estimated value of the document frequency is DF_{jk} and the real value is a number falling in the range $[0,1]$

which contains the same information as the statement:

The real value of the document frequency is a number in the range $[0,1]$.

The only logical conclusion is that the estimate DF_{jk} clearly has to be considered as non-information without a measure for its reliability, i.e. uncertainty. So, the estimation has to be refined in order to produce this information about the uncertainty. This refinement is done by introducing a statistical (Type-A) uncertainty estimation.

1. partition the training set T_j randomly in N subsets $T_j^n, n \in 1..N$ each containing $\frac{C_j}{N}$ documents, such that

$$\forall n, m \in [1, N] \; n \neq m \Rightarrow T_j^n \cap T_j^m = \emptyset, \bigcup_{n=1}^{N} T_j^n = T_j$$

2. determine the N DF_{jk}^n's of the subsets T_j^n, treating them as separate independent training sets.

$$DF_{jk}^n = \frac{D_{jk}^n}{C_j^n} = N\frac{D_{jk}^n}{C_j} \tag{6}$$

3. determine DF_{jk} by taking the mean of these as an estimate for the "real" document frequency:

$$\overline{DF}_{jk} = \frac{1}{N} \sum_{n=1}^{N} DF_{jk}^n = \frac{D_{jk}}{C_j} = DF_{jk} \tag{7}$$

which turns out to be exactly the same as the counted estimate of DF_{jk} above.

4. determine (the extra information about) the reliability of DF_{jk} by taking the reliability of the DF_{jk} as the uncertainty in DF_{jk}.

$$u(DF_{jk}) = \frac{s_{jk}}{\sqrt{N-1}} = \sqrt{\frac{1}{N(N-1)} \sum_{n=1}^{N} (DF_{jk}^n - \overline{DF}_{jk})^2} \tag{8}$$

since there is again a natural variability in the DF_{jk}^n.

The measurement result is given by the set of associations $DM_j = \{[t_k \mid [DF_{jk}, u(DF_{jk})]]\}$ for category j, which contains no loss of information against the counted estimate, but additional information about the reliability of the measurement. The total information over all categories is given by the set

$$DM^\star = \{\{DM_j\}\}$$

2.5   Noise and Information

As mentioned above, the estimated term frequencies are a priori probabilities of the terms in a class-dependent manner. They are certainly valued between zero and one. For this type of boundary condition, under the assumption that the "real" quantity is single valued, and with known mean estimate and uncertainty, the worst case distribution is the Beta distribution.

$$P(x|a,b) = \frac{(1-x)^{b-1}\, x^{a-1}}{B\,(a,b)}$$

In terms of the estimated mean and its uncertainty, the parameters a and b are given by

$$a = -\frac{m\left(u\,(m)^2 + m^2 - m\right)}{u\,(m)^2}$$

and

$$b = \frac{(m-1)\left(u\,(m)^2 + m^2 - m\right)}{u\,(m)^2}$$

where m is the estimated mean and $u(m)$ the uncertainty.

It is clear that the boundary conditions on the mean imply boundary conditions on the uncertainty. One is trivial: $u(m) > 0$. The other one is given by the fact that $a > 1$ and $b > 1$ must hold, since otherwise the distribution function diverges at zero, giving infinite probabilities. Solving a and b for this boundary condition gives

$$u\,(m) < m\sqrt{-\frac{m-1}{m+1}}$$

and

$$u\,(m) < (1-m)\sqrt{-\frac{m}{m-2}}$$

or

$$u\,(m) < \min\left(m\sqrt{-\frac{m-1}{m+1}}, (1-m)\sqrt{-\frac{m}{m-2}}\right)$$

with "min" the usual minimization function. We shall call $k = m/u(m)$ the k-factor or "quality" of the data.

2.6   Noisy Term Elimination

The smaller k is, the greater the chance that the data is noise. The bigger k, the more certain it is that the value really contains information about a term. So k can be considered as a measure for the *quality* (not the significance) of the information.

It is advisable to remove the noise from the data before processing it further, because otherwise noise may propagate through the entire process. In particular, a learning process which is amplifying significant data and suppressing insignificant data can not itself distinguish between noise and information. Unless the learning process inherently filters noise, noise will then be randomly amplified or suppressed.

As a rule of thumb, noise reduction with $Q = 1.4$ would remove about 60% of the terms; a value of $Q = 2$ would remove about 95% and $Q = 3$ about 98% of the terms. These crude estimates are based on the assumption that for $k > 2$, the normal distribution should be a reasonable approximation to the Beta distribution. For combined term selection setting $Q = 1.4$ should be a reliable way to obtain high quality data, when sufficient data is available.

2.7   Uncertainty-Based Term Selection

In categorizing documents based on the terms occurring in them, any technique for term selection will tend to eliminate noisy terms, and therefore noisy term elimination is also a technique for term selection.

We have experimented with the use of uncertainty in the term frequency for term selection, selecting for each class j only the terms k with $\frac{TF_{jk}}{u(TF_{jk})} > Q$. This is expected to improve the *quality* of the information while reducing the number of terms. For estimating the *significance* of this information other estimates are available, e.g. information gain (IG). Two approaches to term selection can therefore be distinguished:

- *information quality*, measured e.g. by uncertainty (UC)
- *information significance*, measured e.g. by IG or χ^2.

These criteria are in principle independent, and can be combined.

3   Experimental Approach

We have performed a large scale experiment, comparing

- six term selection criteria
- applied to three different corpora
- using two classification algorithms.

The measurements at the end of this paper are the result of 3-way cross validation: the corpora were divided randomly into three equal subsets. Three measurements were done, taking each subset in turn as test set and the other two as train set. The three results were averaged.

3.1   Six Term Selection Criteria

Six different criteria were investigated, of which the first has been described in this article while four others can be found in somewhat varying forms in literature (see the overview in [14]). The last one is not a serious criterium but it will provide a baseline. They are:

- UC - UnCertainty
  the ratio between the term frequency and its uncertainty, described above
- TF - Term Frequency
  $\frac{1}{|T_j|} P(t_k|C_j)$ estimated from the term frequencies
- DF - Document Frequency
  $\frac{1}{|T_j|} P(t_k|C_j)$ estimated from the document frequencies
- IG - Information Gain
  as in [14]
- SX - Simplified Chisquare
  as in [14]
- RD - Random.

3.2   Three Corpora

The corpora used in the following experiments each contain a large number of mono-classified documents (each document belongs to precisely one class) in many classes.

1. The *Reuters mono* corpus is a random selection of 9090 pre-classified documents from the well-known Apte subset of the Reuters 21578 corpus [2]. The documents are short newspaper articles very unevenly distributed over 66 classes. The largest class acq comprises about 25% of the documents.
2. The EPO1F corpus (see [9,8]) consists of 16000 patent applications in English, pre-classified into 16 disjoint classes (*clusters* of directorates) with a thousand training examples each. The collection has a size of 461.1 M-bytes. Of these documents we used 8000, chosen at random.
   The corpus is very homogeneous in document size, and evenly distributed over the classes. The documents have been pre-classified with the greatest care by experts in their respective domain. The full text documents (avg 4580 words) are in descriptive prose and contain some non-linguistic material like tables and formulae.
3. The EPO1A corpus contains the abstracts of the documents in EPO1F distributed evenly over the same classes. We used 9600, chosen at random. The abstracts, with an average length of 129 words, are in descriptive prose without tables or formulae.

The properties of these corpora can be summarized as

corpus identifier	number of terms	properties
Reuters mono	26288	small documents, wide variation in class size
EPO1A	18208	small documents, all classes same size
EPO1F	82347	large documents, all classes same size

We use keywords as terms. The only pre-processing applied to the documents was the replacement of capital letters by the corresponding small letters (decapitalization) and the removal of special characters. In particular, no stemming was performed and no stop list was applied. We relied on the term selection to eliminate redundant features.

3.3   Three Algorithms

The well-known Rocchio algorithm [13,5] is the typical workhorse for document retrieval and classification in Information Retrieval. It is based on the Vector Space model and computes a classifier essentially as a vector of term weights.

The less well-known Winnow is a heuristical learning algorithm, iterating repeatedly over the training documents in order to obtain an optimal linear separator between relevant and non-relevant documents (for the underlying theory see [7]).

In terms of the admirable exposition given in [6], what we have implemented is the *Balanced Winnow* algorithm with the *thick threshold* heuristic. We have made a slight improvement to its speed of convergence by using *normalized term strengths* to initialize the Winnow weights.

3.4   The Measure of Accuracy

The measure of Accuracy used here is the *F1 measure*, a kind of average of Precision and Recall defined by

$$F1 = \frac{2}{\frac{1}{Precision} + \frac{1}{Recall}}$$

which is *micro-averaged* over the classes, meaning that the number of relevant documents selected (RS) are summed over all classes, and similarly for RNS, NRS and NRNS. This measure favors the large classes over the small ones, but it can be argued that it gives a useful overall view. Using the F1-value as Accuracy measure attaches equal importance to Precision and Recall.

3.5   Varying the Number of Terms

We are going to measure the Accuracy at various numbers of terms. Two ways of choosing the number of terms are available:

1. (global) choosing a given number of terms from the corpus and using these terms for each class
2. (local) choosing for each class a given number of terms, not necessarily using the same set of terms for each class.

We choose for a mixed approach, first selecting the best k terms per class but then training on the union of the terms selected.

Both Winnow and Rocchio make an essential use of negative terms, terms indicating that the document does NOT belong to the class: Winnow does that by training both positive weights w_j^+ and negative weights w_j^- for term j, and Rocchio by the γ term in the formula (originally included for incorporating negative feedback). Therefore we have to make sure that not only terms predicting strongly for the class are retained, but also enough terms predicting against it. That is why we use this mixed approach.

By allowing a large number of terms per class, we can also model the absence of term selection.

3.6   Mono- or Multi-classification?

Even though all documents are mono-classified, we make no use of the fact that each test document should belong to precisely one class but rather allow it to be assigned to several classes (between zero and three). Not using this information lowers the Accuracy achieved somewhat, because not all information is used, but it actually provides a harsher test, which is also relevant to multi-classification. Thus, although we are training 16 independent classifiers we also take into account the interaction between them (by looking at the combined set of terms and by multi-classifying the test data).

4   Experimental Results

The three pages of graphs at the end of this article show our main results, providing for each of the three corpora and for both the Rocchio and Winnow algorithms a comparison of the five term selection criteria, with RD as baseline.

A typical graph looks like the following sketch:

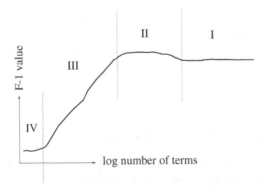

This sketch shows four phases or regions, obtained when successively reducing the number of terms per class:

I   a region in which the reduction of the number of terms has practically no effect. Not even for the random elimination of terms (RD)! This shows that there is a lot of redundancy in the documents and explains why OCR errors (knocking out a small random fraction of the occurrences of terms) have no important influence on classification Accuracy.

II a longer region (one or two orders of magnitude) where the Accuracy may actually increase slightly (a few percent points) when reducing the number of terms, reaches some optimum and decreases again. The effect is somewhat more pronounced for Rocchio than for Winnow, showing that the latter algorithm is better at disregarding spurious terms.

III an exponential decrease in Accuracy, whose position and steepness depends on the term selection criterium and the corpus, and

IV a rebound where the number of terms gets too small to distinguish between the classes, consistent with a random choice of classes.

In the lower end of the graph, the variance is large, but not enough to hide this trend.

Note that in some of the graphs at the end, the horizontal axis is logarithmic and represents the *total number of terms selected*, whereas in others the scale is linear and represents the *number of terms selected per class*. These numbers are related, depending on the corpus and the selection algorithm, e.g. (for Reuters mono):

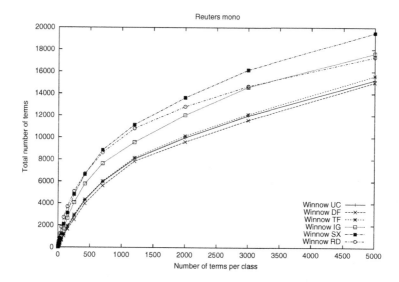

It appears that SX and IG choose more diverse terms per class than the others (so that the union over all classes is larger), which partly explains their success.

Notice that RD also chooses more diverse terms than UC, but obviously not very good ones.

4.1   Comparison

What we are looking for is the term selection criterium which (consistently across corpora and classification algorithms) achieves the best Accuracy at the lowest number of terms.

The first thing that strikes the eye about the graphs in the appendices is the great length of the regions I and II: the number of terms can be reduced by 2-3 orders of magnitude without a reduction in Accuracy or even with a slight gain (Cf. [15]). Surprisingly few terms are actually needed to characterize a class and distinguish it from others.

At high numbers of terms there is little to choose between the criteria, but at low numbers of terms a clear picture emerges: SX performs best followed by IG, then DF and TF, and UC is the weakest. It should however be realized that when performing term selection for performance reasons there is no necessity to remove as many terms as possible. For both Winnow and Rocchio the complexity of training is roughly proportional to the size of the corpus times the number of classes. This holds in particular for the collection of the statistics on which the terms selection criteria are based, so that the reduction in the training and testing time achieved by reducing the number of terms per class is limited.

Winnow achieves consistently better Accuracy than Rocchio. The differences between the three corpora are small. In particular, using SX, each corpus needs less than 50 terms per class.

4.2   UC Term Selection

As a term selection criterium UC is rather weak, especially when taking into account that it needs more complicated statistics than DF and TF, which can be implemented more efficiently. On the other hand, it behaves more stably than TF and DF, whose effect depends more strongly on the corpus.

Obviously, UC does not predict very well which are the good terms to use – but that is not what it was designed for: it should be good at eliminating noisy terms. The other algorithms will actually have a similar noise-reducing effect (a noisy term is never a good predictor for a class) but in distinction to the other terms selection criteria UC has the advantage that it can be parameterized with a desired Quality level Q, rather than by an estimate of the number of terms needed for each class, which depends in an unpredictable way on the corpus.

The reason for UC's somewhat disappointing behaviour may lie in the fact that we took into account the uncertainty in the term frequency only, disregarding other sources of uncertainty.

The relation between the Q-value chosen for UC and the Accuracy achieved is illustrated vividly by the following graph (Winnow and Rocchio on Reuters mono). In distinction to the others, this measurement was done in mono-classification, that is, taking into account the information that each document belongs to precisely one class. The Accuracy is therefore higher than in the other graphs.

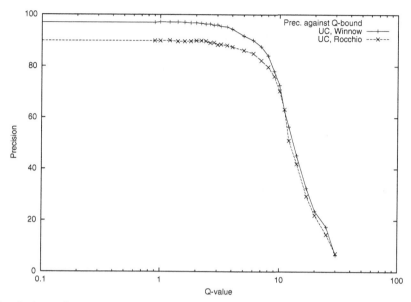

It is obvious that noise reduction with Q = 2 is a reliable, although not very aggressive, form of term selection, suitable for both small and large corpora, with an expected reduction of the number of terms by 95%. This is a form of term selection that you can install and forget – reducing the number of parameters that an integrator or user of the classification system has to specify.

4.3   Hybrid Term Selection

Since noise reduction and term selection are complementary ideas, it should be possible to combine them in a form of *hybrid term selection*: on a per-class basis, first eliminate noisy terms and then select the most predictive terms by another criterium. The noisy terms can then be eliminated from the statistics on which the term selection criterium is based, which may slightly improve precision and definitely reduces the memory needed.

This hybrid approach was inspired by a remark in a paper on term clustering by [3]. In an experiment on the Reuters-21578 test-set, they found that after applying term selection, clustering achieved better precision with fewer terms than without this selection, which they attributed to the elimination of noisy terms by the term selection algorithm.

We have investigated the effect of this hybrid approach, using UC with Q = 1.4 and Q = 2.0 for noise reduction followed by each of the six term selection algorithms, and also showing the case Q = 0.0 for comparison. The following graphs (for Reuters mono) are typical.

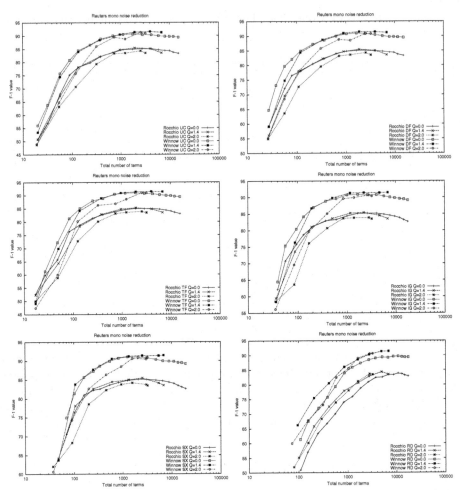

Noisy term elimination with Q = 1.4 followed by term selection is marginally better than term selection alone, achieving slightly better Accuracy, even in combination with UC itself. There may also be some gains in performance. Noise removal with Q =2.0 is not useful, because it seems to eliminate some terms which are needed at low numbers of terms.

5   Conclusion and Outlook

We have derived a new term selection method UC, based on the elimination of noisy terms, rather than on the selection of significant terms. We have compared its effect very thoroughly with other term selection methods from literature, using three different corpora and two different classification algorithms. UC does not yield more accurate results than other term selection criteria, especially for very low numbers of terms, but it is very reliable and consistent in its behaviour.

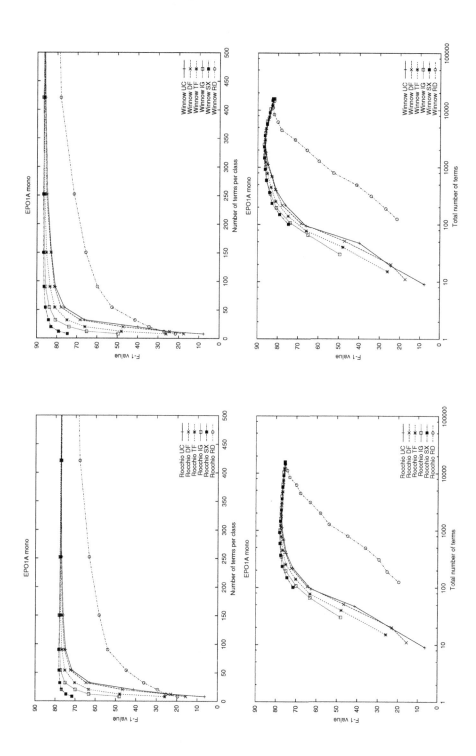

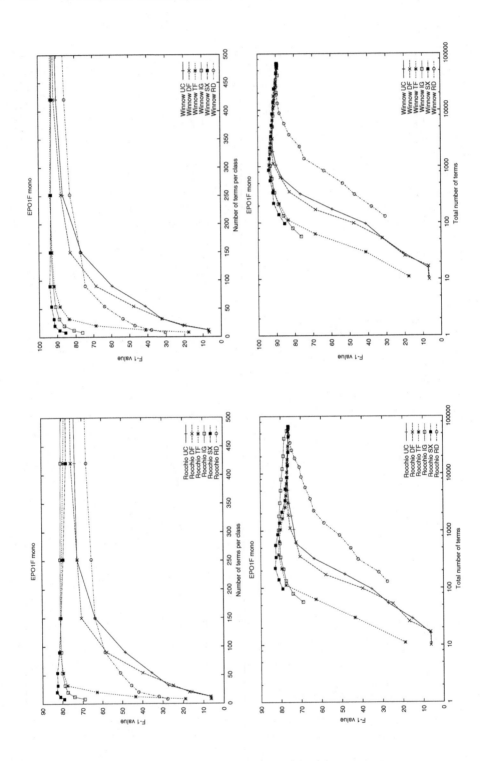

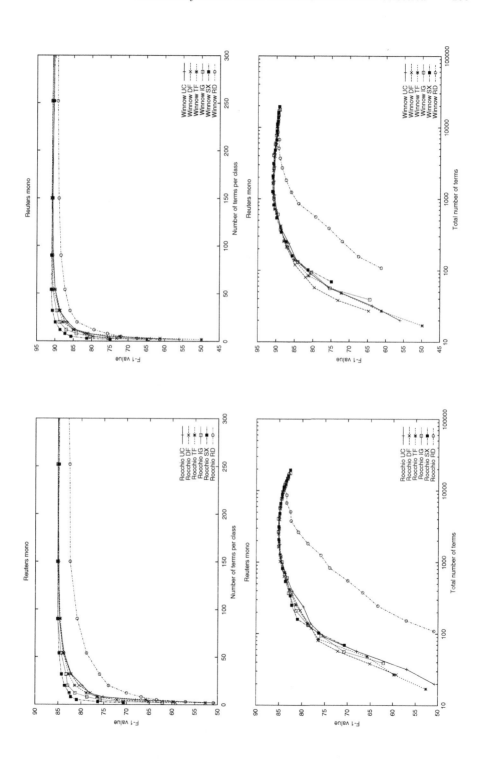

UC is controlled by one parameter, the Quality, which is not dependent on either the classification algorithm used or on the dataset. In particular, when using UC it is not necessary to guess how many terms will be needed, in distinction to other methods. This makes UC ideal as an "install-and-forget" technique for term selection.

We have also described a hybrid term selection method, first removing noisy terms and then selecting the terms with the highest information quality. It showed only marginal improvements in Quality over straight term selection. This may be caused by the fact that we take only one source of Uncertainty into account, the variability of term frequencies.

This paper is actually a first exercise in the application of measurement theory to Information Retrieval. We are currently investigating more serious applications:

- measuring uncertainty in document scores
- measuring entropy and uncertainty in class profiles
- developing more objective techniques for comparing the quality of categorization algorithms

and others.

References

1. ISO/TAG4/WG3, (R. Cohen, P. Clifford, P. Giacomo, O. Mathiesen, C. Peters, B. Taylor, K. Weise), *Guide to the expression of uncertainties in measurement*, ISO publication ISBN-92-67-10118-9.
2. Apté, C. and Damerau, F. (1994) Automated learning of decision rules for text categorization. In: *ACM Transactions on Information Systems* 12(3):233-251, 1994.
3. L. Douglas Baker and Andrew Kachites McCallum, Distributional clustering of words for text-classification, In: Proceedings SIGIR 98, pp. 96-103.
4. E. Richard Cohen, Uncertainty and error in physical measurements, At: The International summer school of physics "Enrico Fermi", SIF Course CX, Metrology at the frontiers of physics and technology, Lerici (Italy), 27 June - 7 July 1989.
5. W.W. Cohen and Y. Singer (1999), Context-sensitive learning methods for text categorization. *ACM Transactions on Information Systems 13*, 1, 100-111.
6. I. Dugan, Y. Karov, D. Roth (1997), Mistake-Driven Learning in Text Categorization. In: *Proceedings of the Second Conference on Empirical Methods in NLP*, pp. 55-63.
7. A. Grove, N. Littlestone, and D. Schuurmans (2001), General convergence results for linear discriminant updates. Machine Learning 43(3), pp. 173-210.
8. C.H.A. Koster, M. Seutter and J. Beney (2000), Classifying Patent Applications with Winnow, Proceedings Benelearn 2001, Antwerpen, 8pp.
9. M. Krier and F. Zaccà (2001), Automatic Categorisation Applications at the European Patent Office, International CHemical Information Conference, Nimes, October 2001, 10 pp.
10. L. D. Landau, E.M. Lifschitz, Lehrbuch der theoretischen Physik V, Statistische Physik Teil 1, Akademie Verlag Berlin, 1979.

11. David D. Lewis, An evaluation of Phrasal and Clustered representations on a Text Categorization task, Fifteenth Annual International ACM SIGIR, Copenhagen, 1992.
12. H. Ragas and C.H.A. Koster, Four classification algorithms compared on a Dutch corpus, Proceedings SIGIR 98, pp. 369-370.
13. J.J. Rocchio (1971), Relevance feedback in Information Retrieval, In: Salton, G. (ed.), *The Smart Retrieval system - experiments in automatic document processing*, Prentice - Hall, Englewood Cliffs, NJ, pp 313-323.
14. Fabrizio Sebastiani, Machine learning in automated text categorization, ACM Computing Surveys, Forthcoming, 2002
    `http://faure.iei.pi.cnr.it/~fabrizio/Publications/ACMCS02.pdf`,
15. Yiming Yang and Jan Pederson (1997), Feature selection in statistical learning of text categorization. In: ICML 97, pp. 412-420.

A Graphical User Interface for Structured Document Retrieval

Jesús Vegas[1], Pablo de la Fuente[1], and Fabio Crestani[2]

[1] Dpto. Informática
Universidad de Valladolid
Valladolid, Spain
jvegas@infor.uva.es
pfuente@infor.uva.es
[2] Dept. Computer and Information Sciences
University of Strathclyde
Glasgow, Scotland, UK
fabioc@cs.strath.ac.uk

Abstract. Structured document retrieval requires different user graphical interfaces from standard Information Retrieval. An Information Retrieval system dealing with structured documents has to enable a user to query, browse retrieved documents, provide query refinement and relevance feedback based not only on full documents, but also on specific document structural parts. In this paper, we present a new graphical user interface for structured document retrieval that provides the user with an intuitive and powerful set of tools for structured document searching, retrieved list navigation, and search refinement. We also present the results of a preliminary evaluation of the interface which highlights strengths and weaknesses of the current implementation and suggests directions of future work.

1   Introduction

Standard Information Retrieval (IR) treats documents as their were atomic entities, indexing and retrieving them as single objects. However, modern IR needs to be able to deal with more elaborate document representations, like for example documents written in SGML, HTML, or XML. These document representation formalisms enable to represent and describe documents said to be *structured*, that is documents that are organised around a well defined structure. New standards in structured document representation compel IR to design and implement models and tools to index and retrieve documents according to the given document structure. This area of research is known as *structured document retrieval*. This means that documents should no longer be considered as atomic entities, but as aggregates of interrelated objects that need to be indexed, retrieved, and presented both as a whole and separately, in relation to the user's needs.

IR systems are powerful and effective tools for accessing documents by content. A user specifies the required content using a query, often consisting of a

F. Crestani, M. Girolami, and C.J. van Rijsbergen (Eds.): ECIR 2002, LNCS 2291, pp. 268–283, 2002.

natural language expression. Documents estimated to be relevant to the user need expressed in the query are presented to the user through an interface. A good interface enables the IR process to be interactive, stimulating the user to review a number of retrieved documents and to reformulate the initial query, either manually or, more often, automatically, using relevance feedback. Given the complexity of the IR task and the vagueness and imprecision of the expression of the user information need and document information content, interactivity has been widely recognised as a very effective way of improving information access performance [10].

In structured document retrieval, the need for a good interface between user and system becomes even more pressing. Structured documents are often long and complex and it has been observed that a certain form of disorientation occurs in situations where the user does not understand why certain documents appear in the retrieved list [5]. The length and structural complexity of such documents makes it difficult for the user to capture the relationship between the information need and the semantic content of the document. This user disorientation makes the task of query reformulation much harder, since the user has first to understand the response of the system and then to choose if any of the retrieved document is a good enough representation of the information need to provide the system with precise relevance feedback. This added difficulties obviously increase the cognitive load of the user and decrease the quality of the interaction with the system [3].

A possible solution to this problem in structured document retrieval is to provide the IR system interface with *explanatory* and *selective feedback* capabilities. In other words, the system should be able to explain the user, at any moment, why a particular document has been estimated as relevant and where the clues of this estimated relevance lie. In addition, the user should then be able to select for relevance feedback only those parts of the document that are relevant to the information need and not the entire document, has it is done in standard IR. Being able to focus on the parts of the document that makes it appear relevant, without losing the view of the relationships between these parts and the whole document, the user's cognitive load is reduced and the interaction is enhanced in quality and effectiveness.

The consideration that the design and implementation of improved structured document retrieval visualisation interfaces provide an effective contribution to the solution of this problem is the starting point of the work presented here. In this paper we present the current stage of implementation and evaluation of a graphical user interface of a structured document retrieval system. This work is part of a wider project aimed at the design, implementation, and evaluation of a complete system for structured document retrieval. The system combines a retrieval engine based on an aggregation-based approach for the estimation of the relevance of the document, with an interface with explanatory and selective feedback capabilities, specifically designed to the structured document retrieval task. In this paper we present only the work concerned with the interface.

The paper is structured as follows. In section 2 we highlight the importance and the difficulty of the design of graphical user interfaces for information access. In section 3 we explain the characteristics of the specific information access task that we are targeting: structured document retrieval. In section 4 we present a new graphical user interface for hierarchically structured document retrieval. The retrieval model currently used in conjunction with the interface is presented in 5, even though this part of our work is only at a very early stage. A first evaluation of the graphical user interface is presented in section 6. Finally, section 7 summarises the conclusions of this work and provide an outline of future work.

2   Graphical User Interfaces for Information Access

A great deal of work has been devote in IR to the design of user interfaces. It is well recognised that information seeking is a vague and imprecise process. In fact, when users approach an information access system they often have only an imprecise idea of what they are looking for and a vague understanding of how they can find it. The interface should aid the users in the understanding and expression of the information need. This implies not simply helping the users to formulate queries, but also helping them to select among available information resources, understand search results, reformulate queries, and keep track of the progress of the whole search process.

However, human-computer interfaces, and in particular graphical user interfaces (GUI), are less well understood than other aspects of IR, because of the difficulties in understanding, measuring, and characterising the motivations and behaviours of IR users. Nevertheless, established wisdom combined with more recent research results (see [2][pp. 257-322] for an overview of both) have highlighted some very important *design principles* for GUIs for information access systems.

GUIs for information access should:

- provide informative feedback;
- reduce working memory load;
- provide functionalities for both novice and expert users.

These design principles are particularly important for GUIs for IR systems, since the complexity of the IR task requires very complex and interactive interfaces.

An important aspect of GUIs for information access systems is *visualisation*. Visualisation takes advantage of the fact that humans are highly attuned to images and visual information. Pictures and graphics can be captivating and appealing, especially if well designed. In addition, visual representation can communicate some information more rapidly and effectively than any other method. The growing availability of fast graphic processors, high resolution colour screens, and large monitors is increasing interest in visual interfaces for information access. However, while information visualisation is rapidly advancing in areas such as scientific visualisation, it is less so for document visualisation. In fact, visualisation of inherently abstract information is difficult, and visualisation of textual information is especially challenging. Language and its written representation, text, is the main human means of communicating abstract ideas, for which there is no obvious visual manifestation [18].

Despite these difficulties, researchers are attempting to represent some aspects of the information access process using visualisation techniques. The main visualisation techniques used for this purpose are icons, colour highlighting, brushing and linking, panning and zooming, and focus-plus-context [2][257-322]. These techniques support a dynamic, interactive use that is especially important for document visualisation.

In this paper we will not address these techniques in any detail. We will just use those that are most suitable to our specific objective: structured document retrieval. The distinctive characteristics of this task are described in the next section.

3   Structured Document Retrieval

Many document collections contain documents that have complex structure, despite this not being used by most IR systems. The inclusion of the structure of a document in the indexing and retrieval process affects the design and implementation of the IR system in many ways. First of all, the indexing process must consider the structure in the appropriate way, so that user can search the collection both by content and structure. Secondly, the retrieval process should use both structure and content in the estimate of the relevance of documents. Finally, the interface and the whole interaction has to enable the user to make full use of the document structure. In the next section we report a brief and abstract taxonomy of IR systems with regards to the use of content and structure for indexing and retrieval. This will help us to identify what kind of operations should an interface for structured document retrieval provide the user with. For a more detailed discussion on the types of operations necessary for structured document retrieval see [19].

3.1   Use of Content and Structure in IR Systems

From a general point of view, we have nine types of IR systems, depending on the use of content and/or structure in the indexing, querying and processes. We can identify them with two sets of two letters: two letters for the indexing and two for the querying process. We use C and S to indicate the use of content or structure, respectively. The nine types of IR systems are showed in Table 1. In this table we indicate what kind of retrieval function the system would need (the function f) and what kind of input the user can provide to the querying (the arguments of the function f, c or s), where the first argument refers to indexing and the second to querying.

The different types of IR systems are the following:

Table 1. Taxonomy of IR Systems respect the use of Content/Structure

indexing	querying		
	C	CS	S
C	$q = f_c(c)$	$q = f_c(c, s)$	-
CS	$q = f_{c+s}(c)$	$q = f_{c+s}(c, s)$	$q = f_{c+s}(s)$
S	-	$q = f_s(c, s)$	$q = f_s(s)$

(C,C) In this type of systems, indexing is carried out only with the content of the documents, so either the structure is not taken in account, or the documents are unstructured. Since the structure has not been considered in the indexing, querying can only be related to the content of the documents. This is the most common type of IR systems, and all the classic IR models (vector space model, probabilistic, etc.) have been designed to work with this kind of systems.

(CS,CS) This type of systems index document content in relation to document structure, so that the index contains indications of how a document content is arranged in the document. The user can then query the system for content with the ability to specify the structural elements in which the content should be found. This enables a higher degree of precision in the search. Some models have been proposed for this kind of IR systems, but few implementations exists.

(S,S) This type of systems index documents only in relation to their structure, not content, and querying can only be related to structure. So, this type of systems are useful only when the queries are exclusively about structure. Models for this systems are very simple, and given the very limited and specific use of these systems, only few implementation exists.

(CS,C) This type of systems index documents content in relation to document structure, but users are not able to specify structural information in the querying. In other words, document structure is used in an implicit way; the user is not aware of document structure, but it is used in the relevance evaluation to achieve better retrieval performance. In this category of IR systems we can include a number of advanced systems aimed at collections where the structure is specified in the document markup (e.g. SGML, HTML, XML, etc.). In addition, in this category we find most Internet crawlers, that use information about hyper links, titles, etc. of the HTML pages to better rank the retrieved set [3].

(CS,S) This type of systems index document content in relation to document structure, but querying can only uses the structure of documents. This kind of systems may not seem very useful, but they may be valuable components of (CS,CS) systems, where there is a need to use document similarity from a structural point of view.

(C,CS) This type of IR systems index documents by content, but allow queries to specify structure too. Clearly, the system cannot answer completely the query, since to structural information is not contained in the index. The user will have to browse the documents retrieved to find those that respond to the structural requirements of the query.

(S,CS) This is other "incomplete" type of IR systems, because the index contains only part of the information needed to answer the query. In this case, the index only holds information about the structure, while the systems enables querying by both structure and content. Users will have to browse the documents retrieved to find those that respond to the content requirements of the query.

The systems of type **(S,C)** and **(C,S)** are "void", since it is impossible to query a system for information not contained in the index.

From the above classification it is clear that different kinds of systems make available different functionality to the user. In this respect, we can say that an IR system is *competent* if all kinds of queries allowed can be answered completely, and *incompetent* if not. In addition, we need to consider the resources used by the system (e.g. computing time and memory space) to make available to the user the possibility of querying by content and/or structure. This is somewhat reflected in the amount of information contained in the index. We can qualify an IR system as *oversized* if its index contain more information than are necessary to answer the queries. On the other hand, if an IR system has the right amount of information and no more in its index we will qualify is as *fitted*.

With regard the Table 1 the types of IR systems in the main diagonal are both competent and fitted. The systems of type (CS,C) and (CS,S) systems are competent, but oversized. The system of type (C,CS) and (S,CS) systems are incompetent, but fitted.

Notice that only a fraction of the types of systems presented in Table 1 have been studied and implemented. These are systems of type (C,C) and (CS,CS). In our work we aim at designing and implementing a system that is of type (CS,C) for novice users, with the possibility of functioning as a (CS,CS) system for more advanced users. Some initial results of this work have been presented in [19]. This system comprises a retrieval engine that is both competent and fitted, with an interface that facilitates querying by structure and content, hiding the complexity of expressively naming the structural elements in the query and in the relevance feedback.

3.2   Structured Document Retrieval Operations

In order to enable querying both content and structure in a competent and fitted way, an IR system need to posses the necessary primitives to index effectively the documents and to enable a user to specify content and structural elements in the query. In our work we have analysed both. However, given the scope of this paper we will only discuss the querying primitives and operations.

Querying by content and structure can only be achieved if the user can specify in the query *what* he/she is looking for, and *where* this should be located in the required documents. The what involves the specification of the content, while the where is related to the structure of the documents. A great amount of work in IR has gone into letting the user specify in the most natural way the content of the information need. The tendency in IR is to let the user specify as freely as possible the information need, using a natural language query [3,2]. This has been proved to be more effective in the IR task than complex query languages (e.g. Boolean or relational database systems).

Considerably less effort has been devoted in designing systems that allow the user to specify in the most natural way the structural requirements (the "where") of the information need. It is obvious that the user can give structural specifications only if he/she knows the typical structure of a document in the collection. The problem is not trivial if the collection is not homogeneous with regards to the document structure. The case of the Web is the most conspicuous. In this case the user is only allowed very limited kinds of structural queries, mostly related to the structural elements that are almost always present in a Web page, i.e. page title, links, etc.. On the other hand, links and other structural elements are used by Web search engines in the ranking in a way that is completely transparent to the user (see for example [12,8]). In other cases, when the documents structure is not homogeneous or poor, automatic structuring techniques can be employed to present the user with a browsable structure that is particularly effective in the case of long documents (see for example [16, 1]). However, even if the collection is homogeneous in structure, the necessity of specifying the structural requirements in the query often negates the advantages of natural language querying.

It has been recognised that the best approach to querying structured documents is to let the user specify in the most natural way both the content and the structural requirements of the desired documents. This can be achieved by letting the user specify the content requirement in a natural language query, while enabling the user to qualify the structural requirements through a graphical user interface. A GUI is well suited to show and let the user indicate structural elements of documents in the collection. In addition, as already pointed out in Section 1, the complexity and the resulting user's cognitive load of querying for structured documents can be greatly reduced by designing interfaces that have explanatory and selective feedback capabilities. Such interface not only lets the user specify both content and structural requirements of the required documents, but also shows the user why and where a document has been found relevant, giving the user the ability to feedback to the system relevance assessments that are similarly selective. We have presented the design of one such interface for hierarchically structured documents in [6]. In the next section we will briefly describe this interface with an example of a query session.

4   A GUI for Structured Document Retrieval

A GUI for effective structured document retrieval should enable a user to specify the required content and structure in a natural way. In addition, the GUI should: a) provide informative and explanatory feedback to user; b) capture user selective relevance feedback; c) provide functionalities for both novice and expert users. The interface we have designed has the following characteristics:

- it enables the modelling of hierarchically structured documents, that is of the most common type of long structured documents;
- it allows the user to forget about structural elements, if the user wishes so, but still informs the user of the use the system makes of the structure, which is a suitable interaction for novice users and for (C,CS) systems;
- it allows the user to chose the structural elements the system should consider as most important, which is a suitable interaction for advanced users and (CS,CS) systems;
- it allows the user to provide inclusive or selective relevance feedback by indicating or not which structural part of the document should be considered most relevant;
- it provides the user with a view of the overall search interaction with the system, giving the user a sense of where the search is going to and enabling the user to go back to any past stage of the search process.

A first implementation of the GUI has been carried out at the University of Valladolid. The implementation is in Java, working under the Linux operating system (but potentially portable to other operating systems, given the characteristics of Java).

A the core of the GUI is the representation of a single structured document. A document is represented using an iconic representation called *docball*. An example of a docball with a corresponding hierarchically structured document is depicted in Figure 1. Using a docball it is possible to represent the different structural elements of the document: the whole document (the inner circle), or its sections and subsections (the outer circles), down to the smallest elements that the system designer decides to represent (the outermost circle). The docball also represents the way structural elements of the document are hierarchically included one into another and enables the user to select any element with the touch of the mouse. The selection process is governed by the document structure, so that the selection of a section (at any level) implies the selection of all its subsections, with the innermost circle implying the selection of the whole document. This document representation is similar in concepts to the Tree-Maps proposed by Shneiderman in [17] and it has been proved to be intuitive to users.

In [6] we presented in details the design and describe the visual elements of the GUI. In this paper we will remind the reader of them through an example of user interaction with the current implementation of the GUI. The example refers to a user querying the same document collection used in the evaluation presented in section 6, that is a collection of Shakespeare plays.

Figure 2 shows the GUI for novice users. The GUI shows a query area, in which the user can write the text of the query and select the structural level of interest (in this case the act level). Just below the query area is the query history area, where the results of each query is presented. The user can select how many hits should be displayed (10 in the figure). There is also a document display

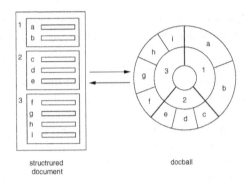

structrured
document

docball

Fig. 1. Visualisation of a structured document.

area, that shows the text of the document and the docball representation of the document. The specific structural element selected in the query history area is displayed and also highlighted in the docball. The docball shows in different colours the parts of the document that are most relevant and by moving the mouse on top of any structural element in the docball the text of that element is displayed and so is its relevance estimate to the query. Visualised documents can be displayed in XML, text, or XSL format using the view buttons.

Fig. 2. Visualisation of query results at the "act" structural level.

The user can ask that hits for the same query be displayed ranked in relation to another structural level (for example the scene level) as depicted in figure 3. This new interaction becomes part of the query history, so that the user can always go back to the previous retrieved list. The selection on a new structural level is highlighted in the docball area.

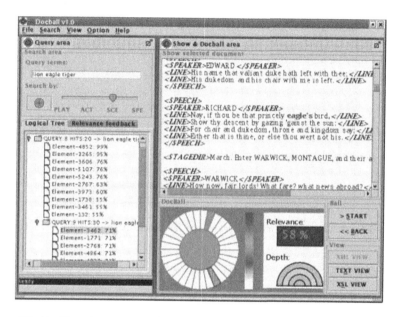

Fig. 3. Visualisation of query results at the "scene" structural level.

Figure 4 show the user expanding the window with the query history and providing relevance feedback on one retrieved element. Pressing the search button activates the relevance feedback at that structural level and elements similar to the one indicated as relevant by the user are retrieved and displayed in a new retrieved list (Query 10).

At any time in the query session the user can go back to a previous retrieved list and analyse any structural element of the retrieved document. The start and back buttons can be used to move quickly in the query history and can also be used to move in the hierarchical structure of the document. In fact, the user can zoom into a specific structural level at any time (using one of the mouse buttons) asking the system to display only relevance information related to that level of the docball. This is particularly useful in the case of document that are highly structured and with many elements at some level.

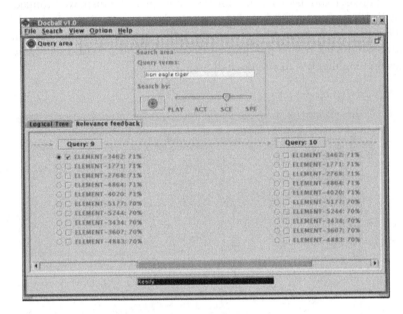

Fig. 4. Query history and relevance feedback at the "scene" structural level.

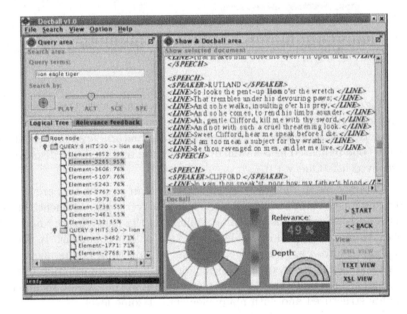

Fig. 5. Zooming on a scene.

5 Modelling Structured Document Retrieval

At this stage, our work is mainly directed towards the design, implementation, and evaluation of the GUI. Nevertheless, in order to evaluated the GUI effectively using a task-oriented methodology we need a retrieval engine. Since we could not wait for our more methodological and theoretical work to be implemented, we decided to use a rather simplistic approach to structured document retrieval. This approach, tailored to hierarchically structured documents, consists in producing in response to a query as many rankings as are the hierarchical structural levels of the documents. The user can then choose the ranking that seems more appropriate to the level of specificity required by the information need. So, for example, if a user is interested in a paragraph about a particular topic, the entire retrieved list can be viewed ranked by the estimated relevance of paragraphs, while if the user is interested in a chapter about that topic, the entire retrieved list can be ranked by estimated relevance of chapters. Ties are dealt by ranking equally relevant structural elements by the estimated relevance of the structural level directly below in the hierarchy.

This approach is rather simplistic, but at the current stage of our work it has a number of advantages. First, it can be implemented with any existing classical IR model, like for example the Vector Space Model [15] or any variation of the Probabilistic Model [7]. Once the level of specificity (or granularity) of the document has been specified (e.g. chapter, section, subsection, paragraph, etc.), any classical model can index and rank the text fragments as they were individual documents. In other words, this approach enables to implement a (C,CS) system using a model designed for a (C,C) system. Secondly, indexing and ranking at different levels of specificity can be carried out using concurrent processes and the retrieved sets can be buffered for a fast presentation to the user. This enables the user to switch quickly and effortlessly from one ranked list to another, providing the kind of specificity of presentation of results that one would expect from a (CS,CS) system without the complexity of expressing structural requirements in the query. Finally, this approach enables the evaluation of the relevance estimate for every structural element of the documents. This data is necessary for the colouring of the docballs of the GUI, which provide the user with a clear visual indication of which structural elements of a document are most relevant.

We are fully aware of the inefficiencies of this approach, but at the current stage of our work we are not concerned with these issues.

6 Evaluation

We are currently evaluating the proposed GUI following a typical formative design-evaluation process (similar to [9]). The process consists in carrying out a first implementation based on the original design, evaluating this implementation, and use the result of the evaluation to refine the design, so that a new improved implementation can be carried out and re-evaluated.

The first prototype GUI is currently being evaluated both at the University of Valladolid and at the University of Strathclyde following a task-oriented and user-centred evaluation methodology. The evaluation methodology is very similar to the one developed in the context of the Esprit "Mira" Project [14].

The first stage of the evaluation was carried out in the University of Valladolid in October 2001. The evaluation involved 10 users with varying degree of expertise in using retrieval tools and GUIs. The user were librarians and graduate students of the Department of Computer Science. All users were proficient in English and had no linguistic difficulties in carrying out the evaluation.

The document collection used in the evaluation was the XML version of 4 Shakespeare plays. This collections is available in the public domain. Each play is hierarchically divided in acts, scenes, and speeches. There are other intermediate structural elements, but they were not considered appropriate to be used in this evaluation, since they referred to characters in the play, scene descriptions, etc., which would have required some considerable background knowledge of Shakespeare plays by the part of the users. Given the small size of this collection, we decided to use the act as the default "document" level. The collection comprises 37 acts, divided in 162 scenes and 5300 speeches.

The evaluation consisted of three tests. The first test evaluated the effectiveness of the GUI indirectly by giving users 5 tasks to carry out which involved searching the collection of documents and locating some specific document parts. The tasks were simple questions whose answer was to be found in one or more acts, scenes or speeches. Users had a limited amount of time to carry out the tasks, which started after users had followed an example of a session in which all the functionalities of the GUI were briefly explained. The second test was more directly related to evaluating the user understanding of the docball visual element of the GUI, after the first test was carried out. It involved asking users to: a) depict a docball representing a specific document, and b) explain the structure of a document from its docball representation. The documents and docballs given to the users were unrelated and different from those present in the collection used in the first test. Finally, the third test comprised a questionnaire with 46 short questions concerning the appearance, querying and navigation functionalities and usability of the interface. The questionnaire aimed at capturing users' judgements and personal considerations.

A presentation of all the details of the results of the evaluation is outside the scope of this paper. We will present only the major findings and the most important indications on how to improve the GUI in future work.

In the first test 8 out of 10 users were able to correctly accomplish all 5 tasks. The remaining two users were able to accomplish only 4 tasks in the time limit. A feature of the GUI that all users utilised was the level selection bar, which enabled users to select any structural element of a document at any level. This made it easier for users to assess the relevance of the document under consideration. On the other hand, one feature that was used rarely (by only 2 users) was relevance feedback. The reason for this can be related to the fact that users were not familiar which such feature, being it uncommon in other information access systems like, for example, web search engines.

The second test showed that all users understood the GUI and in particular the graphical representation of the structured document. Users had no difficulties in drawing a docball for any specific structured document presented to them and also had no difficulties in inferring a document structure given a docball. Of course, we were quite pleased with this result, that shows that the docball metaphor at the center of the GUI is a very natural and clear representation of the document structure.

Finally, he analysis of the users comments in the questionnaire will require some time to be fully accomplished. Nevertheless, we feel we can extract the following observations.

- The presence of a single query box and button together with the possibility of identifying the query level graphically was considered positively by most users.
- The query tree representing the history of the query sessions was considered non-intuitive and difficult to understand and use. This was mainly due to the limited amount of information it presents to the users about documents.
- All users appreciated the docball metaphor and its use for document structural level selection and navigation.
- The response time of the system was too long and often annoyed users. This was due to the current implementation of the GUI which is Java based and has not been optimised yet.

Therefore, this first evaluation has confirmed that the docball structured document representation and the GUI are intuitive and easy to use. However, there are still a number of directions to explore to improve the usability of the GUI.

Based on the results of this evaluation we are improving the GUI to overcome some of its limitations. A new evaluation will be carried out as soon as a new improved version of the GUI will become available. One of the difficulties in evaluating any system or GUI for structured document retrieval is related to the limited availability of collections of structured documents. Although there is a large amount of documents that are structured in nature, they are either not publicly available or not marked up at the appropriate level of detail (e.g. TREC documents). A possible solution to this problem would be to create a collection of structured documents from a subset of some exiting test collection (see for example [20]). However, this approach is deemed to produce a very artificial document collection that, though valid for a search engine evaluation, would not be adequate to a user-centred and task-oriented evaluation. In addition, we found that only documents in SGML and XML have the tags necessary to clearly identify the structural elements of the documents. Documents in HTML are too irregular and not sufficiently marked up.

7   Conclusions and Future Work

We presented a graphical user interface for structured document retrieval. An initial evaluation of the interface shows that it provides the user with an intuitive and powerful set of tools for hierarchically structured document searching, retrieved list navigation, and search refinement.

The work presented in this paper is part of wider work aimed at the design, implementation, and evaluation of a complete system for structured document retrieval. The system will combine a retrieval engine based on an *aggregation-based approach* to the estimation of the relevance of the document, with an interface with explanatory and selective feedback capabilities specifically designed to the structured document retrieval task. While work on the interface is at an advanced stage, the design and implementation of the retrieval engine still requires much theoretical and methodological work. A number of approaches are currently being explored. They range from heuristically driven modifications of the Vector Space Model to take into account different terms weights for different structural elements (work inspired by [20]), to more theoretically driven work using a formal framework to combine the relevance evidence of different structural elements. This latter direction, inspired by results presented in [11,13,4], seems the most exciting to us.

References

1. M. Agosti, F. Crestani, and M. Melucci. On the use of Information Retrieval techniques for the automatic construction of hypertexts. *Information Processing and Management*, 33(2):133–144, 1997.
2. R. Baeza-Yates and B. Ribeiro-Nieto. *Modern Information Retrieval*. Addison-Wesley, Harlow, UK, 1999.
3. R. Belew. *Finding Out About: A Cognitive Perspective on Search Engines Technology and the WWW*. Cambridge University Press, Cambridge, UK, 2000.
4. G. Bordogna and G. Pasi. Flexible representation and querying of heterogeneous structured documents. *Kibernetika*, 36(6):617–633, 2000.
5. Y. Chiaramella. Information retrieval and structured documents. In M. Agosti, F. Crestani, and G. Pasi, editors, *Lecture on Information Retrieval*, volume 1980 of *Lectures Notes in Computer Science*, pages 291–314. Springer-Verlag, Heidelberg, Germany, 2001.
6. F. Crestani, P. de la Fuente, and J. Vegas. Design of a graphical user interface for focussed retrieval of structured documents. In *Proceedings of SPIRE 2001, Symposium on String Processing and Information Retrieval*, pages 246–249, Laguna de San Rafael, Chile, November 2001.
7. F. Crestani, M. Lalmas, C.J. van Rijsbergen, and I. Campbell. Is this document relevant? ...probably. A survey of probabilistic models in Information Retrieval. *ACM Computing Surveys*, 30(4):528–552, 1998.
8. M. Cutler, Y. Shih, and W. Meng. Using the structure of HTML documents to improve retrieval. In *Proceedings of the USENIX Symposium on Internet Technologies and Systems*, pages 241–251, Monterey, CA, USA, December 1997.

9. D. Egan, J.R. Remde, L.M. Gomez, T.K. Landauer, J. Eberhardt, and C.C. Lochbaum. Formative design-evaluation of SuperBook. *ACM Transactions on Information Systems*, 7(1):30–57, 1989.
10. P. Ingwersen. *Information Retrieval Interaction*. Taylor Graham, London, UK, 1992.
11. D. Kerkouba. Indexation automatique et aspects structurels des textes. In *Proceedings of the RIAO Conference*, pages 227–249, Grenoble, France, March 1985.
12. J.M. Kleinberg. Authoritative sources in a hyperlinked environment. In *Proceedings of the Ninth Annual ACM-SIAM Symposium on Discrete Algorithms*, pages 668–677, San Francisco, CA, USA, January 1998.
13. M. Lalmas and E. Moutogianni. A Dempster-Shafer indexing for the focussed retrieval of a hierarchically structured document space: Implementation and experiments on a web museum collection. In *Proceedings of the RIAO Conference*, Paris, France, April 2000.
14. A.M. Pejtersen and R. Fidel. A framework for work centred evaluation and design: a case study of IR and the Web. Working paper for Mira Workshop, Grenoble, France, March 1998.
15. G. Salton. *Automatic information organization and retrieval*. McGraw Hill, New York, 1968.
16. G. Salton and J. Allan. Automatic text decomposition and structuring. In *Proceedings of the RIAO Conference*, volume 1, pages 6–20, Rockefeller University, New York, USA, October 1994.
17. B. Shneiderman. Tree visualization with tree-maps: 2-d space-filling approach. *ACM Transactions on Graphics*, 11(1):92–99, 1992.
18. R. Spence. *Information Visualization*. Addison-Wesley, Harlow, UK, 2001.
19. J. Vegas Hernández. *Un Sistema de Recuperatión de Informatión sobre Estructura y Contenido*. Ph.D. Thesis, Departamento de Informática, Universidad de Valladolid, Valladolid, Spain, 1999.
20. R. Wilkinson. Effective retrieval of structured documents. In *Proceedings of ACM SIGIR*, pages 311–317, Dublin, Ireland, July 1994.

The Accessibility Dimension for Structured Document Retrieval

Thomas Roelleke[1,2], Mounia Lalmas[2], Gabriella Kazai[2], Ian Ruthven[3], and Stefan Quicker[4]

[1] HySpirit GmbH, Postfach 30 02 58, Dortmund 44232, Germany
roelleke@hyspirit.com
http://www.hyspirit.com
[2] Department of Computer Science, Queen Mary, University of London, London E1 4NS, England
{thor,mounia,gabs}@dcs.qmul.ac.uk
http://qmir.dcs.qmul.ac.uk
[3] Department of Computer and Information Sciences, University of Strathclyde, Glasgow G1 1XH, Scotland
Ian.Ruthven@cis.strath.ac.uk
http://www.cs.strath.ac.uk
[4] Informatik VI, University of Dortmund, Dortmund 44221, Germany
quicker@ls6.cs.uni-dortmund.de
http://ls6-www.cs.uni-dortmund.de/ir/

Abstract. Structured document retrieval aims at retrieving the document components that best satisfy a query, instead of merely retrieving pre-defined document units. This paper reports on an investigation of a *tf-idf-acc* approach, where *tf* and *idf* are the classical term frequency and inverse document frequency, and *acc*, a new parameter called *accessibility*, that captures the structure of documents. The *tf-idf-acc* approach is defined using a probabilistic relational algebra. To investigate the retrieval quality and estimate the *acc* values, we developed a method that automatically constructs diverse test collections of structured documents from a standard test collection, with which experiments were carried out. The analysis of the experiments provides estimates of the *acc* values.

1 Introduction

In traditional information retrieval (IR) systems [18], retrievable units are fixed. For example, the whole document, or, sometimes, pre-defined parts such as paragraphs constitute the retrievable units. The *logical structure* of documents (chapter, section, table, formula, author information, bibliographic item, etc) is therefore "flattened" and not exploited. Classical retrieval methods lack the possibility to interactively determine the size and the type of retrievable units, that best suit an actual retrieval task or user preferences.

Current research is aiming at developing retrieval models that dynamically return document components of varying complexity. A retrieval result may then

F. Crestani, M. Girolami, and C.J. van Rijsbergen (Eds.): ECIR 2002, LNCS 2291, pp. 284–302, 2002.

consist of several entry points to a same document, whereby each entry point is weighted according to how it satisfies the query. Authors such as [17,6,13,15, 8] have developed and implemented such approaches. Their models exploit the content and the logical structure of documents to estimate the relevance of document components to queries, based on the aggregation of the estimated relevance of their related components. These models have been based on various theories (e.g. fuzzy logic [3], Dempster-Shafer's theory of evidence [13], probabilistic logic [17,2], and Bayesian inference [15]). What these models have in common is that the basic components of their retrieval function are variants of the two standard term weighting schemes, term frequency (*tf*) and inverse document frequency (*idf*). Evidence associated with the logical structure of documents is often encoded into one or both of these dimensions.

In this paper, we make this evidence explicit by introducing the "accessibility" dimension, denoted by *acc*. This dimension measures the strength of the structural relationship between document components: the stronger the relationship, the more impact has the content of a component in describing the content of its related components (e.g. [17,6]). We refer to the approach as *tf-idf-acc*. We are interested in investigating how the *acc* dimension affects the retrieval of document components of varying complexity.

To carry out this investigation, we require a framework that explicitly captures the content and the structure of documents in terms of our *tf-idf-acc* approach. We use a probabilistic relational algebra [9] for this purpose (Section 2). Our investigation also requires test collections of structured documents. Since relevance assessments for structured documents are difficult to obtain and manual assessment is expensive and task specific, we developed an automatic approach for creating structured documents and generating relevance assessments from a flat test collection (Section 3). Finally, we perform retrieval runs for different settings of the accessibility dimension. The analysis provides us with methods for estimating the appropriate setting of the accessibility dimension for structured document retrieval (Section 4).

2   The *tf-idf-acc* Approach

We view a structured document as a tree whose nodes, called *contexts*, are the components of the document (e.g., chapters, sections, etc.) and whose edges represent the composition relationship (e.g., a chapter contains several sections). The *root* context of the tree, which is unique for each document, embodies the whole document. *Atomic* contexts are document components that correspond to the last elements of the composition chains. All other nodes are referred to as *inner* contexts.

Retrieval on structured documents takes both the logical structure and the content of documents into account and returns, in response to a user query, document components of varying complexity (root, inner or atomic contexts). This retrieval methodology combines querying - finding which atomic contexts match the query - and browsing along the documents' structure - finding the level of complexity that best matches the query [5]. Take, for example, an article with five sections. We can define a retrieval strategy that is to retrieve the whole article if more than three of its sections are relevant to the query. Dynamically returning document components of varying complexity can, however, lead to user disorientation and cognitive overload [6,7,10]. This is because the presentation of document components in the retrieval result does not take into account their structural proximity within the documents. In the above example, depending on the assigned retrieval status values, the article and its sections could be displayed at different positions in the ranking.

To reduce user disorientation and cognitive overload, a retrieval strategy would be to retrieve (and therefore display to the user) *super-contexts* composed of many relevant *sub-contexts* before - or instead of - retrieving the sub-contexts themselves. This strategy would prioritise the retrieval of larger super-contexts from where the sub-contexts could be accessed through direct browsing [6,5]. Other strategies could favour smaller, more specific contexts, by assigning smaller retrieval status values to large contexts.

To allow the implementation of any of the above retrieval strategies, we follow the aggregation-based approach to structured document retrieval (e.g. [17,11,2, 15,6,8]). We base the estimation of relevance, or in other words, we compute the retrieval status value (RSV) of a context based on a content description that is derived from its content and the content of its sub-contexts. For this purpose, we *augment* the content of a super-context with that of its sub-contexts. The augmentation process is applied to the whole document tree structure, starting with the atomic contexts, where no augmentation is performed, and ending with the root context.

In this framework, the browsing element of the retrieval strategy is then implemented within the method of augmentation. By controlling the extent to which the sub-contexts of a super-context contribute to its representation we can directly influence the derived RSVs. Via the augmentation process we can also influence the extent to which the individual sub-contexts contribute to the representation of the super-context. This way certain sub-contexts, such as titles, abstracts and conclusions, etc. could be emphasised while others could be de-emphasised.

We model this impact of the sub-contexts on the super-context by expanding the two dimensions, term frequency, *tf*, and inverse document frequency, *idf*, standard to IR, with a third dimension, the **accessibility dimension**, acc[1]. We refer to the influencing power of a sub-context over its super-context as the sub-context's importance. **What the *acc* dimension represents, then, is the degree to which the sub-context is important to the super-context.**

---

[1] The term "accessibility" is taken from the framework of possible worlds and accessibility relations of a Kripke structure [4]. In [12], a semantics of the *tf-idf-acc* is defined, where contexts are modelled as possible worlds and their structure is modelled through the use of accessibility relations.

In the remainder of this section we show, by means of probabilistic relational algebra defined in [17,9], how this dimension can be used to incorporate this qualitative notion of context importance for structured document retrieval.

2.1   Probabilistic Relational Algebra

Probabilistic Relational Algebra (PRA) is a language model that incorporates probability theory with the well known relational paradigm. The algebra allows the modelling of document and query representations as relations consisting of probabilistic tuples, and it defines operators, with similar semantics to SQL but with probabilistic interpretations, which allow the description of retrieval strategies.

Document and query modelling. A PRA program describing the representation of a structured document collection uses relations such as *term*, *termspace*, and *acc*. The *term* relation represents the *tf* dimension and consists of probabilistic tuples in the form of *tf_weight term(index_term,context)*, which assign *tf_weight* values to each (*index_term, context*) pair in the collection (e.g. index terms that occur in contexts). The value of *tf_weight* $\in [0,1]$ is a probabilistic interpretation of the term frequency. The *termspace* relation models the *idf* dimension by assigning *idf* values to the index terms in the collection. This is stored in tuples in the form of *idf_weight termspace(index_term)*, where *idf_weight* $\in [0,1]$. The *acc* relation describes the document structure and consists of tuples *acc_weight acc(context_p,context_c)*, where *context_c* is "accessible" from *context_p* with a probability *acc_weight*[2].

A query representation in PRA is described by the *qterm* relation which is in the form of *q_weight qterm(query_term)*, where the *q_weight* describes the importance of the query term, and *query_term* are the terms composing the query.

Relational operators in PRA. Similarly to SQL, PRA supports a number of relational operators. Those used in this paper are SELECT, PROJECT, JOIN, and UNITE. Their syntax and functionalities are described next.

- **SELECT[*criteria*](*relation*)** returns those probabilistic tuples of *relation* that match the specified *criteria*, where the format of *criteria* is $col-umn=$[3]a_value. For example, SELECT[\$1=sailing](*termspace*) will return all those tuples from the *termspace* relation that have the term "sailing" in column one. To store the resulting tuple in a relation we use the following syntax: *new_relation* = SELECT[*criteria*](*relation*). The arity of the *new_relation* is equal to the arity of *relation*.

---

[2] On a conceptual level there is no restriction on which contexts can access which other contexts, so this formalism can be adopted to describe networked architectures. In this study, however, we only deal with tree type structures where *context_p* and *context_c* form a parent-child (super-context and sub-context) relationship.

[3] Also $<, >, \leq$, etc.

- **JOIN[$column1=$column2](relation1,relation2)** joins (matches) two relations and returns tuples that contain matching data in their respective columns, where *column1* specifies a column of *relation1* and *column2* relates to *relation2*. The arity of the returned tuples is the sum of the arity of the tuples in *relation1* and *relation2*. For example, *new_term* = JOIN[$1=$1] (*term,termspace*) will populate *new_term* with tuples that have the same value in the first column. The format of the resulting tuples is *new_weight new_term (index_term, context, index_term)*, where the value of *new_weight* is derived from the values of *tf_weight* and *idf_weight* (e.g. based on probability theory [9]).

- **PROJECT[columns](relation)** returns tuples that contain only the specified columns of *relation*, where the format of *columns* is $*column1*,$*column2*, etc. For example, *new_term* = PROJECT[$1,$3] (JOIN[$2=$2](*term,acc*)) returns all *(index_term,context_p)* pairs where the *index_term* occurs in *context_p*'s sub-context. This is because the JOIN operator returns the tuples *new_weight(index_term,context_c,context_p,context_c)*, where *context_p* is the super-context of *context_c*. Projecting column one and three into *new_term* results in *new_weight new_term(index_term,context_p)*.

- **UNITE(relation1,relation2)** returns the union of the tuples stored in *relation1* and *relation2*. For example, *new_term* = UNITE (*term*, PROJECT [$1,$3] (JOIN[$2=$2] (*term,acc*))) will produce a relation that includes tuples of the *term* relation and the resulting tuples of the PROJECT operation. The probabilities of the tuples in *new_term* are calculated according to probability theory (see [9]).

Based on the relations describing the document and query space and with the use of the PRA operators we can implement a retrieval strategy that takes into account both the structure and the content of the documents by augmenting the content of sub-contexts into the super-context, where the augmentation can be controlled by the *acc_weight* values.

Retrieval strategies. We first model the classical *tf_idf* retrieval function. For this, we use the JOIN and PROJECT operations of PRA.

$tfidf\_index$ = PROJECT[$1,$2](JOIN[$1=$1](*term,termspace*))
$retrieve\_tfidf$ = PROJECT[$3](JOIN[$1=$1](*qterm,tfidf_index*))

Here, the first function computes the *tf_idf* indexing. It produces tuples in the form of *tf_idf_weight tfidf_index(index_term,context)*. The *tf_idf_weight* is calculated using probability theory and the independence assumption as $tf\_weight \times idf\_weight$. The second function joins the query terms with the *tfidf_index* terms and produces the retrieval results in the form of *rsv retrieve_tfidf(context)*. The RSVs given in *rsv* are calculated according to probability theory assuming disjointness with respect to the term space (*termspace*) as follows:

$$rsv(context) = \sum_{query\_term_i} q\_weight_i \times tf\_weight_i(context) \times idf\_weight_i$$

We use next the *acc* relation to take the structure into consideration. We *augment* the content of the super-context by that of its sub-contexts. This is modelled by the following PRA equation.

$tfidfacc\_index = \text{PROJECT}[\$1,\$3](\text{JOIN}[\$2=\$2](tfidf\_index, acc))$

The augmented relation consists of tuples of the form *tfidfacc_weight tfid-facc_index (index_term, context_p)* where *context_p* is the super-context of *context_c* which is indexed by *index_term*. The value of *tfidfacc_weight* is calculated as $tf\_idf\_weight \times acc\_weight$ (assuming probabilistic independence). Based on the *tfidfacc_index* we can now define our retrieval strategy for structured documents.

$tfidfacc\_index = \text{PROJECT}[\$1,\$3](\text{JOIN}[\$2=\$2](tfidf\_index, acc))$
$retrieve\_tfidfacc = \text{PROJECT}[\$3](\text{JOIN}[\$1=\$1](qterm, tfidfacc\_index))$
$retrieve = \text{UNITE}(retrieve\_tfidf, retrieve\_tfidfacc)$

The RSVs of the retrieval result are calculated (by the UNITE operator) according to probability theory and assuming independence:

$$
\begin{aligned}
rsv(context) &= P(retrieve\_tfidf(context) \ OR \ retrieve\_tfidfacc(context)) \\
&= P(retrieve\_tfidf(context)) + P(retrieve\_tfidfacc(context)) - \\
&\quad P(retrieve\_tfidf(context) \ AND \ retrieve\_tfidfacc(context)) \\
&= P(retrieve\_tfidf(context)) + P(retrieve\_tfidfacc(context)) - \\
&\quad P(retrieve\_tfidf(context)) \times P(retrieve\_tfidfacc(context))
\end{aligned}
$$

Since the weight of *tfidfacc_index* is directly influenced by the weight associated with *acc*, the resulting RSVs is also dependent on *acc*.

2.2   Example

Consider the following collection of one document doc1 composed of two sections, sec1 and sec2. Terms such as sailing, boats, etc. occur in the collection:

0.1 *term*(sailing, doc1)
0.8 *term*(boats, doc1)
0.7 *term*(sailing, sec1)
0.8 *term*(greece, sec2)
0.4 *termspace*(sailing)
0.3 *termspace*(boats)
0.2 *termspace*(greece)
0.1 *termspace*(santorini)
0.8 *acc*(doc1, sec1)
0.6 *acc*(doc1, sec2)

We take the query "sailing boats", represented by the following PRA program.

qterm(sailing)
qterm(boats)

Given this query and applying the classical *tf_idf* retrieval function (as described in the previous section) to our document collection we retrieve the following document components.

0.28 *retrieved_tfidf*(doc1)
0.28 *retrieved_tfidf*(sec1)

Both retrieved contexts have the relevance status value of 0.28. The above retrieval strategy, however, does not take into account the structure of the document, e.g. that sec1 which is about sailing is part of doc1. From a user's point of view, it might be better to retrieve first - or only - doc1 since sec1 can be accessed from doc1 by browsing down from doc1 to sec1. Let us now apply our *tf_idf_acc* retrieval strategy. We obtain:

0.441 *retrieve*(doc1)
0.28 *retrieve*(sec1)

This shows that the RSV of doc1 increases when we take into account the fact that doc1 is composed of sec1, which is also indexed by the term "sailing". This is done using the structural knowledge stored in *acc*. This demonstrates that by using our third dimension, *acc*, we obtain a ranking that exploits the structure of the document to determine which document components should be retrieved higher in the ranking.

In designing applications for structured document retrieval, we are faced with the problem of determining the probabilities (weights) of the *acc* relation. In our retrieval applications so far, constant *acc* values such as 0.5 and 0.6 were used. However we want to establish methods to derive estimates of the *acc* values. To achieve this, we require test collections with controlled parameters to allow us to derive appropriate estimations of the *acc* values with respect to these parameters. In the following section we present a method for creating simulated test collections of structured documents that allow such an investigation.

3   Automatic Construction of Structured Document Test Collections

Although many test collections are composed of documents that contain some internal structure [19,1], relevance judgements are usually made at the document level (root contexts) or at the atomic context level. This means that they cannot be used for the evaluation of structured document retrieval systems, which would require relevance judgements at the root, atomic *and* inner levels.

Our investigation requires several test collections of structured documents with different characteristics (e.g. depth and width of document tree structure). These will enable us to investigate the *acc* dimension under different conditions. Since relevance assessments for structured documents are difficult to obtain and manual assessment is expensive and task specific, it was imperative to find a way to automatically build such test collections. We developed a methodology that allowed us to create diverse collections of structured documents and automatically generate relevance assessments. Our methodology exploits existing standard test collections with their existing queries and relevance judgements so that no human resources are necessary. In addition our methodology allows the creation of all test collections deemed necessary to carry out our investigation regarding the effect of the *acc* dimension for structured document retrieval.

In Section 3.1 we discuss how we created the structured documents, in Section 3.2 we discuss how we decided on the relevance of the document components, and finally, in Section 3.3 we show the results of the methodology using the CACM collection[4].

3.1   Construction of the Documents

Our basic methodology is to *combine* documents from a test collection to form simulated structured documents. That is to treat a number of original documents from the collection as components of a structured document. A simplified version of this strategy was used in [13]. In the remainder of this section we shall present a more sophisticated version, and deal with some of the issues arising from the construction of simulated structured documents. To illustrate our methodology, we used a well known small standard test collection, the CACM test collection.

Using the methodology of combining documents, it is possible to create two types of test collections: *homogeneous* collections in which the documents have the same logical structure and *heterogeneous* collections in which the documents have varying logical structure. In our experiments, Section 4, we use these collections to see how the values of *acc* compare for the two types of collections.

By controlling the number of documents combined, and the way documents are combined, it is also possible to generate different types of structured documents. We used two main criteria to generate structured documents. The first criterion is *width*. This corresponds to the number of documents that are combined at each level, i.e. how many contexts in a document, and how many sub-contexts per context. The second criterion is *depth*. This corresponds to how many levels are in the tree structure. For example a document with no sub-contexts (all the text is at one level) has depth of 1, a document with sub-contexts has depth 2, a document with sub-sub-contexts has depth 3, and so on. Using these criteria it is possible to automatically generate test collections of structured documents that vary in width and depth.

For the experiments we describe in Section 4 we constructed eight homogeneous collections of structured documents. The types of logical structure are

---

[4] The collection has 3204 documents and 64 queries.

shown in Figure 1. Pair (EE), Triple (EEE), Quad (EEEE), Sext (EEEEEE) and Oct (EEEEEEEE) are composed of root and atomic contexts only. These test collections will be useful in estimating the acc values based on the width criterion. The other collections Pair-E ((EE)E), Pair-2 ((EE)(EE)) and Triple-3 ((EEE)(EEE)(EEE)) have root, inner and atomic contexts. These collections are useful for estimating the acc values based on the depth criterion. Collections of each type were built from the CACM test collection where documents of the test collection, referred to as "original documents", were used to form the atomic contexts.

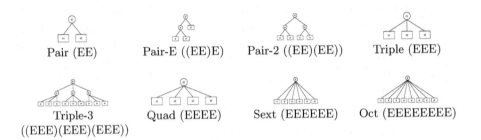

Pair (EE)   Pair-E ((EE)E)   Pair-2 ((EE)(EE))   Triple (EEE)

Triple-3   Quad (EEEE)   Sext (EEEEEE)   Oct (EEEEEEEE)
((EEE)(EEE)(EEE))

Fig. 1. Types of logical structure

We also created one *heterogeneous* test collection, referred to as Mix, which is composed of a mixture of Pair (EE) and Triple (EEE) documents.

We should note here that we are aware that the structured documents created in this manner often will not have a meaningful content and may not reflect term distributions in real structured documents. Nevertheless the use of simulated documents does allow for extensive investigation, Section 4, to provide initial estimates for the acc values. We are currently using these estimates in our current work on a real test collection of structured documents (XML-based documents). We are not, therefore, suggesting that we can use the artificially created test collections as substitutes for real documents and relevance assessments. Rather we use them as a test-bed to obtain estimates for parameters that will be used in more realistic evaluations. As mentioned before, the necessity of using artificial test collections comes from the lack of real test collections.

One of the advantages of our approach is that we can automatically create collections diverse in type and size. However we must take steps to ensure that the created collections are realistic and of manageable size to allow experimentation.

With a straight combinatoric approach, we can derive from a collection of N original documents the possible number of structured documents would be N^2 over 2 for the Pair type of collection (that is about 5 million documents for the 3204 documents of the CACM collection). Therefore we require methods to cut down the number of actual documents combined. In the particular experiments we carried out, we used two strategies to accomplish this: discarding "noisy" documents and minimising "dependent" documents. These strategies are based on the assumption that a document which has not been explicitly marked relevant to a query is considered not-relevant. Both strategies are based on an analysis of the atomic contexts of the structured documents, i.e. the original documents from the CACM collection.

(1) **Discarding "noisy" documents:** If a document's sub-contexts are a mixture of relevant and non-relevant contexts for all queries in the collection then the document is considered to be noisy.

That is, there is no query in the collection for which all sub-contexts are relevant or all sub-contexts are non-relevant. We discard all noisy documents from the collection. This does not mean that we are only considering structured documents where all sub-contexts are in agreement; we simply insist that they are in agreement for at least one query in the collection[5].

(2) **Minimising "dependent" documents:** With a straight combination approach we also have the problem of multiple occurrences of the same atomic concepts (the original documents in the test collection appearing many times). This could mean that our simulated structured documents may be very similar - or *dependent* - due to the overlap between the sub-contexts.

Our second approach to cutting down the number of created documents is therefore to minimise the number of dependent documents.

We do not, however, want to eradicate multiple occurrence completely. First, multiple occurrence mimic real-world situations where similar document parts are used in several documents (e.g. web, hypertext, digital libraries). Second, exclusive usage of an atomic context requires a procedure to determine which atomic context leads to the "best" structured document, which is difficult, if not impossible to assess.

The way we reduce the number of multiple occurrences is to reduce the repeated use of atomic contexts that are *relevant* to the same query. That is, we do not want to create many structured documents that contain the same set of relevant contexts.

Our basic procedure is to reduce the number of documents whose atomic contexts are all relevant to the same query, i.e. composed of components that are all relevant to the query. The reason we concentrate on relevant contexts is that these are the ones we use to decide whether the whole structured document is relevant or not, (see Section 3.2).

For each atomic context, e_i, which is relevant to a query, q_j, we only allow e_i to appear in one document whose other atomic contexts are all relevant to q_j. This reduces multiple occurrences of e_i in documents composed entirely of relevant atomic contexts. As there may be many structured documents containing e_i whose atomic contexts are relevant, we need a method to choose which of these documents to use in the collection. We do this by choosing the document with

---

[5] This approach can be extended to define the degree of noise we allow in the collection.

the lowest noise value. This means that we prefer documents that are relevant to multiple queries over documents that are only relevant to one query. If more than one such documents exists we choose one randomly.

Both these steps reduce the number of structured documents to a manageable size.

3.2   Constructing the Relevance Assessments

We have so far described how we created the structured documents and how we cut down the potential number of documents created. What we have now to consider are the queries and relevance assessments. The queries and relevance assessments come from the standard test collections that are used to build the simulated structured documents. However, given that a structured document may be composed of a mixture of relevant and non-relevant documents, we have to decide when to classify a root context (structured document), or an inner context, as relevant or non-relevant.

Our approach defines the relevance of non-atomic contexts as the aggregation of the relevance of their sub-contexts. Let a non-atomic context d be composed of k sub-contexts $e1, ..., ek$. For a given query, we have three cases: all the sub-contexts $e1$ to ek are relevant; all the sub-contexts are not relevant; and neither of the previous two cases holds. In the latter, we say that we have "contradictory" relevance assessments. For the first two cases, it is reasonable to assess that d is relevant and d is not relevant to the query, respectively. In the third case, an aggregation strategy is required to decide the relevance of d to a query. We apply the following two strategies:

- *optimistic relevance*: d is assessed relevant to the query if at least one of its sub-contexts is assessed relevant to the query; d is assessed non-relevant if all its sub-contexts are assessed non-relevant to the query.
- *pessimistic relevance*: d is assessed relevant to the query if all its sub-contexts are assessed relevant to the query; in all other cases, d is assessed non-relevant to the query.

Variants of the above could be used; e.g., d is considered relevant if 2/3 of its sub-contexts are relevant [11]. We are currently carrying out research to devise strategies that may be closer to user's views of relevance with respect to structured document retrieval[6].

The point of using different aggregation strategies is that it allows us to investigate the performance of the *acc* dimension when using different relevance criteria. For example, the optimistic strategy corresponds to a loose definition of relevance (where a document is relevant if it contains any relevant component) and the pessimistic strategy corresponds to a strict definition of relevance (where all components must be relevant before the structured document is relevant).

---

[6] For instance, in an experiment related to passage retrieval, some relevant documents contained no parts that were individually assessed relevant by (expert) users [20]. See [14] for a survey on the notion of relevance in IR.

3.3   Example

In the previous sections we have shown how we can use existing test collections to create collections of structured documents. These collections can be of varying width and depth, be based on differing notions of relevance and be of identical or varying structure (homogeneous or heterogeneous). The flexibility of this methodology is that it allows the creation of diverse collection types from a single original test collection.

The collections we created for the experiments reported in this paper were based on the CACM collection. We have described the collection types, we shall now examine the collections in more detail to show the differences between them.

Table 1 shows the number of root, inner and atomic contexts for the collections. As it can be seen, the homogeneous collections display a relationship between the atomic contexts and root and inner context. For instance, the Pair collection has twice as many atomic contexts as root contexts, the Triple collection has three times as many atomic contexts as root contexts, etc. This does not hold, however, for the heterogeneous Mix collection, which is combined of a mixture of document types.

Table 1. Number of contexts

Coll.	Num. Root	Num. Inner	Num. Atomic	Total Num.
Pair	383	0	766	1149
Pair-E	247	247	741	1235
Triple	247	0	741	988
Quad	180	0	720	900
Pair-2	180	360	720	1260
Triple-3	66	198	594	858
Sext	109	0	654	763
Oct	80	0	640	720
Mix	280	0	700	980

One of the ways we cut down the number of created structured documents was to reduce the number of multiple occurrences of atomic contexts. As shown in Table 2, we do not exclude all multiple occurrences, however such occurrences are rare. For, example, in the Triple-3 collection, 20 of the original 3204 documents are used three times among the 594 atomic contexts.

The above two measures are independent of how we decide on the relevance of a context, i.e. whether we use the optimistic or pessimistic aggregation strategy. The choice of aggregation strategy will affect the number of relevant contexts. As an example we show in, Figure 2, the number of relevant root contexts when using the Pair collection, (full figures can be found in [16]). As it can be seen, for the optimistic aggregation strategy we have almost twice as many relevant root

Table 2. Multiple occurrence of contexts

Occurrence frequency	1	2	3	4	5	6
Pair	398	86	33	14	7	1
Pair-E	392	82	31	14	6	1
Triple	392	82	31	14	6	1
Quad	388	82	28	12	6	1
Pair-2	391	84	32	11	3	1
Triple-3	336	83	20	8	0	0
Sext	362	74	22	12	6	0
Oct	352	75	21	11	5	1
Mix	366	85	27	12	7	0

contexts (average 15.53 per query) as for the pessimistic aggregation strategy (average 7.85 per query). This demonstrates that the aggregation strategy can be used to create collections with different characteristics.

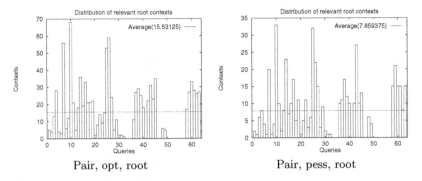

Pair, opt, root   Pair, pess, root

Fig. 2. Distribution of relevant contexts

In this section we described the creation of a number of collections based on the CACM collection. In the following section we investigate the *acc* dimension using these collections.

4   Experiments

Using the different types of collections, and their associated properties, we carried out a number of experiments to investigate the accessibility dimension for the retrieval of structured documents. With our set of test collections of structured documents and their various and controlled characteristics, we studied the effect of different *acc* values on the retrieval quality. We targeted the following questions:

1. Is there an optimal setting of the *acc* parameter for a context with n sub-contexts? (Section 4.1). An optimal setting is one which gives the best average precision.
2. With high *acc* values, we expect large contexts to be retrieved with a higher RSV than small contexts. What is the "break-even point", i.e. which setting of *acc* will retrieve large and small contexts with the same preference? (Section 4.2)

4.1   Optimal Values of the Accessibility Dimension

For all our constructed collections, for increasing values of *acc* (ranging from 0.1 to 0.9), we computed the RSV of each context, using the augmentation process described in Section 2. With the obtained rankings (of root, inner and atomic contexts) and our relevance assessments (optimistic or pessimistic), we calculated precision/recall values and then the average precision values. The graphs in Figure 3 show for each accessibility value the corresponding average precision. We show the graphs for Pair, Pair-E and Mix only. All graphs show a "bell shape". The optimal accessibility values and their corresponding maximal precision values are given in Table 3.

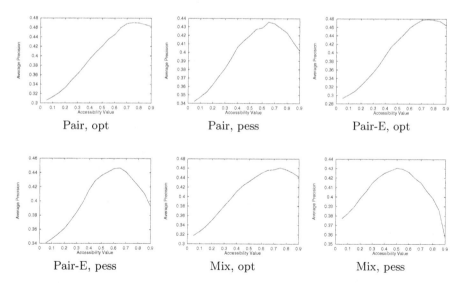

Fig. 3. Accessibility values and corresponding average precision values

Looking at Pair, Triple, Quad, Sext and Oct, we can see that the optimal accessibility values decrease with the number of sub-contexts. This holds for

Table 3. Optimal accessibility values and corresponding maximum precision

collection	Optimistic relevance max. av. precision	acc	Pessimistic relevance max. av. precision	acc
Pair	0.4702	0.75	0.4359	0.65
Triple	0.4719	0.6	0.4479	0.45
Quad	0.455	0.55	0.4474	0.35
Sext	0.4431	0.45	0.4507	0.25
Oct	0.4277	0.35	0.4404	0.2
Pair-2	0.4722	0.8	0.4556	0.6
Pair-E	0.4787	0.75	0.4464	0.65
Triple-3	0.4566	0.65	0.4694	0.4
Mix	0.4608	0.75	0.4307	0.5

both relevance aggregation strategies. The acc value can be approximated with the function

$$acc = a \cdot \frac{1}{\sqrt{n}}$$

where n is the number of sub-contexts. The parameter a depends on the relevance aggregation strategy. With the method of least square polynomials (see Appendix), values of a are 1.068 and 0.78 for optimistic and pessimistic relevance assessments, respectively.

The optimal acc values obtained for Pair and Triple are close to those of Pair-2 and Pair-E, and Triple-3, respectively. This indicates that for depth-two collections (Pair-2, Pair-E, Triple-3) we can apply the above estimates for acc independently of the depth of the collection, indicating that approximations based on the number of sub-contexts seem appropriate.

The acc value for Mix used the same fixed accessibility values for all documents, whether they were Pair or Triple documents. This could be considered as "unfair", since, as discussed above, the setting of the acc for a context depends on the number of its sub-contexts. Therefore, we performed an additional experiment, where the acc values were set to 0.75 and 0.6, respectively, for contexts with two and three sub-contexts in the optimistic relevance case, and 0.65 and 0.45 for the pessimistic case. These are the optimal accessibility values obtained for Pair and Triple (see Table 3). The average precision values are 0.4615 and 0.4301 for optimistic and pessimistic relevance assessments, respectively. Compared to the values obtained with fixed accessibility values (0.4608 and 0.4307, respectively), there is no significant change. An experimental setting with a more heterogeneous collection would be more appropriate for comparing fixed and variable settings of the acc value.

From the results on the homogeneous collections, we conclude that we can set the acc parameter for a context according to the function $a \cdot \frac{1}{\sqrt{n}}$ where a can be viewed as the parameter reflecting the relevance aggregation strategy.

4.2   Large or Small Contexts

One major role of the accessibility dimension is to emphasise the retrieval preference of large vs small contexts. For example, contexts deeper in the structure (small contexts) should be retrieved before contexts upper (large contexts) in the structure when specific contexts are preferred to more exhaustive contexts [6]. The *acc* value gives powerful control regarding exhaustiveness and specificity of the retrieval. With small *acc* values, small contexts "overtake" large contexts, whereas with high *acc* values large contexts dominate the upper ranks.

For demonstrating and investigating this effect, we produced for each collection with our *tf-idf-acc* method defined in Section 2 a ranked list of contexts for different *acc* values, ranging again from 0.1 to 0.9. For each type of contexts (atomic, inner and root), we calculate its average rank over all retrieval results for a collection. These average values are then plotted into a graph in relation to the accessibility values. Figure 4 shows the obtained graphs for Oct, Triple-3 and Mix. In all graphs, the root context curve starts in the upper left corner, whereas the atomic context curve starts in the lower left corner. For instance, we see that for the Oct collection, the "break-even point" is around 0.1 and 0.2 for pessimistic relevance assessment.

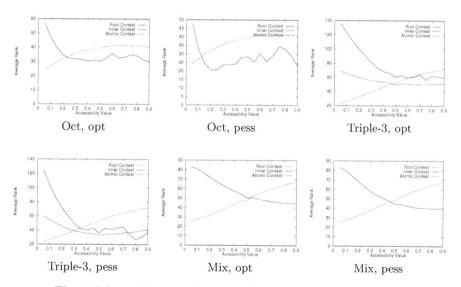

Fig. 4. Effect of the accessibility on the types of retrieved contexts

With the Triple-3 collection we obtain three break-even points for root-inner, root-atomic, and inner-atomic. Whereas the average rank of inner nodes does not vary greatly with varying *acc* values, the effect on root and atomic contexts is similar to the effect observed with the Oct collection, but with different break-even points values (e.g. around $0.4 - 0.5$ for optimistic relevance assessment).

For the Mix collection the break-even-point locates around 0.5, a higher value than that for the Oct collection.

Whereas as in Section 4.1, the maximum average precision leads to a setting of *acc*, the experiments regarding small and large contexts provide us with a second source for setting the *acc* value, one that controls the retrieval of exhaustive vs specific document entry points.

5   Conclusion

In this work we investigated how to explicitly incorporate the notion of structure into structured document retrieval. This is in contrast to other research, (e.g. [3, 15,8,20]), where the structure of a document is only implicitly captured within the retrieval model. The advantage of our approach is that we can investigate the effect of differing document structures upon the success of structured document retrieval.

Our approach to structured documents ranks document contexts (document components of varying granularity) based on a description of their individual content augmented with that of their sub-contexts. Therefore a document's context encapsulates the content of all its sub-contexts taking into account their importance. This was implemented using PRA, a probabilistic relational algebra. In our model, and implementation, we quantitatively incorporated the degree to which a sub-context contributes to the content of a super-context using the *acc* dimension, i.e. higher *acc* values mean that the sub-context contributes more to the description of a super-context.

We carried out extensive experiments on collections of documents with varying structure to provide estimates for *acc*. This investigation is necessary to allow the setting of *acc* to values that will facilitate the retrieval of document components of varying granularity.

The experiments required the development of test collections of structured documents. We developed a methodology for the automatic construction of test collections of structured documents using standard test collections with their set of documents, queries and corresponding relevance assessments. The methodology makes it possible to generate test collections of structured documents with varying width and depth, based on differing notions of relevance and with identical or varying structure.

The analysis of the retrieval results allowed us to derive a general recommendation for appropriate settings of the *acc* value for structured document retrieval. The *acc* values depend on the number of sub-contexts of a contexts, and the relevance assessment aggregation strategies. They also depend on the required exhaustiveness and specificity of the retrieval. These results are being used as the basis for an evaluation on a real structured document collection.

References

1. BAEZA-YATES, R., AND RIBEIRO-NETO, B. *Modern Information Retrieval*. Addison Wesley, 1999.

2. BAUMGARTEN, C. A probabilistic model for distributed information retrieval. In *Proceedings of ACM-SIGIR Conference on Research and Development in Information Retrieval* (Philadelphia, USA, 1997), pp. 258–266.

3. BORDOGNA, G., AND PASI, G. Flexible querying of structured documents. In *Proceedings of Flexible Query Answering Systems (FQAS)* (Warsaw, Poland, 2000), pp. 350–361.

4. CHELLAS, B. *Modal Logic*. Cambridge University Press, 1980.

5. CHIARAMELLA, Y. Browsing and querying: two complementary approaches for multimedia information retrieval. In *Proceedings Hypermedia - Information Retrieval - Multimedia* (Dortmund, Germany, 1997). Invited talk.

6. CHIARAMELLA, Y., MULHEM, P., AND FOUREL, F. A model for multimedia information retrieval. Tech. Rep. Fermi ESPRIT BRA 8134, University of Glasgow, 1996.

7. EDWARDS, D., AND HARDMAN, L. Lost in hyperspace: Cognitive navigation in a hypertext environment. In *Hypertext: Theory Into Practice* (1993), pp. 90–105.

8. FRISSE, M. Searching for information in a hypertext medical handbook. *Communications of the ACM 31*, 7 (1988), 880–886.

9. FUHR, N., AND ROELLEKE, T. A probabilistic relational algebra for the integration of information retrieval and database systems. *ACM Transactions on Information Systems 14*, 1 (1997).

10. IWEHA, C. *Visualisation of Structured Documents: An Investigation into the Role of Visualising Structure for Information Retrieval Interfaces and Human Computer Interaction*. PhD thesis, Queen Marty & Westfield College, 1999.

11. LALMAS, M., AND MOUTOGIANNI, E. A Dempster-Shafer indexing for the focussed retrieval of hierarchically structured documents: Implememtation and experiments on a web museum collection. In *6th RIAO Conference, Content-Based Multimedia Information Access* (Paris, France, 2000).

12. LALMAS, M., AND ROELLEKE, T. Four-valued knowledge augmentation for structured document retrieval. Submitted for Publication.

13. LALMAS, M., AND RUTHVEN, I. Representing and retrieving structured documents with Dempster-Shafer's theory of evidence: Modelling and evaluation. *Journal of Documentation 54*, 5 (1998), 529–565.

14. MIZZARO, S. Relevance: The whole story. *Journal of the America Society for Information Science 48*, 9 (1997), 810–832.

15. MYAENG, S., JANG, D. H., KIM, M. S., AND ZHOO, Z. C. A flexible model for retrieval of SGML documents. In *Proceedings of ACM-SIGIR Conference on Research and Development in Information Retrieval* (Melbourne, Australia, 1998), pp. 138–145.

16. QUICKER, S. Relevanzuntersuchung fur das Retrieval von strukturierten Dokumenten. Master's thesis, University of Dortmund, 1998.

17. ROELLEKE, T. *POOL: Probabilistic Object-Oriented Logical Representation and Retrieval of Complex Objects - A Model for Hypermedia Retrieva*. PhD thesis, University of Dortmund, Germany, 1999.

18. VAN RIJSBERGEN, C. J. *Information Retrieval*, 2 ed. Butterworths, London, 1979.

19. VOORHEES, E., AND HARMAN, D. Overview of the Fifth Text REtrieval Conference (TREC-5). In *Proceedings of the 5th Text Retrieval Conference* (Gaitherburg, 1996), pp. 1–29.
20. WILKINSON, R. Effective retrieval of structured documents. In *Proceedings of ACM-SIGIR Conference on Research and Development in Information Retrieval* (Dublin, Ireland, 1994), pp. 311–317.

Appendix: Least Square Polynomials

Consider the experimental values of *acc* in relation with the square root of the number of sub-contexts. Assuming $a \cdot \frac{1}{\sqrt{n_i}}$ where n_i ranges in the set $\{2, 3, 4, 6, 8\}$ is the function for estimating the optimal accessibility values, we apply least square polynomials as follows for calculating a.

$$err(a) = \sum_i \left(y_i - a \cdot \frac{1}{\sqrt{n_i}} \right)^2$$

$$\frac{err(a)}{\delta a} = 2 \cdot \sum_i \left(y_i - a \cdot \frac{1}{\sqrt{n_i}} \right) \cdot \frac{1}{\sqrt{n_i}}$$

$$0 = \sum_i \left(y_i \cdot \frac{1}{\sqrt{n_i}} - a \cdot \frac{1}{n_i} \right)$$

$$a \cdot \sum_i \frac{1}{x_i} = \sum_i y_i \cdot \frac{1}{\sqrt{n_i}}$$

$$a = \frac{\sum_i y_i \cdot \frac{1}{\sqrt{n_i}}}{\sum_i \frac{1}{n_i}}$$

Building Bilingual Dictionaries from Parallel Web Documents

Craig J.A. McEwan[1], Iadh Ounis[1], and Ian Ruthven[2]

[1] Department of Computing Science, University of Glasgow, G12 8QQ

[2] Department of Computer and Information Sciences, University of Strathclyde, G1 1XH

Abstract. In this paper we describe a system for automatically constructing a bilingual dictionary for cross-language information retrieval applications. We describe how we automatically target candidate parallel documents, filter the candidate documents and process them to create parallel sentences. The parallel sentences are then automatically translated using an adaptation of the EMIM technique and a dictionary of translation terms is created. We evaluate our dictionary using human experts. The evaluation showed that the system performs well. In addition the results obtained from automatically-created corpora are comparable to those obtained from manually created corpora of parallel documents. Compared to other available techniques, our approach has the advantage of being simple, uniform, and easy-to-implement while providing encouraging results.

1 Introduction

The content of the Internet is changing from being mainly in the English language to being multi-lingual [11]. At the moment English speakers are the largest group of Internet users, but the number of non-English speaking Internet users is increasing rapidly. For example, it is estimated that by 2005, over 70% of the online population will be non-native English speakers [6].

The Internet is therefore becoming an important source for multi-lingual information, necessitating the development of effective multi-lingual information access tools. This paper describes the development of a system for automatically creating bilingual dictionaries to support these information access tools. The bilingual dictionary can then be put to a variety of uses including Cross-Language Information Retrieval (CLIR) [7]. Furthermore, we examine the potential of using the web as a source of parallel translated documents for the automatic construction of bilingual dictionaries. If the web can be used as a source for parallel documents, then it will allow the development of low-cost, but high quality, translation systems for CLIR.

F. Crestani, M. Girolami, and C.J. van Rijsbergen (Eds.): ECIR 2002, LNCS 2291, pp. 303-323, 2002.

Our system is composed of three components, comprising three distinct and independent stages. Firstly a collection stage sends a query to a search engine and retrieves the documents from the search engine results links. The second stage uses the HTML tags of the web documents to filter and align the English and Spanish text into parallel sentences. The final stage involves the translation of the words from the parallel blocks. This is achieved by finding word pairs that co-occur in many sentences. The translation stage also incorporates the construction of the dictionary itself. The languages chosen for this implementation are English and Spanish because of the availability of expert evaluators, but the system can be adapted for use with any pair of languages.

Our intention is to provide a system that will automatically cover the whole construction of a dictionary from the initial gathering of parallel documents to the translation of words. However, we must ensure that the documents collected automatically are of sufficient quality. Hence we compared the techniques for creating a dictionary on two sets of data: an automatically collected corpus of parallel web documents of unknown quality and a manually collected corpus of parallel documents that are good quality translations. The evaluation of the two dictionaries created indicates that the automatic corpus produces a dictionary that is of similar quality to the dictionary produced by the manual corpus. This result requires further investigation, but indicates that it may be possible to generate good quality bilingual dictionaries from rapidly collected parallel corpora of unknown quality.

The paper is structured as follows. In section 2 we briefly summarise earlier studies and discuss how our work relates to these. Section 3 discusses the data we collected to construct our dictionary and the means by which we collected the data. In sections 4 and 5 we deal with how we process the documents and in section 6 we discuss how we construct the bilingual dictionary. In section 7 we describe the evaluation of the system and in sections 8 and 9 we conclude with a discussion of our approach and options for future work.

2 Related Work

The idea of building bilingual thesaurus structures using parallel or comparable texts (i.e. comparable on the basis of the similarity between the topics they address [12]) is not new. Comparable texts are usually easier to find or build than parallel texts (i.e. translation equivalent). However, they require appropriate alignment tools to extract cross-language equivalencies. Sheridan and Ballerini [17] created a multilingual similarity thesaurus by aligning news stories from the Swiss news agency (SDA) by topic label and date, and then merging them to build the similarity thesaurus. The alignment process used by Picchi and Peters [13] relies on some contextual information derived from a multilingual machine readable dictionary (MRD). The bilingual MRD is used to establish the links between contexts over languages. The above approaches do not necessarily apply to all pair of languages. Moreover, they are corpus-based techniques and as such they tend to be very application-dependent.

Parallel texts have been used in several studies on CLIR [2] [5] [8] [18]. In [8], the Latent Semantic Indexing reduction technique has been applied on a relatively small parallel text (i.e. translation equivalent) collections in English with French, Spanish, Greek and Japanese. The effectiveness of this approach has not been demonstrated on large collections of data. In [18], a corpus-based bilingual term-substitution thesaurus, called EBT was proposed. In [2], a thesaurus has been constructed from parallel texts using co-occurrences information. QUILT [5] integrates traditional, glossary-based machine translation technology with IR approaches into a Spanish/English CLIR system. These approaches use parallel collections that are domain-specific and/or costly to obtain. In fact, one of the problems with using parallel texts is the difficulty to find cheap, available, generic, large and reliable parallel texts.

Recently, there have been some attempts to collect cheap parallel texts from the Web. Resnik [14][15] was among the first researchers to investigate methods to collect parallel/translated text from the Web. He uses queries to the AltaVista search engine together with HTML tags to detect potential candidate documents on the Web. His approach can be seen as a filtering process allowing identification of high quality syntactically similar translated documents. Indeed, he did not look into the issue of building a bilingual dictionary from the collected corpus, nor did he investigate the alignment process that would statistically allow such a dictionary to be built. Chen [3], Chen and Nie [4] and Nie et al., [9] all addressed the issue of CLIR using the Web as a source of parallel documents. Their approach was to use a probabilistic translation model based on a training corpus made of parallel documents automatically collected from the Web.

Our approach uses a rather simple but uniform approach for both alignment and translation. We use a simplistic alignment algorithm that only uses the characteristic of the HTML markup in Web documents. For the translation stage, we use: a refinement of the well-established IR EMIM measure for defining the strength of relationships between translated words (instead of using a probabilistic approach [1]). The use of the EMIM technique allows a more accurate interpretation of the co-occurrences information obtained from parallel texts, making it more interesting than the rough co-occurrence technique used in [2]. Moreover, our approach does not need tuning or any other classical pre-operations, as no probabilities have been used. Therefore, like the methodology proposed by Nie et al. [9], it could be seen as a generic methodology for building bilingual dictionaries from the Web, while being cheaper/simpler/ and easier-to-implement. Moreover, it still provides very encouraging results.

3 Collection

We collected two corpora of parallel documents. One corpus was collected manually by finding and comparing parallel documents, and a second corpus was collected automatically by sending a query to the AltaVista search engine.

---

[1] EMIM measures are based on a function that is monotonic to a probabilistic measure. This function avoids the need to estimate probabilities directly, instead it uses values based on the absence or presence of terms in sentences.

The manual corpus was assembled by searching bilingual websites for appropriate documents. An example of the websites reviewed to collect documents for the manual corpus is the European Union website[2]. Parallel documents in English and Spanish from a variety of websites were assessed by bilingual humans for their suitability for inclusion in the manual corpus. Only the text in the parallel documents was assessed, the HTML code of the documents was not considered.

For the automatic collection we tested several different queries to automatically download candidate pair pages in order to determine which query generated the highest number of good quality candidate pairs for the automatic corpus. These queries look for links or anchors from an initial page to its translation page. A query containing *'anchor:spanish version'* will search for pages containing the text 'Spanish version' within HTML anchor tags (Fig. 1).

Additionally, web page authors often use abbreviations for different languages – *en* is the commonest abbreviation for English and *es* is the typical abbreviation for Spanish. Using a query of the form: *'link:*_es.html'* to search for links which include the abbreviation *es.html* in the URL of the Spanish translation page was therefore tried as another method of finding and downloading parallel pages.

However, web page authors use many other abbreviations to identify Spanish pages and the queries for links that end with *'es.html'* encountered many links which were not related to language differences – for instance *_es.html* was frequently used by Environmental Science departments to identify their pages.

After assessing different possibilities, the automatic corpus was collected using the query *'anchor:spanish version'* and searching English pages because this combination produced the least number of erroneous links together with the highest number of result URL addresses. This query finds and downloads parallel pages asymmetrically (Fig. 1). The query searches for web pages in English that have a link containing the text 'Spanish version'. No check is made on the Spanish page to ensure that it has a corresponding link back to the English page.

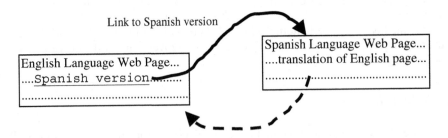

Fig. 1. Model of web page links used to collect the automatic corpus

---

[2] http://europa.eu.int/index_es.htm

Using this approach, a parallel Spanish page is not located for each English document. The reason for the lower number of Spanish pages collected is the variety of different file path possibilities used by web authors to store their Spanish version files which could not be handled by the heuristics employed in the system.

To increase the number of candidate pair pages collected by the system, a different algorithm could be used. There are several different possible ways of doing this. For example, an intelligent crawler could be used to mine through the directory structure of websites where a high concentration of multi-lingual documents occur.

Alternatively, by using a symmetrical approach (Fig. 2), it would be possible to download parallel documents which do not have direct links between them. The query would look for pages with anchors containing the text 'English version' AND 'Spanish version'. The links to the respective versions would be extracted and threads sent to download the candidate pair of pages. Either of these techniques would increase the likelihood of obtaining pairs of documents that were translations of each other [14]

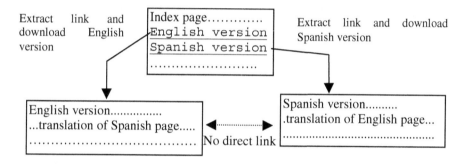

Fig. 2. Symmetrical download model of web page links

Once we have targeted documents that are possible translations of each other – the candidate pair documents - we need to process the documents. This involves filtering the documents to eliminate documents that are not likely to be translations, section 4, and then to align the text that is to be used for creating the dictionary, section 5.

4 Filtering

After the collection of candidate pair documents has been completed, the candidate document pairs are filtered to ensure that they have a reasonable chance of being translations of one another.

Several filters are used:

    i.   *language* filters to prevent documents being classified as belonging to the wrong language, section 4.1,

    ii.   *length* filters to ensure that parallel documents are of approximately similar length, section 4.2,

    iii.   *structural* filters to test whether the HTML mark up code of parallel documents are similar, section 4.3.

4.1 Language Filtering

The first filter for the candidate pair documents is a language check. The document text is compared against a list of stop words in the language that the document is supposed to contain. For example, English language documents are compared against a list of English stop words, and Spanish documents are compared against a list of Spanish stop words. This stage, then, eliminates documents that have been misclassified as belonging to English or Spanish.

The stop word lists themselves have been checked to ensure that no words with the same spelling occur in both the English and Spanish document. This is done to prevent an English document being recognised as Spanish and vice versa. Examples of the words which were removed are '*he*' – pronoun for a male in English, but also first person conjugation of the verb '*haber*' - to have - in Spanish.

If both documents in the pair contain a word from the stop word list of their respective languages, they are assumed to be in the correct language and progress to the length check filter.

4.2 Length Filtering

A length filter is used since it is assumed that very long documents will not be translations of very short documents and vice versa [10]. To determine quantitative parameters for the length filter, 10 pairs of parallel documents of varying lengths were selected at random from the manual corpus. These documents were stripped of their HTML code and the number of words counted. The word counts of these documents showed that the Spanish versions of the documents varied between 1.02 and 1.42 times the length of the English versions.

For the initial runs of the length filter, the system uses 0.9 as the minimum length factor and 1.5 as the maximum length factor. That is, to be considered as a translation, a Spanish document cannot have less than 0.9 times the number of words in its English pair document, nor more than 1.5 times the number of words in its English pair. This is an approximation to filter out candidate pairs of documents that have widely differing lengths, a further length check is done at the sentence alignment stage.

4.3 Structural Filtering

The main advantages of using web documents to build a parallel corpus is that they are part of a large and continually growing source of translated documents which contain HTML mark-up code. The filtering and alignment, section 5, processes assume that parallel documents will have very similar HTML mark up code around the translated text (Fig. 3).

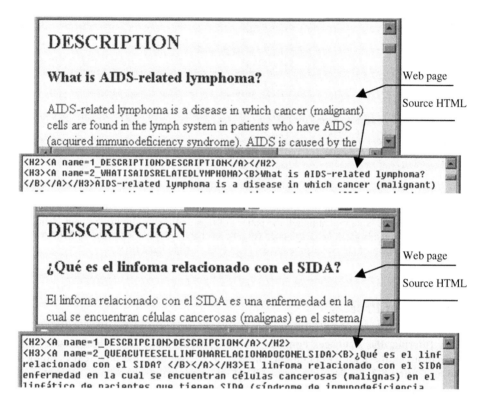

Fig. 3. Web documents and the source HTML code for two parallel translated texts. Note the similar appearance of the web pages and the similarity of the HTML source code for both pages. The text contained in each page is a high quality translation of the other.

Once the system has completed the length filtering it applies a structural filter. Structural filtering uses the HTML tags around the text of the candidate pair documents to test whether the documents are *sufficiently* similar to be considered as parallel translated documents. This approach has been successfully applied to align English: French, English: Spanish and English: Chinese bilingual corpora [3][4][14].

This process is called 'linearisation' [14]. Examples of linearised English and Spanish documents are shown below (Fig. 4).

Once we have the linear sequences of tags and text the system can align the text contained within the tags. We discuss this in the next section.

```
StartTag: HTML
StartTag: HEAD
StartTag: TITLE
Text: AIDS-related lymphoma        StartTag: HTML
EndTag: TITLE                      StartTag: HEAD
StartTag: META                     StartTag: TITLE
StartTag: META                     Text: Linfoma relacionado con el SIDA
StartTag: META                     EndTag: TITLE
StartTag: META                     EndTag: HEAD
StartTag: META                     StartTag: BODY
EndTag: META                       StartTag: P
EndTag: META                       EndTag: P
EndTag: META                       StartTag: CENTER
EndTag: META                       StartTag: B
EndTag: META                       Text: "Linfoma relacionado con el SIDA" is redi
EndTag: HEAD                        StartTag: A
StartTag: BODY                      Text: University of Bonn, Medical Center
StartTag: P                         EndTag: A
Text: "AIDS-related lymphoma"      EndTag: B
Text: University of Bonn, Medi     StartTag: P
StartTag: P                         EndTag: P
Text: AIDS-related lymphoma        StartTag: H1
                                    Text: Linfoma relacionado con el SIDA
                                    EndTag: H1
                                    StartTag: H4
```

Fig. 4. Linear sequence of tags and text for an English and Spanish parallel document pair from the manual corpus. Note that although the pattern of tags and text is similar, it is not identical. In this example, the English language page (Fig. 4, left hand side) has a number of META tags which do not appear on the Spanish language page (Fig. 4, right hand side).

5 Alignment Process

After filtering, the sentences contained within one document are aligned with their translations in the parallel document. In section 5.1, we describe how text is aligned and, in section 5.2, we describe the results of the alignment process on our corpora.

5.1 Aligning Text Blocks

The linear sequence of tags and text for the English language document is compared with the linear sequence of tags and text from the Spanish language document. Web authors may use identical HTML code around the text in parallel translated documents, but this is uncommon even in sites of governmental organisations. It is much more common to have HTML code which is broadly similar but not identical around the parallel texts.

The alignment process relies on matching the HTML tags of the text in the two languages. To quantify the alignment, matching <Start>, <End> and <Text> tags in both languages are counted. In addition, since longer sentences in one language will translate to longer sentences in another language [10], a sentence level word count ensures that short sentences are not aligned against long ones (Fig. 5). Where a <Text> tag in the English document of a pair does not align with a <Text> tag in the Spanish document of the pair, the system searches for the next <Text> tag in the Spanish document.

```
The doctor will cut out (biopsy) small pieces of tissue and look at them under a microscope to se
El médico cortará (biopsia) pequeños pedazos de tejido y los observará en un microscopio para det
This type of staging is called pathologic staging.
Este tipo de clasificación se llama clasificación patológica.
Pathologic staging is usually done only when it is needed to help the doctor plan treatment.
La clasificación patológica por lo general se realiza solamente cuando se necesita para ayudar al
Lymphoma that has started in lymph nodes or other organs of the lymph system.
El linfoma se ha originado en los ganglios linfáticos u otros órganos del sistema linfático.
The lymphoma may have spread from where it started throughout the body, including to the brain or
El linfoma puede haberse diseminado de donde comenzó a todo el cuerpo, incluso al cerebro o a la
Primary central nervous system lymphoma
Linfoma primario del sistema nervioso central
```

Fig. 5. An example of an aligned text file. English and Spanish sentences alternate. Long English sentences align with long Spanish sentences.

If the aligned text strings are similar in length, sentences within the text blocks are identified by searching for full stop characters '.'. One English sentence is then aligned against one Spanish sentence. In this system, it is assumed that one sentence will be translated into one sentence since this occurs in about 90% of sentences in parallel documents [10]. Untranslated sentences, or one sentence translating to 2 sentences account for the remaining 10% of sentences in the parallel documents.

5.2 Results of Filtering and Alignment

In this section we discuss the results of the filtering and alignment process on our two corpora; the automatically retrieved and manually created sets of parallel documents.

Of the 423 candidate pairs collected by the automatic system, 105 pairs passed the three filtering steps described in section 3.

Candidate English and Spanish pairs which do not have a high level of HTML tag matching are discarded by the system. Currently, the threshold for matching tags is set to 60%. That is, 6 out of every 10 English and Spanish lines must have identical HTML tags to be considered translations else the candidate pairs are discarded.

Of the 105 files which passed the language and length filters, 33 were discarded because they fell below the alignment threshold. This leaves 72 aligned text files from the original 423 pairs collected by the automatic collection system.

A corpus of 41 parallel pairs of web pages was collected manually – that is by reading and reviewing both the English and Spanish versions of the documents. If the translation was a good one, the document was included in the manual corpus.

The manual corpus was also filtered and aligned. Of the 41 pairs, 37 pairs passed the language and length filtering stage and of these only 2 were discarded because they fell below the alignment threshold (Fig. 6).

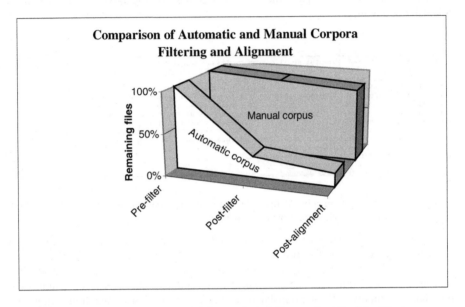

Fig. 6. A graphical comparison of the number of files passing all of the filtering

The high percentage of manual corpus files (88%) which pass filtering and alignment criteria compared with the low percentage (17%) of automatic corpus files which pass all of the filtering and alignment criteria is interpreted to reflect the quality of the translations of the corpora. The manual corpus is a collection of high quality parallel documents that have good translations and very similar HTML code around the text.

These documents were collected from university and governmental websites. The automatic corpus is a collection of web pages from a wide variety of sources. The quality of the translations of the parallel web pages varies from good to poor, and the HTML code around the text is often very different between parallel pages. This results in a low number of files passing all of the filtering and alignment criteria.

The threshold levels for file and sentence length as well as the alignment threshold may be adjusted to allow a greater or lesser number of files pass. Testing the system with different threshold levels for these variables combined with an evaluation of the final bilingual dictionary would be the best way to improve the overall system performance.

6 Building a Dictionary

Once the documents and sentences have been filtered and aligned the system can translate the terms in the sentences. The principal behind the automatic translation of terms is simple – if an English term and a Spanish term both occur in many translated parallel sentences, then the probability that they are translations of one another is higher than an English term and a Spanish term which do not co-occur in many sentences. Automatic construction of thesauri using statistical techniques is a widely used Information Retrieval technique [3][4][16].

The dictionary building stage is divided into three steps; building a matrix of words, section 6.1, normalising the raw co-occurrence scores in the matrix, section 6.2, lastly making a dictionary listing by extracting the Spanish terms with the highest co-occurrence probability for each English term, section 6.3.

6.1 Building a Matrix of English and Spanish Words

The assumption was made in the filtering and alignment stages that a single sentence in English will be translated to a single Spanish sentence. To build the matrix of English and Spanish terms, it is further assumed that a single English term will translate to a single Spanish term. This is clearly not the case for many English and Spanish words, but it is a simplifying assumption that allows us to create a first implementation of our techniques.

Our approach to translating English to Spanish terms is based on statistical co-occurrence techniques. These, in our implementation, depend on the creation of a co-occurrence matrix which shall be described in the remainder of this section.

The word matrix can be imagined as a huge spreadsheet (Fig. 7).

The matrix itself is constructed as follows. For each word in an English sentence, it is assumed that the translation of the word is one of the Spanish terms in the parallel Spanish sentence. Therefore for each English term in the sentence, the co-occurrence score with every term in the parallel Spanish sentence is incremented by one.

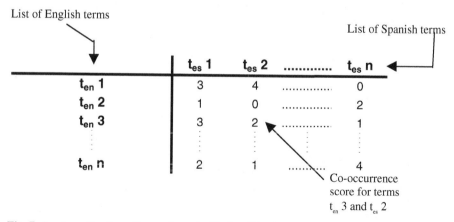

Fig. 7. A schematic view of a word matrix. Each cell in the matrix contains the number of times an English term co-occurs with a Spanish term. $t_{es}i$ is the ith Spanish word, $t_{en}i$ is the ith English word.

We shall illustrate this process below (Fig. 8a-e), using two English sentences 'The dog runs.' and 'The happy dog jumps.' and their Spanish translations '*El perro corre.*' and '*El perro feliz salta.*'.

The stopwords are removed from the sentences leaving 'dog runs' and 'happy dog jumps' and the Spanish versions '*perro corre*' and '*perro feliz salta*'.

	perro	corre
dog	1	1

Fig. 8a. Constructing a word matrix Step 1. After removing English and Spanish stopwords, the first English term 'dog' is added to the matrix with all the remaining Spanish terms in the parallel sentence '*perro corre*' and the co-occurrence score is incremented for each word pair.

	perro	corre
dog	1	1
runs	1	1

Fig. 8b. Step 2. The remaining term in the English sentence is added. The Spanish terms in the parallel sentence are already in the matrix, so only the co-occurrence scores for the new word pairs are incremented

	perro	corre	feliz	salta
dog	1	1	0	0
runs	1	1	0	0
happy	1	0	1	1

Fig. 8c. Step 3. The first term of the second English sentence 'happy dog jumps' is added to the matrix with the Spanish terms from the parallel sentence '*perro feliz salta*'. Since '*perro*' is also already in the matrix, the other new terms '*feliz*' and '*salta*' are added to the matrix and then all of the co-occurrence scores are incremented to 1.

	perro	corre	feliz	salta
dog	2	1	1	1
runs	1	1	0	0
happy	1	0	1	1

Fig. 8d. Step 4. The next English term in the second sentence, 'dog' is added to the matrix with the Spanish terms from the parallel sentence '*perro feliz salta*'. Since all of the English and Spanish terms are already in the matrix, the co-occurrence scores for the English term and all the Spanish terms are incremented.

	perro	corre	feliz	salta
dog	2	1	1	1
runs	1	1	0	0
happy	1	0	1	1
jumps	**1**	**0**	**1**	**1**

Fig. 8e. Step 5. The final term in the second English sentence 'jumps' is added to the matrix and the co-occurrence scores with the terms in the parallel Spanish sentence are incremented.

From the illustrations above (Figs 8a – e) it is clear that the English term 'dog' and the Spanish term *'perro'* have a higher co-occurrence score than the other word pairs in the matrix. It is therefore more likely that the English term 'dog' is translated to *'perro'* than *'corre'*, *'feliz'* or *'salta'*.

When terms from many sentences are added to a matrix, the co-occurrence scores for all of the word pairs in the matrix increment and the contrast between different terms increases.

This trivial example highlights a major drawback with the approach. That is that nouns are likely to be associated with adjectives – words like 'happy' and with verbs – words like 'runs'. In order to distinguish between closely related words, the co-occurrence scores need to be normalised. We shall discuss this in the next section.

6.2 Normalising the Co-occurrence Scores

Normalising the co-occurrence scores is necessary to be able to distinguish between closely related terms in the lists of English and Spanish words. We used the Expected Mutual Information Measure (EMIM) [16] to calculate the degree of association between an English term and a Spanish term in a word pair in the matrix.

The EMIM measure was specifically suggested [16] as a means of calculating term dependencies within a document collection. In our system we re-interpret it for use in calculating how likely a term in one language is to be a translation of a term in another language.

An EMIM score is calculated for each word pair in the matrix, e.g. the terms *'perro'* and *'dog'* (see Fig. 8). The EMIM score is based on values contained within the contingency table shown in (Fig. 9). This contains four main pieces of information regarding the two terms:

    i.   how often both terms co-occur, i.e. how often two aligned sentence contain the terms, value (1) in Figure 9

ii.   how often one term occurs in a sentence and the other term does *not* occur in the aligned sentences, values (2) and (3) in Figure 9

iii.   how often *neither* term occurs in the set of aligned sentences being investigated. This count measures how rare the combination of terms are within the set of aligned sentences, value (4) in Figure 9.

	Spanish term t_{es} j present	Spanish term t_{es} j not present	
English term t_{en} i present	(1)	(2)	(7)
English term t_{en} i not present	(3)	(4)	(8)
	(5)	(6)	(9)

Fig. 9. Contingency table to calculate EMIM values.

The values required to calculate the EMIM scores are obtained from the matrix in the following way:

(1) – matrix score t_{en} i, t_{es} j

(2) – the difference between the maximum score and the matrix score for t_{en} i ((7)-(1))

(3) – the difference between the maximum score and the matrix score for t_{es} j ((5)-(1))

(4) – the part of the total score which is not from either t_{en} i or t_{es} j ((6)-(2) or (8)-(3))

(5) – maximum co-occurrence score for term t_{es} j

(6) – difference between twice the matrix maximum and the t_{es} maximum ((9)-(5))

(7) – maximum co-occurrence score for term t_{en} i

(8) – difference between twice the matrix maximum and the t_{en} maximum ((9)-(7))

(9) – twice the highest co-occurrence score in the matrix.

The EMIM score itself for each word pair is calculated using the following equation:

$$\text{EMIM} = (1)\log\frac{(1)}{(5)(7)} + (2)\log\frac{(2)}{(6)(7)} + (3)\log\frac{(3)}{(5)(8)} + (4)\log\frac{(4)}{(6)(8)} \qquad (1)$$

In this way a number can be assigned to each word pair which is an estimate of the strength of the association between the two terms t_{en} i and t_{es} j. The absolute value of the number is not important, it simply quantifies the association of the two terms t_{en} i and t_{es} j relative to all the other word pairs in the matrix.

It should be noted that the EMIM scores are all **negative** numbers because the denominator of the log term is always greater than the numerator. If the numerator of the log term is 0, then the log term is assigned 0 as its value *e.g.* for the term

$$(x)\log\frac{(x)}{(y)(z)} \text{ if } (x) = 0,\ (x)\log\frac{(x)}{(y)(z)} = 0.$$

None of the denominator terms will be 0 as long as there is at least one word pair in the matrix. Therefore the smaller (more negative) the magnitude of the EMIM value, the greater the degree of normalised co-occurrence between the two terms and the more likely the terms can be regarded as translations of each other.

When the EMIM score has been calculated for each word pair, the original co-occurrence score in the matrix is replaced with the EMIM score.

6.3 Making a Dictionary Listing

A dictionary listing is made by taking each English term and finding each of the co-occurring Spanish terms that have the minimum and second lowest EMIM scores. A dictionary could also have been made by taking each Spanish term and finding an English term or terms with the minimum EMIM score. The system can be easily adapted to generate either or both types of dictionary listing.

The dictionary list of 1687 English terms was generated from the 35 aligned files of the manual corpus. A list of 1047 English terms was generated from the 72 aligned files of the automatic corpus. In the next section we shall evaluate the quality of the translations and the comparative quality of the translations from the two corpora.

7 Evaluation

We chose to evaluate the dictionaries which were created by counting the number of correctly translated words they contain rather than comparing the process of automatic dictionary construction with the corresponding manual process. If an acceptable dictionary can be constructed using our system, then there is no need to consider the construction process used. In this section we shall first describe *how* we evaluate the created dictionaries, section 7.1, and then present the results of the evaluation, section 7.2.

7. 1 Evaluating the Dictionary Lists

The initial hypothesis was that the manual corpus would produce a higher quality dictionary than the automatic corpus because at each stage of the collection, filtering and alignment, and translation the manual corpus documents were higher quality than the automatic corpus (Fig. 10).

Specifically, the manual corpus has a higher ratio of Spanish:English files collected, a higher ratio of files passing all of the filtering and alignment criteria and a higher ratio of words in the dictionary list per document in the corpus. All of these indices are taken to indicate that the manual corpus is of a higher quality than the automatic corpus.

The evaluation experiment consisted of two fluent Spanish speakers reviewing the dictionary listings from both the manual and automatic corpora. These reviewers examined how many correct translations were found in the dictionaries.

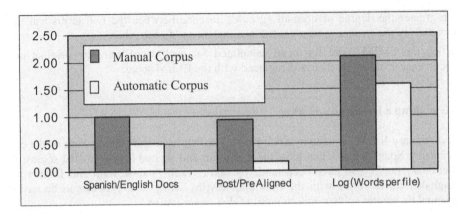

Fig. 10. Comparative statistics for the Manual and Automatic corpora. The histogram indicates that the manual corpus has more Spanish documents per English document than the Automatic corpus, that a far larger proportion of Manual corpus documents passed all of the filtering and alignment stages than was the case for the Automatic corpus, and that on average a document from the Manual corpus provided more words to the dictionary than a file from the Automatic corpus.

For each English term in the listing, if any of the Spanish terms with the minimum or second lowest EMIM score was a good translation of that term, then the count of correct translations was incremented (Fig. 11).

If there was disagreement between the evaluators, a dictionary [1] was used to check the word in dispute.

7.2 Results of the Evaluation

Our system was developed incrementally. The initial version included stopwords and did not remove numbers or words of <4 characters from the dictionary list. Only one term with the minimum EMIM score together with one term with the second lowest EMIM score were incorporated in the dictionary listing. Version 2 removed stopwords, but kept short terms (<4 characters) and again, used only single term with the minimum EMIM and second lowest EMIM scores. Version 3 removed stopwords and words with <4 characters, but only included single terms with the minimum EMIM and second lowest EMIM scores in the dictionary. The final version removed stopwords, only allowed words of >4 characters and included all of the terms with the minimum and second lowest EMIM scores in the dictionary listing.

The removal of stopwords and short words improved the percentage of correct translations slightly (Figure 12). A larger increase in the percentage of correct translations is seen when all of the terms with the minimum and second lowest EMIM scores are collected in the dictionary listing. Collecting all of these translation terms results in a large increase in the number of translation terms as well as the number of correct translations. For example in the first version a total of 1697 English terms were collected from the manual corpus. For each of these terms, 2 Spanish terms were collected resulting in a total of 3394 Spanish words. A total of 612 English terms had a correct translation in the list of Spanish terms (36.1%).

Note no stemming

Good translations – evaluated by human experts

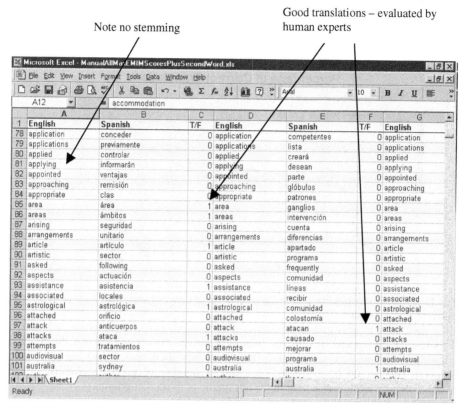

Fig. 11. An example of part of the Manual corpus dictionary listing in an Excel spreadsheet. Note that if any of the Spanish is a good translation of the English term, then the count of good translations increments.

The precision (defined as $\dfrac{number\_of\_correct\_translations}{number\_of\_Spanish\_terms}$) is 18.0%.

In the fourth version, 1688 English terms were collected from the manual corpus. Collecting all of the Spanish terms with either the minimum or the second lowest EMIM score results in the collection of 9136 Spanish terms – a much higher recall than the earlier version. A total of 1048 English terms have a correct translation in the list of Spanish terms (62.1%), but the precision is lower than the earlier versions (11.5%) because of the increase in the number of Spanish terms collected.

There appears then to be some kind of trade-off between number of correct translations and the precision of the translated terms. This balance is similar to the balance between recall and precision that occurs in IR systems.

The results of the evaluation of the final version showed that the manual corpus dictionary contained 1048 good translations out of 1687 English terms which is 62.1% of the total number of terms (Fig. 12). The automatic corpus contains 618 good translations out of 1047 English terms or 59.0% of the total number of terms. It can also be seen that in all of the versions, the percentage of good translations in the manual and automatically collected corpora are about the same (Fig. 12).

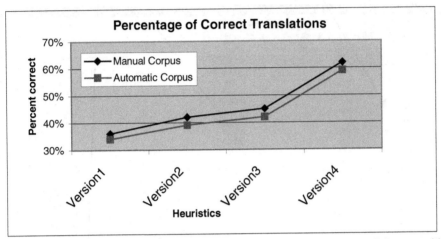

Fig. 12. Graph of the improvement in the percentage of correctly translated English terms with different versions of the system.

This was an unexpected result. As discussed above, we considered that the manual corpora would produce significantly higher quality dictionaries than the automatic corpora. This would be expressed as a higher number of good translations in the manual corpora dictionaries than in the automatic corpora dictionaries.

There are two possible explanations for this – either the alignment in this system is not sophisticated enough to discriminate between high and low quality parallel documents, or it shows that a dictionary can be made by collecting parallel documents from anywhere on the Internet without the need for sophisticated document collection software. A corpus gathered by a quick and simple collection generates a dictionary of similar quality to that of a high quality corpus of parallel documents.

8 Conclusions

The objective of this paper was to design and build a system that would allow the construction of a bilingual dictionary from parallel documents found on the World Wide Web. Any bilingual dictionary created can be put to a variety of uses including Cross Language Information Retrieval (CLIR).

English and Spanish were chosen as the languages for the bilingual dictionary to illustrate our approach. As well as building the dictionaries, an evaluation of the translations contained in the dictionaries was carried out by two bilingual people to assess the quality of the dictionaries produced.

Creating a dictionary requires three distinct and independent steps. Unlike other approaches, which use a combination of techniques, e.g. [3][4][14], our system was a unified system. Firstly a corpus of parallel English and Spanish documents is collected. In this system a query is sent to the AltaVista search engine that then searches for English language web documents containing a link to a 'Spanish version'. To provide a corpus to compare the automatic collection system with, a corpus of 41 parallel documents was also collected manually.

The second step in the process is filtering the document pairs for length and language to ensure that they can be translations of one another, then the HTML tags of the documents are used to align the English and Spanish text. This process was carried out for both the automatic and manual corpora. Overall, a higher percentage of manual corpus documents (88%) passed the filtering and alignment process than documents from the automatic corpus (17%). This indicates that the manual corpus contains English and Spanish documents whose HTML structure is more alike and whose translations are of better quality.

The third step in the dictionary building process is to use statistical techniques to find translations of each of the English words in the corpora. A large matrix of English and Spanish word pairs is used to determine which English and Spanish words are most closely associated with each other in the corpora. The better the association score between the terms in a word pair, the more likely the words are to be translations of one another. The association scores have been normalised using an adaptation of the EMIM technique. A dictionary listing was produced by taking each English term and all of the Spanish terms with the two best association scores for each English word.

The latest version of our system returned a dictionary list from a manual corpus in which 62% of the English words were translated correctly. The automatic corpus dictionary contained 59% of correct translations.

Overall we have shown that it is possible to build a bilingual dictionary by mining parallel web pages. The percentage of good translations of words in the dictionary is relatively low using the current system parameters, but future work would focus on improving the heuristics used at each stage of the process.

The conclusion that an automatically collected corpus of relatively poor quality parallel documents can generate a dictionary that is as good as a dictionary generated by a high quality corpus is interesting. It raises the possibility that high quality dictionaries can be generated quickly and easily from the Internet without the need for sophisticated collection algorithms such as those used by some workers [3][4].

9 Future Work

The current system uses a simple query that retrieves a Spanish language page for up to 67% of the total number of English language pages collected. This percentage could be improved by collecting English pages with links to Spanish pages which themselves also have links back to the original English page. This would improve the likelihood that the pages are translations of one another.

The filtering and alignment stage could be improved by implementing more rigorous language checks. At the moment, the language filtering procedure leads to many English words being included as Spanish terms and vice versa. Removing some of the English words from the Spanish vocabulary and vice versa would improve the final dictionary. Other refinements to the filtering and alignment could include adjusting the length filters to reduce the chance of non-parallel documents passing this stage.

Once the co-occurrence matrix is built, an iteration of the construction process would allow the terms with the highest co-occurrence scores to be selected over other terms in any given sentence. This could improve the mapping between terms compared with the initial co-occurrence matrix where there was no prior knowledge available. Additionally, the percentage of good translations in the dictionary may be improved if a much larger vocabulary is processed because the contrast between association scores for co-occurring terms would be improved if a larger number of sentences containing the co-occurring terms were processed.

All of these improvements are relatively straightforward to implement, and would allow a better test of the dictionary building system.

References

1. Appleton's New Cuyás English-Spanish and Spanish-English Dictionary 5th edition. 1972.
2. Brown, R.D.: Automatically extracted thesauri for cross-language IR: when better is worse, 1st Workshop on Computational Terminology (Computerm), p15-21, 1998.
3. Chen, J.: Parallel Text Mining for Cross-Language Information Retrieval using a Statistical Translation Model. M.Sc. thesis, University of Montreal, 2000. http://www.iro.umontreal.ca/~chen/thesis/node1.html.
4. Chen, J. and Nie, J-Y.: Parallel Web Text Mining for Cross-Language IR. In Proceedings of RIAO-2000: "Content-Based Multimedia Information Access", Paris, 12-14 April 2000.
5. Davies, M.W. and Ogden, W.C.: QUILT, Implementing a large-scale cross-language text retrieval system, 20th International Conference on Research and Development in Information Retrieval (ACM SIGIR'97), Philadelphia, p92-98, 1997.
6. Global Reach website. http://www.glreach.com/globstats/
7. Grefenstette, G. (ed.): Cross-Language Information Retrieval. Kluwer Academic Publisher, 1998.
8. Littman, M.L., and Dumais, S.T. and Landauer, T.K.: Automatic Cross-language Information Retrieval using Latent Semantic Indexing. In Grefenstette, G. (ed.): Cross-language Information Retrieval, Kluwer Academic Publishers, p51-62, 1998.
9. Nie, J-Y., Simard, M., Isabelle, P. and Durard, R.: Cross-Language Information Retrieval based on Parallel Texts and Automatic Mining of Parallel Texts from the Web. In Proceedings of the 22nd International Conference on Research and Development in Information Retrieval (ACM SIGIR'99), Berkeley, p74-81. 1999.
10. Oakes, M.P.: Statistics for Corpus Linguistics. Edinburgh Textbooks in Empirical Linguistics. 1998.
11. Oard, D.: Language Distribution of the Web. Web site for Research Resources on Cross-Language Text Retrieval. http://www.clis2.umd.edu/dlrg/filter/papers/
12. Peters, C. and Sheridan, S.: Multilingual Information Access. In M. Agosti, F. Cresti, and G. Pasi (Eds.): Lectures on Information Retrieval/ESSIR 2000, LNCS 1980, pp. 51-80, 2000.

13. Picchi, E. and Peters, C.: Cross-Language Information Retrieval: A System for Comparable Corpus Querying. In Grefenstette, G. (ed.): Cross-language Information Retrieval, Kluwer Academic Publishers, p81-92, 1998.
14. Resnik, P.: Parallel Strands: A Preliminary Investigation into Mining the Web for Bilingual Text. In Proceedings of the AMTA-98 Conference, October, 1998.
15. Resnik, P.: Mining the Web for Bilingual Text. In Proceedings of the International Conference of the Association of Computational Linguistics (ACL-99), College Park, Maryland, 1999.
16. van Rijsbergen, C.J.: Information Retrieval. 2nd Edition. CD-ROM version, 1999. http://www.dcs.gla.ac.uk/Keith/Preface.html
17. Sheridan, P. and Ballerini, J.P.: Experiments in Multilingual Information Retrieval using the SPIDER system. In Proceedings of the 19th International Conference on Research and Development in Information Retrieval (ACM SIGIR'96), Zurich, p58-65. 1996.
18. Yang, Y. and Carbonell, J.G. and Brown, R.D. and Frederking, R.E.: Translingual information retrieval: learning from bilingual corpora, Artificial Intelligence, 103:323-345, 1998.

Translation-Based Indexing for Cross-Language Retrieval

Douglas W. Oard and Funda Ertunc

College of Information Studies and
Institute for Advanced Computer Studies
University of Maryland, College Park, MD 20742, USA
oard@glue.umd.edu,
and
Department of Computer Science and
Institute for Advanced Computer Studies
University of Maryland, College Park, MD 20742,USA
efunda@cs.umd.edu

Abstract. Structured queries have proven to be an effective technique for cross-language information retrieval when evidence about translation probability is not available. Query execution time is adversely impacted, however, because the full postings list for each translation is used in the computation. This paper describes an alternative approach, translation-based indexing, that improves query-time efficiency by integrating the translation and indexing processes. Experiment results demonstrate that similar effectiveness can be achieved at a cost in indexing time that is roughly linear in the average number of known translations for each term.

1 Introduction

Use of the Internet is increasing rapidly throughout the world, with content in languages other than English now increasing far more rapidly than content in English. For example, Grefenstette found that between 1999 and 2000, English content grew by 800%, German content grew by 1500% and Spanish content grew by 1800% [2]. It is now estimated by some sources that there is more non-English than English text in the visible portion of the Web, and if present trends continue the importance to users of finding materials in languages other than that used in their query will likely continue to increase. This is the goal of Cross-Language Information Retrieval(CLIR) systems: to allow users to present a query in one language and retrieve documents that are written in a different language. Searchers who are able to read more than one language can use the results of such systems directly, formulating queries only once (in their most fluent language). Searchers without the language skills to read the documents that are found can also benefit from CLIR systems, but only if suitable human or machine translation capabilities can be provided. The widespread availability of Web-based translation services now promises at least some degree of support for using documents that are found using CLIR systems—the next challenge is to build and deploy efficient and effective CLIR systems that are compatible with the search system architectures used by high-volume Web search engines.

In CLIR, two alternative architectures have been explored:

F. Crestani, M. Girolami, and C.J. van Rijsbergen (Eds.): ECIR 2002, LNCS 2291, pp. 324–333, 2002.

Query translation, in which the query is translated into that language(s) in which the documents are written.

Document translation, in which the documents are translated at indexing time into the language(s) in which the queries are expected to be posed.

Query translation is the more widely studied approach, at least in part because in experimental settings it is far more efficient to translate the relatively few (perhaps 50) queries than to translate all of the documents. In high-volume production applications the reverse might be true—a substantial speedup in query processing might easily justify additional work at indexing time (particularly if only one query language is to be supported).

Regardless of which architecture is chosen, dictionary-based translation introduces three challenges:

- what to translate (e.g., word roots, words, and/or phrases),
- where to obtain the needed translation knowledge (e.g., extraction from machine readable dictionaries, construction from translation-equivalent (parallel) texts, and/or harvesting Web-accessible bilingual term lists), and
- how that translation knowledge should be used.

In this paper we adopt simple but workable approaches for the first two challenges (we translate words using a single bilingual term list found on the Web) and focus on the third challenge—how the translation knowledge we find in bilingual term lists can be used.

Pirkola observed that the distinction between different query terms and different translations of the same query term should be recognized in the structure of a translated query. Specifically, he suggested treating the translations of a query term as if they were synonyms, demonstrating this by using InQuery's synonym operator (#syn) to group alternate translations and InQuery's weight averaging operator (#sum) to combine the weights from each synonym set into document scores [9]. Pirkola's initial experiments were performed using English queries and Finnish documents; similar results are now available for a broad array of language pairs (c.f., [1,6]). In this paper, we present an alternative to structured queries that achieves a similar effect at indexing time.

The approach to structured query formulation that Pirkola introduced raises two important issues that limit the range of scenarios to which it can be applied:

- The computation required by the InQuery synonym operator is complex, so queries using that operator will be much slower than other approaches to query translation if several alternative translations are known for many of the query terms [5].
- InQuery was designed for commercial applications, so the source code is not available. This limits the ability of researchers to explore variants of the synonym operator that might be better tuned to CLIR applications.

We have addressed these limitations by implementing a computation that closely approximates to that performed by InQuery's synonym operator at indexing time using the freely available MG information retrieval system [11]. In the remainder of this paper we describe the computation performed by the synonym operator in Pirkola's structured query technique, describe our indexing-time implementation, present the results of an experiment to assess the effectiveness and efficiency of our implementation, and identify opportunities for extending this line of research in the future.

2 Structured Queries

The key idea in so-called "bag-of-terms" information retrieval systems such as InQuery is to compute a weight for each term in every document, and then combine the weights for each query term on a document-by-document basis in order to compute a score for each document. These scores can then be used to rank the available documents in order of decreasing likelihood that they satisfy the information need expressed by the query. The computation of term weights can be based on three principal sources of evidence:

Within-document term frequency. Term frequency is the count of the number of occurrences of a given term in a given document, or some monotone function of that count. TF provides a measure of the relative importance of the given term with respect to other terms in the same document. The location of a term within a document can be used to bias the weight given to that term. For example, words appearing in the headline of a news story might receive greater weight, while words that appear in the undisplayed author-assigned metadata fields of a Web page might receive less weight (since they often contain "spam" terms).

Across-document collection frequency. Collection frequency is the count of the number of documents in which a term appears. It is a measure of the degree of specificity of the term with respect to the collection. The most common form of collection frequency measure is Inverse Document Frequency (IDF), which is an information content measure that reflects the degree of surprise associated with finding that a document contains the term.

Length. The length of a document representation is used to normalize the contribution of the first two sources of evidence in a way that facilitates cross-document comparisons. In its simplest form, length might be measured as the number of terms in the document (the sum of the term frequencies), but more complex measures that also account for collection frequency are also commonly used (in so-called "vector-space" systems).

These sources of evidence are typically used to compute the weight of each term in each document in a way that rewards high term frequencies, low collection frequencies, and short lengths.

In CLIR applications, the query and the document use terms from different languages, so some form of translation is needed. The effect of the InQuery synonym operator in Pirkola's structured query method is to compute query-language term weights based on document-language evidence as follows:

$$TF_j(Q_i) = \sum_{\{k|Q_i \in T(D_k)\}} TF_j(D_k) \tag{1}$$

$$CF(Q_i) = \left| \bigcup_{\{k|Q_i \in T(D_k)\}} \{d|D_k \in d\} \right| \tag{2}$$

$$L_k = L_k \tag{3}$$

where Q_i is a query-language term, D_k is a document-language term, $TF_j(X)$ represents the number of occurrences of term X in document j, $CF(X)$ represents the number of documents that contain term X, $T(D_k)$ is the set of query-language translations for document-language term D_k, d is a document, and L_k is the length measure of document k, computed in the same way it would have been if document-language terms were being indexed [3].[1] The effect of these equations is to treat every translation as equally likely and separately estimate the term frequency, document frequency, and length in a manner similar to the way those parameters are computed when stemming is used in a monolingual context. Specifically, the term frequency is the sum of the term frequencies of any possible translation, the collection frequency is the number of documents that contain any translation, and the computation of the length is unchanged. The comparison with stemming is easily seen if "token" is substituted for "translation" in the prior sentence. It is this analogy which motivates our design of an indexing-time analogue for structured queries in the next section.

This way of using document-language evidence has the net effect of suppressing the weight of query-language terms that are associated through translation with *any* common document-language term (i.e., one that appears in many documents). A brief examination of each formula will help to explain why this occurs. The dominant effect results from the CF formula, which can produce a result no smaller than the CF of the most common contributing document-language term. For example, the Spanish term "conducir" is related through translation to the English terms "fly," "go," "pilot," and "drive." Since "go" appears in a great many English documents, "conducir" would receive a high CF and thus a lower term weight if used in a Spanish query.

By contrast, because TF is a within-document measure, the effect of the summation on TF is more often helpful than harmful. Consider the case of the English term "fly," with is related through translation to the Spanish terms "mosca" (a type of insect), "volar" (to travel by airplane), and "conducir" (to pilot an aircraft). Spanish documents that contain "conducir" might also contain "volar." In such cases, summing the term frequencies could produce a beneficial effect by combining the contributions of topically related terms. By contrast, since documents about airplanes rarely mention insects, the set of Spanish documents that contain "mosca" is unlikely to contain either of the other two terms. The few cases in which unrelated translations do occur in the same document will indeed have the effect of giving a query-language term more weight than it deserves, but such cases are likely to be sufficiently rare to have little net effect on retrieval results.

It is computationally expensive to compute term weights in this way at query time because the postings file must be traversed to compute the union in equation 2. The time required to perform this computation increases with both the number of translations for each term, and with the number of documents in which each translation is found. In an earlier study we found that structured queries required about 8 times longer than a corresponding monolingual query [7], although that factor undoubtedly varies with the number of translations that are known for each query term. It is equation 2 that is responsible for this delay, since computing the union requires that access to the postings file. Since the postings file is typically so large that it must be stored on disk, the number of disk accesses that are required to process each query is increased.

---

[1] InQuery actually computes the sum and the union over the document-language translations of the query terms, but because bilingual term lists can be thought of as a set of reversible translation pairs, our formula is equivalent.

A more efficient variant of structured queries has been implemented in the Queens College PIRCS system [4]. In that implementation, the union in equation 2 is replaced by:[2]

$$CF(Q_i) = \sum_{\{k|Q_i \in T(D_k)\}} CF(D_k) \qquad (4)$$

where Q_i is a query-language term, D_k is a document-language term, $CF(X)$ represents the number of documents that contain term X, $T(D_k)$ is the set of query-language translations for document-language term D_k, d is a document. This formula computes the sum of document frequencies of each term in the query. The document frequency of each term is the number of documents containing a term whose one of the translations is the query term.

If near-synonyms rarely occur among the translations used in the dictionary, this equations 2 and 4 will compute similar values. With a richer dictionary that contains more near-synonyms, equation 4 would tend to overestimate the collection frequency if the near-synonyms often occur within the same document. We are not aware of any experiments in which this approach has been compared with the computation that is implemented by InQuery's synonym operator.

3 Translation-Based Indexing

The goal of the indexing stage in an information retrieval system is to preprocess the document collection to create an index structure that can be efficiently searched to obtain a value (known as a "term weight") for each document that contains a query term. If stemming will be used at query time in a monolingual system, then it is the term weights associated with stems (rather than surface forms) that would normally be indexed. In a CLIR system, the natural extension of this idea is to index the term weights associated with translations (or, if queries will be stemmed, the weights associated with stems of translations). The key question is therefore how such term weights should be computed. This is the focus of translation-based indexing.

Translation-based indexing requires access to a machine readable bilingual dictionary (or some other form or translation lexicon) in which the source language is the language in which the documents are written and the target language is the language in which the queries will be posed. The key idea is simply to index every possible translation of each document-language term.

We modified the August, 1999 release of the Managing Gigabytes (MG) system (mg-1.2.1) to incorporate translation-based indexing.[3] The changes were localized to the inversion steps in the first and second pass of the indexing process. In each case, we replaced each document-language word with all of its target (query) language translations. Since there are often several translations of a single term, the second pass (in

---

[2] Personal communication with K.L. Kwok.

[3] Source code for MG is available under the GNU public license at http://www.cs.mu.oz.au/mg/ and our modifications are available at http://tides.umiacs.umd.edu.

which the postings file is built) results in more disk accesses, and hence slower indexing, when translation-based indexing is used. The expected slowdown is:

$$t_c/t_m > c * f \tag{5}$$

where t_c is the time required for translation-based indexing, t_m is the time required for document-language indexing, c is the fraction of the terms for which a translation is known (the "by-token" coverage of the dictionary with respect to the collection being indexed), and f is the "fanout" of the dictionary, the average number of translations that are known for each term. The expected indexing time is somewhat greater than the right hand side of the formula would indicate because fanout is normally computed on a by-type basis, giving common terms (which typically have more translations) the same weight as rare terms. We also made some minor modifications to MG to accommodate languages other than English.

MG's implementation of vector space retrieval systems perform length normalization in a manner different from InQuery's inference network model. In InQuery, document length is incorporated in weight computations by computing a ratio between the term frequency and the document length. Equation 3 therefore results in an appropriate computation with document-language terms. MG, by contrast, normalizes for document length in a way that further increases the relative weight of terms with low collection frequencies. This is accomplished using cosine normalization as follows:

$$w'_{j,k} = \frac{w_{j,k}}{\sqrt{\sum_k w_{j,k}^2}} \tag{6}$$

where $w'_{j,k}$ is the normalized weight for term j in document k and $w_{j,k}$ is the corresponding weight before length normalization. This difference in length normalization strategies precludes a straightforward analytical comparison between structured queries and translation-based indexing, so we have conducted some experiments to characterize the effect.

4   Evaluation

We performed a preliminary evaluation to characterize the efficiency and effectiveness of our implementation. We used the 161 MB collection of 44,013 1994 French Le Monde news articles from the Cross-Language Evaluation Forum (CLEF-2000) collection. For each of the 40 topics, we formed three queries: short (all words from the title field), medium (all words from the title and description fields), and long (all words from the title, description and narrative fields).

Figure 1 shows the effect of adding translation-based indexing on the time required to index a collection in MG on a 750 MHz Sun Blade workstation with 1 GB of physical memory. We used a French-English dictionary (referred to as "Dict1" in Table 1) that has an average of 2.1 English translations per French term by type (25,037 unique French terms, 52,475 English translations) and 85% by-token coverage of the French document collection (14.2 million / 16.6 million tokens). The observed effect on indexing time

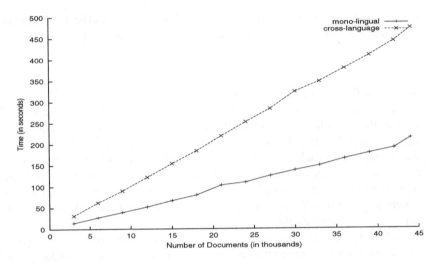

Fig. 1. Indexing time (in seconds) with and without translation-based indexing.

is consistently just over a factor of two, which matches well with our expectations $(t_c/t_m > 0.85 * 2.1)$.

The effectiveness results in Table 1 also behave about as we would expect, with mean uninterpolated average precision increasing with query length from 0.10 (for title queries) to 0.13 (for title/description/narrative queries). These results are about one-third of the mean average precision obtained by MG in a monolingual condition (with French queries; 0.26 and 0.31, respectively), and are consistent with results obtained when using structured queries with InQuery. The relatively poor cross-language performance in this case reflects some deficiencies in our initial implementation (e.g., we did not remove accents when retaining untranslated terms, and we tried no morphological variants if the surface form of a French term was not found in the dictionary) and the relatively poor coverage of the dictionary that we chose. To partially characterize the effect of dictionary coverage, we reran both systems with a second French-English dictionary and achieved a somewhat better results from translation-based indexing (0.14 and 0.15, respectively). From this we conclude that our present implementation of translation-based indexing achieves results that are similar to those achieved by a comparable implementation of structured queries.

5   Future Work

Clearly, the next thing that we need to do is compare the relative performance of translation-based indexing under a broader range of conditions (bilingual dictionaries and test collections), and with a broader set of contrastive conditions (e.g., balanced translation [6] and the PIRCS variant of structured queries). As part of this effort, we intend to integrate additional features such as orthographic normalization for untranslated terms, phrase translation, and backoff translation [10], all of which are known to improve retrieval effectiveness.

Table 1. Uninterpolated mean average precision for different query lengths (T=title queries, TD=title/description queries, TDN=title/description/narrative queries).

		InQuery Dict1	MG Dict1	InQuery Dict2	MG Dict2
Monolingual	T	0.29	0.26	0.29	0.26
	TD	0.33	0.28	0.33	0.28
	TDN	0.36	0.31	0.36	0.31
Structured	T	0.10		0.10	
Queries	TD	0.12		0.12	
	TDN	0.13		0.13	
Translation-	T		0.10		0.14
Based	TD		0.11		0.14
Indexing	TDN		0.13		0.15

The existence of a freely available system for translation-based indexing will also make it possible to explore several other potentially promising lines of inquiry:

- Post-translation resegmentation. Term translation sometimes yields multiword expressions, but it is well known from monolingual retrieval experiments that indexing the constituent words of a multiword expression can be beneficial. In the context of translation-based indexing, this creates a credit assignment problem in which the weight computed for a multiword expression provides a basis for computing the weights of the constituent words.
- Context-sensitive translation. If sharp syntactic and semantic constraints are available, the set of possible translations for the same document-language term could be varied based on this evidence. Queries, which are often short, typically offer less scope for this sort of analysis, so context-sensitive approaches would naturally favor a document translation architecture.
- Weighted summation for term frequency. If the relative likelihood of alternative translations is known, the contribution of each translation to the sum operator could be weighted appropriately.
- Proportional representation for collection frequency. If the relative likelihood of alternative translations is known, the contribution of each translation to the union operator could be apportioned appropriately.
- Multilingual indexing. Translation-based indexing could conceivably be extended to support multiple query languages by using a merged bilingual term list to identify the translations in each language that should be indexed. Open questions regarding this approach include whether the occurrence of the same string with different meanings in two query languages would adversely affect retrieval effectiveness, and whether present approaches to document length normalization would need to be adapted to accommodate the richer document representations.

6   Conclusion

Translation-based indexing offers a new capability, but like many new ideas it augments, rather than replaces, what came before. When only a single query language must be supported, translation-based indexing offers a way of achieving a substantial reduction in query execution time without adversely affecting retrieval effectiveness. Structured queries, by contrast, offer greater flexibility at query time, both because users can potentially help in the translation process (c.f. [8]), and because a broad range of query languages can easily be supported. Perhaps the most lasting contribution of this work, however, will be the availability of a freely available implementation of translation-based indexing in a state-of-the-art retrieval system—something that we hope will inspire further work along the lines outlined above.

Acknowledgments. The authors are grateful to Gina Levow and Clara Cabezas for assistance with the implementation of balanced translation, Dina Demner-Fushman for providing dictionary coverage statistics, and Jianqiang Wang for his help with InQuery. This work has been supported in part by DARPA cooperative agreement N660010028910.

References

1. Lisa Ballesteros and W. Bruce Croft. Resolving ambiguity for cross-language retrieval. In C.J. Van Rijsbergen W. Bruce Croft, Alistair Moffat, editor, *Proceedings of the 21st Annual International ACM SIGIR Conference on Research and Development in Information Retrieval*, pages 64–71. ACM Press, August 1998.
2. Gregory Grefenstette and Julien Nioche. Estimation of emglish and non-english language use on the www. In *Content-Based Multimedia Information Access*, April 2000.
3. Jaana Kekäläinen and Kalervo Järvelin. The impact of query structure and query expansion on retrieval performance. In *Proceedings of the 21st Annual International ACM SIGIR Conference on Research and Development in Information Retrieval*, pages 130–137, August 1998.
4. K. L. Kwok. NTCIR-2 chinese, cross-language retrieval experiments using PIRCS. In Noriko Kando, editor, *Proceedings of the Second NII Test Collection Information Retrieval Workshop*. 2001. http://ir.cs.qc.edu.
5. Douglas W. Oard, Gina-Anne Levow, and Clara Cabezas. CLEF experiments at the University of Maryland: Statistical stemming and backoff translation strategies. In *Working Notes of the First Cross-Language Evaluation Forum (CLEF-1)*, September 2000. http://www.glue.umd.edu/~oard/research.html.
6. Douglas W. Oard and Jianqiang Wang. NTCIR-2 ECIR experiments at Maryland: Comparing pirkola's structured queries and balanced translation. In Noriko Kando, editor, *Proceedings of the Second NII Test Collection Information Retrieval Workshop*. 2001. http://www.glue.umd.edu/~oard/research.html.
7. Douglas W. Oard, Jianqiang Wang, Dekang Lin, and Ian Soboroff. Trec-8 experiments at maryland: Clir, qa and routing. In *Eight Text Retrieval Conference*, November 1999.
8. William C. Ogden and Mark W. Davis. Improving cross-language text retrieval with human interactions. In *Proceedings of the 33rd Hawaii International Conference on System Sciences*, January 2000. http://crl.nmsu.edu/~ogden.

9. Ari Pirkola. The effects of query structure and dictionary setups in dictionary-based cross-language information retrieval. In *Proceedings of the 21st Annual International ACM SIGIR Conference on Research and Development in Information Retrieval*, pages 55–63, August 1998.
10. Philip Resnik, Douglas Oard, and Gina Levow. Improved cross-language retrieval using backoff translation. In *First International Conference on Human Language Technologies*, 2001. http://www.glue.umd.edu/~oard/research.html.
11. Ian H. Witten, Alistair Moffett, and Timothy C. Bell. *Managing Gigabytes*. Morgan Kaufmann, San Francisco, second edition, 1999.

A Retrospective Evaluation Method for Exact-Match and Best-Match Queries Applying an Interactive Query Performance Analyser

Eero Sormunen

University of Tampere, Department of Information Studies
FIN 33014 University of Tampere, Finland
eero.sormunen@uta.fi

Abstract. A retrospective method for the performance comparison of Boolean and best-match queries is introduced. The method is based on the interactive optimisation of queries by a group of test searchers using a query performance analyser. The case experiment focused on comparing the maximum effectiveness of Boolean exact-match queries, and structured and unstructured best-match queries. The experiment verified the problems in maintaining precision of Boolean queries at high recall levels. Interesting similarities were also observed between structured and unstructured best-match queries giving new light on the results of earlier studies. The case experiment showed that the proposed evaluation method yields more elaborated results in comparisons than earlier query-centred methods.

1 Introduction

Different types of queries are a challenge for experimental evaluation methods. Depending on the IR model upon which the IR system is based, the query might be a Boolean expression, a vector with weights for each term, a natural language sentence or a bag of words [24]. The comparisons of best-match and exact-match Boolean systems are rare. This is not a surprise since experimenters are facing the problem of diversely developed evaluation methods. Traditional test designs are often IR model specific.

Finding an appropriate performance measure for the comparison is one problem. Boolean IR systems retrieve unordered document sets matching exactly the query, and performance is typically measured by two overall figures, precision and recall averaged across the test topics. Best-match systems rank documents in order of decreasing probability of relevance, and performance is measured by averaging precision at some standard points of operation, e.g. fixed recall levels $R_{0.1}...R_{1.0}$. The comparison of results is difficult between IR models [9]. Another major problem is how the experiment dealing with different matching models should be designed.

F. Crestani, M. Girolami, and C.J. van Rijsbergen (Eds.): ECIR 2002, LNCS 2291, pp. 334-352, 2002.

1.1 Boolean and Best-Match Queries: Query-Centred Experiments

The study by Salton et al. [16] is a classical experiment comparing queries of different IR models. The effectiveness of Boolean queries, vector-based queries, and extended Boolean queries (based on the p-norm model) was compared. All queries were composed from the same set of query terms (a set of single terms). In the extended Boolean queries, connectives (AND, OR) were softened, and in the vector-based queries the effect of operators was completely abolished. All query results were ranked using the tf·idf formula – also within the result sets of Boolean queries. The same retrieval software was used for all queries by tuning only the p parameter changing the interpretation of Boolean operators. Precision at standard recall levels could be used as a performance measure. The main finding was that extended Boolean and vector-based queries outperformed traditional Boolean queries.

Paris & Tibbo [12] made a similar experiment by formulating candidate Boolean queries for each of the 100 search topics in the CF test collection using nine protocols. One or a few candidate queries were generated by each protocol. Among other things, protocols guided to vary the number of conjunctions in search for "optimal" Boolean formulations. "Optimal" queries were required to achieve full or nearly full recall at maximum level of precision. Best-match queries were derived from the Boolean queries found optimal by excluding AND operators. Phrases and disjunctive structures were retained for best-match queries. Performance was measured by the overall average precision and by the E measure calculated from high recall queries (R_{ave}=0.98-0.99). The main finding was that Boolean queries slightly outperformed best-match queries.

The problem in the above experiments is that they neglected some essential differences between IR systems. Queries compared were forced to contain the same set of terms, and an equivalent structure (if possible). As can be seen from the results, comparisons are sensitive to the strategies adopted in query formulation. Salton's approach is not fair to Boolean queries. The number of conjunctions in Boolean queries derived from the topic descriptions in natural language tends to be high (i.e., query exhaustivity was high). In queries without expansion, precision collapses already at low recall levels because of the exact-match requirement [2, 20]. Similar drop is not likely to happen in best-match queries. In the latter study [12], Boolean queries contained few conjunctions (i.e., query exhaustivity was low) to guarantee high recall. Best-match queries were punished since higher query exhaustivity could have improved their performance [22].

The conclusion from the query-centred experiments is that queries should be designed separately for different matching models to guarantee fair comparison. Empirical support for this view was published in [18] questioning the results of an experiment by Tenopir and Shu [26].

1.2 Boolean and Best-Match Comparisons: User-Centred Experiments

Boolean and best-match systems have also been compared by using real searchers to formulate Boolean queries and by using automatic procedures to generate best-match queries [11], or by using real searchers for both Boolean and best-match systems [7]. Ranking algorithms were not applied in these experiments for Boolean queries. Precision and recall were calculated for each query at the document cut-off value equalling the size of the Boolean query result, and averaged over all search topics. In a similar study by Turtle [27], the novelty of documents was used as the ranking criterion in Boolean queries. Average precision at the standard recall levels could be used as the performance measure. However, the idea of using novelty as a topical relevance criterion has not received general acceptance [11]. Hersh et al. also made a series of user-centred experiments in TREC-7 and TREC-8 applying instance recall as an effectiveness measure [8].

Queries can be formulated for all matching methods compared by real users but the effects of user-related variables on system related variables are difficult to control. This is not a major problem if the goal is to measure the overall performance of a given user group in a given retrieval environment, see [7]. However, the control of user related variables becomes an issue when the goal is to study the core characteristics of IR systems based upon different matching models. Another problem is that the systematic differences in queries are hard to analyse. Users can select any query terms or query structures they like inducing unnecessary variation in resulting queries.

1.3 The Goals and Motivation of This Study

Both query-centred and user-centred experiments described above have shared similar research goals. They were attempts to reveal the overall superiority of one IR model over the other (see examples in [4]). On the other hand, justified views have been presented that overall performance differences between different IR methods are small [8, 11, 15]. The variation of performance differences from one search topic to another has been suggested as a relevant starting point for future comparisons [12].

Professional search experts have also raised interesting questions: When do best-match queries perform best? When Boolean queries work better? What are appropriate query formulation strategies for an IR system based on particular matching model? See [3] and [25]. These questions are timely since modern IR systems support both Boolean and best-match queries as an integrated functionality. The trend towards IR systems where the user may select between a bag of words queries (simple mode) and structured queries (advanced mode) is clear in the World Wide Web. However, the present implementations vary a lot and Boolean operators are often supported in a restricted way.

This paper presents a new method for controlled comparisons of queries based on different matching models and the results of a case study applying the method. The basic ideas behind the proposed method are:

1. Queries are formulated and optimised separately for each IR method. This gives a fair basis for comparisons.

2. The queries used in the comparison are derived from an *inclusive query plan* designed for each search topic. The total set of queries that can be derived from the inclusive query plan is called *query tuning space*. Since queries for all IR models are derived from joint query plans, uncontrolled variation in resulting queries can be reduced.

3. Optimisation requires that relevance data is available and used in the query formulation process. This means that the proposed method is *retrospective*, see [14]. Harter [6] was the first to propose a method for searching optimal query formulations on basis of relevance data.

4. An interactive Query Performance Analyser (QPA) is used as an interactive tool by which the users are able to efficiently and conveniently search for optimal formulations in query types investigated. QPA gives instant visual feedback of the effectiveness of queries formulated [21].

The paper is organised in the following way. Section 2 will explain the basic concepts of the method. Section 3 describes the case study conducted to demonstrate the proposed method. The findings of the case study and the experiences got from the proposed method are discussed in Section 4.

2 A New Method for Query Comparisons

Traditional query-centred experiments employed single queries having an equivalent structure for all systems compared. To overcome the restrictions of fixed queries we introduce a facet-based approach to represent query plans, all queries in the query tuning space and optimal queries.

2.1 A Facet-Based Framework for Query Structures

The notion of *facet* has been adopted in the Boolean IR literature to represent the relationship between query structures and search topics as expressed information needs. A facet is a concept (or a family of concepts) identified from, and defining one exclusive aspect of a search topic. The notion of facet helps to identify query terms that play a similar semantic role, and are interchangeable in a query or a text. Terms within a facet are naturally combined by Boolean disjunctions. Facets themselves present the exclusive aspects of desired documents. Thus, a natural interpretation for facets is Boolean conjunction or negation [5, p. 76-81].

We need two additional concepts to characterize the structure of Boolean queries. *Query exhaustivity* (*Exh*) is simply the number of facets that are exploited in a query. *Query extent* (*QE*) measures the broadness of a query, e.g. the average number of query terms used per facet. The structural properties, exhaustivity and extent, are illustrated in Figure 1. For example, in the query *(image retrieval OR CBIR) AND (experiment OR test OR evaluation)*, query exhaustivity *Exh*=2 and extent *QE*=2.5. The exhaustivity and extent of unstructured queries can be calculated by mapping query terms to the facets of a query plan.

The changes made in query exhaustivity and in query extent to achieve appropriate retrieval goals are called query tuning. The range within which query exhaustivity and query extent can change sets the boundaries for query tuning. In Figure 1, query exhaustivity may be tuned from 1 to n, and extent from 1 to $(k+l+ ...+m)/n$. Figure 1

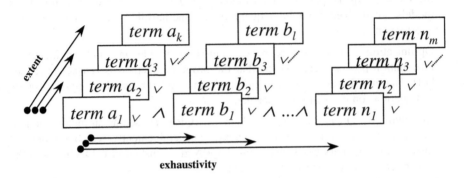

Figure 1. The structural dimensions of a query for a search topic containing n identifiable facets.

actually represents a model of an inclusive query plan. The inclusive query plan is always one interpretation of a search topic, and there is no way to guarantee that it is a complete one (if there is such). However, it is based on a controlled work of a search expert, and gives a common platform to compare the behaviour of different query types, see [18].

Query tuning space consists of all queries that can be derived from the inclusive query plan. Assuming the order of facets fixed (as we do in tin this study) the size of the query tuning space can be computed using the formula

$$N_{QTS} = \left(2^k -1\right)+\left(2^k -1\right)\cdot\left(2^l -1\right)+...+\left(2^k -1\right)\cdot\left(2^l -1\right)\cdot...\cdot\left(2^m -1\right)$$

where k, l, and m are the number of query terms for different facets of the inclusive query plan (see Figure 1). For instance, if we assume a query plan consists of 5 facets and 5 query terms per each facet, the number of optional queries is 31 for the first facet, i.e. at $Exh=1$. Further, 31x31=961 optional queries are available for $Exh=2$, 31x31x31=29,791 for $Exh=3$, 31x31x31x31= 923,521 for $Exh=4$, and 28,629,151 for $Exh=5$. In the given example, the size of the query tuning space is 29,583,455. The risk of combinatorial explosion is obvious as soon as the exhaustivity and extent of inclusive query plans grow.

2.2 Query Optimisation with QPA

Sormunen [18, 19] introduced a heuristic algorithm for optimising Boolean queries at standard recall levels. In the same study, it was shown that the optimisation of queries could be made interactively by real searchers exploiting the Query Performance Analyser. Of course, the interactive optimisation is realistic only in small and medium sized query tuning spaces. The advantage of interactive optimisation is that the constraints of optimisation can be conveniently changed from one experiment to another by giving the searchers new guidelines. The real power of the searcher-based optimisation is that heuristics requiring common sense and searching expertise can be applied.

The Query Performance Analyser is a web-based tool developed at the University of Tampere for the performance analysis and visualisation of individual queries. On top of a laboratory test collection, the tool offers immediate performance feedback in form of recall-precision curves. The searcher is able to study, in a convenient and effortless way, the effects of any query modifications. The performance data for all queries are stored automatically, and the precision of optimal queries at a particular recall level can be checked easily [21].

The use of QPA[1] is quite straightforward and intuitive. After selecting the search topic, the database, and the IR system to be used, the user enters the query formulation page. (S)he types in the query using the query language of the target IR system (here the Inquery search language). After the query has been processed in the IR system and query results downloaded, the recall-precision figures are computed, and the resulting P/R graph is automatically presented to the user.

QPA displays the resulting P/R graph highlighted together with the best results achieved in earlier queries. Thus, the user sees immediately after executing a query whether or not any progress has been made. If the average precision over all recall levels exceeds that of earlier queries, the query is automatically assigned to the "Hall of Fame". Actually, any precision curve can be presented in the background as a reference. Basic data of all queries are stored in to a log file.

2.3 Performance Measures

Performance of queries based upon different IR models can be measured and presented in several comparable ways but only two of these support the idea of separately optimised queries (instance-based metrics omitted here). Salton et al. [16] assumed that all query results are ranked by using the tf·idf formula. This is a simple and convenient method when the IR system supports the ranking also in Boolean queries, e.g. [1, 16]. In WWW, ranking of Boolean query results is common, see e.g. AltaVista (URL: www.altavista.com). Ranked Boolean queries are not genuine Boolean queries but they are realistic since they are based on the exact-match principle.

Another option is to optimise Boolean queries at standard points of operation, e.g. at fixed recall levels $R_{0.1}$-$R_{1.0}$ [18]. In this case, a P/R curve is interpolated from several Boolean queries found optimal at a particular recall level. The combined P/R curve is compared to the P/R curve of a single optimised best-match query. This approach is more complex than the approach used by Salton and the validity of comparisons based on a group of Boolean queries and a single best-match query may be questioned.

---

[1] See the demo of QPA: http://www.info.uta.fi/~lomise/pinball3.5/pinball3.5.html.

3 A Case Study

The goal of the case study was to compare the effectiveness and characteristics of Boolean queries, structured probabilistic queries and unstructured probabilistic queries all optimised separately on basis of full relevance data.

3.1 Research Questions

The research questions of the study were:

1. *General performance characteristics.* Are there differences in the average performance capability between Boolean queries, structured best-match queries and unstructured best-match queries? The tentative hypothesis was that the effectiveness of structured best-match queries should be highest since it combines weighting from the best-match IR models with the query structures of the Boolean IR model but avoids the pitfalls of exact matching.

2. *Query exhaustivity and extent.* How exhaustivity and extent vary in queries optimised separately for different query categories? An earlier experiment showed that high recall could be achieved in Boolean queries only by reducing dramatically the exhaustivity of queries [19, 20]. It has also been suggested that, in best-match queries, higher exhaustivity could be used to maintain precision in high recall searching [22]. Unstructured queries have usually suffered from query expansion [10]. Thus, the extent of optimal unstructured queries should be lower than in other queries.

3. *Performance characteristics at different exhaustivity levels.* How exhaustivity is related to performance in different query categories? Different search topics contain a varying number of searchable facets, and real users identify and apply all or some of them in the query formulation process. An interesting question is, which of the query categories most likely leads to the highest effectiveness at a given exhaustivity level.

3.2 Methods and Data

Test Collection

The test environment is a text database containing Finnish newspaper articles operated under the InQuery retrieval system (version 3.1). The database contains 53,893 articles published in three Finnish newspapers. For the database there is a collection of 35 topics, which are 1-2 sentences long, in the form of written information need statements. For the topics of the collection there is a recall base of 17,337 articles, which fall into four relevance categories. The base was collected by pooling the result sets of thousands of different queries formulated from the topics in different studies, using both exact-match, and best-match retrieval [10, 18].

In addition, the test collection provides inclusive query plans that were designed by an experienced search analyst. One of the goals in inclusive query planning was to identify all searchable facets for each search topic. The mutual recall capability of facets was estimated to find one fixed facet order to be used in experiments [18].

A subset of 18 search topics was used in this experiment. For this subset, the results of a comprehensive text analysis of all relevant documents are available, i.e. how query plan facets have been expressed [18]. Thus, the subset of the test collection provides several extraordinary features: reliable relevance data, inclusive query plans including an ordered set of facets, and occurrence data how query plan facets have been expressed in relevant documents.

Inquery

The easiest way to design a test setting is to optimise queries in a retrieval system that supports three query categories:

1. Boolean queries: Exact-match Boolean queries creating a distinct result set are supported.

2. Structured best-match queries: Facet-based query structures are supported in ranking documents but exact-match is not required.

3. Unstructured best-match queries: Facet-based query structures may be dismissed.

All this was available in InQuery.

InQuery is a best-match retrieval system but it also allows retrieval of strict Boolean result sets. All result sets, whether agreeing Boolean conditions or best-match queries, are ranked. InQuery is based on Bayesian inference networks and it supports a wide range of operators, including strict Boolean AND, OR, NOT and proximity operators as well as various best-match operators. For details, see [1, 27].

Query Plans

Inclusive query plans designed in the earlier research project for the test collection [18] were used as a starting point of query plans in the present study. The ordered set of facets was taken as a frame for query plans but query terms used in the earlier experiment were replaced by expressions identified in the facet analysis of relevant documents. Collecting query terms in this way guaranteed that all terms occur at least in some training set documents, and on an equal basis for all search topics. In addition, the idea was to create a reference for a study of real users trying to capture best query terms without any external help (an idea for a future experiment).

A critical issue in retrospective evaluation is the risk of over-fitting [14]. The problem is that the optimum may be found on basis of unpredictable document features like spelling errors or rarely used expressions. One technique minimising the effects of over-fitting is to use different documents for optimising queries (*a training set*) and testing their performance (*a test set*).

The 661 relevant documents for the 18 search topics were divided into two groups by taking a systematic sample. The sample used as the training set consisted of 335 articles. The rest of documents (326 articles) were used as the test set for performance measuring.

Query terms for each query plan facet were selected through the following process:

1. A list of all expressions used to represent a facet in the training set documents was composed.

2. Complex phrases not very likely search terms such as "chemical, biological and nuclear weapons" or "arms factory and armoury" were excluded.

3. Expressions occurring only in one relevant document were excluded.

The aim of pruning the original list was to make query plans more manageable for test searchers. Expressions appearing rarely in texts are neither likely to appear as query terms in real searching situations.

The average exhaustivity of query plans was 3.9 ranging from 2 to 5. The total number of query terms accepted was 452, which corresponds to 25 query terms per query. The average extent of queries was 6.4 ranging from 1 to 20. Facets related to named persons and organizations provided quite few query terms. Since the names of persons and organizations are usually quite good query terms both in terms of recall and precision, their facets are typically ranked first in query plans. Thus, the average number of query terms was as low as 4.8 for the first facets (i.e. Exh=1) while ranging between 5.9 and 7.6 terms in other facets.

The three versions of query plans were generated and stored as a text file to make the work of test searchers as convenient as possible. Operator #band is a strict Boolean AND; #and is a 'soft' Boolean operator giving a product of the weights of all keys or InQuery expressions within its scope. All operands within the #syn are treated as instances of one search key. #sum gives an average of the weights of its operands. #n is a proximity operator requiring its operands within n words in given order.

Operators *#band* and *#and* were used to connect facets in Boolean and structured queries, respectively. Operator *#syn* was used to combine query terms within facets. In unstructured queries, all query terms were combined by the default operator *#sum*, except for phrases. The proximity operator *#5* was used for phrases in all query types. The use of proximity operators is not common in experiments using unstructured queries, but can be justified when queries are formulated manually.

Optimisation

Three test searchers, all competent users of the InQuery system and the Query Performance Analyser, were selected as query optimisers. They were given written guidelines, and the procedure of optimisation was also explained in an introductory session. After this all test searchers made some optimisations to train themselves, and a new meeting was held to clarify the details of the procedure.

The optimisation was conducted in two stages. First, each test searcher got a set of six search topics, and an overall time limit of 6 hours per search topic in optimisation. After all searchers had completed their work, each searcher was given three search topics optimised by two other searchers. The idea of the second round was to check syntactic and technical errors in optimisation results as well as find more optimal queries. A time limit for performing the second round was 2 hours per search topic.

The test searchers were advised to seek optimal queries separately at each exhaustivity level, and test at least 10 query versions for each exhaustivity level and query type. Boolean queries were optimised first, next structured queries, and finally unstructured queries. The order of query types was not rotated but the searchers were encouraged to return to optimise earlier query types if any doubts raised in course of the work.

A separate copy of QPA was used for the optimisation of different query types, and the searcher could make direct comparison only within a query category but not between them. The measure of effectiveness used in comparing queries was precision averaged across recall levels $R_{0.1}$-$R_{1.0}$. All queries with time stamps, user ids, and measured precision averages were automatically stored into a log file. The best queries overall were available on the "Hall of Fame" but this file typically contained only optimal queries for one exhaustivity level. Best queries for other exhaustivity levels had to be checked from the log file.

The use of two stage optimisation turned out to be useful since two major syntactic errors affecting substantially the optimisation results were observed, and could be corrected. The other aim of redundant work was to reveal "blind spots" in optimisation procedures adopted by individual searchers. The second searcher could improve 16 (23%) of the Boolean, 23 (32%) of the structured, and 22 (31%) of the unstructured queries. In one search topic, the effectiveness of queries improved substantially but most improvements did not have practical importance.

The total number of queries attempted per search topic was about 520 for Boolean, 280 for structured and 350 for unstructured queries. The number of attempts per a search topic ranged from 77 to 3050. These figures correlated with the size of query tuning space. For instance, the query plan for the former topic (77 attempts) contained 2 facets and 13 query terms while the latter (3050 attempts) contained 5 facets and 52 query terms.

Test Runs and Data Analysis

The three series of queries achieving the highest average precision over all recall levels at each exhaustivity level were collected from the log files. The relevant documents of the training set were <u>not</u> removed from the test database but they were excluded by using the operator *#bandnot* of InQuery. Actual test queries were of the form *#bandnot(Q_{opt} #syn(n_1, n_2 ...n_m))*, where Q_{opt} is the optimised query, and n_1, n_2 ...n_m are id-numbers for relevant documents belonging to the training set.

Query exhaustivity and extent data was gathered from the lists of optimal queries. Standard tools available for InQuery were used to collect and analyze performance data. We compared the performance as average precisions at standard recall levels and grand precision averages over recall levels. Statistical significance was tested with Friedman two-way analysis by ranks using both types of precision averages.

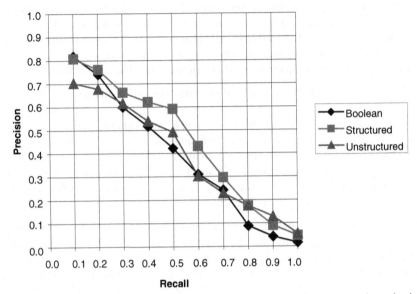

Fig. 2. Average performance of optimised Boolean, structured and unstructured queries in the test set (18 search topics).

3.3 Results

Performance and Structure of Optimal Queries

Structured best-match queries performed somewhat better than the other queries (Figure 2). The average precision in structured queries was 0.07 above Boolean and 0.06 above unstructured best-match queries but the differences observed were not statistical significant. At the lowest recall levels, the precision of Boolean queries achieved that of structured queries while, at the highest recall levels, Boolean queries were not as effective as the best-match queries. It turned out that the observed lower precision of Boolean queries at highest recall levels was statistically significant (see Table 1).

The results gave partial support to our tentative hypothesis that structured queries should perform better than other query categories since they combine weighting and query structures but avoid pitfalls of exact-matching. The success of Boolean queries at the lowest recall level may sound surprising but this phenomenon has a test environment based explanation. Even in the strict Boolean mode, InQuery ranks the documents within the result set. Boolean queries enjoyed similar weighting benefit as structured queries. At the highest recall levels, the precision of Boolean queries fell below that of other queries because the exact-match requirement rejects completely some of the relevant documents.

The stalemate between structured and unstructured queries at the highest recall levels was not in line with the tentative hypothesis. A potential explanation for equal performance may relate to the characteristics of documents that are retrieved only at the highest recall levels, the least retrievable documents [18]. Typical of the least retrievable documents is that they either do not contain searchable expressions for one or more query facets, or the expressions used in the text do not match terms used in the query. In addition, the number of expression occurrences is lower in least retrievable documents. The least retrievable documents do not provide much evidence for weighting based on term occurrences or on co-occurrence of facets.

Table 1. The results of the statistical significance tests (Friedman) for precision differences: B=Boolean, S=structured best-match, U=unstructured best-match queries. Significance levels: * denotes $p<0.05$, ** $p<0.01$, and *** $p<0.001$, respectively.

Recall	Best Queries Overall	Best Queries (Exh=1)	Best Queries (Exh=2)	Best Queries (Exh=3)	Best Queries (Exh=4)
0.1	-	-	B,S>U**	-	-
0.2	-	-	B,S>U*	-	-
0.3	-	-	-	-	-
0.4	-	-	B>U**	-	-
0.5	-	-	-	-	-
0.6	-	-	-	-	S,U >B**
0.7	-	-	-	-	S,U >B***
0.8	S>B*	-	-	S,U>B***	S,U >B***
0.9	S,U>B*	-	-	S,U>B***	S,U >B***
1.0	S,U>B**	-	S,U>B***	S,U>B***	S,U >B***
Average	-	-	B,S>U*	-	S>B*

Structural Characteristics of Optimised Queries

The average exhaustivity and extent of optimised queries is presented in Figure 3. It turned out that the exhaustivity of Boolean queries was only about 2.8 while rose to 3.6 in structured queries and up to 3.7 in unstructured queries. The measured exhaustivity difference was statistically significant between the Boolean and best-match queries but not between structured and unstructured queries. The average extent of queries was highest in unstructured queries (3.5), lowest in the structured queries (3.0), and quite high in Boolean queries (3.3). Extent differences were not statistically significant in this data set. Thus the discussion to follow is focused on query exhaustivity.

The low exhaustivity of the Boolean queries was not a surprise since the requirement of exact-match limits the use of facets. If full recall is required, the exhaustivity of queries may drop below 2 (see [20]) implying that many Boolean queries optimal for high recall searching employed only one facet. In this study, Boolean queries were not required to retrieve all relevant documents, and the optimum was found at a higher level of exhaustivity leading to higher average precision across fixed recall levels than single facet queries. In structured and unstructured queries, the average exhaustivities were very close to the maximum (3.9).

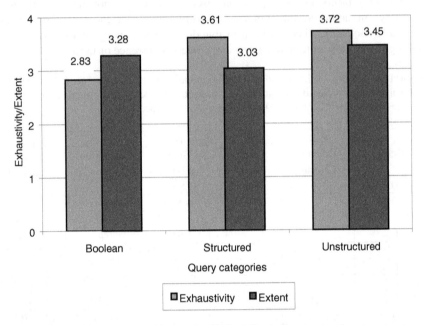

Fig. 3. Average exhaustivity and extent of optimised Boolean, structured and unstructured queries (18 search topics).

In the Boolean queries, 20 out of the 71 facets were not employed in optimal queries. In 11 search topics, at least one facet was neglected but in seven search topics all facets were exploited. In 6 search topics, the exhaustivity of Boolean queries was equal to or more than 4. This is just to emphasize the contradiction of average results and individual queries. Sometimes expressions for several facets of a query co-occur in most relevant documents but it is also common that only one or two facets could be employed.

In the structured queries, the number of neglected facets was only 6/71 in 4 search topics, and in the unstructured queries the number was 4/71 facets in 4 search topics, respectively. The results suggest that in structured or unstructured best-match searching all searchable facets should be employed. All six facets that were rejected in the optimisation process were quite general and difficult to express by query terms of any discriminating power.

Optimal Queries on Different Exhaustivity Levels

The aim of comparing optimal queries at different exhaustivity levels is to comprehend better the behaviour of different query types when the number of available or employed facets varies. Figure 4 presents a comparison of queries optimised at low exhaustivity levels 1 and 2.

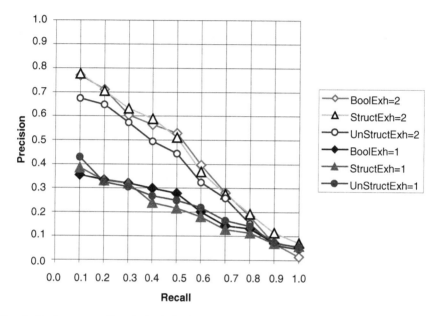

Fig. 4. Performance of optimised Boolean, structured and unstructured queries at low exhaustivity levels Exh=1-2 (18 search topics).

If only one facet is employed, no clear performance differences between the query types were observed. The difference in averages was less than 0.02 and overall differences or differences at individual recall levels were not statistically significant (Table 1). The average precision of queries was well below the optimum presented in Figure 2 except at the highest recall levels $R_{0.9}$ - $R_{1.0}$. If the goal of searching is to retrieve all relevant documents, single facet queries may be as competitive as any more focused best-match queries of higher exhaustivity (precision varies from 0.054 to 0.056). The top of the ranked list may be richer of relevant documents in multi-facet queries but the last relevant document has always a very low rank. Overall, precision was quite low for all query types and for all exhaustivity levels at the highest recall levels.

At the level *Exh=2*, the average precision of Boolean and structured queries was slightly above (0.05 - 0.06) the precision of unstructured queries. The role of query structures is advantageous both in strict and soft sense. At the highest recall level $R_{0.9}$ - $R_{1.0}$, the effect of strict AND-operators drops the precision of Boolean queries and they are no more competitive with best-match queries. The above results turned out to be statistically significant (see Table 1). The precision curve for the Boolean queries reached its maximum position at exhaustivity level 2. In other words, one could see Exh=2 as the default value for exhaustivity in optimal Boolean searching. Of course, other factors may lead to increase or decrease exhaustivity in individual cases but,

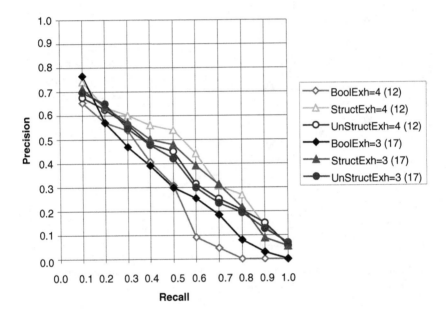

Fig. 5. Performance of optimised Boolean, structured and unstructured queries at high exhaustivity levels Exh=3-4 (12-17 search topics).

anyway, the over-exhaustivity of queries is a major performance risk in Boolean searching, see [18].

Figure 5 presents the P/R graphs for the exhaustivity levels 3 and 4. When three or four facets were employed, the precision of Boolean queries fell clearly below the precision of other query types. This was especially clear at $R_{0.5}$ and above. At the lowest recall level, Boolean queries were still competitive. The average precision was again higher in structured queries than in unstructured queries (difference 0.03-0.05), but at the lowest and at the highest recall levels the difference was negligible. However, the difference observed between best-match queries was not statistically significant (see Table 1).

4 Discussion and Conclusions

4.1 Findings of the Case Experiment

The results of the case experiment corroborated the findings in [18, 19, 20] suggesting that the requirement of exact-match in traditional Boolean queries leads to the fall of precision in high recall searching. In this study, we could compare Boolean queries and best-match queries, and verify that the decline of effectiveness is associated with the exhaustivity of queries. Over-exhaustivity is an effectiveness risk in the formulation of Boolean queries. The fall of precision was steadier in best-match queries.

Although Boolean queries were less effective than the others, all query types suffered from low effectiveness at the highest recall levels $R_{0.9}$-$R_{1.0}$. Even under the idealized conditions (a homogeneous and relatively small collection of documents, query terms from relevant documents, optimisation with full relevance data) precision fell close to or below 10 percent. This result gives a chance for a pessimistic prognosis in high-recall searching of large databases like web indexes.

Earlier experiments based on predictive evaluation methods have shown that structured queries benefit of query expansion but unstructured queries suffer from the increase of query extent [10]. Similar benefit of query structures has been observed in CLIR experiments where queries are expanded in the translation process and translations induce a lot of 'garbage' [13, 23]. Our results suggest that there is difference neither in average precision nor in average extent between unstructured and structured best-match queries.

In the present experiment, all query terms were justified expressions for the query plan facets, and were representative for the relevant documents of the training set. In addition, all query terms that did not improve the effectiveness of queries were very likely to be rejected in the optimisation process. This is not the case in predictive evaluation where queries tend to contain also very poor or even harmful query terms. The role of the query structure is to minimize the effect of noise generated by these terms [10].

The sensitivity of optimised queries to the effects of poor query terms was tested by adding up to 5 broad terms to each facet of optimal queries. It turned out that precision fell more in the Boolean and structured queries than in unstructured queries. One could conclude that the proposed evaluation method and highly idealised query plans emphasise different aspects of the same phenomenon. The results suggest that if an optimal set of query terms covering all relevant facets (high exhaustivity) is found, the structure of queries brought by operators do not have a role in improving performance. The situation may be different in real life queries where the set of optimal query terms is extremely difficult to discover.

4.2 Retrospective Evaluation and the Use of QPA

The image of the retrospective evaluation method as applied by Shaw [17] and criticized by Robertson [14] has been very poor. The work by Sormunen [18, 19] partially based on the ideas of Harter [6] justified that the retrospective approach can be used reasonably in analyzing the performance capability and structures of Boolean queries. This study expanded the use of the retrospective approach to the comparison of Boolean and best-match queries. Another difference was that now query optimisation was based totally on the interactive use of the Query Performance Analyser.

Over-fitting in optimising queries with the help of full relevance data is a justified fear but this fear should not be overemphasized. The use of separate training and test sets is a simple solution to solve the problem although it increases the amount of work. Even a more important question is how experiments are designed and the number of uncontrollable variables is reduced. The role of query plans as a solid framework for the query tuning space, and the control of the optimisation process are key issues in this respect. The more there are degrees of freedom in the query optimisation process, the more difficult it is to make valid inference on query structures.

The use of the Query Performance Analyser was not comprehensively evaluated as an optimisation tool but the first impressions were encouraging. The number of query modifications compared by the searchers was substantial. In predictive evaluation and in traditional experimental designs, an equal versatility of queries is difficult to achieve. The advantage of QPA is that it supports also the detailed analysis of query results, see [18]. An obvious danger in the optimisation is that test searchers easily get excited of "game playing". In hunt for higher scores, test persons may forget the actual goals of their work. For instance, we noticed that at those exhaustivity levels which the highest performance was achieved, more candidate queries were composed than at other exhaustivity levels.

4.3 Final Remarks

The basic idea and the procedure of the proposed evaluation method for the comparison of different types of queries were illustrated above including a case experiment. The evaluation method proposed is query-centred but is more elaborated than earlier query-centred approaches applied in [12,16]. The differences in overall effectiveness of exact-match and best-match at high recall levels could be identified. In addition, through the proposed method one could analyse the dynamics of query tuning.

One obvious limitation in the case experiment was (in addition to the small number of test topics) that query terms of a facet could be selected in any combination. This makes the analysis of query extent differences difficult since it is mixed with variation in performance of individual query terms. The order of query terms in the facets of a query plan should have a fixed order to eliminate the effect of term replacement. The order of terms could be based, for example, on their descending or ascending document frequency (df) in the database.

Acknowledgements. The author is grateful to Jaana Kekäläinen, Jussi Koivisto, Erkka Leppänen and Katja Nirkkonen for their contribution in the experiment. The members of the FIRE group have also helped to improve the manuscript.

The *Inquery* search engine was provided by the Center for Intelligent Information Retrieval at the University of Massachusetts.

References

1. Allan, J., Callan, J., Croft, W.B., Ballestros, L., Broglio, J., Xu, J. & Shu, H. (1997). INQUERY at TREC 5. In: Harman, D.K. & Voorhees, E.M. (Eds.) *Information technology: The Fifth Text REtrieval Conference (TREC-5)*. Gaithersburg, National Institute of Standards and Technology, 119–132.
2. Blair, D.C. & Maron, M.E. (1985). An evaluation of retrieval effectiveness for a full-text document retrieval system. *Communications of the ACM* (28)3, 289-299.
3. Feldman, S. (1996). Testing Natural Language: Comparing DIALOG, TARGET, and DR-LINK. *Online* 20(6), 71-79.
4. Frants, V.I., Shapiro, J., Taksa, I. & Voiskunskii, V.G. (1999). Boolean Search: Current State and Perspectives. *Journal of the American Society of Information Science* 50(1), 86-95.
5. Harter, S.P. (1986). *Online Information retrieval*. Orlando: Academic Press.
6. Harter, S.P. (1990). Search Term Combinations and Retrieval Overlap: A Proposed Methodology and Case Study. *Journal of the American Society for Information Science* 41(2), 132-146.
7. Hersh, W.R. & Hickam, D.H. (1995). An Evaluation of Interactive Boolean and Natural Language Searching with Online Medical Textbook. *Journal of the American Society for Information Science* 48(7), 478-489.
8. Hersh, W., Turpin, A., et al. (2001). Challenging conventional assumptions of automated information retrieval with real users: Boolean searching and batch retrieval evaluation. *Information Processing & Management* 37(), 383-402.
9. Keen, E.M. (1992). Presenting results of experimental retrieval comparisons. *Information Processing & Management* 28(4), 491-502.
10. Kekäläinen, J. & Järvelin, K. (1998). The impact of query structure and query expansion on retrieval performance. In: Croft, W.B., Moffat, A., et al. (Eds.), *Proceedings of the 21st Annual International ACM SIGIR Conference on Research and Development in Information Retrieval* (ACM SIGIR '98). New York, NY: ACM Press, pp. 130-137.
11. Lu, X.A., Holt, J.D. & Miller, D.J. (1996). Boolean System Revisited: Its Performance and its Behaviour. In: Harman, D.K. (Ed.) *The Fourth Text REtrieval Conference (TREC-4)*. Gaithersburg, National Institute of Standards and Technology, 459–473.
12. Paris, L.A.H. & Tibbo, H.R. (1998). Freestyle vs. Boolean: A comparison of partial and exact match retrieval systems. *Information Processing & Management* 34(2/3), 175-190.
13. Pirkola A. (1998). The effects of query structure and dictionary setups in dictionary-based cross-language information retrieval. In: Croft, W.B., Moffat, A. et al. (Eds.), *Proceedings of the 21st Annual International ACM SIGIR Conference on Research and Development in Information Retrieval* (ACM SIGIR '98). New York, NY: ACM Press, pp. 55-63.
14. Robertson, S.E. (1996). Letter to the Editor. *Information Processing & Management* 32(5), 635-636.
15. Robertson, S.E. & Thompson, C.L. (1990). Weighted searching: The CIRT experiment. In: Jones, K.P. (Ed.), *Informatics 10 – Prospects for Intelligent retrieval*. London: Aslib, p. 153-165.

16. Salton, G., Fox, E.A. & Wu, H. (1983). Extended Boolean Information Retrieval. *Communications of the ACM* 26(11), 1022-1036.
17. Shaw, W.M. (1995). Term-relevance computations and perfect retrieval performance. *Information Processing and Management* 31(4), 491-498.
18. Sormunen, E. (2000a). *A method for measuring wide range performance of Boolean queries in full-text databases.* Doctoral Thesis. Acta Electronica Universitatis Tamperensis, URL: http://acta.uta.fi/pdf/951-44-4732-8.pdf. Tampere: University of Tampere, 2000.
19. Sormunen, E. (2000b). A novel method for the evaluation of Boolean query effectiveness across a wide operational range. In: Belkin, N.J., Ingwersen, P. and Leong, M.-K: eds. *Proceedings of the 23rd Annual International ACM SIGIR Conference on Research and Development in Information Retrieval.* New York, NY: ACM, 2000, 25–32.
20. Sormunen, E. (2001) Extensions to the STAIRS Study - Empirical Evidence for the Hypothesised Ineffectiveness of Boolean Queries in Large Full-Text Databases. *Information Retrieval* 4(3/4):257-274.
21. Sormunen, E., Keskustalo, H. & Halttunen, K. (2001a). Query Performance Analyser - a interactive tool for bridging information retrieval research and education. Submitted for publication in *Information Retrieval.*
22. Sormunen, E., Kekäläinen, J., Koivisto, J. and Järvelin, K. (2001b). Document text characteristics affect the ranking of the most relevant documents by expanded structured queries. *Journal of Documentation* 57(3):358-374.
23. Sperer, R. & Oard, D.W. (2000). Structured translation for cross-language information retrieval. In: Belkin, N.J., Ingwersen, P. and Leong, M.-K: eds. *Proceedings of the 23rd Annual International ACM SIGIR Conference on Research and Development in Information Retrieval.* New York, NY: ACM, 2000, 120-127.
24. Tague-Sutcliffe, J. (1992). The pragmatics of information retrieval experimentation, revisited. *Information Processing and Management* 28(4), 467-490.
25. Tenopir, C. & Cahn, P. (1994). TARGET & FREESTYLE: Dialog and Mead join the relevance ranks. *Online* 18(3), 31-47.
26. Tenopir, C. & Shu, M.E. (1989). Magazines in full text: uses and search strategies. *Online Review* 13 (2), 107-118.
27. Turtle, H. R. (1990). *Inference networks for document retrieval.* Ph.D. dissertation. Computer and information Science Department, University of Massachusetts. COINS Technical Report 90–92.

Genre Classification and Domain Transfer for Information Filtering

Aidan Finn, Nicholas Kushmerick, and Barry Smyth

Smart Media Institute, Department of Computer Science, University College Dublin
{aidan.finn, nick, barry.smyth}@ucd.ie

Abstract. The World Wide Web is a vast repository of information, but the sheer volume makes it difficult to identify useful documents. We identify document genre is an important factor in retrieving useful documents and focus on the novel document genre dimension of subjectivity. We investigate three approaches to automatically classifying documents by genre: traditional bag of words techniques, part-of-speech statistics, and hand-crafted shallow linguistic features. We are particularly interested in domain transfer: how well the learned classifiers generalize from the training corpus to a new document corpus. Our experiments demonstrate that the part-of-speech approach is better than traditional bag of words techniques, particularly in the domain transfer conditions.

1   Introduction

There is a vast amount of information on the WWW, but the potential of the Web as an instant information source is being hampered. There are likely to be thousands of documents with content relevant to any particular query, and different users issuing the same query will have differing information needs. Current WWW search services take a "one size fits all" approach, which takes little account of the user's individual needs and preferences. Each user's information need may be satisfied by a different subset of the set of documents returned by a search. We believe that content alone is insufficient for determining document relevance.

Traditionally, information retrieval has focused on content analysis. More recently, link analysis, latent semantic indexing and collaborative filtering have been used to improve retrieval. However genre analysis has not been widely explored.

The genre of a document reflects the style of language used in the document. Genre can be used to retrieve documents that are written in a style relevant to a particular user. In small homogeneous collections of documents, genre may be quite similar across the document collection. However in a large heterogeneous document collection such as the WWW, identifying the genre of a document can significantly contribute to retrieving the most relevant documents for a particular user. Genre analysis is therefore a valuable tool in the construction of personalised retrieval and filtering systems.

F. Crestani, M. Girolami, and C.J. van Rijsbergen (Eds.): ECIR 2002, LNCS 2291, pp. 353–362, 2002.
© Springer-Verlag Berlin Heidelberg 2002

In this paper we apply machine learning techniques to automatic genre classification. We investigate three approaches, namely bag of words (BOW), part-of-speech (POS) tagging and hand-crafted text statistics. We evaluate these three approaches on one particular genre identification task: classifying news articles according to whether they present the authors opinion or report fact. We conclude that all three sets of features can be used to classify documents into our chosen genre, but that BOW produces the most brittle classifier while POS produces the most general.

2   Document Genre

The term "genre" is difficult to define. It is a frequent term in popular culture. Music is divided into genres based on differences in style, e.g. blues, rock or jazz. Sample genres from popular fiction include science fiction, mystery and drama. Genres are often vague concepts with no clear boundaries and need not be disjoint. For a given subject area there are is no fixed set of genre categories. Identifying a genre taxonomy is a subjective process and people may disagree about what constitutes a genre, or the criteria for membership of a particular genre.

In this paper, when we refer to genre, we are referring to the *text genre* of a document. Informally, the text genre of a document refers to the style of text used in that document. We view a genre as a class of documents that arises naturally from study of the language style and text used in the document collection. Genre is an abstraction based on a natural grouping of documents written in a similar style and is orthogonal to topic.

The readability of a document could be considered a genre classification. A tabloid newspaper generally has higher readability than a broadsheet. Different users searching for information will require different levels of readability. The level of technical detail in a document can be considered another genre class. An engineer searching for information on a topic would probably require a different document than a journalist searching for information on the same topic. Users generally are not looking for all information on a certain topic but rather certain kinds of information about that topic. By identifying the genre of a document, we can further reduce the set of documents that have relevant content to a set of documents that have both relevant content and are from genres that are appropriate to the users current information need.

3   Personalised News Filtering

Our focus is information filtering services for the personalised retrieval of online news articles. Such services should:

- promptly retrieve and classify new articles appearing on the WWW;
- employ classification techniques that scale gracefully and transfer easily to new subject domains; and

– combine content classification with other techniques that will improve personalised retrieval.

Personalisation can take place along several dimensions. Content can be used to recommend documents to users based on their previous interests. Collaborative filtering recommends documents based on the fact that other similar users found them interesting.

We have identified genre analysis as another technique that facilitates improved personalisation. Genre analysis can be used to recommend documents that are written in a style that the user finds interesting. We consider genre to be complimentary to content as a method of recommendation. The two used in conjunction with each other can improve the quality of a user's recommendations.

Personalised retrieval of online news articles presents several challenges that we believe cannot be met by content analysis alone.

– Volume: Numerous news articles appear on the web every day. Many of these may be relevant to the user, but we can only recommend a small amount. Therefore it is important to identify the most relevant. Genre analysis can filter out documents that are unlikely to be interesting to the user.
– Timeliness: Many news articles are only relevant for a short time before they become obsolete. Genre analysis does not directly address this problem but can be used to reduce the number of articles to be considered and identify good candidates for recommendation.
– Interestingness/Appropriateness: An information filtering service should find documents that the user is interested in, and genre analysis may be relevant to differentiating between documents that all relate to the correct topic, but that the user nevertheless does not view as equally interesting.

In the remainder of this paper we focus on the task of genre identification. We identify a particular genre classification task: that of subjectivity classification and evaluate three different approaches to genre classification. We focus our experiments on the task of identifying whether a document reports objectively or presents the opinion of its author. We are also exploring other genre classification tasks such as the amount of assumed technical expertise necessary to read a document and the level of detail in a document[3]. Each of these genres have clear applications for web search services and recommender systems.

3.1 Related Work

Karlgren [4] performs various experiments analyzing stylistic variation in texts for information retrieval purposes. His experiments use a corpus of documents from the Wall Street Journal and a set of queries from the Text Retrieval Conference (TREC) to investigate various word-based and text-based statistics for the purpose of improving retrieval results. In other work, Karlgren et al [5] propose a genre scheme for web pages and outline a search interface prototype that incorporates both content and genre.

Argamon et al [1] use frequency of function words and POS trigrams to classify documents according to style.

The SOMLIB system [7] is a Digital Library system that organizes documents by content, where documents on similar topics but of different genre are visualized as books of different colors. In this system, the genre classes arise through clustering the documents using shallow text features.

Wiebe [8] investigates subjectivity classification at the sentence level and indicates that adjectives are representative of subjectivity. We expand this to document-level classification and explore other parts of speech.

4   Subjectivity Classification

The genre class we investigate is whether a document presents the opinion of its author or reports facts. This is a common distinction in newspaper articles and other media. Many news articles report some significant event objectively. Other articles offer the author's opinion. These often take the form of columns or editorials. This genre class is particularly useful for filtering news articles because a user may have a preference for articles of each of these genre classes at different times. Consider the example of financial news. Financial news sites publish many articles each day. Articles of genre class fact may be reporting the latest stock prices and various events that are likely to influence the stock price of a particular company. Articles of genre class opinion may give the opinions of various financial analysts as to the implications of the events of the day for future stock prices. Different users at different times may be better served by articles from one genre or the other. It would be a useful service for the user to be able to filter or retrieve documents from each of these genre classes.

Table 1 show a selection of document extracts from our three subject domains. A human reader can recognize a subtle difference in style between extracts from articles of genre class opinion and articles of genre class fact. We investigate techniques for automating this classification.

Our aim in constructing the classifier is to maximize accuracy both within a single domain and across domains. To this end we use datasets from three subject domains: Football, Politics and Finance[1]. We are interested in how well a classifier trained on documents in one domain performs in another.

5   Document Representation

Our experiments used documents from three domains in order to evaluate accuracy and domain transfer. A corpus of documents was spidered from the web and each document was manually classified as being either opinion or fact. The distribution of articles across subject domain and genre class is shown in Table 2.

---

[1] Our document corpus is available to the research community at http://www.smi.ucd.ie/hyppia

Table 1. Examples of fact and opinion articles from our three domains.

	Fact	Opinion
Football	Liverpool have revealed they have agreed a fee with Leeds United for striker Robbie Fowler - just hours after caretaker boss Phil Thompson had said that contract talks with the player were imminent.	The departure of Robbie Fowler from Liverpool saddens me but does not surprise me. What did come as a shock, though, was that the club should agree terms with Leeds, one of their chief rivals for the Championship.
Politics	Al Gore picked up votes Thursday in Broward County as election officials spent Thanksgiving weekend reviewing questionable presidential ballots.	Democrats are desperate and afraid. The reality that their nominee for President has a compulsive tendency to make things up to make himself look good is sinking in.
Finance	In a move that sent Enron shares higher after days of double-digit declines, Dynegy confirmed Tuesday that it is in talks to renegotiate its $9 billion deal to buy its rival.	The collapse of Enron is hard to believe, and even harder to understand. But in retrospect, there are some valuable lessons in the whole mess.

Table 2. Corpus Details.

Subject Domain	Opinion	Fact	Total
Football	174	177	351
Politics	144	145	289
Finance	56	100	156

We used C4.5 [6], a widely used algorithm for decision tree induction[2]. We investigated three approaches to identifying the genre of a document: bag of words (BOW), part-of-speech tagging (POS) and hand-crafted shallow linguistic features.

5.1   Bag of Words

The first approach represented each document as a bag of words. In the BOW representation, a document is encoded as a feature vector, with each element in the vector indicating the presence or absence of a word in the document. This approach was used as a baseline to determine how well a standard keyword based learner performs on this task. This approach led to feature vectors that are large and sparse.

---

[2] We performed initial experiments using five machine learning algorithms: OneR, KNN, Naive Bayes, C4.5 and PART. No algorithm was obviously best for these classification tasks but C4.5 performed consistently well.

5.2   Part-of-Speech

The second approach uses the output of Brill's part-of-speech tagger [2] as the basis for its features. It was anticipated that the POS statistics would reflect the style of the language sufficiently for our learning algorithm to distinguish between different genre classes. A document is represented as a vector of 36 POS features, one for each POS tag, expressed as a percentage of the total number of words for the document.

5.3   Hand Crafted Features

Our third approach used a set of hand-crafted features. Some of these are features mentioned in related work that intuitively seem suited to the task of subjectivity classification, while others were selected from examination of the training data for the Football and Politics domains. Many of the features could be used for other genre identification tasks but some are specific to the task of identifying subjective documents. In total there were 76 features. Examples include counts of certain stop-words, counts of various punctuation symbols, and text statistics such as average sentence length, number of long words and keywords that indicate subjectivity within the domain.

6   Results

Our experiments are designed to measure accuracy within a single domain and across domains. While accuracy within domain is important we emphasize domain transfer measurements when distinguishing between feature-sets. We wish to measure how well each feature-set performs when evaluated on data from subject domains outside that of the classifiers training data. By measuring domain transfer, we aim to identify feature-sets that generalize well to unseen subject domains. Concentrating evaluation on intra-domain accuracy alone can lead to classifiers that are brittle and perform badly when presented with data from new subject domains.

Accuracy for single domain experiments was evaluated using tenfold cross-validation. Domain transfer was evaluated by training the classifier in one subject domain and testing it in another. We evaluated three feature-sets. Figure 1 shows accuracy for Single Domain Experiments. Figures 2 and 3 show evaluation of domain transfer. The legend on the vertical axis shows the documents used for training followed by the documents used for testing. For example, Football_Politics indicates that the classifier is trained on the Football dataset and tested on the Politics dataset. The horizontal axis shows classification accuracy. On the legend, POS indicates the that POS statistics were used as features, BOW indicates that keywords were used as features and HC indicates that hand-crafted text statistics were used as features.

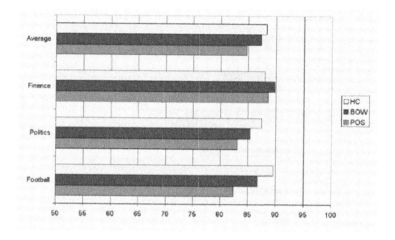

Fig. 1. Single Domain Experiments

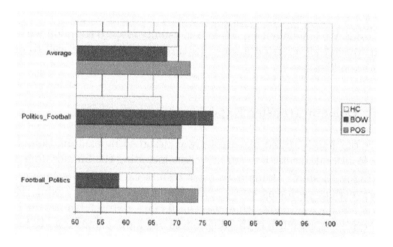

Fig. 2. Domain Transfer Experiments excluding Finance Domain

6.1 Single Domain Experiments

In the single domain experiments (Figure 1), the hand-crafted features perform best with average accuracy of 88%. POS statistics performs worst (85%), BOW achieves average accuracy of 87%. On average there is little difference in accuracy between the three classifiers when evaluated in a single domain. This indicates that subjectivity within a single domain can be accurately identified using any of the three representations.

Note that on average the hand-crafted features perform best but are actually worst in the finance domain. This is consistent with the fact that some of the hand-crafted features were designed by examination of the Football and Politics

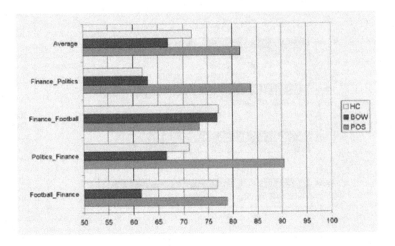

Fig. 3. Domain transfer experiments for the Finance Domain

datasets. We conclude that while it is usually easy to come up with a feature-set that works well, crafting a set of features that generalize well to other domains is more difficult.

6.2   Domain Transfer Experiments

Since our hand-crafted feature-set was designed by examination of the Football and Politics datasets, we examine cases including the finance domain separately.

Figure 2 shows domain transfer results excluding the finance domain. On average POS performs best (72%), HC is second (70%), while BOW is worst (68%). For experiments that use the finance dataset (shown in Figure 3) this pattern is repeated, but the differences are more significant. POS is again best (82%), HC is second (72%) and BOW is last (67%).

In the domain transfer experiments, the POS features perform significantly better. The BOW features perform worst. This indicates that while keywords can be used to identify subjective documents, a model built using these features is more closely tied to the document collection used for training. Intuitively we would expect that the classifier built using the POS statistics as features would have a more general model of what constitutes genre than one built using keywords or domain-specific hand-crafted features.

The classifier built using hand-crafted text statistics performs better than the keyword classifier but worse than the POS classifier. Shallow text statistics have the advantage of being easy and inexpensive to compute. We believe that many of these features would be useful for identifying genres other than our opinion/fact task.

Note that, as predicted the HC features perform worse relative to the POS features when a third domain is considered. Specifically, the HC features obtain

94% of POS's accuracy excluding the finance domain, but only 82% of POS's accuracy when the finance domain is included.

The BOW approach performs similarly to the other two approaches in single domain experiments but is inferior when domain transfer is evaluated. POS statistics and shallow text statistics are both good feature-sets for this particular genre identification task. Shallow text statistics perform best in single domain experiments, while POS statistics perform best in domain transfer experiments. It must be remembered that the hand-crafted features were designed with our classification task in mind and after examination of some of the training data from two of the domains. Therefore the hand-crafted features have an inherent advantage for this particular classification task. We expect that the utility of each technique depends on the particular genre at hand and that a combination of the feature-sets might be suitable for a general genre classifier.

POS statistics and bag of word based features can be generated automatically. However, the selection of hand-crafted features requires human involvement and these features may not transfer well to a new domain. When building a classifier to identify a different genre class some of the hand-crafted features used here would be useful. Other features would need to be gleaned from examination of the target genre.

7   Conclusion

With the explosion of information on the Web, personalised information retrieval and filtering is necessary to reduce the growing information overload problem. Current approaches generally use content analysis to decide if a document is relevant or not. Text genre is a valuable method for ensuring that users are presented with information that most suits their needs. We have described a novel genre identification task, namely whether a document is fact or opinion based, and applied machine learning techniques to the problem. Our experiments demonstrate that features based on POS statistics can be used to identify the genre of documents, particularly in the important transfer scenario, in which the classifier is trained and tested on different corpora.

We wish to extend our genre taxonomy to include more genres which enhance personalised news retrieval. Other genres include whether a document is highly detailed or brief and the level of topic expertise assumed by the author. For review articles our approaches may be applicable to deciding whether the review is positive or negative. These genres will then be incorporated into a personalised news retrieval and recommendation system.

Currently the amount of effort involved in building a genre classifier is significant. We wish to investigate semi-supervised methods of learning such as active learning based on small amounts of training data.

Acknowledgments. This research was funded in part by grant N00014-00-1-0021 from the US Office of Naval Research. Experiments were performed using the Waikato Environment for Knowledge Analysis (WEKA).

References

1. Shlomo Argamon, Moshe Koppel, and Galit Avneri. Routing documents according to style. In *First International Workshop on Innovative Information Systems*, 1998.
2. Eric Brill. Some advances in transformation-based parts of speech tagging. In *AAAI*, 1994.
3. Maya Dimitrova, Aidan Finn, Nicholas Kushmerick, and Barry Smyth. Web genre visualisation. Submitted to Conference on Human Factors in Computing Systems, 2002.
4. J. Karlgren. Stylistic experiments in information retrieval. In T. Strzalkowski, editor, *Natural Language Information Retrieval*. Kluwer, 1999.
5. Jussi Karlgren, Ivan Bretan, Johan Dewe, Anders Hallberg, and Niklas Wolkert. Iterative information retrieval using fast clustering and usage-specific genres. In *Eight DELOS workshop on User Interfaces in Digital Libraries*, pages 85–92, Stockholm, Sweden, 1998.
6. Ross Quinlan. *C4.5: Programs for Machine Learning*. Morgan Kaufman, 1993.
7. A. Rauber and A. Muller-Kogler. Integrating automatic genre analysis into digital libraries. In *First ACM-IEEE Joint Conf on Digital Libraries*, 2001.
8. Janyce M. Wiebe. Learning subjective adjectives from corpora. In *AAAI*, 2000.

Author Index

Lecture Notes in Computer Science

For information about Vols. 1–2205
please contact your bookseller or Springer-Verlag